OXFORD ENGLISH MONOGRAPHS

LEGITIMATE HISTORIES

Scott, Gothic, and the Authorities of Fiction

FIONA ROBERTSON

CLARENDON PRESS · OXFORD

Oxford University Press, Great Clarendon Street, Oxford OX2 6DP
Oxford New York
Athens Auckland Bangkok Bogota Bombay Buenos Aires
Calcutta Cape Town Dar es Salaam Delhi Florence Hong Kong Istanbul
Karachi Kuala Lumpur Madras Madrid Melbourne Mexico City
Nairobi Paris Singapore Taipei Tokyo Toronto Warsaw
and associated companies in
Berlin Ibadan

Oxford is a registered trade mark of Oxford University Press

Published in the United States
by Oxford University Press Inc., New York

ISBN 0-19-811224-6

Printed in Great Britain
by Antony Rowe Ltd.
Chippenham

FOR MY PARENTS,
John and Denise Robertson

Acknowledgements

I thank the Principal and Fellows of Hertford College, Oxford, for the post-doctoral Baring Research Fellowship which I held from 1987 to 1990 and which enabled me to continue work on Scott. This study is in most conceivable senses the product of my involvement with Hertford College over many years. I also thank my family, especially my parents, whose support and enthusiasm have been unfailing, and my brother Struan Robertson, who has worked in the past on literary Gothic but now specializes in a somewhat terser style.

Scott's favourite way of dealing with intellectual debts was to present them in terms of personal friendships and conversations. Appropriately, my interpretation of his fiction owes a great deal to the friends and colleagues who have listened and argued back. From undergraduate work onwards I have been fortunate in the guidance of Julia Briggs and Tony Cockshut. Marilyn Butler and Roy Park supervised the D.Phil. thesis on which this book is based, while Paul Hamilton and Andrew Hook were helpful and constructive examiners. On a less formal level, Penny Fielding has joined in more ponderings about Scott than anyone else; and while teaching at Pembroke College, Oxford, between 1985 and 1987, I was able to draw on the varied literary expertise of David Fleeman, Nicholas Mann, and Eric Stanley. Kay Langdale read through the entire work in its first completed form and saved it from death by semicolon. More recently, I have been grateful for the comments and suggestions of Oxford University Press's two anonymous readers, and for the stimulus provided by my colleagues and students at the University of Durham. Michael O'Neill helpfully commented on an intermediate version of Chapter 1. At Trevelyan College, George Marshall has been generous in his friendship and encouragement.

The broader intellectual and cultural preoccupations which shape this study are charted wherever possible in the text and the notes, but the impact of a few scholarly works calls for special mention here. My work has benefited greatly from the many new readings of Gothic over the last fifteen years, especially those by

viii ACKNOWLEDGEMENTS

David Punter, Ronald Paulson, Margaret Anne Doody, and Judith Wilt. They have made it possible for me to leave a great deal unsaid. It has also, of course, benefited from a more general revival of interest in Scott's novels and poetry, which has produced many important studies in recent years. Of them all, Judith Wilt's *Secret Leaves* was the one which most convinced me that there was a way forward, but it would have been difficult to proceed at all without the work of Peter Garside, F. R. Hart, Jane Millgate, and Alexander Welsh. The varied topics of debate raised at the Fourth International Scott Conference in Edinburgh, 1991, proved stimulating in the final stages of my work, when I was able to reshape my sense of a critical audience for Scott and Scott scholarship through discussions with Carol Anderson, James Chandler, Graham Tulloch, and Chris Worth. I appreciate the new sense of direction they gave me.

F.R.

Durham, 1993

Contents

Abbreviations

Caleb Williams	William Godwin, *Things as They Are; or, The Adventures of Caleb Williams*, 3 vols. (London, 1794)
Confessions	James Hogg, *The Private Memoirs and Confessions of a Justified Sinner: Written by Himself: With a Detail of Curious Traditionary Facts, and Other Evidence, by the Editor* (London, 1824)
Fatal Revenge	Charles Robert Maturin, *Fatal Revenge; or, The Family of Montorio: A Romance*, 3 vols. (London, 1807)
Frankenstein	Mary Wollstonecraft Shelley, *Frankenstein; or, The Modern Prometheus*, 3 vols. (London, 1818)
Italian	Ann Radcliffe, *The Italian; or, The Confessional of the Black Penitents: A Romance*, 3 vols. (London, 1797)
Johnson	Edgar Johnson, *Sir Walter Scott: The Great Unknown*, 2 vols. (London, 1970)
Journal	*The Journal of Sir Walter Scott*, ed. W. E. K. Anderson (Oxford, 1972)
Letters	*The Letters of Sir Walter Scott*, ed. H. J. C. Grierson *et al.*, Centenary Edition, 12 vols. (London, 1932–7)
Lockhart	John Gibson Lockhart, *Memoirs of the Life of Sir Walter Scott, Bart.*, 2nd edn., 10 vols. (Edinburgh, 1839)
Melmoth	Charles Robert Maturin, *Melmoth the Wanderer: A Tale*, 4 vols. (Edinburgh, 1820)
Milesian	Charles Robert Maturin, *The Milesian Chief: A Romance*, 4 vols. (London, 1812)
Monk	Matthew Gregory Lewis, *The Monk: A Romance*, 3 vols. (London, 1796)
MPW	*The Miscellaneous Prose Works of Sir Walter Scott, Bart.*, ed. J. G. Lockhart, 28 vols. (Edinburgh, 1834–6)
Old English Baron	Clara Reeve, *The Old English Baron: A Gothic Story*, 2nd edn. (London, 1778)
Otranto	Horace Walpole, *The Castle of Otranto: A Gothic*

	Story (1764, 1765), ed. and introd. W. S. Lewis (Oxford, 1964, 1982)
PW	*The Poetical Works of Sir Walter Scott, Bart.*, ed. J. G. Lockhart, 12 vols. (Edinburgh, 1833–4)
Recess	Sophia Lee, *The Recess; or, A Tale of Other Times*, 3 vols. (London, 1785)
Romance of Forest	Ann Radcliffe, *The Romance of the Forest: Interspersed with Some Pieces of Poetry*, 3 vols. (London, 1791)
Scott–Maturin Correspondence	*The Correspondence of Sir Walter Scott and Charles Robert Maturin With a Few Other Allied Letters*, ed. Fannie E. Ratchford and William H. McCarthy, Jr. (Austin, Tex., 1937)
Sicilian Romance	Ann Radcliffe, *A Sicilian Romance*, 2 vols. (London, 1790)
Udolpho	Ann Radcliffe, *The Mysteries of Udolpho, A Romance; Interspersed with Some Pieces of Poetry*, 4 vols. (London, 1794)
WN	Sir Walter Scott, Bart., *The Waverley Novels*, 48 vols. (Edinburgh, 1829–33)
Women	Charles Robert Maturin, *Women; or, Pour et Contre: A Tale*, 3 vols. (Edinburgh, 1818)

A Note on Texts

Gothic fiction has been extensively, but not comprehensively or uniformly, reprinted in recent years. I have preferred the authority of the first printed edition, wherever available, and when later editions do not provide indispensable additional information. When they do, as in the case of *The Castle of Otranto*, I have used a modern edition which includes all the relevant information. For ease of general reference, and wherever possible, the Bibliography includes in square brackets brief details of the most reliable modern reprints of the Gothic novels referred to. Editions of individual Waverley Novels, similarly, are no substitute for an authoritative single collected edition, and I have preferred the text of the 1829–33 Magnum Opus edition to the various nineteenth-century reprints and revisions of it. In order to indicate more precisely the pace of reaction to Scott's work and to Gothic, I have included information on the dates of contemporary reviews even when it is not bibliographically necessary. All references to Shakespeare's works are to the Riverside edition.

That it was a daylight ghost, surprisingly angular in his attitudes, and for the most part spread out on three chairs, did not make it any easier. Daylight only made him a more weird, a more disturbing and unlawful apparition.

(Joseph Conrad, *Victory*, 1915, Part II, ch. 6)

Catherine's library was select; and its state of dilapidation proved it to have been well used, though not altogether for a legitimate purpose; scarcely one chapter had escaped a pen and ink commentary—at least, the appearance of one—covering every morsel of blank that the printer had left.

(Emily Brontë, *Wuthering Heights*, 1847, ch. 3)

Very lately, however, the writer chanced to look them over with feelings very different from those of the adventurous period of his literary life during which they had been written, and yet with such as perhaps a reformed libertine might regard the illegitimate production of an early amour. There is something to be ashamed of, certainly; but, after all, paternal vanity whispers that the child has a resemblance to the father.

(Walter Scott, Advertisement to *The House of Aspen*, 1829)

Introduction

IN his *Familiar Anecdotes of Sir Walter Scott* (1834), James Hogg describes a visit which he made with Scott and a group of Scott's friends to 'the wilds of Rankleburn' in the summer of 1801. During the expedition Hogg joined in a search for relics of the Scotts of Buccleuch, and in particular for 'a font-stone of blue marble' which, according to local tradition and the authority of Satchells ('the most fabulous historian that ever wrote', as Hogg declares, quietly loading the terms), lay hidden among the ruins of an old church. The party searched in vain until one recess yielded it not a font but a suitably mysterious relic by way of substitute. This story seems to promise the reader a quasi-mystical end such as the discovery of the magical book of Michael Scott in *The Lay of the Last Minstrel* or the discovery of the long-buried heart of the Abbot Ambrosius in the frame narrative of *The Monastery*. In fact, the end of the Rankleburn quest more closely resembles the anticlimactic identification of 'Aiken Drum's Lang Ladle' in *The Antiquary*:

As there appeared, however, to have been a sort of recess in the eastern gable, we fell a turning over some loose stones, to see if the baptismal font was not there, when we came to one-half of a small pot encrusted thick with rust. Mr. Scott's eyes brightened and he swore it was part of an ancient consecrated helmet. Laidlaw, however, fell a picking and scratching with great patience until at last he came to a layer of pitch inside, and then, with a malicious sneer, he said, 'The truth is, Mr. Scott, it's nouther mair nor less than an auld tar-pot, that some of the farmers hae been buisting their sheep out o' i' the kirk lang syne.' Sir Walter's shaggy eye-brows dipped deep over his eyes, and, suppressing a smile, he turned and strode away as fast as he could, saying, that 'we had just rode all the way to see that there was nothing to *be* seen.'[1]

---

[1] This passage, included in printed but not in manuscript versions of the *Familiar Anecdotes*, is repeated from Hogg's *Memoir of the Author's Life*. It is quoted here from James Hogg, *Memoir of the Author's Life* and *Familiar Anecdotes of Sir Walter Scott* (1834), ed. Douglas S. Mack (Edinburgh, 1972), 139. The reference to Satchells comes from p. 138.

The most obvious attraction of Hogg's anecdote is that its presentation both of Scott and of the quest for historically significant material seems so familiar. Hogg mocks the questing poet, though affectionately, because Scott proves so ready to recognize and to register his own absurdity. In doing so he captures exactly the image of Scott—self-deprecating, pragmatic, good-humoured—which has become standard in biographical and literary-historical tradition and which has done so much to exclude his works from what are still commonly regarded as mainstream Romantic aesthetics. Hogg's anecdote also suggests something of the ironic sense of history which shapes Scott's work. When read in the broader context of works such as Keats's 'Ode on a Grecian Urn' and Shelley's 'Ozymandias', it mocks the search for antique objects which have been invested with intense spiritual or even mystical significance, and insists on a commonsensical deflation of romantic images of the past. Such ironies can be paralleled many times in Scott's writings.

Less obviously, Hogg's anecdote is also paradigmatic of another, literary, displacement. Searching among the recesses of a dilapidated building, Scott thinks he has discovered an emblem of the lost past. The recess, however, unlike the caverns, dungeons, and secret passageways of Gothic fiction in the tradition of Walpole, Radcliffe, and Lewis, yields neither a remnant of the body (a mouldered skeleton) nor a remnant of the text (an old manuscript). Instead, it offers up a symbol of a male past, military and ecclesiastical, 'an ancient consecrated helmet'. Adding the deflation of historical to the deflation of literary romance, this heroic remnant is in turn exposed as a relic of continuing peasant labour, a tar-pot for branding sheep. Finally, Scott sums up the incident in terms which can be paralleled to his recognition of disappointment and frustration in the narrative structures of Radcliffe's fiction, 'a narrative where the imagination has been long kept in suspense, and is at length imperfectly gratified by an explanation falling short of what the reader has expected'.[2] Turning away, he concludes: 'we had just rode all the way to see that there was nothing to *be* seen'.

This study focuses on the relationship between Scott's texts and the narrative strategies and conventions of late eighteenth- and

---

[2] *MPW* iii. 375.

early nineteenth-century Gothic, in order to elucidate the narrative complexities of the Waverley Novels, their interplays of different forms of narratorial and historical authority, and the special narratorial status of the 'Author of *Waverley*'. It addresses, therefore, all three of the issues just raised in relation to Hogg's anecdote of the recess and the tar-pot: the construction and reception of a 'Walter Scott' who can stand detachedly on the margins of Romantic studies, to be included or not as the critical agenda dictates; the problematic status of the historical and the means of historical enquiry and authentication; and the literary transgressiveness of the Waverley Novels, defined as the narratorial and descriptive processes by which they both suggest and continually redefine generic vocabularies. In organizing these three arguments around a reinterpretation of Gothic it also aims to show that previous estimations of Gothic's significance in Scott's work have been unduly motif- and subject-orientated and have not adequately registered the complications introduced by style and structure.

As several recent studies (taking their cue from Foucault) have suggested, 'Walter Scott' is a complex construction of authorial and critical preoccupations which inevitably privileges certain types of authorial endeavour over others. From the earliest reviews onward, for example, critics have tended to view Scott as a 'natural' rather than as a 'literary' writer, and have been correspondingly distrustful of the heavily stylized parts of Scott's writing, including characters, descriptions, episodes, and entire subplots which are so conventional that they seem to ask to be read within ironic or even apologetic inverted commas. David Brown, for example, suggests at the end of his reading of *Waverley* that the apparently inferior parts of Scott's works are the result of his falling back on derivative literary models which are 'inconsistent with the temper of his own imagination'.[3] However, any attempt to essentialize the 'temper' of Scott's imagination is defeated by the variety and experimentation of the Waverley Novels. Their titles alone demonstrate his unwillingness to be restricted to any one literary manner. He draws back from extending his disquisition on the implications of titles in the first chapter of *Waverley*, declaring: 'I could proceed in proving the importance of a title-

[3] David Brown, *Walter Scott and the Historical Imagination* (London, 1979), 30.

page, and displaying at the same time my own intimate knowledge
of the particular ingredients necessary to the composition of
romances and novels of various descriptions.'[4] One must assume,
therefore, that he had reasons for teasing the public with titles like
The Black Dwarf, *The Monastery*, and *Castle Dangerous*. In
the novels themselves, character-types, settings, and plots familiar
from Gothic vie for attention with others commonly regarded as
truer to 'the temper of his imagination'. The Indian sub-plot of
Guy Mannering; or, The Astrologer (a subtitle which immediately
marks a new direction from *'Tis Sixty Years Since* the year before)
adds the conventions of Gothic to the other romance elements
evaluated in the novel. Modelling herself into a sort of Madame
Montoni without reflecting that this implies both her own death
and the persecution of her daughter, Guy Mannering's wife 'called
her husband in her heart a tyrant until she feared him as such, and
read romances until she became so enamoured of the complicated
intrigues which they contain, as to assume the management of a
little family novel of her own, and constitute her daughter, a girl
of sixteen, the principal heroine'.[5] In *The Antiquary*, Scott's
next novel, the Gothic Glenallans coexist with the Wilkie-esque
Mucklebackits (and indeed are tightly bound to them by the plot).
Later, *Rob Roy* contains secret passageways and fathers raised from
the dead as well as discussions of the Highland economy and mercantile ethics, while the Radcliffean waif Lady Hermione is as
important a player as her stolid protector George Heriot in *The
Fortunes of Nigel*. Consistently, however, critics have regarded the
Mucklebackits, the Highland economy, and George Heriot as
somehow closer to Scott's 'true' genius than the Glenallans, secrets,
and Lady Hermione, and have imposed standards of artistic and
political homogeneity on the Waverley Novels which those novels
then conspicuously fail. This study does not propose to smooth
over the differences of tone and style in Scott's work, or to effect
reconciliations between competing novelistic conventions which
seriously challenge the authority of the rational and normative
voice of the 'Author of *Waverley*' as it sorts and grades competing

---

[4] WN i. 11.
[5] WN iii. 179. *The Mysteries of Udolpho* is a useful context here, but it is also
rewarding to read the Indian sub-plot of *Guy Mannering* in relation to the anatomy
of a marriage destroyed by jealousy in Godwin's novel *Fleetwood* (1805), which
Scott reviewed so derisively in the *Edinburgh Review*.

orders of experience and expression. The effectiveness of the narrating voice in the Waverley Novels is difficult to estimate if one continues to filter out critically the problems (social, generic, structural) which most exercised Scott authorially.

It is also important to avoid filtering out the novels which have not been thought to add much to Scott's reputation. The internal canon which is implicit in much Scott criticism has selected for special attention a small group of Waverley Novels (*Waverley* to *The Bride of Lammermoor*, plus *Redgauntlet*), leaving many others awaiting even a fairly elementary interpretation. This study draws on the full range of Scott's work, in implication if not always in detail, approaching its idiosyncrasies via interpretation of canonically marginal texts such as *The Pirate* and *Peveril of the Peak* while drawing attention to the importance of margins and boundaries (imaginative, hermeneutic, and historical as well as generic) in individual novels. Working from a conviction that a change of emphasis and a widening of discussion is necessary at the present stage in the reception of Scott's work, it has more to say about *The Fortunes of Nigel* and *Anne of Geierstein* than about *Waverley*, and more about the frame narrative of *The Fair Maid of Perth* than about the frame narrative of *Old Mortality*. It also aims to throw some light on the construction of the Scott canon itself, and, in particular, to show how influential Scott's own directions have been in guiding readers along the interpretative routes he came to favour. Probably the most familiar critical assumption about Scott is that he became a great writer by accident, enjoying a popularity and degree of influence throughout the nineteenth century which were entirely disproportionate to the care he took over his work. Surveying previous critical readings of *Rob Roy*, for example, A. N. Wilson finds himself concluding that Scott's critics have been 'simply too clever' for him.[6] Yet Scott has had a powerful and lasting impact on the way in which his works are read, and towards the end of his career he made clear though never explicit decisions about the presentation of his fiction as he formed it into a coherent, though disparate, collection of narratives to be passed on to the next generation of readers.

The revaluation which is proposed in this study questions,

[6] A. N. Wilson, *The Laird of Abbotsford: A View of Sir Walter Scott* (Oxford, 1980), 184.

therefore, several of the founding tenets of Scott's current critical reputation. The triumph of the Mucklebackits over the Glenallans, George Heriot over Lady Hermione, is on the most obvious level a triumph of what is seen as historical realism over the clichés of extravagant romance. Scott's critical reputation, especially since the publication of Georg Lukács's study *The Historical Novel* in 1937, has been inseparable from the claim that he should be regarded as the inventor of historical fiction. In studies of the development of this sub-genre it has sometimes seemed obvious to draw a line between the pseudo-historical fiction of the eighteenth century and the new form invented by Scott, distinguished for most critics by its factual specificity; by its sense of a relationship between past and present which it highlights in prefaces, notes, and narratorial comment; and most of all by its desire to make the past appear familiar rather than strange. This division between pseudo-history and the real thing did not seem obvious to Scott. His critical analyses of such works as Walpole's *The Castle of Otranto* openly reject simple distinctions of this kind, and he insists in theory as well as in practice on the interdependence of history and fictional form. He prefaces *Ivanhoe*, for example, with an astute and knowing Dedicatory Epistle from one antiquary to another, reflecting on the problems of combining history and fiction, and on the novelist's duties to his historical material. Instead of emphasizing the educative value of historical fiction, the preface to the most influential novel of the nineteenth century suggests that historical fiction may not only depend upon but also perpetuate the reader's ignorance—that it might be an escape from and denial of history rather than a new medium for analysing it.

Scott's consciousness of the part played by literary convention in creating what he wanted to be a personally and popularly satisfying medium of analysis is clearly demonstrable in two novels which, like *Ivanhoe*, set out to re-imagine well-known historical figures: Mary, Queen of Scots in *The Abbot* and Elizabeth I in *Kenilworth*. Viewed in terms of Gothic, *The Abbot* includes variations on the motifs of the nunnery, the evil female gaoler/abbess, the escape from prison, and the disguised monk. The situation of Queen Mary, like that of Burke's Marie Antoinette, draws on readers' familiarity with literary accounts of imprisoned femininity (and indeed there are similarities between Scott's depiction of Mary in *The Abbot* and his description of Marie Antoinette facing the Parisian crowd in his 'Preliminary View of the French Revolution' in the 1827 *Life of Napoleon*).[7] The most telling literary context for his next novel, *Kenilworth*, meanwhile, is Sophia Lee's Elizabethan romance *The Recess*, in which Leicester has to account to his queen for another secret marriage, this time not to Amy Robsart but to Matilda, one of the novel's two imaginary heroines. Cumnor Hall is a variant of the Recess of the earlier novel's title (and like it is simultaneously haven and prison), while Scott's determination not to denigrate the historical character of Elizabeth may have been reinforced by the villainous part she plays in the love-triangles of *The Recess*. Scott's novel seems to be much more securely 'historical' than Lee's, or at least has been accepted as such in most criticism. As a historical figure Amy Robsart is externally verifiable, which cannot be said for Lee's notorious invention of twin daughters for Mary, Queen of Scots. As the heroine of *Kenilworth*, however, she is deployed in a blatantly anachronistic series of events. Scott's readers may have smoothed over the joins between history and fiction in these novels, but Scott himself seems to be more interested in drawing attention to them.

The questions about the status and value of historical fiction which are repeatedly raised in the Waverley Novels become much more significant when examined in the context of literary Gothic, much of which was engaged in exploring the same aesthetic and historiographical questions. The recognition of cultural difference and change (what Coleridge termed the conflict between the 'two great moving principles' of human life),[8] which is so fundamental to the effect of the Waverley Novels, was implicit from the first in the relationship between modern reader and past custom deliberated by Walpole in the two prefaces to *The Castle of Otranto* in 1764 and 1765. This study proposes that Gothic modes of history were not preparations for the real thing but ways of presenting the past and imaginative responses to the past which

---

[7] *The Life of Napoleon Buonaparte, Emperor of the French: With a Preliminary View of the French Revolution*, 9 vols. (Edinburgh, 1827), i. 196: 'the reviled, persecuted, and denounced Queen stood before them, her arms folded on her bosom, with a noble air of courageous resignation'.

[8] *Coleridge's Miscellaneous Criticism*, ed. Thomas Middleton Raysor (London, 1936), 341–2.

survive in the Waverley Novels—indeed, as in *The Abbot* and *Kenilworth*, intrude into, complicate, and fashion them, in whole or in part.

The process described here in such combative terms might be glossed as a struggle for generic identity, of a kind discussed increasingly frequently by historians of the Romantic novel. The title of this study, accordingly, draws attention to the different types of legitimacy and processes of legitimation (cultural as well as formal) at work in the Waverley Novels. As Ina Ferris has recently reminded us: 'Questions of generic propriety and hierarchy are rarely matters of simply literary interest, and Scott and his contemporaries were well aware of the cultural implications of genre.'[9] Establishing legitimacy for a cultural form means validating, authenticating, an origin; for example, by validating as source a particular author, a specific historical moment, or a reliable repository of information. It is inseparable from broader cultural constructions of authority.

Like Gothic fictions since Walpole's *Castle of Otranto* (1764)— a story of usurpation and retribution—and like the romance narratives on which Gothic is modelled, the Waverley Novels are literally histories of restored legitimacy. In *The Antiquary* (1816), the double taint of illegitimacy and incest must be removed from the Glenallan line and the true heir restored to his inheritance. At the end of *The Abbot* (1820), Roland Graeme's parents must be shown, against all the odds, to have been married after all. In *The Surgeon's Daughter* (First Series of *Chronicles of the Canongate*, 1827), the evil brother, Richard Middlemas, is never legitimized and never redeemed from villainy. All these novels tell not merely of miraculous recoveries of life and fortune but also of the restoration of something which is regarded as socially and legally just. The familiar romance plot of legitimate restoration which is so common in Gothic has an obvious political relevance in the years following 1814. The Waverley Novels appeared between the first Treaty of Paris (May 1814) and the first Reform Act in Britain (1832)—that is, between the settlement which began to restore legitimate monarchies in several European states, and the first

---

[9] *The Achievement of Literary Authority: Gender, History, and the Waverley Novels* (New York, 1991), 139. In her important study of Scott's construction of a new type of literary authority Ferris makes no attempt to address the generic complications introduced by Gothic, viewing the historical novel as primarily a development of the 'regional tale' pioneered by Maria Edgeworth and Lady Morgan.

great broadening of the parliamentary franchise in Britain. As several recent critics have insisted, the Waverley Novels are distinctively post-Revolutionary fictions, telling stories of providential restoration for individuals and nations.[10] They address in self-protectively conventional fictional guises questions which are analogous to those which exercised European leaders in debating the two treaties of Paris in 1814 and 1815 and throughout the Congresses of major powers which took place between 1814 and 1822: questions about the nature and value of monarchy, the place of ideology in practical politics, the wisdom of intervention in the affairs of other states, and the balance of power within, and between, nations. They also bear directly on political and constitutional issues debated in Britain over the same period. Scott did not need to think back to Paris in 1789 in order to discuss 'the behaviour of the rabble in the brutal insanity of the Queen's trial', to the Jacobin Club to reinforce his fears of coteries and conspiracies, or to the Illuminati to prompt his suspicions of the Roman Catholic priesthood, 'whose unrivalled dexterity and activity are increased by the rules which detach them from the rest of the world'.[11] In a specifically Scottish context, moreover, the first

---

[10] Critics who discuss Scott's work in the context of revolution include John P. Farrell, *Revolution as Tragedy: The Dilemma of the Moderate from Scott to Arnold* (Ithaca, NY, 1980), ch. 2; Marilyn Butler, *Romantics, Rebels and Reactionaries: English Literature and its Background* (Oxford, 1981), 109–12; Judith Wilt on *Quentin Durward* in *Secret Leaves: The Novels of Walter Scott* (Chicago, 1985), ch. 2; George Dekker, *The American Historical Romance*, Cambridge Studies in American Literature and Culture (Cambridge, 1987), 8–11. F. R. Hart discusses the historical conditions of questions of authority and legitimacy in the Waverley Novels, 'Scott's Endings: The Fictions of Authority', *Nineteenth-Century Fiction*, xxxiii (1978–9), 48–68. In 'The Audience for Romanticism: Walter Scott in France, 1815–51', *European History Quarterly*, xiv (1984), 21–46, Martyn Lyons argues (pp. 36–7): 'Novels like *The Heart of Midlothian* were based on a system of values which strongly echoed those promoted by French legitimism after 1815.'

[11] The trial of Queen Caroline (Aug. and Sept. 1820), recalled in Scott's *Journal* in Oct. 1826, p. 218; and see also *Letters*, vi. 235 for his opinion of the Queen's conduct in 1820. Graham McMaster comments on the Queen Caroline affair in *Scott and Society* (Cambridge, 1985), ch. 4. Scott comments on the 'Merry doings in London', the Cato Street Conspiracy, *Letters*, vi. 140, 178. Scott's suspicions of the Roman Catholic priesthood, which are especially marked in his letters and *Journal* when the question of Catholic Emancipation was on the political agenda, are quoted from a letter to Southey in 1807, *Letters*, i. 400: see also ii. 312, xi. 93, 130–1, 141–5, and *Journal*, 474–5, 533 (this last being the statement of half-formed artistic intent in Mar. 1829: 'I meditate doing something on the popish and protestant affray').

great period of his popularity as a novelist was also the period which witnessed the meeting of Glasgow radicals in Thrushgrove Field in October 1816; the local espionage of Alexander Richmond who reported oaths and conspiracies which the lord advocate, Alexander Maconochie (from 1819 Lord Meadowbank, the same who in 1827 announced Scott's authorship of the Waverley Novels), reported to such effect in the House of Commons in February 1817; the Scottish 'state trials' of 1817, which aimed to prove accusations of radical conspiracy but which revealed far more about governmental conspiracy and the urge to convict; and the so-called Radical War in 1820.[12]

The term 'legitimate', therefore, most immediately conjures up the political context of Scott's work, asking what counts as a legitimate history for Britain within the rapidly changing European framework of Scott's time, and for Scotland after its first (Ossianic) creation of a romantic identity and cultural history. In *Life on the Mississippi* in 1883, Mark Twain claimed that the French Revolution 'broke the chains of the *ancien régime* and of the Church' which were then promptly reforged by Scott and his 'enchantments'. Twain's Scott is a culpable reactionary who sets the world in love again with (among other things) 'decayed and degraded systems of government'.[13] Scott clearly supported the restoration of the Bourbon monarchies and celebrated, after the rule of 'force' exemplified first by the Terror and later by Napoleon, a government founded on 'law'. Making one of his favourite Shakespearian tags significantly more legalistic, he writes to Matthew Weld Hartstonge in April 1814, commenting on the settlements of 1814: 'The moderation of the Allied Princes has something peculiarly graceful in it—and gives much lustre by the contrast between lawful rule, and right supremacy, compared to military usurpation.'[14]

The translation of these views into fiction, however, is not

---

[12] On the lord advocate's judgements in the trials of Jan. 1817 in Selkirk, and Scott's reactions to the radical unrest of the times, see *Letters*, iv. 362, 369, 384–5.

[13] Mark Twain, *Life on the Mississippi* (1883), introd. James M. Cox (Harmondsworth, 1984), 327. Ch. 46 of *Life on the Mississippi* is devoted to Scott and his influence in the American South: see also the foundered steamboat *Walter Scott* in *The Adventures of Huckleberry Finn* (1884), ed. and introd. Peter Coveney (Harmondsworth, 1966), 129. Dekker discusses Scott's influence on the South in *American Historical Romance*, 272–333.

[14] *Letters*, iii. 428. The phrase is 'aweful rule, and right supremacy' from *The Taming of the Shrew*, v. ii. 109.

always either clear or direct. Scott presents his novels as loyalist fictions (a direction which is even clearer in the Magnum Opus, with its fulsome dedication to George IV), but there are problems and contradictions in his stance. As Hazlitt argues in his essay on Scott in *The Spirit of the Age* (1825), the element of romance works against the grain of the political message:

Through some odd process of *servile* logic, it should seem, that in restoring the claims of the Stuarts by the courtesy of romance, the house of Brunswick are more firmly seated in point of fact, and the Bourbons, by collateral reasoning, become legitimate! In any other point of view, we cannot conceive how Sir Walter imagines 'he has done something to revive the declining spirit of loyalty' by these novels. His loyalty is founded on *would-be* treason: he props the actual throne by the shadow of rebellion.[15]

Both Scott's emphasis on loyalty and Hazlitt's criticism of a spirit of political reaction which seems to him disingenuously dependent on fantasies of treason, attempt to single out governing principles in insistently pluralist novels. Hazlitt is right, however, to seize both on the importance of legitimate inheritance in Scott's work and on the difficulties of making fictional plots espouse personal political convictions. The 'actual throne' is not so easy to prop by 'the shadow of rebellion'. Nor is the 'principle of legitimacy' itself simple to apply. As Hazlitt recognizes in citing the competing legitimacies of the Brunswicks in Britain and the Bourbons in France and Spain (legitimacies which rested on significantly different principles of monarchy), fictions supporting the claims of one family may not coincide with fictions enhancing the appeal of legitimacy itself as a political principle. Lukács encounters similar problems when looking at Scott's relationship to the fictions of legitimacy. Lukács argues that the ideological struggle against the French Revolution produced a shallow contrast between capitalism and feudalism which became 'the war-cry of legitimist Romanticism',[16] although he emphatically denies that Scott idealized feudal societies in the way which he finds characteristic of Chateaubriand and the German Romanticists. Of the form of

[15] *The Complete Works of William Hazlitt*, Centenary Edition, ed. P. P. Howe, 21 vols. (London, 1930–4), xi. 65.
[16] Georg Lukács, *The Historical Novel* (1937), trans. Hannah and Stanley Mitchell (London, 1962), 23.

pseudo-history developed by supporters of the Bourbon Restoration
and the Holy Alliance, Lukács argues: 'The ideal of Legitimism is
to return to pre-Revolutionary conditions, that is, to eradicate
from history the greatest historical events of the epoch.'[17] Scott is
not this type of legitimist, however univocally the Waverley
Novels may sometimes seem to declare their politics.

The Waverley Novels are, then, histories of legitimacy in terms
both of plot and of declared political orientation. They are also
fictions which repeatedly question their own legitimacy *as* histories
and as legitimate products of the 'Author of *Waverley*' as final
authority and source. There has always been a close, though
under-examined, relationship between the plurality and flexibility
of Scott's work and the difficulty of fixing upon him a defined
authorial identity. According to Lukács, the only explanation for
the oddities of Scott's work was a divided psychology, a creative
life and social self ideologically opposed: a man who 'became a
great realist despite his own political and social views'.[18] Some
nineteenth-century readers of Scott cherished more complicated
explanations for the diversity of the Waverley Novels. If the novels
were several and varied, so, conceivably, was the author. Of the
many contemporary explanations of the magical productivity of
the 'Author of *Waverley*', one of the most bizarre is recorded in
Lockhart's *Life of Scott*, as an anecdote passed on to Scott's friend
Maria Edgeworth by an American correspondent in 1824: 'The
theory prevalent in her own neighbourhood was, it seems, that the
authorship was a joint-stock business—Sir Walter being one of
the partners, and the other an unfortunate lunatic, of whose
papers he had got possession during a lucid interval.'[19] Scott
himself was attracted to the metaphor of the joint-stock company
as a way of representing the sources of his work (as he demonstrates in the frame narrative of *Tales of the Crusaders* in 1825),
and it usefully emphasizes the competing voices and authorities in
his fiction. His 'other' partner, the 'unfortunate lunatic', rebels
throughout his fiction against the tones of sober reason which are
clearly audible in such works as the review 'On the Supernatural
in Fictitious Composition; and particularly on the Works of
Ernest Theodore William Hoffmann' (1827), in which Scott firmly

---

[17] Ibid. 24.   [18] Ibid. 59.   [19] Lockhart, vii. 226.

subordinates the thrills of supernatural fiction to the satisfactions of historical enquiry: 'We could willingly have spared some of his grotesque works of *diablerie*, if we had been furnished, in their place, with the genuine description of the attack upon, and the retreat from Dresden, by the allied army, in the month of August, 1813.'[20] This is an important comment, not least because it shows succinctly the resistance which Scott is capable of mounting against any attempt to idealize the imaginative at the expense of the factual.

It also helps to explain one major omission from this study. The subordination of the supernatural to the historical and cultural, evident in Scott's review of Hoffmann, is particularly significant in those parts of the Waverley Novels which might be expected to challenge the rational narrative voice most pressingly. As Hogg laments in his short story 'The Mysterious Bride', first published in 1830, belief in the supernatural was waning: 'Even Sir Walter Scott is turned renegade and with his stories made up of half-an-half like Nathaniel Gow's toddy is trying to throw cold water on the most certain though most impalpable phenomena of human nature.'[21] These 'half-an-half' stories are full of narratorial tensions, opportunities, and crises. Coleridge's complaint about *The Pirate* is often quoted to suggest the contradictions of Scott's use of the supernatural:

Sir Walter relates ghost stories, prophecies, presentiments, all praeter-supernaturally fulfilled; but is most anxious to let his readers know, that he himself is far too enlightened not to be assured of the folly and falsehood of all that he yet relates as *truth*, and for the purpose of exciting the interest and the emotions attached to the belief of their truth . . .[22]

Ruskin, as so often, follows Coleridge closely when he complains in the third part of *Modern Painters* about Scott's inability to believe in his own ghosts, and about the apologetic manner in which he explains them away. It is significant, however, that Coleridge's complaint concentrates not on Scott's ghosts but on

---

[20] *MPW* xviii. 299.

[21] *James Hogg: Selected Stories and Sketches*, ed. Douglas S. Mack, The Association for Scottish Literary Studies, No. 12 (Edinburgh, 1982), 145.

[22] Coleridge, *Misc. Crit.* 332. Coleridge makes a very similar point when pondering the effect of the Bodach Glas in his marginalia on *Waverley*, p. 322.

his manner of narrating them. The 'Author of *Waverley*' gives his readers thrills which, he then insists, are their own fault, nothing whatsoever to do with the suddenly detached and official tones of the narrator. When considering Scott's links with Gothic, previous critics have concentrated almost exclusively on motifs such as the presence of the supernatural or the setting of the haunted castle to the exclusion of matters of style, tone, context, and narrative pattern. This study therefore omits to comment on Scott's spectres as if they were evidence in themselves of links with Gothic, and attends instead to the narrative ploys used to introduce, accommodate, isolate, and explain them.

The final legitimacy with which this study is concerned is the construction of a critical tradition, not just by critics of the present day but also, and pressingly, by Scott and his contemporaries. Something of Hazlitt's, Peacock's, or Percy Shelley's conviction that the poetry of the post-Revolutionary period signalled a new beginning can be detected in the novel's concern with origins in the late eighteenth and first part of the nineteenth centuries. Scott was construed by his contemporaries, somewhat surprisingly, as a novelist without origins except in the legends and traditions of oral culture. As some of his authorial disguises and feints suggest, he was fascinated by the role of the newcomer, always tempted to re-enact and rewrite the moment when, with the unmarked shield of *Waverley*, he made his entry into the lists of fiction. Critics, reviewers, and (especially influential) biographers have frequently endorsed this view. A great deal of nineteenth-century commentary on Scott implicitly or explicitly validates a particular tradition for the novel; a tradition which privileges the representational conventions of realism over those of romance. When eighteenth- and early nineteenth-century commentators on the history of fiction looked back, however, it was romance which they emphasized, as is clear from Clara Reeve's *The Progress of Romance* (1785) and John Dunlop's *History of Fiction* (1814). For Scott, too, as he demonstrates in his 1824 'Essay on Romance', the sources of romance and 'real history' were one and the same. The reception of Scott's work is, then, responsive to changing conceptions of the subject-matter and stylistic conventions deemed appropriate to the novel as a distinct literary genre. Such changing conceptions, however, smooth over the disruptions of form and tone which are actually going on in Scott's work. All too frequently, the critical

legitimization of the nineteenth-century novel has involved imposing a stultifying homogeneity on the Waverley Novels, and a
single voice on their author. I hope to show locally and precisely
the difficulties created in those novels by the intrusiveness of the
self-consciously expendable trappings of populist fiction.

Scott also deserves to be (but has so far failed to become) a piv-
otal figure in studies of how the novel transformed itself in terms
of class and gender in the early nineteenth century. Literature of
the Romantic period, and particularly its fiction, has recently been
described by Gary Kelly as 'a field of struggle for self-definition of
the classes who produced and consumed literature, principally the
professional middle classes', and as a representation of a 'national'
culture.[23] Other critics have viewed the diffusion of Gothic in even
starker terms. Tania Modleski has examined Gothic and other
fantasy literature as a way of 'inoculating' society against what
it fears most.[24] Rosemary Jackson argues that some nineteenth-
century novelists who adapt Gothic in effect betray its potential
for subversion, reclaiming its conventions for bourgeois ideology.
As both Modleski and Jackson recognize, gender is a complicating
factor in this progress towards respectability. Many recent com-

---

[23] Gary Kelly, 'The Limits of Genre and the Institution of Literature: Romanticism between Fact and Fiction', in *Romantic Revolutions: Criticism and Theory*,
ed. Kenneth R. Johnston *et al.* (Bloomington, Ind., 1990), 158–75 (158). Kelly's
case for the new conceptions of genre and audience in this period is clearly
indebted to the main precursor of this type of analysis, Raymond Williams in
Culture and Society 1780–1950 (1958; repr. with postscript Harmondsworth,
1963), esp. ch. 2. Also relevant to the present discussion are Kelly's argument that
there was a gender split between 'high' and 'low' literary forms (an argument easily
extended to the critical reception of Gothic and Waverley Novels), the moves by
fiction to appropriate the factual discourses of history and antiquarianism as part
of the redemption of the 'mere novel' (p. 165), and fiction's relegation of 'commercial' literature to the margins (p. 161): 'Because it seemed to transcend mere
professional, practical writing while itself remaining a kind of writing, it could
validate or legitimate the entire culture of writing while concealing the fact that
that culture was the property of only one part of society.' In *An Exemplary History
of the Novel: The Quixotic versus the Picaresque* (Chicago, 1981), Walter L. Reed
identifies what he calls a 'protocol of displacement' in a novel's relationship to
other novels, and argues that the rules of the novelistic form prevent the acknowledgement of debt (p. 4): 'The novel is a type of literature suspicious of its own
literariness; it is inherently antitraditional in its literary code.'
[24] *Loving With a Vengeance: Mass-Produced Fantasies for Women* (1982; repr.
New York, 1988). Modleski draws on Roland Barthes' suggestion in his essay
'Operation Margarine': 'One inoculates the public with a contingent evil to prevent
or cure an essential one.' See *Mythologies* (1957), selected and trans. Annette
Lavers (New York, 1972), 42–3.

mentators on the early development of the novel have demonstrated that the history of fiction validated in the nineteenth century was a masculine tradition. Scott's place in this history is suitably chivalric, his role being to rescue the novel from a creeping feminization which was particularly noticeable in the production and consumption of Gothic. Even in his own critical remarks on Gothic, it is noticeable that Radcliffe is allowed to be great not as a novelist but as a 'poetess', a dealer in sentiment and gentility. Eugenia C. DeLamotte has recently objected to the way in which many studies of Gothic emphasize male practitioners of the form, while Kate Ferguson Ellis attempts to relocate it in a politics of the domestic. The marginalization of female Gothic is not just a construction of recent critics, but (like its apolitical psychologizing) a process of literary and social realignment to which early practitioners actively contributed. The way in which critics of his own time, and ever since, have separated Scott's historical novels from the falsities of Gothic is of importance to this type of analysis of how the genre established itself and the kind of distancing tactics it employed.

The six chapters of this study bring Scott and Gothic together in several different ways. Chapter 1 examines the reception and interpretation of Scott's work, analysing the traditions of criticism which have worked to separate him from Gothic, and paying particular attention to the metaphor of health which has dominated them. Scott always chose to present himself as a casual writer, neither jealous nor ambitious; and his texts as casual constructions, neither sustained nor complete. The image of the likeable gentleman amateur, in turn, has profoundly influenced critical estimates of his work, which have always been inclined to present him as 'a man only extraordinary by the depth of his ordinariness',[25] making him (as Carlyle was quick to grasp and to exploit) unusually vulnerable to guilt by association with the ethics and aesthetics of the dominant culture ('the every-day mind').[26] Critical discussions of the texts, too, have been dominated by appeals to the normative and quotidian, and Scott's fissured novels eased into unity and wholeness (not to say wholesomeness). The final section

---

[25] Wilson, *Laird of Abbotsford*, 8.
[26] *The Works of Thomas Carlyle*, Centenary Edition, ed. H. D. Traill, 30 vols. (London, 1896–9), xxix. 75.

of this chapter deals in summary form with Scott's immediate contacts with Gothic novels and novelists, and identifies key issues in his critical writings on them. Gothic is notoriously difficult to isolate as a literary style in other works, and in Scott's case it tends to come mingled with the influences of the taste for German sensationalism in the 1790s, his editorial interests in medieval literature, and his experimentation in ballad. It has also tended to be played down in key accounts of Scott's intellectual development. Lockhart's *Life of Scott*, for example, presents him as an avid reader who is somehow never moved to take imaginative issue with what he reads, and a youthful collaborator of Matthew Lewis's who has already learned from Shakespeare all he needs to know about historical representation. By bringing together a wide range of Scott's comments on Gothic, this section of the argument demonstrates that Scott was not merely a passive inheritor of Gothic subjects and styles, but instead was actively involved in debating and promoting them.

The subjects and styles of Gothic itself are the focus of the second chapter, which aims to interpret Gothic in a way which establishes parameters for the analysis of the narrative and historio-graphical techniques of the Waverley Novels. It brings together Gothic's dual preoccupations with history and narrative, relating both to anxieties of literary origin by way of the figure of the recess. The frame narrative of *The Monastery*, which describes the search for the lost heart of the Abbot Ambrosius (originally intended to be the heart of Robert Bruce) in the ruins of St Mary's at Kennaquhair, makes architecture the focus of a search which is really about ways of telling, or narrating.[27] So, too, in Gothic, narrative and historical processes are repeatedly figured as tortuous approaches through hidden subterranean passageways to a secret which may finally be revealed, but which can never be an adequate recompense for the terrors of the quest. The interpretation of Gothic in this chapter is allusive rather than exhaustive, and it does not engage in the kind of comparative analysis which would allow it to claim that the techniques and preoccupations which it highlights in late eighteenth-century Gothic are exclusive to that form. It does, however, emphasize certain matters rather more

[27] See WN xxi. 355 and the note to the Magnum Opus edition (xxi. 357–8) on the original scheme for the novel and the heart of Robert Bruce.

than has been done in previous criticism, paying particularly close attention to devices of historical authentication in Gothic, to questions of literary and historical origin, and to the problems which arise when Gothic conventions intrude into non-Gothic works.

Chapter 3 returns in detail to the frame narrative of *The Monastery*, and several other types of paratext in the Waverley Novels, in order to focus on the careful constructions of authenticity which, for many readers, mark the difference between Waverley Novels and Gothic. Since authenticity presupposes authority, the apparent absence of authority during the years of Scott's anonymity has recently received a great deal of attention from critics, who have analysed in detail Scott's habit of 'keeping you all this while in the porch, and wearying you with long inductions', as Dr Dryasdust describes it in the Prefatory Letter to *Peveril of the Peak*.[28] The frame narratives of the first editions of the Waverley Novels, with their extended play between competing antiquaries, amateur historians, and gentlemen of leisure of varying degrees of dignity and trustworthiness, are now well-charted demonstrations of the complex interplay of authority and authenticity in Scott's work. It is fitting that comparable critical discrimination should be shown when considering Scott's later, more seductive, and more lastingly authoritative, authenticating voice: that is, the autobiographical voice introduced in the Magnum Opus edition, in which Scott creates an authorial persona whose pronouncements about origins and authority have been more difficult to refute than those of Peter Pattieson or Dr Jonas Dryasdust.

The remaining chapters turn in detail to individual Waverley Novels. Their discussions are weighted towards novels which have previously received little critical attention, although I have been conscious that one of the most effective ways of dismissing Gothic elements in Scott has been the implication that they infiltrate only his weakest novels. For this reason I include discussion of works like *The Heart of Midlothian*, *Rob Roy*, and *Redgauntlet*, which are staples of previous scholarship and which also, therefore, present the opportunity to consider interpretative difficulties alongside the critical traditions which have so far worked either to neutralize or more simply to lament them. Continuing Chapter 3's

---

[28] *WN* xxviii, pp. lxvii–lxviii.

interest in the creation of different types of narratorial authority in the Waverley Novels, each ensuing chapter analyses the functions of Gothic elements in particular novels, providing practical demonstrations of the argument that the elevation of the rational voice of the 'Author of *Waverley*' into the sole voice of Scott is a misrepresentation of the conflict of styles and tones characteristic of his fiction. Chapter 4 examines Scott's techniques of secrecy and suggestion in *The Pirate*, *Rob Roy*, and *Peveril of the Peak*, arguing that Scott draws on his readers' familiarity with a literature of terror while allowing them, if they choose, to categorize it as literary and therefore secondary to the main purposes (moral and political) of his art. It also argues for a strategic and self-aware use of Gothic conventions, which are not to be equated either technically or psychologically with anything 'repressed' by the 'dominant' aesthetic of these novels. Developing these ideas, Chapter 5 provides five sample case-studies of the ways in which Gothic complicates the social, political, and historical interpretations of individual works. Finally, Chapter 6 and the Conclusion examine two of Scott's most interesting experiments in historicism and the fictional patterns of Gothic, *Redgauntlet* and *Woodstock*, regrouping in the process some of the study's governing preoccupations: with texts, bodies, and experiments, with narrative as approach and delay, and with the relationship between authority and authenticity. *Redgauntlet* shows that Gothic, far from invalidating the novel's claim to be taken seriously as a re-creation of a past era, acts both as catalyst and as means of expression for Scott and for his hero, Darsie Latimer. In the best traditions of politicized Gothic, Darsie tells a story of authority which must be resisted and which thinks itself absolute, and in order to convey its fearfulness he draws on his readers' familiarity with the conventions of terror-fiction. In several Waverley Novels, from *Old Mortality* to *The Surgeon's Daughter*, a narrative of historical and social particularity struggles against a psychological language of possession and fatalism. In *Redgauntlet* and *Woodstock*, this struggle is shown to be an inescapable part of the imaginative assimilation and modern redescription of the past. Just as *The Abbot* tells the story of Mary, Queen of Scots as if she were an Emily St Aubert being pressed to sign documents giving up her estate (and in so doing fits her into a tradition of heroineship which helps to ensure her survival as an icon of Romantic culture), so Gothic provides models for *Redgauntlet* and *Woodstock* which make them not inauthentic histories but histories necessarily narrated according to the literary conventions of their time.

I

The Healthy Text: Scott, the Monsters, and the Critics

Were one to preach a Sermon on Health, as really were worth doing, Scott ought to be the text.

(Thomas Carlyle, 1838)[1]

THIS chapter is a study in the pervasiveness of critical metaphor and its powers of exclusion. It begins with two of the most celebrated of all nineteenth-century appraisals of Scott: Carlyle's assessment of 'our *healthiest* of men' in his review of the first six volumes of Lockhart's *Life of Scott* in 1838; and Mark Twain's attack on Scott in *Life on the Mississippi* in 1883. To these it adds another description of Scott which has not been celebrated at all: Lady Charlotte Bury's contemporary account in her *Diary Illustrative of the Times of George the Fourth*, which was published in 1838–9. The terms in which Bury and Carlyle praise and Twain disparages Scott highlight the way in which Scott's works, and the image of Scott as a robust and manly writer, became entangled in the course of nineteenth-century criticism with notions of moral and spiritual healthiness. The association between the Waverley Novels, moderation, and good health is not just a hackneyed convention of Victorian ideology but a complex of unexamined assumptions about the nature of Scott's art (and, indeed, the purpose of all art) which have impeded certain types of literary analysis and have brought Scott's work into what seems a natural alignment with some literary works rather than with others. Historically, Scott criticism has been dominated by three metaphors—the 'natural', the 'healthy', and the 'sane'—which veer between medical, moral, and aesthetic values and to each of which the reputation of Gothic is unassimilable. Although few modern critics would make explicit appeals to the healthiness of Scott's work,

---

[1] Unsigned review of the first six vols. of Lockhart's *Life of Scott*, first printed in *London and Westminster Review*, xxviii (1838), 293–345; repr. in Carlyle, *Works*, xxix. 22–87 (51).

images of the organically coherent text, uncontaminated by external influences incompatible with its essential self, are still used to belittle those parts of the Waverley Novels which draw most clearly on the conventions of sensationalist literature and the vogue for horrid mystery. In the most recent comprehensive biography of Scott, for example, Edgar Johnson describes Scott's reaction against *The House of Aspen* in the following revealing terms: 'In fact by this time Scott was recovering from the German measles that had mottled English literature with a rash of Gothic melodrama. He was to move steadily away from the monstrous absurdities of its horrors and in the direction of good sense.'[2] The word-play here is understandably irresistible, but it has a long and interesting intellectual history.

One of the key arguments of this chapter is that Scott's critics, far from being 'too clever for him' (in A. N. Wilson's phrase), have been remarkably responsive to the authorial role he fashioned for himself. It is only fair, therefore, to point out at the start of this analysis Scott's own stated preference for an aesthetic governed by moderation, proportion, and common sense. No author of the early nineteenth century more strenuously opposed, in life and art, the image of the Romantic artist in agony—as debilitated tuberculor or ineffectual angel—or seemed more decisively to have brought to a conclusion the Romantic debate on the sanity of true genius. Explicitly avowing an aesthetic and a politics of moderation, the Waverley Novels publicly warn of the fate of the victims of 'enthusiasm' and excess. In private, Scott's *Journal* and letters confidently endorse the value of self-restraint, while the biographical traditions which support his literary reputation throughout the nineteenth century firmly establish him as the icon of normality for his own and future ages. ('A man only extraordinary by the depth of his ordinariness', one recalls, also from Wilson.) Appeals to the moral and intellectual healthiness of literary works were common in the aesthetics of the mid-nineteenth century and had long been a feature of the reception of the Waverley Novels.[3] According to Lockhart, for example, Scott was

---

[2] Johnson, 186. New attention to the metaphor of monstrosity, of a kind which serves as useful commentary on such remarks as Johnson's, is paid by Chris Baldick in 'The Politics of Monstrosity', ch. 2 of *In Frankenstein's Shadow: Myth, Monstrosity, and Nineteenth-Century Writing* (Oxford, 1987).

[3] The fullest account of the reception of Scott's work, with references to the concentration on 'healthiness', is given by James T. Hillhouse in *The Waverley Novels and Their Critics* (Minneapolis, 1936), esp. p. 217.

characterized by a 'firm healthiness of feeling', a 'sustained and masculine purity of mental vigour'.[4] Scott himself, likewise, commonly discussed literary creativity in terms of bodily well-being, describing several of his works as 'apoplectic' or 'smelling of apoplexy',[5] and condemning *The Black Dwarf* for being just as stunted and misshapen as its central character. Among such analogies between the healthy body and the healthy text, however, Carlyle's influential remarks have acquired an uncommon force. In Carlyle's review Scott, with Cobbett as ally, triumphs over a 'sickly' age as the embodiment of the healthy imagination. Underlying Carlyle's praise, however, is an energetic dissatisfaction with the adequacy of such standards for art. Scott, he complains, lacks what he describes as any 'spiritual' purpose. His works have no moral significance. Carlyle's assessment of Scott manages simultaneously to celebrate Scott at the expense of his contemporaries as the epitome of moral and artistic healthiness and to suggest that such healthiness can never be quite enough to produce great works of literature. Scott is a useful prop for an attack on the false literary sensibilities of his contemporaries, but the inevitable implication of Carlyle's review is that it is not enough for the artist or his work to be comfortably in communion with the everyday impulses and beliefs of his society. Health becomes bourgeois, banal.

No other critic conveys quite such an intricate view as Carlyle of the desirability and the limitations of the healthy imagination. Many of Scott's critics in the mid to late nineteenth century endorse much more vigorously the virtues of artistic healthiness. Like Carlyle's, however, their praise frequently leaves Scott vulnerable to charges of mediocrity and complacency. In his biography of Scott, published in 1870, George Gilfillan confidently

[4] In his review of the Galignani edition of *Lives of the Novelists, Quarterly Review*, xxxiv (Sept. 1826), 349–78 (377). The association between healthiness and manliness has recently been analysed by Ina Ferris in *The Achievement of Literary Authority*. Especially relevant to the present discussion are ch. 8 and pp. 92–4, 242–6 (in which Ferris discusses the contrast between Scott and Byron in terms of health and fever: Byron seems close to Gothic here). Ferris's main case is that Scott legitimized novel-reading as well as novel-writing as a manly practice, and some parts of her analysis of the way in which the Waverley Novels were received, especially in the reviews, usefully complement the concerns of this chapter, which was written before her study was published.
[5] According to Scott, the 'apoplectic' novels (the term an allusion to the Archbishop's apoplexy in *Gil Blas*) are *Rob Roy* (*Letters*, v. 50), *Peveril of the Peak* (vii. 281, 308), *Tales of the Crusaders* (ix. 179), *Woodstock* (ix. 363).

links Scott's style to his physical well-being, and repeats accounts
of how Scott composed his novels before breakfast, 'a practice to
which some have ascribed in part the limpid clearness, temperate
calm, freshness, and healthiness of his style'.[6] Similarly, Ruskin's
Scott never wrote a bad word except when he was ill, and for
Walter Bagehot the tone of his imagination made the Waverley
Novels ideal resources for the sickroom.[7] One needs to re-create
something of this consensus in order to appreciate the shock-value
of Twain's rhetoric in *Life on the Mississippi*. In the course of his
attack on Scott for negating all the social gains of the French
Revolution, Twain refers to what he calls 'the Sir Walter disease'
which had infected the thinking, manners, and social structures of the American South. Twain's attack has prompted many
defences, but no one has paid much attention to the corrosive
force of his reference to 'the Sir Walter *disease*', which challenges
the most fondly held of all nineteenth-century beliefs about
Scott.

Both Carlyle and Twain sound confident in their diagnosis of
Scott's work. The cultural associations of (dull?) healthiness and
(creative?) illness create something of a crisis of representation,
however, when Scott's fervent admirer Lady Charlotte Bury comes
to describe his physical appearance in her *Diary Illustrative of the
Times of George the Fourth*. The passage is an interesting instance
of the complications caused by analogies between body and imagination. Bury is torn between her desire to see Scott's genius hand-
somely embodied and her appreciation of a singularity which does
not fit conventional notions of beauty. She first allows herself
sentimental regret that men of such ability should not be 'more
sightly', confessing her disappointment at Scott's homely appearance. She concludes, however, by finding 'something I think graceful in Walter Scott's hitch; it would be a pity he should walk like
any body else'.[8] Bury's dilemma comes to seem typical of a recurrent problem in Scott criticism. Does the critic choose to celebrate

[6] George Gilfillan, *Life of Sir Walter Scott, Baronet* (Edinburgh, 1870), 77.
[7] Review of *The Waverley Novels*, *The National Review*, vi (Apr. 1858),
444–72.
[8] *Diary Illustrative of the Times of George the Fourth, Interspersed with
Original Letters from the late Queen Caroline, and from Various Other Distinguished Persons*, 4 vols., vols. iii and iv ed. John Galt (London, 1838–9), iii.
153–4.

Scott's healthy integrity or besmirch it in the hope of producing more intellectually provocative interpretations?[9]

The first two sections of this chapter set out to trace the history of this choice and to suggest some of its implications. Lest Edgar Johnson's account of the 'German measles' seem an isolated example of the continuing association between Gothic and disease, however, it is worth citing a few instances which bring into focus the kind of aesthetic and moral judgement critics have sometimes thought themselves to be making when considering the Waverley Novels and Gothic as related literary forms. In 1960 Leslie A. Fiedler separated Scott from Gothic in terms of their relative healthiness. *The Bride of Lammermoor*, the only Waverley Novel to produce 'the authentic sadist shudder' of Gothic, is, according to Fiedler, 'rather the creation of his illness than of his will'.[10] Fiedler's account appeared long before the dismantling of what might be called the delirium theory of the composition of *The Bride of Lammermoor*, but his (this time openly disapproving) reliance on an aesthetic of healthiness is clear. Going further still, the whole genre of historical fiction, initiated and championed by Scott, becomes for Fiedler a return to cleanliness after the infection of Gothic:

The historical romance is the 'cleanest' of all sub-genres of the novel thus far, the creation of a self-conscious attempt to redeem fiction at once for respectability and masculinity. The acclaim which greeted Scott is surely due in part to a sense in the bourgeois community that the novel in his hands at long last had become fully acceptable, not merely 'pure' but patriotic, too.[11]

Metaphors of health and purity have been used many times since Fiedler to justify the neglect of much of Scott's later work, and they continue to support the common assumption that the earlier Waverley Novels are 'fresher', more natural, than the later pro-

[9] An interesting example of a critic writing in Scott's defence after critical equations of genius with neurosis had excluded him from attention is C. S. Lewis's address as President of the Edinburgh Sir Walter Scott Club in 1956. Lewis complains that critics now want to discover *angst* in Scott in order to take him seriously as an artist. He finds the 'blue devils' confined to Scott's private writings, however: *Sir Walter Scott 1771–1832: An Edinburgh Keepsake*, ed. Allan Frazer (Edinburgh, 1971), 99.
[10] Leslie A. Fiedler, *Love and Death in the American Novel* (1960; rev. edn. London, 1967), 172.
[11] Ibid. 170.

ducts of financial necessity. At a much more advanced stage of scholarship, similar tastes may underlie recent editorial moves to purge Scott's texts of the encrustations of later revisions, additions, explanatory notes, and introductions, and to restore to them what is somewhat optimistically regarded as their original freshness. Healing the body of Scott's texts is a complicated manœuvre editorially, for reasons which differ from novel to novel. Critically, it is important to be alert to any supporting aesthetic which perpetuates some of the oldest preoccupations of Scott scholarship.

Bearing Charlotte Bury's descriptive dilemma in mind, however, the following discussion does not set out simply to reverse the value judgements of the metaphor of healthiness and to equate either excess or limitation with artistry. The usefulness, and dangers, of disease as a metaphor for creativity are pertinently addressed by Susan Sontag in her essay *Illness as Metaphor* (1978), which contrasts the cultural associations of tuberculosis and cancer. These distinctions, and the characteristics Sontag accords them, are useful in working through the implications of the metaphors of healthiness in Scott criticism and biography. Sontag notes of the image of the artist as tuberculor:

> Many of the literary and erotic attitudes known as 'romantic agony' derive from tuberculosis and its transformation through metaphor.... 'When I was young,' wrote Théophile Gautier, 'I could not have accepted as a lyrical poet anyone weighing more than ninety-nine pounds.' (Note that Gautier says lyrical poet, apparently resigned to the fact that novelists had to be made of coarser and bulkier stuff.)[12]

Sontag makes no mention of Scott, but the terms in which she describes the prototypical novelist here cannot fail to recall him, particularly in his incarnation as 'Eidolon' in the frame narratives of *The Fortunes of Nigel* and *Peveril of the Peak*. To adapt the terms of Sontag's essay as a whole, Scott might be seen to contradict the model of the artist as tuberculor, imagined as the victim of excess passion, but to come close to the model of the (usually non-artistic) victim of cancer, imagined as the disease of repression. Sontag quotes Blake's 'Proverbs of Hell' in support of her analysis of the victim of cancer: 'He who desires but acts not,

---

[12] Repr. in *Illness as Metaphor* and *Aids and its Metaphors* (Harmondsworth, 1991), 30.

breeds pestilence.' In an understandable reaction against earlier convictions of Scott's healthiness, much Scott criticism of recent years seems over-enamoured of the repressed forces of anger, ambition, and greed in his writings and psyche. The attention paid to Williamina Belsches or to Scott's relationship with his father exposes assumptions just as powerful and distorting as those proposed by Carlyle for his sermon on Health, with Scott as text.

1. The New-Discovered Continent

When Joanna Baillie wrote her 'Lines on the Death of Sir Walter Scott' in November 1832, she not only praised Scott's 'virtuous', 'pure' writings, but also took special care to distinguish them from the moral and representational distortions of sensationalist literature:

> Not so with those where perverse skill pourtrays
> Distorted, blighting passions; and displays,
> Wild, maniac, selfish fiends to be admired,
> As heroes with sublimest ardour fired.
> Such are, to what thy faithful pen hath traced,
> With all the shades of varied nature graced,
> Like grim cartoons, for Flemish looms prepared,
> To Titian's or Murillo's forms compared . . .[13]

Baillie's image of Scott complements Hazlitt's portrait of the conservative, inartificial artist, 'only the amanuensis of truth and history'.[14] It is also in keeping with Carlyle's 'healthy' Scott of 1838, sent by Nature 'in the sickliest of recorded ages, when British Literature lay all puking and sprawling in Werterism, Byronism, and other Sentimentalism tearful or spasmodic (fruit of internal *wind*)'.[15] The consensus after his death, and in reaction to details of his life, therefore, was that Scott's 'faithful pen' had rescued literature from excess and perversity. Scott's transformation into the Victorian icon of normality required that he be set expressly in opposition to the experiments of Gothic. 'Their

---

[13] *The Dramatic and Poetical Works of Joanna Baillie* (London, 1851), 792–4 (793).

[14] Hazlitt, *Works*, xi. 63, and see p. 61: 'All is fresh, as from the hand of nature'.

[15] Carlyle, *Works*, xxix. 39.

naturalness is their main charm, with which they will win their
way to posterity', proposes one early memoir, considering the
Waverley Novels as a group.[16] For David Vedder also, writing in
1832, the success of *Waverley* could be traced to Scott's 'natural'
genius.[17] For many Victorian readers, Scott was the central
exponent of normative, moderate, aesthetics: a powerful position
politically, as well as aesthetically, encouraging an acceptance of
Scott's interpretations of history and society as sane and equable.

So why did Scott's works become so closely associated with a
mid-Victorian aesthetic of health, and what part did Scott himself
play in setting his works in the context of an aesthetic which
valued nature over culture, inspiration over imitation?

The critical division between Scott and Gothic set in early,
despite the comments of some contemporary observers who
thought them closely linked. Wordsworth instinctively grouped
Guy Mannering with 'modern novels of the Radcliffe School',
while the *Augustan Review* compared its 'mysterious incidents'
and 'darkness of coloring' to *Caleb Williams*.[18] More commonly,
however, as John Murray's relieved endorsement of *Waverley*
illustrates, the Waverley Novels were hailed as a return to sanity
after false and irresponsible horrors. Murray wrote to his wife in
1814: 'Pray read *Waverley*, it is excellent. No dark passages; no
secret chambers; no wind howling in long galleries.'[19] Sounding a
moralistic note to be heard many times afterwards, Francis Jeffrey
argued in his review of *Waverley* in November 1814 that 'the
secret of this success' is that the unknown author is 'a person of
genius; and that he has, notwithstanding, had virtue enough to
be true to nature throughout'.[20] Scott himself was keen to dif-
ferentiate his works from others of their type on the grounds of

[16] *The Genius and Wisdom of Sir Walter Scott, Comprising Moral, Religious,
Political, Literary, and Social Aphorisms, Selected Carefully from his Various
Writings: With a Memoir* (London, 1839), p. xiii.
[17] *Memoir of Sir Walter Scott, Bart. With Critical Notices of His Writings:
Compiled from Various Authentic Sources* (Dundee, 1832), 21–2. Vedder traces
the development of the novel form before Scott (pp. 18–19) without mentioning
Gothic novelists, but records a conversation with Dr Pichot on Lewis, Radcliffe,
Walpole, and Maturin (p. 49).
[18] *The Letters of William and Dorothy Wordsworth: The Middle Years Part II,
1812–1820*, ed. E. de Selincourt, rev. Mary Moorman and Alan G. Hill, 2nd edn.
(Oxford, 1970), 232; review of *Guy Mannering*, *Augustan Review*, i (July 1815),
228–33 (228).
[19] Quoted by Amy Cruse, *The Englishman and his Books in the Early Nineteenth Century* (London, 1930), 226.
[20] *Edinburgh Review*, xxiv (Nov. 1814), 208–43 (208).

their increased truth to 'nature'. In the opening chapter of *Waverley* he declares: 'It is from the great book of Nature, the same through a thousand editions, whether of black-letter, or wire-wove and hot-pressed, that I have venturously essayed to read a chapter to the public.'[21] (He is unable to make even this declaration, however, without displaying the antiquarian's interest in historical specifics, here the specifics of typesetting methods.) In the review of the first series of *Tales of My Landlord*, which he wrote with Erskine and Gifford to discourage suspicions that he was the author of *Waverley*, he argues that the unknown writer had attended more to human psychology and historical detail than to 'the involutions and developement of the story'. Other novelists of the time, he claims, 'sought for assistance chiefly in the writings of their predecessors. Baldness, and uniformity, and inanity are the inevitable results of this slovenly and unintellectual proceeding. The volume which this author has studied is the great book of Nature.'[22]

The authority of the 'great book of Nature' in the reception of the Waverley Novels owes much to the critical ground established by responses to Scott's earlier work as poet and ballad-collector. Looking back on *Minstrelsy of the Scottish Border* in 1838, Carlyle was to think of Scott's work as 'a new-discovered continent in Literature'.[23] In 1870 George Gilfillan traced in Scott's poetry the 'healthful influence' of the *Minstrelsy*, and early reviewers of the poetry comment on its 'beauty and originality' and the 'vigour and originality of poetical genius'.[24] The Waverley Novels, in turn,

---

[21] *WN* i. 14.

[22] *Quarterly Review*, xvi (Jan. 1817), 430–80 (468); for details of the attribution of much of this review to Scott, see Hillhouse, *The Waverley Novels and their Critics*, 17 n.

[23] Carlyle, *Works*, xxix. 50. See comments in reviews of *Minstrelsy of the Scottish Border*, *British Critic*, xix (June 1802), 570–6; *Edinburgh Review*, i (Jan. 1803), 395–406, esp. description of the ballads as not highly polished, but 'exhibiting the true sparks and flashes of individual nature' (p. 399); *Monthly Review*, NS xlii (Sept. 1803), 21–33; *Scots Magazine*, lxiv, 3rd ser. i (Jan. 1802), 68–70, praising the introduction, notes, and the pathos and energy of the 'rude' productions (p. 69).

[24] Reviews of *The Lay of the Last Minstrel*, *British Critic*, xxvi (Aug. 1805), 154–60 on 'the beauty and originality of the poetry' (p. 155); *Eclectic Review*, ii, pt. 1 (Mar. 1806), 193–200, on the 'vigour and originality of poetical genius' (p. 20). Even the disapproving review in *Critical Review*, 3rd ser. v (July 1805), 225–42, concedes that 'In the rough but spirited sketch of the marauding borderer, and in the *naiveté* of his last declaration, the reader will recognize some of the most striking features of the ancient ballad' (p. 230).

were received as innovative and unique. They came to readers without an acknowledged author and without a literary past. George Allan, recalling this early period of historical fiction in 1834, claimed that *Waverley* 'was of an entirely distinct species of fictitious composition from any that had ever preceded it', the first to combine history and imaginary characters and events.[25] As Croker states in his review of *Waverley*, the quality of the work was felt to derive 'not from any of the ordinary qualities of a novel, but from the truth of its facts, and the accuracy of its delineations'.[26] These first reviewers noted literary debts, but, especially in the early years of his fame, regarded them as insignificant when weighed against his originality. Reviewers were indignant when, later in his career, Scott offended against this reputation. One especially scathing review of *St Ronan's Well* declares: 'such a writer, we say, has no right to have recourse to the exhausted subjects of bigamist noblemen, death-bed repentances, accomplished sons, and injured mothers'.[27]

The tendency to detect in the Waverley Novels a turning-point in the history of the novel has its own historical context and explanation. In an age which was becoming more interested in the genealogy of the novel, and in which works like Dunlop's *The History of Fiction* and Scott's own 'Lives' of the novelists formed part of a developing debate, many commentators and critics sought clear patterns of development in the tastes of the age. It seemed to many that a revolt against the enthusiasm for Gothic had taken place on a roughly educational or evolutionary model (and one with a distinct gender bias), by which adult common sense had supplanted childish and womanish fancy. Scott had rescued the

[25] *Life of Sir Walter Scott, Baronet; with Critical Notices of His Writings* (Edinburgh, 1832–4), 339. The anonymously published *Genius and Wisdom* agrees that the 'productions of Scott are virtually novelties in our literature' on the same grounds (p. xxxv).
[26] See commendation of 'that original and native poet' in the review of *Waverley*, *British Critic*, NS ii (Aug. 1814), 189–211 (211); the opening remark of Jeffrey's review of *Waverley*, *Edinburgh Review*, xxiv. 208–43; the assertion in the review attributed to Croker, *Quarterly Review*, xi (July 1814), 354–77 (377): the comparable reception of *Guy Mannering*, *Scots Magazine*, lxxvii (Aug. 1815), 608–14, esp. p. 609; *Augustan Review*, i. 228–33; *Monthly Review*, NS lxxvii (May 1815), 85–94.
[27] *British Critic*, NS xxi (Jan. 1824), 16–26 (17). The same novel is described as a 'sickly, misbegotten imp' in *New European Magazine*, iv (Jan. 1824), 54–61 (55).

public from Gothicism, with some help from Maria Edgeworth and, more rarely admitted, Jane Porter. Even critics who did not admire the Waverley Novels accepted that Scott had made a great difference to a degenerating fictional tradition. It is debatable whether Charles Lamb had Scott in mind when he wrote in 'The Sanity of True Genius' of the 'happier genius' who had 'expelled for ever the innutritious phantoms' of the Minerva Press.[28] Other commentators, however, certainly made this connection. Lady Louisa Stuart, one of Scott's most perceptive and challenging correspondents, wrote to him in April 1826 in mock despair over Mary Shelley's novel *The Last Man*:

> Since the wonderful improvement that somebody who shall be nameless, together with Miss Edgeworth and one or two more, have made in novels, I imagined such stuff as this had not ventured to show its head, though I remember plenty of it in the days of my youth. So for old acquaintance-sake I give it welcome. But if the boys and girls begin afresh to take it for sublime and beautiful, it ought to get a rap and be put down.[29]

The alliance between Scott and Edgeworth, of course, was no sudden insight of Lady Louisa's, but had been proposed by Scott himself at the end of *Waverley*, when a novel which on one level is about crises in personal identity, entrapment, and the remorselessness of historical change, instead neatly assimilates itself to the new departures in social historiography represented by novels of national and regional manners.

As part of criticism's quest for origins and progress, some observers assumed that public enthusiasm for the Waverley Novels had ruined the market for Gothic. *A Letter, Containing Some Remarks on the Tendency and Influence of the Waverley Novels on Society* (1832), observes:

> few are those who, from their own private knowledge, may not affirm to what total oblivion the 'Castle Spectre,' or the 'Haunted Tower,' or any bearing such titles, are for ever consigned. The 'Family Vault' has long received the 'Queen of Ghost Stories and Subterranean Horrors,' together

---

[28] *The Works of Charles and Mary Lamb*, ed. E. V. Lucas, 7 vols. (London, 1903–5), ii. 187–9 (188). Lamb refers to the 'silver fork' novels as well as to Gothic.

[29] *Lady Louisa Stuart: Selections from her Manuscripts*, ed. James A. Home (Edinburgh, 1899), 229.

with her numerous train of imitators. For this change in the character of
our reading, I think we must confess ourselves mainly beholden to the pen
of Walter Scott. Our change has been by no means abrupt; we were
hardly rid of the old love before we were gradually on with the new.[30]

'Gradually' is an important concession, but in any case the commentator's aim is not to applaud Scott but to show that both types
of novel are responsible for moral deterioration. He presents the
shift in taste as a change of degree, not of kind:

We changed from falsehood to partial truth only: like the awakening
sleeper, we unclosed, in part only, our morning shutter, and so we
exchanged that which was glaringly and decidedly unreal, for that which
might possibly be imagined as real. This was the first step in our con-
version. This is the simple history of our change from Mrs. Radcliffe and
Co. (unless Miss Jane Porter be allowed an intermediate consideration) to
the Author of the 'Tales of my Landlord.'[31]

The author of the *Letter* argues against the moral tendency of the
Waverley Novels, and therefore groups them with a more disreputable tradition. It was much more common, in a drive to
secure the respectability and masculinity of the novel, to separate
them from it. In the most telling of all summaries of Scott's
relationship to Gothic, this division is emphatically declared by
Lewis's biographer, Margaret Baron-Wilson, whose *Life and Correspondence of M. G. Lewis* was published in 1839, the year after
Carlyle's inspired review of Lockhart:

The novels of the 'wizard of the north,' following, as they did, the
talented but worldly-minded productions of Miss Edgworth, happily an-
nihilated the class of works among which that of Lewis was so prominent. They proved that the deepest and most thrilling interest was to be
invoked and sustained, without the aid of the wild or supernatural; while
the sympathies were awakened by historical associations, and kept alive
by natural delineations of ordinary life. Imparting, as the Scotch novels
did, a more solid and healthy tone to the taste of 'light readers,' the

---

[30] *A Letter, Containing Some Remarks on the Tendency and Influence of the
Waverley Novels on Society, From a Clergyman of the Church of England to a
Younger Brother* (London, 1832), 4. The tendency of this work is clear from its
epigraph and closing quotation from Jeremiah 6: 30 ('Reprobate silver shall men
call them'). See also 'Timothy Touchstone' (pseud.), *A Letter to the Author of
Waverley, Ivanhoe, &c. &c. &c. on the Moral Tendency of those Popular Works*
(London, 1820).
[31] *Tendency and Influence of the Waverley Novels*, 5.

monstrous and supernatural in fiction—having done their worst—were quietly consigned to the graves from which they might be said to have originally sprung.[32]

For Scott's own most influential biographer, the conviction that Scott had revolutionized the practice and reputation of novel-writing became central to the creed:

He has widened the whole field to an extent of which none that went before him ever dreamed; embellished it by many original graces, as exquisite at least as any that their hands had introduced; and ennobled it by the splendours of a poetical imagination, more powerful and more exalted by far than had ever in former days exerted its energies elsewhere than in the highest of the strictly poetical forms—epic and tragic.[33]

This claim, made in Lockhart's review of the pirated Galignani edition of *Lives of the Novelists*, was a logical extension of the consensus of opinion at the time of the publication of the Waverley Novels. His *Life of Scott*, in turn, authoritatively validated that claim for future readers and critics.[34]

The *Life of Scott* examines the aspects of Scott's art which are explicable as direct products of his life and personality, and it is not concerned to establish any precise aesthetic context, unless this context is so distanced that it constitutes a statement of value rather than an analysis of artistic allegiance. (Acceptable literary contextualizing is permitted when Lockhart comes to mention Shakespeare, Cervantes, and Dryden, for example.) Lockhart's emphasis on natural genius was neither accidental nor automatic, as a comparison with another of his biographical projects demonstrates. In his *Life of Burns* (1828), Lockhart argues that Burns was better acquainted with literary convention than might be expected, was less of a heaven-taught ploughman and more of a

---

[32] *The Life and Correspondence of M. G. Lewis, Author of 'The Monk,' 'Castle Spectre,' &c. With Many Pieces in Prose and Verse, Never Before Published*, 2 vols. (London, 1839), i. 175–6; published anonymously, but authorship claimed in her later work *Our Actresses; or, Glances at Stage Favourites, Past and Present* (1844).

[33] *Quarterly Review*, xxxiv (Sept. 1826), 376–7.

[34] Some impression of the importance of Lockhart in shaping later presentations of Scott is given by John Gibson, *Reminiscences of Sir Walter Scott* (Edinburgh, 1871), 3. See also Andrew Lang, *Sir Walter Scott*, Literary Lives, ed. W. Robertson Nicoll (London, 1906), p. viii: 'All other books on Scott are but its satellites, and their glow, be it brighter or fainter, is a borrowed radiance.'

reader.[35] In the *Life of Scott*, in contrast, he isolates his subject from the common round of literary knowledge and exchange. Lockhart makes it clear that Scott paid careful attention to the techniques of other writers: 'Those who observed him the most constantly, were never able to understand how he contrived to keep himself so thoroughly up to the stream of contemporary literature of almost all sorts, French and German, as well as English.'[36] Even so, he offers no analysis of the possible effects of such reflection. On the one hand, he notes Scott's 'propensity to think too well of other men's works'. On the other, he ascribes the weakest parts of Scott's work to the influence of 'the practice of vulgar romancers' and 'the German taste'.[37]

Lockhart's use of the tag 'German' repays closer attention. The villainizing of German literature of the 1790s, which is obvious in Lockhart's account of what he suspects to be the weakest parts of Scott's work, had of course been anticipated by Scott himself in nearly every letter of later years which reflects on the 'German-mad' period of his youth.[38] Even so, the taints of 'Germanism' which proved most useful to Lockhart in explaining away incongruous aspects of Scott's literary experimentation reveal much more about the tastes of the late 1830s than about those of the 1790s. Some hints about the unsuitability of 'German' taste in the

[35] *Life of Robert Burns*, Constable's Miscellany of Original and Selected Publications in the Various Departments of Literature, Science, and the Arts, No. 23 (Edinburgh, 1828), on education, pp. 14–18, on reading, pp. 21, 35–6, and a summary of the effect of his reading, pp. 309–10. Scott approved of Lockhart's treatment of Burns (*Journal*, 486).

[36] Lockhart, viii. 62; Lockhart makes a similar point when discussing *Ballantyne's Novelist's Library*, vi. 270. This impression is justified by Scott's numerous reviews, and references to newly published works in his letters and *Journal*. For the reviews, see *MPW* xviii; see *Journal*, 213 (Ainsworth), 114 (Austen), 507 (Ferrier), 213, 215, 672 (Horace Smith), 219, 231, 232–3, 233–4, 415, 420 (James Fenimore Cooper), 304 (Thomas Hamilton), 298, 323–4 (Robert Ward), 314 (Disraeli), 268, 270 (Mrs Johnstone), 152–3, 161, 587, 608 (Galt), 114 (Lady Morgan).

[37] Lockhart, x. 247, vii. 117–18, vi. 256. R. P. Gillies agreed with Lockhart that Scott discovered good in second-rate novels, *Recollections of Sir Walter Scott, Bart.* (London, 1837), 168.

[38] *Letters*, i. 124, ii. 89, 495, x. 250, 282–3, 331, xii. 449–50. See Lockhart, i. 276–8, 280, and on Scottish material used in the German manner in 'Glenfinlas', ii. 25: also Scott's comments on late 18th-cent. German drama, *MPW* vi. 381–6; 'Essay on Imitations of the Ancient Ballad', *PW* iv. 36–44, the argument reinforced by Allan, *Life of Sir Walter Scott*, 63, on German literature arousing the 'dormant imagination of the nation'.

context of 'natural' art at the time of the *Life of Scott* are suggested by Wordsworth's 1842 manuscript note, appended to the third poem in his *Memorials of a Tour in Scotland, 1803* ('Thoughts Suggested the Day Following, on the Banks of Nith, Near the Poet's [Burns's] Residence'). Wordsworth comments on his reading of the 'natural' Burns and Cowper, 'whose writings, in conjunction with Percy's *Reliques*, powerfully counteracted the mischievous influence of Darwin's dazzling manner, the extravagance of the earlier dramas of Schiller, and that of other German writers upon my taste and natural tendencies'.[39] Wordsworth's comment suggests that a particular kind of 'German' taste was incompatible with the desired model of a natural artist. Some indication of the enduring appeal of this model, and its incompatibility with the image of the Germanist, is given by the terms in which Ruskin contrasts Scott and Carlyle in *Praeterita* (1885–9):

> It is farther strange to me, even now, on reflection—to find how great the influence of this double ocean coast and Cheviot mountain border was upon Scott's imagination; and how salutary they were in withdrawing him from the morbid German fancies which proved so fatal to Carlyle...[40]

The underlying model of Scott's healthiness is striking, as is the emphasis on fresh air. Ruskin assumes that Scott was protected from Germanism by the way in which his temperament responded to and accorded with his native environment.

It is worth emphasizing that there is nothing inevitable or automatic in Lockhart's tilts at German literature in the *Life of Scott*. They are part of a process which constructs Scott as a self-inspired and peculiarly *native* writer, and they may seem a surprising tactic given Lockhart's own involvement in the transmission of German writing during this period. Lockhart was a notable German scholar, contributing with R. P. Gillies to the 'Horae Germanicae' for *Blackwood's Edinburgh Magazine* from 1819 onwards. However, this 'Blackwoodian' Germanism—more in-

---

[39] *The Poetical Works of William Wordsworth*, ed. E. de Selincourt and Helen Darbishire, 5 vols. (Oxford, 1940–9), iii. 442.

[40] *Praeterita: Outlines of Scenes and Thoughts Perhaps Worthy of Memory in my Past Life* (1885–9), introd. Kenneth Clark (London, 1949), 510. On the importance of imaginative health for Ruskin, see C. Stephen Finley, 'Scott, Ruskin, and the Landscape of Autobiography', *Studies in Romanticism*, xxvi (1987), 549–72.

formed, more critically aware, and more acceptable in literary
circles—was very different from the brief popularity of German
melodramatic and sentimental plays in the 1790s, summarily dis-
credited by 'The Rovers; or, The Double Arrangement' for *The
Anti-Jacobin; or, Weekly Examiner* in 1798. Associating Scott's
Germanism with this earlier disreputable type, Lockhart took
defensive action. The *Life of Scott* defuses a potential problem
with a mixture of frank avowal and assurances that Scott's judgement improved as he grew older. After describing the reasons for
Scott's fascination with German materials, Lockhart notes that
William Erskine, always anxious that Scott should regulate his
imagination, tried to curb his enthusiasm with 'unmerciful severity
as to the mingled absurdities and vulgarities of German detail'.
He adds: 'That it was not accompanied with entire success, the
readers of the Doom of Devorgoil, to say nothing of minor blem-
ishes in far better works, must acknowledge.'[41] Lockhart's emphasis sits awkwardly beside Scott's own 'Essay on Imitations
of the Ancient Ballad' (1830), when the German language and
literature seem to have freed themselves from the levelling reputation of the 1790s and to have acquired emphatically anti-French
connotations. The German language is like English, he thinks, in
its 'manly force of expression'. The literature, also, is sympathetic,
unlike the neo-classical tastes of the French.[42] Instead of basing
his defence on similar politically charged associations, the *Life of
Scott* keeps Scott's interest in German literature closely within the
bounds of what F. R. Hart has called 'Lockhart's Coleridgian
theme: the sanity of true genius'.[43]

In some ways, as the example of German literature and its
reputation demonstrates, the *Life of Scott* is, inevitably and fruit-
fully, an exercise in artistic updating, a re-marketing of Scott for a
new generation of readers. The *Life of Scott* is in this sense the
logical continuation of Scott's own project in the Magnum Opus
edition. Lockhart offers a personal interpretation of the origins
and progress of Scott's imagination, but he also writes as Scott's

[41] Both from Lockhart, i. 280. For a discussion of the dramatic models and
sources of *The Doom of Devorgoil*, see my 'Castle Spectres: Scott, Gothic Drama,
and the Search for the Narrator', in *Scott '91*, ed. J. H. Alexander and David S.
Hewitt (Edinburgh, forthcoming).
[42] *PW* iv. 25.
[43] F. R. Hart, *Lockhart as Romantic Biographer* (Edinburgh, 1971), 245.

son-in-law and executor, and he is protective of Scott's personal
and literary reputation. The *Life of Scott* corrects several rumours
about Scott's life and opinions, including rumours that *Waverley*
sold slowly and that George IV treated Scott with coldness. In
reaction to Hogg's *Anecdotes of Sir W. Scott* (the first version of
Domestic Manners and Private Life of Sir Walter Scott), which
Lockhart read in March 1833, it plays down any sense of literary
equality and collaboration between Scott and Hogg, relegating
Hogg to the position of 'happy child' among the Edinburgh literati
and notably conflicting with other accounts of the friendship,
such as those given in George Allan's *Life* and the memoirs of
James Skene and William Laidlaw.[44] 'Literature, like misery,
makes men acquainted with strange bed-fellows', muses Lockhart,
deftly registering through *The Tempest* the class-determined access
to literature which allies him with Scott against the common
enemy.[45]

However, it would be misleading to fix upon 'Oedipus Lockhart' all responsibility for the version of Scott which emerges from
the *Life of Scott*.[46] It was not Lockhart's purpose to offer a
comprehensive account of Scott's art or of its origins. Scott had
already provided details of his literary inspirations and motivation
in the introductions and notes of the Magnum Opus, which,
for financial as well as artistic reasons, it was inadvisable to
supersede. To some extent, Lockhart's interference with Scott's
letters shows that the *Life of Scott* was a revisionist interpretation

[44] Allan, *Life of Sir Walter Scott*, 198–205; William Laidlaw, *Recollections of
Sir Walter Scott (1802–1804)*, ed. James Sinton, Transactions of the Hawick
Archaeological Society (Hawick, 1905), 3–6; and the impression of banter and
equality in the early years in *The Skene Papers: Memories of Sir Walter Scott
(c.1832)*, ed. Basil Thomson (London, 1909), 38. In contrast, the impact of
Lockhart's presentation is crudely apparent in Gilfillan's comments on the 'monstrous *mesalliance*', *Life of Sir Walter Scott*, 53, and Archibald Stalker's comments
on 'the outrageous Hogg', *The Intimate Life of Sir Walter Scott* (London, 1921),
55.
[45] Lockhart, ii. 173, adapting *The Tempest*, II. ii. 41. The version of Hogg's
memoirs to which Lockhart reacted so violently (and with so little obvious cause)
has been reprinted as *Anecdotes of Sir W. Scott*, ed. Douglas S. Mack (Edinburgh,
1983). See also Mack, 'Hogg, Lockhart, and *Familiar Anecdotes of Sir Walter
Scott*', *Scottish Literary Journal*, x/1 (May 1983), 5–13.
[46] The phrase is Graham McMaster's, in *Scott and Society*, 6, but the belief that
Lockhart secretly disliked Scott and did his best in his *Life* 'to dishero him', as
Carlyle puts it (*Works*, xxix. 32), can be traced back to the very earliest reception
of his biography.

of Scott's personality and art according to Lockhart's own perceptions, but it was also very conservative. Its opening narrative is
Scott's own, the brief 'Ashestiel Autobiography' of 1808, which,
in a tone of dignified reticence, Scott claims to have written so
that 'the public may know from good authority all that they are
entitled to know of an individual who has contributed to their
amusement'.[47] The statements, and the vaunted authority, of this
opening document set perceptible limits to Lockhart's endeavour,
especially in relation to the early years in which, in best Words-
worthian fashion, readers assume Scott's imagination to have been
shaped. Lockhart appears unwilling to set up theories of Scott's
imagination which might overshadow or contradict those already
set out by Scott. Instead, he simply gives up this dominant space in
his biography to Scott's own narrative.

It is the power of Scott's own self-invention, therefore, which
emerges most strongly from an analysis of Lockhart's *Life*. Lockhart reinforces rather than invents an image when he celebrates
Scott as 'the last and greatest of the Border Minstrels', a writer
who drew his primary inspiration from the traditions of Scottish
legend, history, and folklore. He repeats the account of the growth
of imaginative powers which Scott gives in the Epistle to Erskine,
an account which emphasizes the influence of early surroundings,
romance tales, and local legend, the 'poetic impulse given, | By the
green hill and clear blue heaven'.[48] Scott did not need Wordsworth's endorsement for these ideas, but after the publication of
The Prelude in 1850 his account of himself, supplemented by
Lockhart, must have been all the more instantly recognizable as a
portrait of the Romantic artist. Similarly, Lockhart's silence on the
subject of literary exchange and context, which is incompatible
with his insistence on Scott's wide reading, is less surprising when
set beside Scott's own comments on these matters. Although he
consistently makes light of the artistic design and ambitions of

[47] Lockhart, i. 2. On Lockhart's revisions, see Hart, *Lockhart*, ch. 5, esp. pp.
199–236.
[48] *PW* vii. 137. Lockhart quotes the Epistle, i. 110–12, and recommends it, p.
110, as 'a picture of the dawning feelings of life and genius, at once so simple, so
beautiful, and so complete'. Kathryn Sutherland's discussion in 'Defining the Self in
the Poetry of Scott and Wordsworth', *Scott and His Influence: The Papers of the
Aberdeen Scott Conference, 1982*, ed. J. H. Alexander and David S. Hewitt,
Association for Scottish Literary Studies Occasional Papers, No. 6 (Aberdeen,
1983), 51–62, is relevant.

his work, Scott's comments about his own creativity emphasize freedom from artistic rule and a regard for 'nature' rather than for literary convention. In his letters he emphasizes the easy inclusiveness of his 'light & loose sort of poetry', which he claims to regard as a 'pleasure-walk' for taking in fine views.[49] Much of his theorizing about imagination and self-expression, especially in the Epistles written to introduce the cantos of *Marmion*, is a declaration of creative independence. In keeping with this notion of his creative autonomy, Scott works hard to distinguish his work from the current output of fiction. In the first chapter of *Waverley*, he assures his readers that this is to be no 'Tale of other Days' or 'Romance from the German', with a profligate abbot, oppressive duke, and all the machinery popularized by *The Monk*.[50] In fact, Scott's working practice was consistently more deliberate and more consciously literary than his theories of creativity choose to suggest. One of the few details which he gives about his methods of composition suggests that his imagination was sustained and prompted by other literature, of whatever quality: 'When I find myself doing ill or like to come to a still stand in writing I take up some slight book, a novel or the like, and usually have not read far ere my difficulties are removed and I am ready to write again.'[51] All his personal statements deny that he took his work seriously, but the internal evidence of the novels suggests that he continually reflected, privately and in print, on the nature and extent of his commitment to writing.[52] His self-image was never an adequate summary of his literary interests or speculative opinions. Whatever Scott may have said about disregarding his fame, reputation mattered intensely to him, as is obvious in the *Journal* whenever it was threatened: 'They cannot say but what I had the *crown*.'[53]

Although they were given new impetus by Carlyle's response to the details provided in Lockhart's *Life of Scott*, the metaphors

[49] *Letters*, i. 353, iii. 30: see also ii. 69, 278, 348, iii. 191, *Journal*, 86, 215: and the development of this as a theory of romance narrative, in review of Southey's and W. S. Rose's translations of *Amadis de Gaul*, *MPW* xviii. 1–43.

[50] *WN* i. 10–11.

[51] *Journal*, 391.

[52] For denials of seriousness, see e.g. *Journal*, 6, 32, 50, 97, 416, 433, 526, 554 ('Get a good name and you may write trash'); on plots, 86, 214–15, 433.

[53] *Journal*, 393. See also 26, 62, 404, 523, 548, 554 (on fame in context), 65, 77, 129, 138, 491 (for Scott's defensiveness about his popularity).

around which so much critical discussion of Scott has clustered may be found in earlier reviews of the Waverley Novels and poetry, and are prominent in Scott's own presentation of himself as the artist of 'nature'. This self-presentation is especially marked in the review of the First Series of *Tales of My Landlord*. That the metaphors take on new life of their own after Carlyle's rewriting and resituating of Lockhart, and that Lockhart had created an image of Scott which was more in keeping with the tastes of the late 1830s than with those of (say) the 1810s, does not alter the fact that Scott himself made the primary decision to align his works with nature rather than with culture. Lockhart's chariness about Scott's literary debts is also entirely in keeping with Scott's skilfully underplayed presentation of himself as an original artist. Discussing his use of historical fact in contrast to his competitors, he hints in the *Journal* that it might be difficult to uncover his borrowings: 'Another thing in my favour is that my contemporaries steal too openly. . . . When I *convey* an incident or so I am [at] as much pains to avoid detection as if the offence could be indicted in literal fact at the Old Bailey.'[54] If one distinguishes further between two broad types of literary debt, a debt to tradition and received (perhaps historical) story, and a debt to particular texts by individual writers, one sees that Scott's apparent openness about the sources of his work is concentrated within the first category. It is not surprising that Lockhart should have followed the instincts so shrewdly demonstrated in the notes and introductions of Scott's Magnum Opus edition, to create a closed system of self-reference and self-validation.

The *Life of Scott*, therefore, is authoritative, but historically specific in terms of the literary traditions it is prepared to continue and the images of creativity it chooses to recognize. If one moves on from Lockhart to the generations of critics who have accepted him as the most authoritative guide to Scott's life and work, the alienation of Gothic from that life and work becomes all the more apparent. Lockhart's *Life of Scott* was written at a time when the critical reputation of Gothic was especially low. Radcliffe and Lewis (as Baron-Wilson's biography of Lewis amply demonstrates) were no longer regarded as either innovative or exciting. Scott had internalized so much of their example that he had forgotten it.

----

[54] *Journal*, 215.

Lockhart, with more lofty models of British and classical genius in mind, simply ignored it. For many readers of Lockhart, Scott's process of 'makin' himsell a' the time' was indeed achieved without outside help. This splendid isolation, however, was to have less than happy consequences for critical estimates of Scott's work. The image of an 'Oedipus Lockhart' trivializes both Lockhart's motivations in the *Life of Scott* and the importance of the interpretations he presents there. The meshing of critical opinions from periods as diverse as the 1790s and the 1830s clearly presented him with problems in selection and emphasis, as the denigration of German literature suggests. Even so, several of the problems which have beset critics up to the present day in convincing a wider readership to look seriously again at Scott stem from judgements made locally and for identifiable historical reasons in the *Life of Scott*.

2. *The Titanic Incompetent*

Lockhart's authoritative statements in the *Life of Scott*, with the commentary they encouraged, made a decisive impact on critical evaluations of Scott in the late nineteenth and early twentieth centuries. When Scott's novels first appeared they did not even have a securely assigned author, never mind the mass of details about that author's personal life which Lockhart was able to provide. Towards the end of Scott's career (as discussed in Chapter 3), the Magnum Opus edition had begun to supply these details; but the Magnum Opus is, importantly, a sporadic autobiography, and it subordinates the revelation of personality to the revelation of context and tradition. Lockhart's *Life of Scott* imposes pattern and decisively integrates the life, work, and environment. A useful comparison might be made with the first publications of *Jane Eyre* and *Wuthering Heights* and the rereadings of these works in the biographical contexts which were made possible by Elizabeth Gaskell's *Life* of Charlotte Brontë and Charlotte Brontë's 1850 introduction to *Wuthering Heights*.

A few examples will make clear the particular aspects of the Scott tradition which have hampered analyses of Scott's relationship to Gothic. Leslie Stephen's enthusiasm for the Waverley Novels as a 'breath from the Cheviots' is a particularly vivid instance of the attractive combination of ideas reinforced by Lockhart.[55] George Gilfillan, as already cited, envisages Scott writing 'amid the freshness of morning nature, with the sound of the Tweed in his ears, or the sun smiting the Castle rock before his eyes'.[56] The difficulty of asserting disharmonies either in Scott's thinking or in his literary debts is suggested by John Patten's insistence: 'Scott's nature was a perfectly harmonised organism. There were no ragged edges to his character, and he was not plagued with "the artistic temperament." So completely healthy was he that whatever he did, he did it with all his might.'[57] Scott's personal health and harmony comes potently associated, in some commentaries, with the health and harmony of a sentimentalized Scotland. Only in later commentaries is Scott's work linked to an energizing *dis*harmony, whether it be the disharmony of Scottish culture and language analysed by Edwin Muir, or the further disharmonies raised by critics (including MacDiarmid) of Muir's own romantic sense of nation.[58] On a smaller scale, critics continued to admire Scott's healthily generous appraisals of rival writers. 'Absence of all literary envy and jealousy was one of the most striking features of his character', according to G. R. Gleig's Lockhartian *Life of Sir Walter Scott* (1871).[59] More generally, Margaret Ball takes a strongly Lockhartian line in the only extensive study of Scott as a critic of literature, commenting on his 'admirable freedom from literary jealousy' as an 'innate virtue which he deliberately increased by cultivation'.[60] Another survivor

---

[55] Carlyle, *Works*, xxix. 38–40; Leslie Stephen, 'Hours in a Library No. 3— Some Words About Sir Walter Scott', *Cornhill Magazine*, xxiv (Sept. 1871), 278–93 (293).

[56] Gilfillan, *Life of Sir Walter Scott*, 33. A similarly sentimental description of Scott and the Tweed is given in George King Matthews, *Abbotsford and Sir Walter Scott* (London, 1853), 112.

[57] John A. Patten, *Sir Walter Scott: A Character Study* (London, 1932), 137.

[58] 'His picture of life had no centre, because the environment in which he lived had no centre.' (Muir, *Scott and Scotland: The Predicament of the Scottish Writer* (London, 1936), 12.) Muir's account was itself attacked by MacDiarmid, *Lucky Poet: A Self-Study in Literature and Political Ideas* (London, 1943), 199–204. See also Paul Henderson Scott's revision of Muir in *Walter Scott and Scotland* (Edinburgh, 1981); and the view of Scottish culture in David Craig, *Scottish Literature and the Scottish People 1680–1830* (London, 1961), esp. 222–3, 230.

[59] *The Life of Sir Walter Scott: Reprinted with Corrections and Additions from the Quarterly Review* (Edinburgh, 1871), 133, first printed in 1868.

[60] *Sir Walter Scott as a Critic of Literature* (1907; repr. Port Washington, NY, 1966), 81.

was the notion that Scott had banished the 'innutritious phantoms' from literature. George Saintsbury, introducing extracts from 'Tales of Mystery' in 1891, maintains that Lewis's 'best real claim to fame is the stimulus which he administered to Walter Scott's literary tendencies'; while Caroline Spurgeon, introducing *The Castle of Otranto* in 1907, expresses surprise that Scott should have taken Walpole's work seriously.[61]

In the 1920s and 1930s, interest in a newly labelled and documented 'Gothic' fiction began to develop, led by Montague Summers, Edith Birkhead, and Eino Railo. These critics located in Gothic a new psychological truth, an appeal to permanent human emotion now conceived in post-Freudian rather than post-Wordsworthian terms. It appeared that the subconscious, freed from moral constraint, might have its own representative fiction, and this fiction appeared increasingly alien from the work of the 'Border Minstrel'. As Birkhead concludes, when turning from Gothic fiction to Scott in her study *The Tale of Terror*: 'We leave the mouldy air of the subterranean vault for the keen winds of the moorland.'[62] These pioneering critics of Gothic, especially Railo, frequently suggest links between Gothic and the Waverley Novels, but only in motif and incidental atmosphere. The 'essential' Scott remained untouched by such parallels. According to Clara McIntyre, 'Scott owed much to both Mrs. Radcliffe and Lewis, though the tone of his mind was too healthy to allow him to follow them very far.'[63] Other critics accepted that Scott was, as Norman Collins tellingly expressed it, 'infected' by the tastes of his early years, but accorded him the heroic role of having rescued fiction from them.[64] One reason for the persistence of Lockhart's views in this period may have been the resurgence of specifically biographical celebrations published in and just after 1932, the centenary of Scott's death, including studies by Grierson, Pope-

---

[61] Saintsbury, ed., *Tales of Mystery: Mrs. Radcliffe—Lewis—Maturin*, The Pocket Library of English Literature, i (London, 1891), p. xxii; *The Castle of Otranto, with Sir Walter Scott's Introduction*, pref. Caroline F. E. Spurgeon, The King's Classics (London, 1907), p. ix.

[62] *The Tale of Terror: A Study of the Gothic Romance* (London, 1921), 156. Birkhead goes on to echo Hazlitt: 'He creates romance out of the stuff of real life.'

[63] 'The Later Career of the Elizabethan Villain-Hero', *PMLA* xl (1925), 874–80 (879).

[64] *The Facts of Fiction* (London, 1932), 135–6.

Hennessy, Buchan, Muir, Carswell, and Cecil.[65] Anchoring the work even more firmly than before in the life, these critics surely, though unintentionally, separated it from the new approaches being used for the analysis of Gothic.

More recently, treatment of Scott in relation to Gothic has had an uneven and unfocused history. There are many asides on the presence of Gothic elements in Scott's work, and a few longer discussions, nearly all sharing a tendency to look at motifs rather than narrative, the details of superstition rather than the precondition of suspense. Despite extensive revaluations of Gothic in recent years, it has retained many of its older connotations of the ridiculous, the jaded, and the historically naïve when used as a shorthand term for undesirable elements in the Waverley Novels. Those critics who accept Gothic as a shaping force in the Waverley Novels still tend to regard it as something which Scott transformed, made culturally and historically credible. What might have been a disconcerting presence in Scott's writing is thereby assimilated with as little trouble as possible to the dominant preoccupations of Scott scholarship.

Four main assumptions underpin the various critical examinations, whether they be brief or extensive, of Scott's links with Gothic. One assumption places the Waverley Novels automatically on a higher literary plane than any attained by Gothic fiction. Another assumes just the opposite, that Gothic becomes innovative and daring precisely in those areas of psychological, social, and literary exploration where Scott's conservatism, both social and literary, is most restrictive. A third, middle line grants Scott an experimentalist's interest in a burgeoning new literary form, but only at the cost of (variously) flippancy or obtuseness. A fourth, the most persistent of all (and sufficiently distinct to be identifiable as a separate trend, though strictly a subsection of the first), is the division between serious and superficial types of historicity common in post-Lukácsian readings of Scott. There are problems with all four.

---

[65] The survival of sentimental views of Scott is suggested by the later crop of biographical studies in and around 1971, the bicentenary of Scott's birth, including MacNalty's *Sir Walter Scott: The Wounded Falcon* in 1969, Moray McLaren's *Sir Walter Scott: The Man and Patriot* in 1970, and Carola Oman's *The Wizard of the North: The Life of Sir Walter Scott* in 1973. Sentiment did not, of course, elude Edgar Johnson's work of 1970.

Working from the first assumption, that Scott's fiction was immeasurably superior to Gothic, critics suggest that Scott resorted to Gothic simplifications when he was ill or uninspired; that, as his mind and fortunes failed, he relied more heavily on Gothic formulas, trusting to popular enthusiasm for sensationalist fiction and abandoning scruples about artistic integrity.[66] According to this argument, the supposedly 'undigested' Gothic of his weaker moments merely testifies to Scott's willingness to please his public, while, by contrast, his best writing transforms Gothic into historical and psychological realism. Walter Freye's dissertation on Gothic influence in Scott (1902) is symptomatic of key underlying assumptions. Freye readily accepts the importance of Gothic *taste* in Scott's life, declaring: 'Strawberry Hill, Fonthill Abbey and Abbotsford are successive manifestations of the same spirit.'[67] Freye lists borrowings from Gothic, some of them strikingly direct, in the poems. Of Gothic influence throughout Scott's career, however, he claims: 'Of course it is most apparent in Scott's first works, those in verse, and less striking in his prose, the Waverley-Novels.'[68] This assumes a pattern of development essentially the same as that proposed by Lockhart. Even J. H. Maddox's much later study of the influence of Gothic on Scott, Charlotte Brontë, and Dickens (1970) assumes that Scott adapted Gothic to the pattern of realistic fiction, 'naturalizing' Gothic by transforming supernatural curses into forces of historical and cultural disharmony. And for David Daiches, addressing the Sir Walter Scott Club in 1965, Scott is to be congratulated for saving himself from Gothic 'by drinking at the living waters of a genuine Scottish pastoral tradition', by which, he explains, he means the history and folklore of the Scottish Borders rather than literary pastoral (a questionable division).[69] There are still recent accounts of how Scott saved the Middle Ages from Gothicism and replaced Rad-

---

[66] See Herbert J. Merrill, 'A Reappraisal of Sir Walter Scott: His Commercial Motivation and His Reliance Upon Formula Fiction for Popular Markets', Ph.D. Dissertation (Indiana University, 1957), 97–139, and the argument that Gothic elements increase as Scott's ability fades, p. 128. David Brown argues, similarly, that Scott 'fell back' on Gothic horrors when his historical imagination failed (*Historical Imagination*, 187).

[67] Walter Freye, 'The Influence of "Gothic" Literature on Sir Walter Scott', Inaugural Dissertation (Rostock, 1902), 14.

[68] Ibid. 17.

[69] Frazer, *Edinburgh Keepsake*, 139.

cliffe's and Lewis's 'parody of medievalism' with 'figures of flesh and blood'.[70] Several critics who assume that Gothic can only be a degraded literary form conclude that its presence in Scott's work inevitably weakens his claims to be taken seriously as a writer. It comes as a shock to Robin Mayhead in his influential 1968 study of Scott that the characterization of George Staunton in *The Heart of Midlothian* so closely approximates to Radcliffean stereotype.[71]

Alternatively, Gothic is assumed to have qualities of daring and dash which make the Waverley Novels seem unduly conformist and cautious. Working from this assumption, critics suggest that Scott included Gothic elements in his work without any conviction that they could be psychologically or symbolically significant. Too timid to develop the insights into evil and psychological collapse which he undoubtedly possessed, he ignored or even impeded the development of a psychologically more complex Gothic. The most persuasive exponent of this view is Leslie Fiedler. Fiedler throws down an irresistible gauntlet for the present study when he declares that the historical novel as a distinct genre, and the Waverley Novels in particular, constitute a masculine, scientific, and genteel version of Radcliffean Gothic. For Fiedler, Scott is conservative, Gothic radical, and the Waverley Novels remain 'healthy' (his term) only because they are unable or unwilling to see the importance of the alternative: 'The trappings of the gothic seemed to him part of the popular author's stock in trade; the meanings of the gothic were alien to him.'[72]

A middle line, implicit in this last comment by Fiedler, is the argument that Scott, the 'happy prisoner' of literary tradition, unpretentiously drew on whatever fictional conventions pleased him.[73] This seems to exculpate Scott from the charge that he degraded his work by including inferior material, but it does so only at the expense of his seriousness about his art. Herbert J. Merrill, for example, argues that Scott adopted Gothic merely to ensure sales, without troubling to revise or redirect the form.[74]

[70] Allan Massie, 'Scott and the European Novel', in *Sir Walter Scott: The Long-Forgotten Melody*, ed. Alan Bold (London, 1983), 95.
[71] Robin Mayhead, *Walter Scott*, Profiles in Literature Series (London, 1968), 3–7.
[72] Fiedler, *Love and Death*, 172.
[73] Wilson, *Laird of Abbotsford*, 75; McMaster on Gothic as one of Scott's 'quarries', *Scott and Society*, 24.
[74] Merrill, 'Reappraisal of Sir Walter Scott', 139.

The presence of Gothic is commonly used to support the charge that Scott was artistically unreliable, unable to sustain serious imaginative effort without descending into literary clichés of sensationalism and suspense. This flaw in his art proceeded, critics suggest, from a failure of confidence and commitment. Such an approach produces not just Norman Collins's Scott, 'the Titanic incompetent', and David Cecil's writer of 'careless greatness', but also, more recently, Robert C. Gordon's Scott, 'a great novelist with a weak aesthetic conscience', and George Levine's Scott, a fundamentally flawed writer who 'adored what he could not believe in'.[75] There have been more positive emphases on the literary conventions adopted by Scott. Always less judgemental, and often very fruitful, were links proposed by critics of eighteenth- and nineteenth-century medievalism, a trend reinforced by Northrop Frye's attention to shared narrative patterns in romance, especially in *The Secular Scripture* (1976).

A special problem besets the works which transformed Scott criticism in the 1960s by showing, after Lukács, the importance of his *historical* imagination. According to Lukács, Scott's new brand of historical fiction, the product of the French Revolution and the Revolutionary wars, must be distinguished clearly from seventeenth- and eighteenth-century works with historical themes (he instances Scudéry and Calpranède) by its attempt to create 'an artistically faithful image of a concrete historical epoch'.[76] Works like *The Castle of Otranto*, in contrast, turned history into 'mere costumery'. 'What is lacking in the so-called historical novel before Sir Walter Scott is precisely the specifically historical, that is, derivation of the individuality of characters from the historical peculiarity of their age.'[77] Lukács spends considerable time in the section of his work devoted to Scott in elaborating what he means by the notion of historical 'faithfulness', arguing strongly that it inheres not in antiquarian detail or a clutter of allusions to historical events, but, much more fundamentally, in the *charac-*

---

[75] Collins, *Facts of Fiction*, 134; David Cecil, *Sir Walter Scott*, The Raven Miscellany (London, 1933), 60; George Levine, *The Realistic Imagination: English Fiction from Frankenstein to Lady Chatterley* (Chicago, 1981), 82; Robert C. Gordon, *Under Which King? A Study of the Scottish Waverley Novels* (Edinburgh, 1969), 1.

[76] Lukács, *Historical Novel*, 15.

[77] Ibid.

terization of individuals, 'the authenticity of the historical psychology of his characters, the genuine *hic et nunc* ... of their inner motives and behaviour'.[78] His examples are carefully selected, of course, an issue to which I return in Chapter 5 when examining those sections of Scott's novels which do not seem to work by such rules. In the history of Scott's severance from Gothic, however, Lukács's work is decisive. Lukács makes a special point of discrediting attempts to trace influences on Scott from the pseudo-historical romances of the eighteenth century. He specifically dismisses Radcliffe and other 'second- and third-rate writers' from Scott's literary inheritance on the grounds that they can bring us 'not a jot nearer to understanding what was *new* in Scott's art, that is in his historical novel'.[79] According to critics following Lukács, Scott's innovation was to write historical fiction which reproduced a coherent, credible, and consistent image of a specific historical era, not the vague impression of the past acceptable in fictions which concentrated upon situations of terror. Gothic, of course, is singled out in such analyses, even when it rather than Scott is the focus of the critic's interest. In his influential article on Gothic in 1969, Robert D. Hume declares that history in Gothic is merely a prop for the imagination and that 'history' in the Waverley Novels is something quite different: 'If wearing a wool tie makes me a sheep, then *The Recess* is a Gothic novel. The novels of Jane Porter and Scott are the first novels whose *basis* is a specific historical setting.'[80]

Scott scholarship benefited enormously from the new direction given by Lukács, and in recent years it has gradually freed itself from the greatest danger posed by Lukács's case for Scott, which was a simplified critical model of historical verisimilitude (not used, in fact, by Lukács, but a temptation for those who followed his suggestions about Scott). Of post-Lukácsian treatments of the problem of a Gothic strain in Scott, the most stimulating are Leslie Fiedler's comments in *Love and Death in the American Novel*, already mentioned; Francis Hart's essay on Scottish Gothic; David Punter's reading of *The Bride of Lammermoor* in his survey of Gothic tradition; interpretations of the same novel by George

[78] Lukács, *Historical Novel*, 65.
[79] Ibid. 29.
[80] Hume, 'Gothic versus Romantic: A Revaluation of the Gothic Novel', *PMLA* lxxxiv (1969), 283.

Levine and, more recently, by James Kerr; and Daniel Cottom's selection of Radcliffe, Scott, and Austen as his examples of 'the civilized imagination'. Most important of all are David Morse's attention to Scott's mingled preoccupations with superstition, madness, and imprisonment, and Judith Wilt's brief comments on Scott on her way to looking at Gothic in Austen, Eliot, and Lawrence.[81]

The most common critical position, however, is still that Scott and Gothic may be separated with some confidence on the grounds of historical realism, and even, as David Punter extends it, on the grounds of Scott's whole moral-political orientation as an artist. Punter's suggested resolution of the Gothic issue in the ghost scene in *The Bride of Lammermoor* is important and extremely revealing:

> The impression received of realism from a book like *Bride of Lammermoor* is not likely to be due to knowledge on the part of the reader that 'history really was like that', but to the feeling that Scott is not trying to derive any particular advantage from distortion. If it could be said non-pejoratively, one would want to say that Scott's novels are singularly pointless...[82]

It is difficult to say 'pointless' non-pejoratively, and also difficult to forget that Carlyle had rested his case against Scott on precisely the same argument a century before. Punter's study, of course, aims to provide a coherent account of the long and complex history of Gothic, and it may seem unfair to single out this particular passage. Implicit in Punter's comment on *The Bride of Lammermoor*, however, are many of the problems which the present study seeks to address. It is a significant comment, also, precisely because Punter's work on Gothic is so wide-ranging and so authoritative. The Waverley Novels achieve their influential sense of historical realism, Punter implies, not by reference to readerly knowledge or any determinable relationship to historical

[81] More combative than substantive, disputing Mario Praz's discussion of Scott, Gothic, and the supernatural in his *The Hero in Eclipse in Victorian Fiction*, trans. Angus Davidson (London, 1956), 54–6: 'as if there were no more morally serious or adventurous use of the Gothic in Scott and Austen than making the world safe for the bourgeois', Judith Wilt, *Ghosts of the Gothic: Austen, Eliot and Lawrence* (Princeton, NJ, 1980), 102 n.

[82] David Punter, *The Literature of Terror: A History of Gothic Fictions from 1764 to the Present Day* (London, 1980), 164.

fact, but instead through a convincingly neutral narrative voice. According to Punter, Gothic mythologizes *about* the past while Scott writes about the myths *of* the past. Working with a similar division between types of fictitious history, James Kerr's recent study fully acknowledges the importance of Gothic as a model for the Waverley Novels, and suggests that the Waverley Novels act as a 'counterfiction' to Gothic in which the literary structures and conventions of Gothic are preserved and modified only to be dismissed:

To grasp properly the place of Scott's fiction in literary history, we must see his novels as a countergenre to the Gothic, in which the forms of the Gothic are taken up and rendered as the conventions of an obsolescent literature, and at the same time preserved and modified. The forms of Gothic romance are represented in Scott's writing in order to be defamiliarized and then historicized.[83]

This depends on the novels deemed to be representative, of course, and Kerr's choice is revealingly conservative: *Waverley, Old Mortality, The Heart of Midlothian, The Bride of Lammermoor,* and *Redgauntlet.*

One critic of Scott who rarely mentions Gothic has been a great influence on the proposals for Gothic narratology put forward in this work. Alexander Welsh's study of anxiety and 'tentative fiction' in the Waverley Novels is free of the motif-fixation which limits so many discussions of Gothic in Scott, and comes much closer to the narrative effects of Gothic which this study attempts to isolate. Welsh comments:

Incidents of the plot do not befall the passive hero so much as threaten him. Because so many threatened events never do come to pass, the entire fiction takes on a tentative aspect.... Rather than report things, the Waverley Novels conceive possible conditions and events that are frankly projections of the mind of author and reader alike.[84]

---

[83] James Kerr, *Fiction against History: Scott as Storyteller* (Cambridge, 1989), 5–6.

[84] Alexander Welsh, *The Hero of the Waverley Novels,* Yale Studies in English, No. 154 (New Haven, Conn., 1963), 189. See the quotation from John Dunlop in the opening section of my next chapter, and George Saintsbury's comment on *Udolpho* ('Emily is conducted with the most appalling apparatus through scene after scene in which nothing can really be said to happen at all'), in his introd. to *Tales of Mystery,* p. xvi.

There could be few better descriptions of one important strand in Gothic writing. Gothic is the classic form of 'tentative fiction', in Welsh's sense. In Radcliffe's novels, in particular, everything is threatened, but few things actually happen, creating a common emotional currency—anxiety—between protagonist and reader. The next chapter gives an interpretation of the narrative strategies of Gothic in terms which (like several recent readings) are indebted to Welsh's suggestions.

In summary, the discomfort created in critical circles by the notion of a Gothic Scott has both a history of its own and a place in the much larger problem of the reception of the Waverley Novels both within Scott's lifetime and afterwards. The construction of a legitimate critical history for the Waverley Novels turns out, unsurprisingly, to have its own unformulated agenda, which at its most simple is the denial of significant influence from earlier fiction. The rehabilitation of Gothic has worked in just the opposite way, as critics strive to show that it was not the outrageous new departure from literary convention which many of its first reviewers, for their own moralistic reasons, tended to suggest. The divergence of these two traditions of critical reception, moreover, may be seen as a response to the terms in which Scott chose to promote himself as artist, which, taken up by Lockhart, give to the first chapter of the *Life of Scott* (Scott's own 'Ashestiel Autobiography') an overwhelming authority. The divergence becomes distinctly odd when examined in the context of Scott's own extensive reflections on Gothic as narrative and historiographic experiment, and close association of the springs of his own art with the literary fashions of the 1790s.

3. An Initiated Ghost-Seer

> The influence of fear ... is indeed a faithful and legitimate key to unlock every source of fancy and of feeling.
>
> (Scott's review of *Fatal Revenge*, 1810)[85]

The popular Victorian image of Scott as a Border Minstrel conceals a writer who had a great deal to do with, and to say about,

[85] *MPW* xviii. 169.

Gothic, and whose comments on Gothic are closely related to the development of his own fiction. The main sources of Scott's published critical views on Gothic are the 'Lives' of Walpole, Reeve, and Radcliffe written for *Ballantyne's Novelist's Library* (1821–4), reviews of individual Gothic novels, including Maturin's *Fatal Revenge* for the *Quarterly Review* in 1810 and Mary Shelley's *Frankenstein* for *Blackwood's* in 1818, and the reflections on Lewis in the 'Essay on Imitations of the Ancient Ballad' (written in April 1830 and designed to supplement and extend the 'Remarks on Popular Poetry' for the new *Poetical Works*). There are few references to Gothic writers in the novels themselves, and these few mainly confined to the introductions and notes.[86] To these may be added occasional remarks in letters and the *Journal*, and remarks quoted by Lockhart and other contemporaries. Excluded from the present range of reference are Scott's frequent musings on the use of the supernatural and of materials drawn from the study of folklore and witchcraft.

Scott read widely in tales of terror and wonder throughout his life, admitting in the 'Ashestiel Autobiography' (1808) to an early taste for 'the wonderful and terrible,—the common taste of children, but in which I have remained a child even unto this day'.[87] His awareness of the public excitement which literature could cause was inseparable from his recollections of the vogue for the novels of Radcliffe and Lewis. Looking back in 1830, he still thought that the publication of *The Monk* had created 'an epoch in our literature', and credited Lewis with having changed the course of his own literary fortunes.[88] Lewis's example and encouragement prompted Scott's first published works, and Scott was one of his collaborators in *Tales of Wonder*, although, sensitive to shifts in public taste, he always doubted the success of the collection. Writing to Richard Heber in 1800, he reflected on his contributions to Lewis's (poorly received) venture: 'I am in daily expectation of proofs of such tales of Wonder as I have added to Lewis's stock of *horribles*: my own opinion is that we shall over-

---

[86] *WN* xxiv, p. xi (Radcliffe), i, p. lx (Radcliffe and Lewis), xvi, p. xxxi (Walpole), xli, p. lxiv (Maturin).

[87] Lockhart, i. 37.

[88] *PW* iv. 51, 52–5. In a letter to Constable criticizing Thomas Medwin's *Journal of the Conversations of Lord Byron, etc.* (1824), however, Scott insists that his debt to Lewis was confined to metrical and rhyming effects (*Letters*, viii. 409).

stock the market.'[89] Such doubts, which he shared with other
purveyors of terror- and horror-romance, did not prevent his
using stock conventions when they suited his purposes. When
Scott published, in the second canto of *Marmion* (1808), the most
notorious of all his scenes of Gothic horror (in which the disgraced nun Constance is buried alive in the dungeons of Lindis-
farne), the critical backlash must have convinced him that he was
dealing in somewhat outdated conventions. *The Satirist* suspected
Canto II 'to have been compiled from the jejune stories of Monk
Ghost Lewis, Esq.', and found it to contain 'the same indistinct
throes of abortive horror, the same nonsense of paralysed thought,
the same laughable bombast of turgid expression; its title is over-
flowing, we suppose, with meaning, THE CONVENT!!!'.[90] Horace
Twiss, in his review for *Le Beau Monde*, described Constance as
'exactly what Matilda, in the Monk, would have been, if she had
not turned out to be the devil'.[91] Jeffrey was scathing about those
parts of *Marmion* which reminded him of 'the machinery of a bad
German novel', arguing that the reading public 'we believe, has
now supped full of this sort of horrors; or, if any effect is still to
be produced by their exhibition, it may certainly be produced at
too cheap a rate, to be worthy the ambition of a poet of original
imagination'.[92] For Coleridge, commenting on the earlier narrative

[89] *Tales of Wonder; Written and Collected by M. G. Lewis*, 2 vols. (London,
1801), to which Scott contributed nos. 12, 20, 21, 22, 23. He is quoted from
Letters, xii. 158 (1800), and goes on to say that he will 'keep the Border tales in
view'. For Scott's doubts about *Tales of Wonder*, see also *Letters*, i. 96 (when he
almost regrets contributing), xii. 177 (when he refers dismissively to 'the trifles I
gave Lewis', and seems anxious to dissociate himself from the publication as
a whole). He later claimed, in mitigation, that Lewis's popularity seemed to
guarantee the collection's success ('Essay on Imitations', *PW* iv. 72), and suggested
that Lewis had simply failed to recognize the decline of interest in ballads: 'What
had been at first received as simple and natural, was now sneered at as puerile and
extravagant' (*PW* iv. 74). He escaped from the censure aroused by *Tales of
Wonder* by collecting ballads in his own right (*PW* iv. 77). Scott comments on the
reception of *Tales of Wonder*, and the parody 'Tales of Plunder', *PW* iv. 76.
[90] *The Satirist*, ii (Apr. 1808), 191. More recently, James Reed has described the
plot of *Marmion* as a 'gothic melodrama of trumpery treachery, coincidence and
improbability', *Sir Walter Scott: Landscape and Locality* (London, 1980), 40.
[91] Review signed 'Horatius' and ascribed to Horace Twiss, *Le Beau Monde*, iii
(May 1808), 267.
[92] *Edinburgh Review*, xii (Apr. 1808), 1–35 (9). Scott was fond of using the
same quotation from *Macbeth*, v. v. 13–15 to discuss the vogue for tales of terror,
as in *Letters*, xi. 406, *MPW* xviii. 267. The *Universal Magazine*, NS ix (May 1808),
410, remarks in its review of *Marmion*: 'Mr. Scott is in fact a Mrs. Radcliffe in
poetry, but without her occasional elevations.'

poetry, and thinking particularly of *Marmion*, Scott's willingness
to use familiar material indicated a fatal lack of seriousness and
originality: 'For the rest, whatever suits Mrs Radcliff, i.e. in the
Fable, and the Dramatis Personae, will do for the Poem—with
this advantage, that however thread-bare in the Romance Shelves
of the circulating Library it is to be taken as quite new as soon as
told in rhyme.'[93] Such comments do not support the view that
Scott made use of Gothic conventions merely because they were
expected of him. By 1808 they were clearly unlikely to win critical approval, a point corroborated by Maturin, who, making
his début as a novelist with *Fatal Revenge; or, The Family of
Montorio* in 1807, took special care to explain his reasons for
experimenting with the disgraced form of the terror-romance.
When, in 1818, Maturin came to look back on the failure of *Fatal
Revenge*, he was convinced that the reason lay in its genre: 'the
date of that style of writing was out when I was a boy, and I had
not power to revive it'.[94]

Scott's interest in Gothic clearly went beyond what was expected
of any writer hoping for a wide audience, and indeed survived
unpopularity and critical ridicule. He was always intrigued by
the ways in which Gothic might be made to harmonize with
more scholarly enquiries into folk legend, popular belief, and
the marvellous. He described himself in a letter of 1801 as 'an
initiated Ghost-Seer', and, surveying his career as a whole in a
letter of 1830, recalled the thrills of Radcliffe's supernaturalism
and considered himself 'long both a reader and a writer of such
goodly matters'.[95] As a 'writer' of such matters he was impatient
of attempts to limit the kinds of literary experimentation which
were thought appropriate for him. Irritated by James Ballantyne's
fears that the supernatural elements in *Woodstock* (1826) might
be thought a cheap imitation of Radcliffe, he determined to add a
preface to the novel explaining his purposes, and expostulates in a
letter: 'I can never agree that Mrs Radcliffe any more than Shakespeare is to be a potatoe bogle to scare every poor bird from the

---

[93] *Collected Letters of Samuel Taylor Coleridge*, ed. Earl Leslie Griggs, 6 vols.
(Oxford, 1956–71), iii. 295.
[94] *Women*, i, pp. iii–iv. Maturin also reflects on the nature of his first work in
the preface to *Milesian*, i, pp. ii–iii, v. Maurice Lévy argues that Gothic was more
popular in 1807 than Maturin realized, introd. to his edn. of *Fatal Revenge*, p. viii.
[95] *Letters*, i. 121, xi. 406.

field she is stuck up in and I think I can prove the arrow is fairly aimd—though I may not have hit the mark.'[96] As further evidence of his experimentation in such matters, he published as appendices to the Magnum Opus edition of *Waverley* the fragments 'Thomas the Rhymer' (supposed to be 'in the style of the Castle of Otranto') and 'The Lord of Ennerdale' (in which characters are eager readers of *The Mysteries of Udolpho* and other Gothic fictions, including *The Monk*), both of which can be related back to such experiments in fragmentary Gothic tales as John Aikin's 'Sir Bertrand' (1773) and Nathan Drake's 'Henry Fitzowen' (1798).

In addition to these clear indicators of a sense of shared literary purpose with Gothic writers of the 1790s, Scott's praise played a direct part in the reception of second-generation Gothic writers by the reading public. His review of *Fatal Revenge* marked Maturin as an exception to the general inferiority of terror-fiction, and, although Scott thought that the novel was frantic and ill-judged, he did much for Maturin's confidence and reputation in predicting that his talents would one day 'astonish the public'.[97] He was also one of the few reviewers to perceive the unusual quality of *Frankenstein* when it first appeared in 1818 (although he assumed that Percy Shelley must have written it), and repeated his favourable opinion in his review of Hoffmann in 1827.[98] Both Maturin and Mary Shelley later wrote to him to ask for advice and help with later work, and in Maturin's case this led to a twelve-year correspondence, with intermittent financial assistance and literary guidance. Maturin sent work to Scott for correction and advice, and altered it in accordance with Scott's suggestions. Scott tried to encourage him to 'prune', urged him away from virulent anti-Catholicism (with limited success), and tempted him away from excesses of gloom and violence.[99] Most notably, he helped shape Maturin's runaway success, the play *Bertram* (1816), and persuaded Maturin to abandon a vitriolic preface to the novel *Women; or, Pour et Contre* (1818) in which he avenged him-

[96] *Letters*, ix. 403. Scott reflects on the same accusation in similar form (including the 'potatoe bogle') in his *Journal*, p. 75, but in fact the Preface of *Woodstock* does not contain the planned defence.
[97] *MPW* xviii. 172; Scott's general conclusions about Maturin, 171–2.
[98] *MPW* xviii. 291–2.
[99] *Scott–Maturin Correspondence*, 7, 21–2, 26, 74, 101. Suggestions that Scott's advice influenced Maturin's practice can be found on pp. 32–3, 89–90, 100.

self for Coleridge's attack on *Bertram*, reprinted in *Biographia Literaria*.[100] In private life, he 'always expressed a favourable, though qualified opinion' of Maturin.[101] In his turn, Maturin was so aware of the influence of Scott upon his later work that he was afraid his last novel, *The Albigenses* (1824), would be seen as an imitation of *Ivanhoe*.[102] The links with Mary Shelley were slighter, but significant. Responding to the interest in historical fiction, she experimented with *Valperga* (1823), and, in May 1829, wrote to Scott requesting help with material for *Perkin Warbeck*.[103]

Scott's critical comments have a significance beyond such personal links, however. If literary history as a whole is one way of legitimizing forms which were once threatening, none has been more adroitly appropriated to the categories of the literary in recent years than Gothic itself. Scott was an early initiator of this process, at least in support of those writers of terror-fiction whom he admired as original creators rather than hack imitators. Scott's work on *Ballantyne's Novelist's Library* not only places the texts of writers like Walpole, Reeve, and Radcliffe in the context of a developing novelistic tradition, but also provides a critical context for their work, an opportunity for detailed analysis, contrast, and evaluation. Different ways of handling the supernatural are discussed in relation to Walpole and Radcliffe, for example, making these two 'Lives' effectively complementary. The series as a whole, which may be read as a significant and timely extension of Johnson's project in the *Lives of the Poets*, affirmed the place of prose fiction in the critical and biographical traditions set out by Johnson. Had the scheme been popular, Scott planned to ex-

---

[100] *Letters*, v. 95–8, and 95 n., which quotes Maturin's reply: also *Scott–Maturin Correspondence*, 89–90. Scott thought that nothing would more incline the public to assume the worst about *Bertram* than a display of wounded vanity from Maturin, and that, in any case, nobody would read the *Biographia Literaria*.

[101] Gillies, *Recollections of Sir Walter Scott*, 167. For another contemporary reaction to the relationship between Scott and Maturin, see 'Conversations of Maturin', *New Monthly Magazine*, xix (May and June 1827), 410, and 'Recollections of Maturin', *New Monthly Magazine*, xx (Aug. and Oct. 1827), 147.

[102] 'Conversations of Maturin', 410.

[103] Mary Shelley wrote to thank Scott for his review of *Frankenstein*, *The Letters of Mary Wollstonecraft Shelley*, ed. Betty T. Bennett, 3 vols. (Baltimore, 1980–8), i. 71 (14 June 1818); to ask for information on Warbeck, ii. 77–8 (25 May 1829).

tend its coverage of more recent writers with volumes devoted to Godwin, Holcroft, and Charles Brockden Brown.

Scott's reputation for generosity has undermined his claims to be taken seriously as a literary critic. One reviewer in the *Scotsman* in 1818 remarked that he was 'more, than any other man, prone to admire the works of his cotemporaries'.[104] This generosity led him into occasional embarrassments—as when he had to write a very careful letter to Joanna Baillie explaining and qualifying his public support for Maturin's play *Bertram*[105]—but it usually had the more desirable effect of isolating him from the common round of literary rivalry and protecting his own works from what would then seem ungentlemanly counter-attacks. Even so, habitual generosity can come to look suspiciously like complacency and indifference. Scott's critical comments on Gothic are characteristically generous, and characteristically easy to dismiss as unthinking or superficially polite. Yet they reveal a creative engagement and an awareness of Gothic's weaknesses, as well as its strengths, which is important for his own fiction. The following argument focuses on five main issues: the significance of formula and genre expectation; the terminology of the imaginative and 'poetical', and the conflicts it creates; the unnatural and the improbable; readerly contracts; and historical verisimilitude.

Like many critics of his time, Scott seized on the comic possibilities of predictable Gothic plots when he most wanted to disparage the form. He was thoroughly familiar with the dependable routes of Gothic plotting and scene-setting, as the opening chapter of *Waverley* clearly demonstrates. The most frequently quoted of his remarks on Gothic is the passage in his overview of contemporary fiction written as light relief for the *Quarterly Review* in 1810 (the overview which develops into a receptive but chiding discussion of Maturin's novel *Fatal Revenge*, and which brought Scott in return his first lavishly grateful letter from Maturin). This passage has often been taken in isolation as Scott's final word on

[104] Review of *Tales of My Landlord*, 2nd ser., *The Scotsman*, ii, No. 80 (1 Aug. 1818), 247. Gilfillan comments on Scott's disinterestedness in praising his contemporaries, *Life of Sir Walter Scott*, 193.
[105] *Letters*, iv. 264 (Baillie's letter, 2 July 1816, quoted iv. 262 n.), and note the slur of 'German'. Contrast Scott's letters to Maturin, xii. 349–52, 356–7, and the more balanced account to Daniel Terry, iii. 515, which notes the play's faults, but allows that it has power.

the subject. In fact, it is carefully particular, mocking the conventions of Gothic plotting but notably absolving the originators, Radcliffe and Lewis, of the charge of 'dulness':

The imitators of Mrs Radcliffe and Mr Lewis were before us; personages who, to all the faults and extravagances of their originals, added that of dulness, with which they can seldom be charged. We strolled through a variety of castles, each of which was regularly called Il Castello; met with as many captains of condottieri; heard various ejaculations of Santa Maria and Diabolo; read by a decaying lamp, and in a tapestried chamber, dozens of legends as stupid as the main history; examined such suites of deserted apartments as might fit up a reasonable barrack; and saw as many glimmering lights as would make a respectable illumination . . .

Scott goes on to regret Maturin's decision to immerse himself in this jaded literary style, arguing that his 'taste is so inferior to his powers of imagination and expression, that we never saw a more remarkable instance of genius degraded by the labour in which it is employed'.[106] Scott's comments on *Fatal Revenge*, alternating between praise of 'taste', which Maturin lacks, and 'fire', 'imagination', which he abundantly possesses, are typical of the competing loyalties obvious in many of his comments on literature. His treatment of the corpses scene in Smollett's *Ferdinand Count Fathom* (a proto-Gothic novel for many modern historians of the form) shows his hesitation between the demands of taste and decorum and those of passion and imagination. Scott's first response is to denounce the moral tendency of the work. His second is to endorse its power over the imagination: 'The horrible adventure in the hut of the robbers, is a tale of natural terror which rises into the sublime; and, though often imitated, has never yet been surpassed, or perhaps equalled.'[107] Here, Scott associates imaginative power, the sublime, and the appeal to fear, in a way which clearly reveals his debts to the aesthetic framework established by Burke. Imagination may override good taste. Lack of imagination is the one irredeemable fault, accordingly, as Scott's dismissive remarks about Reeve's *Old English Baron* make clear. When dealing with ghosts and marvels, Scott concludes, the only

---

[106] Both quotations, *MPW* xviii. 162.
[107] *MPW* iii. 137. Scott refers to *The Adventures of Ferdinand Count Fathom*, 2 vols. (London, 1753), i. 132–8.

important limit to an author's daring and invention is the extent
of his or her own talent.[108]

Scott's critical terminology is always evocative rather than analytical, and an appeal to the so-called 'poetical' qualities of novels
is a staple of his comments on Gothic. He declares in his discussion of Smollett: 'Every successful novelist must be more or less a
poet, even although he may never have written a line of verse.
The quality of imagination is absolutely indispensable to him.'[109]
Random comments on Radcliffe, Maturin, and Mary Shelley become much more resonant in such a context:

Mrs Radcliffe has a title to be considered as the first poetess of romantic
fiction, that is, if actual rhythm shall not be deemed essential to poetry.

They [Maturin's novels] might without much expence be printed in a
handsome and popular shape and would be found to contain as much
poetry in the form of prose as any other number of volumes in the English
or any other language.

So concludes this extraordinary tale [*Frankenstein*], in which the author
seems to us to disclose uncommon powers of poetic imagination.[110]

As in the review of *Fatal Revenge*, therefore, Scott praises imaginative inspiration and a 'poetic' style of expression which seem
remarkably detachable from plot and the series of motifs which he
so easily dismisses as clichéd.

These loose appeals to the 'poetical' do not augur well for
Scott's analytical skills as a critic. Fortunately they are supported
by a much more sophisticated awareness of genre and reader
expectation. Unlike many reviewers of contemporary fiction, Scott
made no assumptions about any necessary connection between
one type of fiction and a particular set of moral consequences. In
his review of *Northanger Abbey* and *Persuasion* for the *Quarterly
Review* in 1821, for example, he distinguishes between what he
terms the 'unnatural' and the 'improbable' in fiction in a way
which bears comparison with Todorov's categorization of (respectively) the uncanny and the marvellous, and again looks back to
the aesthetic distinctions suggested in Aikin's and Drake's essays

[108] *MPW* iii. 328–31.
[109] *MPW* iii. 176.
[110] *MPW* iii. 342 (Radcliffe); Scott considered preparing an edition of Maturin's
works, *Letters*, xii. 367–9 (368), although his comments must be judged in the
context of this letter to Maturin's widow; *MPW* xviii. 267.

on the effects of fear. According to Scott's suggestions in the review of Austen, tales of the supernatural may be regarded as 'improbable', but not necessarily as 'unnatural'. As a consequence, palpably unrealistic romances may be less disruptive of ordinary social and moral life than more realistic novels. Not only may 'the supernatural fable' be 'the less mischievous in its moral effects, but also the more correct kind of composition in point of taste'.[111] This assumption that tales of terror can claim their own kind of formal correctness is a promising insight. In his 'Life' of Radcliffe for *Ballantyne's Novelist's Library* Scott argues that Radcliffe's work ought to be appreciated within the limits it establishes for itself, refusing to join the 'hypercritics' in judging Gothic without reference to aims and limitations peculiar to a literature of terror:

The real and only point is, whether, considered as a separate and distinct species of writing, that introduced by Mrs Radcliffe possesses merit, and affords pleasure; for, these premises being admitted, it is as unreasonable to complain of the absence of advantages foreign to her style and plan, and proper to those of another mode of composition, as to regret that the peach-tree does not produce grapes, or the vine peaches.[112]

To this awareness of the demands of individual form Scott added a willingness to accept popular literature as entertainment and solace. Free of the snobbery about Gothic which was common in the reviews, he recognizes it as potentially a widely popular means of communication:

if there were to be selected one particular structure of fiction, which possesses charms for the learned and unlearned, the grave and gay, the gentleman and the clown, it would be perhaps that of those very romances which the severity of their criticism seeks to depreciate. . . . for curiosity and a lurking love of mystery, together with a germ of super-stition, are more general ingredients in the human mind, and more widely diffused through the mass of humanity, than either genuine taste for the comic, or true feeling of the pathetic.[113]

For all the moral and aesthetic condemnation meted out to 'sickly and frantic German novels' and sensationalist literature in the Preface to *Lyrical Ballads*, Wordsworth's interest in finding a literature capable of interesting mankind permanently and of appealing to universal passions is the most fitting context for

[111] *MPW* xviii. 217.   [112] *MPW* iii. 364.   [113] *MPW* iii. 364–5.

Scott's comments. Like Radcliffe and Maturin, Scott emphasizes the power of fear as a 'universal' passion. In a remark which closely resembles the argument of Radcliffe's essay 'On the Supernatural in Poetry', he suggests that 'obscurity and suspense' are 'the most fertile source, perhaps, of sublime emotion; for there are few dangers that do not become familiar to the firm mind, if they are presented to consideration as certainties, and in all their open and declared character; whilst, on the other hand, the bravest have shrunk from the dark and the doubtful'.[114] In his review of *Fatal Revenge*, Scott agrees with the argument of Maturin's preface that the 'influence of fear' is 'indeed a faithful and legitimate key to unlock every source of fancy and of feeling'. He adds, however, perhaps with the Preface to *Lyrical Ballads* in mind, that the most sensitive feelings are those most easily exhausted, and that the continuing effect of terror depends on surprise.[115] Scott shares Wordsworth's unease about the implications of public familiarity with horror, but places the emphasis rather differently, on the challenge which this familiarity presents to literary inventiveness and skill.[116]

Scott's distinction between the improbable and the unnatural in fiction is a useful tool in his appreciation of *Frankenstein*. He argues in his review of *Frankenstein* that novelists ought to preserve psychological probability even in detailing reactions to improbable events, and claims that even fiction which is based on entirely unnatural premises may be governed by strict rules of probability, to support the claims of 'the rules of probability, and the nature of the human heart'.[117] In other words, he clearly endorses the interpretation of *Frankenstein* offered by Percy Shelley in his introduction of 1818, that this novel 'affords a point of view to the imagination for the delineating of human passions more comprehensive and commanding than any which the ordi-

---

[114] *MPW* iii. 368.

[115] *MPW* xviii. 169.

[116] On public familiarity with horror, *MPW* xviii. 170. At dinner with the Lockharts in 1824, Scott discussed the psychological novels of Godwin and Brockden Brown. He held that the sustained portrayal of the 'darker passions' was 'neither a wholesome nor a popular species of literature.... The suggestive manner of treating every subject aims at keeping the mind constantly on the rack of uncertainty.' This technique of suspense was easily exhausted, he thought. (Quoted by Johnson, p. 871, from the report of an American guest, Samuel Griswold Goodrich, in his *Recollections of a Lifetime*, 1857.)

[117] *MPW* xviii. 253–4.

nary relations of existing events can yield'.[118] The possibility that
tales of the supernatural, the fantastic, and the grotesque are
essentially true to the workings of the mind made them a serious
literary form for Scott. In a letter of 1830 to Mrs Hughes, he
recognizes precisely this possibility: 'Every such story on respectable foundation is a chapter in the history of the human mind.'[119]

One of the qualities of Scott's literary criticism which the lingering effects of readings of Romantic literature as individualistic and
egotistical has most obscured is his firm belief in the role of the
reader. Scott's willingness to cater for popular tastes has always
attracted critical anxiety, most notably from Lockhart. Yet it was
always much more than a failure of literary conscience. In some of
his comments on Gothic it develops into a theory about contracts
of expectation between writers and readers. In his discussion
of *Frankenstein*, Scott called these contracts 'a sort of account-
current with the reader'.[120] He contends, in similar vein, that the
reader of *The Castle of Otranto* automatically reads in accordance
with the author's design:

The reader, who is required to admit the belief of supernatural interference, understands precisely what is demanded of him; and, if he be
truly a gentle reader, throws his mind into the attitude best adapted to
humour the deceit which is presented for his entertainment, and grants,
for the time of perusal, the premises on which the fable depends.[121]

Underlying these remarks is a belief that readers have some
imaginative responsibility to the work before them, even if it is
simply a willingness to be entertained. Scott was not the slave of
the popular reader. He believed in a much more positive and
demanding way that artistic effect is culturally specific.

Some of Scott's most interesting remarks on Gothic occur,
as one might expect, on the subject of historical verisimilitude.
Instead of instituting truth to known historical incidents as a
standard by which all kinds of historical fiction must be judged, he
regards the combination of history and fiction as inevitable in any
work which attempts to make medieval subjects accessible and
comprehensible to the reading public. He argues in his 'Life' of

---

[118] *Frankenstein* i, p. viii.
[119] *Letters*, xi. 405. He elaborates on this point, x. 372.
[120] *MPW* xviii. 253.
[121] *MPW* iii. 317, and see the impatience with the over-rational reader in the
footnote on *Gulliver's Travels*.

Reeve, for example: 'He that would please the modern world' must always invest historical fiction with 'language and sentiments unknown to the period assigned to his story; and thus his utmost efforts only attain a sort of composition between the true and the fictitious'.[122] Because the historical romancer necessarily treads a dangerous path between credibility and the reader's knowledge, the reader is led to accept historical inaccuracies simply because he or she is unfamiliar with them.

In the Dedicatory Epistle to *Ivanhoe*, likewise, the imaginary editor Laurence Templeton devotes considerable attention to the wisdom of 'intermingling fiction with [historical] truth', and singles out Walpole as illustration that antiquarians can write romance, in this case 'a goblin tale which has thrilled through many a bosom'.[123] Templeton's liberality is extended in Scott's own reflections on Walpole's art in the 'Life' (originally written for the Ballantyne edition of *The Castle of Otranto* in 1811, and used in a revised form for *Ballantyne's Novelist's Library*), where Scott endorses Walpole's account of the aims and methods as stated in the preface to the second edition of *The Castle of Otranto*, accepting that Walpole's fiction is genuinely historical in approach. James Kerr, in fact, describes Scott's critique of *The Castle of Otranto* as a Bloomian 'strong misreading'.[124] While acknowledging the extravagances of Walpole's imitators, Scott emphasizes the originality and skill required to re-create in the mind of the modern reader the attitudes of feudal times, and the purity and precision of Walpole's language.[125] This point about language becomes especially significant in relation to the discussion in the Dedicatory Epistle to *Ivanhoe* of the degree of accuracy which is essential in historical fiction. Templeton wishes to secure a place for fiction in the description of historical event, but he admits: 'It is true, that this license is confined ... within legitimate bounds.'[126]

[122] *MPW* iii. 333.
[123] *WN* xvi, pp. xxxii, xxxi.
[124] Kerr, *Fiction Against History*, 6.
[125] *MPW* iii. 322–3. See also the significant terms of his praise for *Frankenstein*, *MPW* xviii. 267: 'It is no slight merit in our eyes, that the tale, though wild in incident, is written in plain and forcible English, without exhibiting that mixture of hyperbolical Germanisms with which tales of wonder are usually told, as if it were necessary that the language should be as extravagant as the fiction.'
[126] *WN* xvi, p. xxxviii. This part of Templeton's discussion includes reference to painting as well as to literature.

Setting out the general principle that the historical novelist 'must introduce nothing inconsistent with the manners of the age' of which he writes, Templeton places special emphasis on the novelist's selection of language: 'His language must not be exclusively obsolete and unintelligible; but he should admit, if possible, no word or turn of phraseology betraying an origin directly modern.'[127] In this context, Scott's praise for the choice of language in *The Castle of Otranto*, which has been found outrageously slack by many critics, becomes more interesting. As a linguistic judgement it is imprecise. As a marker of the kinds of aesthetic compromise which Scott considered important for his own work, however, it is perfectly acceptable. It is also another reminder of the all-important part played by the reader in Scott's aesthetic. Historical 'keeping' is not a matter of antiquarian scrupulousness. It is pointless being accurate if that accuracy does not correspond in any way to the reader's preconceptions. What matters to Scott about the language of *The Castle of Otranto* is not that it should be historically accurate but that it should not awaken modern associations in the mind of the reader.

Again, the debate on the methods of historical fiction which the thought of Walpole provokes in both the Dedicatory Epistle to *Ivanhoe* and the 'Life' for *Ballantyne's Novelist's Library* extends into the aesthetic support structures of the Waverley Novels. In the Prefatory Epistle to *Peveril of the Peak*, the 'Eidolon' of the Author declares that although historical romances may mislead poorly informed readers, their aesthetic justification may nevertheless be secure: 'since we cannot rebuild the temple, a kiosk may be a pretty thing, may it not?'[128] There is a clear continuity between the topics of history and fiction debated in the critiques of Gothic novelists in *Ballantyne's Novelist's Library* and the general principles laid down in the frame narratives of the Waverley Novels.

Several other points raised in Scott's criticisms of Gothic novelists are also closely related to the development of his own aesthetic and practice. His views on the validity of supernatural effects in fiction, for example, complement Walpole's explanation that in

---

[127] *WN* xvi, p. xxxix. Joseph Strutt and Thomas Chatterton are Templeton's examples of writers whose choice of exclusively obsolete language destroys the effect of historical coherence.

[128] *WN* xxviii, pp. lxxviii–lxxix.

The Castle of Otranto his interest lay in re-creating the cultural environment in which superstition flourished. Without this cultural and historical context, Scott believed that treatments of the supernatural would quickly become uninteresting, being, in a favourite phrase, 'a spring which is peculiarly apt to lose its elasticity by being too much pressed on'.[129] He declares in a letter to Dr Currie in 1801:

> Ghosts like many other things have of late been put out of fashion by a promiscuous & ill-judged introduction of tales relating to them.... I think the Marvellous in poetry is ill-timed & disgusting when not managed with moderation & ingrafted upon some circumstances of popular tradition or belief which sometimes can give even to the improbable an air of something like probability.[130]

Scott's use of the supernatural came under particularly virulent attack after the publication of *The Monastery*, and his commentary on the explained versus the non-explained supernatural in the 'Lives' of Walpole and Radcliffe continues a process of thinking relevant to his own fiction of the same period. His new doubts about ghosts are obvious in comments in the Introductory Epistle to *The Fortunes of Nigel*, for example. Evidence that the topics discussed in the 'Lives' of Walpole and Radcliffe had a bearing on his handling of the supernatural in his own work comes in the Magnum Opus introduction to *The Pirate* (the novel which irritated Coleridge into making his comments about Scott's dishonest exploitation of supernatural effects). Defending his decision to portray the Zetland islanders as convinced by Norna's delusions of supernatural powers, he concludes:

> Indeed, as I have observed elsewhere, the professed explanation of a tale, where appearances or incidents of a supernatural character are referred to natural causes, has often, in the winding up of the story, a degree of improbability almost equal to an absolute goblin narrative. Even the genius of Mrs Radcliffe could not always surmount this difficulty.[131]

As this comment suggests, the questions about the place of the supernatural in fiction, which carry over from the 'Life' of Wal-

---

[129] *Otranto*, 4; *PW* iv. 72; see also *MPW* iii. 366–7, xviii. 170, *Edin. Annual Reg.* 92–3.
[130] *Letters*, i. 121.
[131] *WN* xxiv, p. xi.

pole to the 'Life' of Radcliffe, are also raised within the novels themselves.

To see Gothic from Scott's perspective, in so far as that perspective may be re-created from the scattered and highly context-specific comments he makes on the form (itself diffuse and complex), is to see an uneven, undeveloped form of mixed potential and achievement. This is especially important when one considers how difficult it is to avoid reading into late eighteenth- and early nineteenth-century Gothic the preoccupations and achievements of later writers within the emerging tradition. If Gothic had been the oddly reputable form of psychological, political, and social investigation which it has come to appear in some recent criticism, it would not have posed such critical and ideological problems—or, perhaps, offered such opportunities—for Scott. Political reflections on Gothic as a potentially subversive form are strikingly absent from Scott's critical reflections. He is preoccupied instead with its formal properties, the demands it makes on readers; and, as I have suggested, with its claims to be accepted as a type of historical fiction.

It is difficult to review in any detail Scott's comments on Gothic and maintain that his obvious openness to the form was the result of either literary complacency or habitual generosity. He is clearly stimulated by the risks it takes, amused when they fail, but unwilling even in extreme cases (and *The Old English Baron* obviously stretched his politeness) to attack it at its most vulnerable points. Nobody was better placed than Scott to demolish its historical pretensions or question its depiction of the workings of superstition. Perhaps the most telling fact of all is the most obvious. *Ballantyne's Novelist's Library* is a selection of what seemed to Scott and his editors to matter most in the past hundred years of fiction. Like Dunlop's *History of Fiction* for the same publishers in 1814, it accepts the literature of terror as a key development in the experiments of the recent past. In *Ballantyne's Novelist's Library*, and through the editorial work of Scott, Gothic is written firmly into a literary history which for the next century tended to write it out again. Scott's critical and cultural canonization during the same period has separated him from the literary inheritance which he himself clearly recognized ('long both a reader and writer of such goodly matters'). If the nineteenth century elevated Scott at the expense of previous experimenters in historical fiction (a very obvious elevation if one considers Jane Porter's reputation), it was partly because Scott had so effectively subsumed them that he had come to seem the sole origin of the romance he bequeathed.

2
Gothic: The Passages that Lead to Nothing

> In the labyrinthine space, many characters alluded to as
> witnesses and well-informed persons appear and are quickly
> relegated to the corner of some street or paragraph. What
> unfolds without fail before the reader's eyes is a kind of
> puppet theater in which real dolls or fake dolls, real and
> simulated life, are manipulated by a sovereign but capricious
> stage-setter. The net is tightly stretched, bowed, and tangled;
> the scenes are centered and dispersed; narratives are begun
> and left in suspension.
>
> (Hélène Cixous on Freud's *Das Unheimliche*)[1]

ONE of the most evocative descriptions of the style of narrative
which this chapter analyses, and which it calls Gothic, is to be
found in Hélène Cixous' account of the pleasures of reading the
Freudian text, *Das Unheimliche*. This is coincidental but appropriate, for Cixous' account draws attention to self-referential and
self-questioning patterns of authority and artifice in the text which,
perhaps more than any other, has shaped twentieth-century interpretations of Gothic.

Nineteenth-century analysts of Gothic used metaphors which
complement those found in Cixous' reading of Freud. The title of
this chapter is a reference to one of the most imaginative of early
nineteenth-century comments on Gothic, a brief aside in John
Dunlop's *The History of Fiction* (1814) which links corridors
and narrative processes, empty vaults and empty conclusions: 'In
short, we may say not only of Mrs Radcliffe's castles, but of her
works in general, that they abound "in *passages* that lead to
nothing."'[2] Dunlop intends this as an elegant conclusion to his
discussion of Gothic, which is brief. Yet his recognition of the

---

[1] 'Fiction and its Phantoms: A Reading of Freud's *Das Unheimliche* (The "Uncanny")', *NLH* vii (1975–6), 525–48 (525).
[2] *The History of Fiction: Being a Critical Account of the Most Celebrated Prose
Works of Fiction, from the Earliest Greek Romances to the Novels of the Present
Age*, 3 vols. (London, 1814), iii. 387.

analogy between the narrative patterns of Gothic and its architectural settings—those descriptions of castles and ruined abbeys, of
locked doors and secret chambers, which privilege what is underground and concealed—is unequalled in contemporary discussions of Gothic and anticipates a common preoccupation of
more recent criticism.[3] Although Dunlop's perception of the links
between narrative and architecture in Gothic is particularly acute,
however, he was not alone in arguing that what was excitingly
new about Gothic was its narrative structure rather than its subject-
matter, its style of description, or even its historical setting.
Coleridge declares in his review of The Mysteries of Udolpho
that Radcliffe's novel builds up expectations which can never be
adequately recompensed by the revelations of the plot; while Scott
attends closely to the principles of narratives based on mystery
and suspense in his 'Life' of Radcliffe. All three critics implicitly
accept that the inadequacy of explanation is less the fault of the
author than a necessary concomitant of narratives of suspense.
They recognize the primary importance of secrecy in generating
literary Gothic.

The four sections of this chapter are divided somewhat arbitrarily because of the complexity of the subject and the profusion
of examples which might be given within each discussion (for
Gothic is nothing if not repetitive). All four sections are concerned
with patterns of disengagement and deferral in Gothic, and with
the problem of origin. Each uses the alliance suggested by Dunlop's
figure of the passages which lead to nothing as a starting-point
for the analysis of different aspects of Gothic narratology and

---

[3] The architectural analogy has dominated criticism of Gothic since the pioneering work of Maurice Lévy in Le Roman 'gothique' anglais, 1764–1824 (Toulouse,
1968). Rosemary Jackson analyses techniques of fragmentation (narrative and
psychological), labyrinthine texts pursuing impossible 'clues', in Fantasy: The
Literature of Subversion (London, 1981), ch. 4. A particularly sustained and
interesting use of the double metaphor is to be found in Jerrold E. Hogle's study,
'The Restless Labyrinth: Cryptonomy in the Gothic Novel', Arizona Quarterly,
xxxvi (1980), 330–58, a reminder of the emptinesses at the heart of Gothic and an
analysis of the passages and crypts as metaphors of narrative. Key analyses of the
narrative structure of Gothic, following J. M. S. Tompkins's comments on the
literature of suspense in The Popular Novel in England, 1770–1800 (London,
1932), are the introductory comments of Robert Kiely in The Romantic Novel in
England (Cambridge, Mass., 1972) and the introd. and ch. 1 of Elizabeth R.
Napier's The Failure of Gothic: Problems of Disjunction in an Eighteenth-Century
Literary Form (Oxford, 1987).

historicity. The first section examines the narrative organization of Gothic, drawing attention to its devices of delay and evasion, and to a narrative style which hesitates between expressing and concealing what it considers to be 'unutterable'. The second focuses on the special kinds of narrative disruption caused by Gothic's fascination with damaged and illegible manuscripts, and on its strategies of historical and authorial authentication. Developing these ideas, the third section then argues that the problem of origins, both historical and literary, dominates the aesthetics of creativity in Gothic. In the preface to the second edition of *The Castle of Otranto*, Walpole claimed that his new type of fiction was an experiment, an attempt to blend the characteristics of the ancient romance and the modern novel. Many critics have disputed the reputable parentage set out in Walpole's preface, describing Gothic instead as a 'bastard genre', a 'mixed grill' of competing literary conventions.[4] Gothic writers themselves were noticeably unsure about the claims which they should make for their fiction, and about the literary ancestry which they should trace for it. Finally, the argument turns to the problems caused for the reader of Gothic by all these strategies of uncertainty and disruption, and considers the reader's active role in constructing his or her own worst fears, psychological and political. A literary form characterized by delay and evasion is not one which might be expected to convey political significance unproblematically, and although that political significance is pervasive and important in Gothic, it is noticeable that many of the critics who have highlighted it have had difficulty in dealing with the formal and stylistic qualities of Gothic as distinct from summaries of its formulaic plots.

It is appropriate to say a little at the outset about the way in which this study defines the term 'Gothic'. Gothic is a type of fiction which invites readers' fears and anxieties in highly stylized mystery-tales, using a limited set of plots, settings, and character-types, and including an element of history. A novel should not be

---

[4] Robert D. Hume and Robert L. Platzner argue for Gothic's 'generic instability' in ' "Gothic versus Romantic": A Rejoinder', *PMLA* lxxxvi (1971), 266–74 (267). Also of interest are Napier's comments in 'Defining Otranto' and on the 'mixed grill' of Gothic (*Failure of Gothic*, 75–8, 126). The best discussions of the literary origins of Gothic are by James R. Foster, *History of the Pre-Romantic Novel in England*, MLA Monographs Series, No. 17 (New York, 1949), chs. 7 and 9; Kiely, *Romantic Novel*, 1–26, and Punter, *Literature of Terror*, ch. 2.

categorized as Gothic if it makes no attempt to situate the events of its plot in a historical setting, however inaccurate or implausible; although it may, of course, be grouped among such significant reworkings of Gothic plotting and setting as *Caleb Williams*, *Jane Eyre*, and *Rebecca*. The distinction is important not just because it allows one to see more clearly Gothic's primary engagement with historical materials but also because it clarifies the purposes of non-Gothic experimentation with Gothic conventions. The decision *not* to deal with injustice and tyranny as if they were problems specific to a safely distanced past is, for example, the whole point of Godwin's reworkings of Gothic in *Caleb Williams*. Similarly, it is important that *Jane Eyre*'s Bertha Rochester is *not* an Italian aristocrat silenced in a nunnery—like one of her prototypes, Laurentini/Agnes in *The Mysteries of Udolpho*—but instead a register of much more immediate sexual and racial crises. These distinctions are also important because Gothic is such an omnivorous literary form. It is awkward and contradictory, constantly questioning and undermining its own conventions, and negotiating its relationship to other types of literature—to drama, for example, in the case of *The Castle of Otranto*, which is never quite sure whether it is a pastiche of *Hamlet* or a revolutionary kind of prose fiction. This uncertainty about its place in literary tradition is signalled by the fact that it had no generally accepted name. Most writers who are now described as 'Gothic' chose not to follow Walpole and Reeve in giving their novels this name. Radcliffe is the most prominent example. A literary hybrid, this nameless fiction adapted settings, characters, and descriptive conventions from a variety of other works. The inspiration drawn from ballads of the supernatural was reinforced by the stylized primitivism of Gray, Chatterton, and Macpherson, and by the preoccupations of the 'graveyard' poets. Interpretations of the narrative structure of *The Faerie Queene* were superimposed on the subject-matter of 'Il Penseroso', 'Eloisa to Abelard', and Jacobean tragedy. Conventions of representing sensibility and a preoccupation with the sexual persecution of heroines were imported from Richardson and his successors. *Hamlet*, *Macbeth*, and *Measure for Measure* provided both character-types and a constant source of explicit narratorial reference. This mixture of forms and conventions has been regarded as both a weakness and a strength, as both predatory and diversely experimental. Such generalizations do not often help with the local instabilities of narratorial tone and descriptive convention discernible from page to page, however. Gothic novelists incorporated previous conventions with a degree of fictional self-consciousness which has yet to be registered fully in critical analysis.

1. The Delayed and the Unutterable: Evasiveness in Gothic Structure and Style

> The rooms *up stairs* may be just habitable, and no more; but the principal incidents must be carried on in *subterraneous* passages. These, in general, wind round the whole extent of the building; but that is not very material, as the heroine never goes through above half without meeting with a door, which she has neither strength nor resolution to open, although she has found a rusty key, very happily fitted to as rusty a lock, and would give the world to know what it leads to, and yet she can give no reason for her curiosity.[5]

Dunlop's aside on the '*passages* that lead to nothing' in Radcliffe's novels is the perfect starting-point for an analysis of narrative strategies which are both frustrating and addictive. Although many Gothic titles explicitly declare the importance of secrets *in* the narrative (as do Francis Lathom's *The Impenetrable Secret, Find It Out!* (1805) and Mary Meeke's '*There Is A Secret, Find It Out!*' (1808)), the ritualization of mystery in Gothic goes much further than this, producing narratives which come to resemble Frank Kermode's description in *The Genesis of Secrecy* of 'something irreducible, therefore perpetually to be interpreted; not secrets to be found out one by one, but Secrecy'.[6] Gothic fiction encourages its readers to seek answers to questions which are never precisely formulated, and forecloses its mysteries with solutions which are rarely satisfying. The narrative structure of *all* Gothic, in fact, follows the principles of 'terror' (suspense) rather than 'horror' (enactment) as they are differentiated in Radcliffe's essay 'On the

---

[5] Part of a 'recipe' for Gothic in 'Terrorist System of Novel Writing', signed 'A Jacobin Novelist', *Monthly Magazine*, iv (Aug. 1797), 104.
[6] Kermode, *The Genesis of Secrecy: On the Interpretation of Narrative*, The Charles Eliot Norton Lectures, 1977–8 (Cambridge, Mass., 1979), 143.

Supernatural in Poetry' (1826). This section is primarily concerned with the narrative strategies of Gothic, although it also seeks to clarify the nature of the secrets to which they lead. For in spite of Dunlop's irritation, the lost subject of Gothic is not quite 'nothing'. In nearly all Gothic fictions the narrative and architectural passages which seem to lead to nowhere in fact lead to the secret past, whether that secret past is personal (the discovery of a mother, a father, alive or in skeletal form) or cultural (the barbarisms of feudal society, of 'monkish superstition'). The powerful opening chapters of *A Tale of Two Cities* ('*Recalled to Life*') develop out of a kind of literature in which the past is repeatedly dug up, shown to be not dead but simply imprisoned; or, like the corpse of Cly, found even more terribly to be absent.

The approaches to history which Gothic repeatedly figures, in its tantalizing passageways, vaults, and ruins, sometimes lead literally to the rediscovery of a family past, the lost origins of the hero or heroine. In Radcliffe's early novel, *A Sicilian Romance* (1790), the heroine finds her way through the secret passageways underneath the family castle to the prison-chamber of her supposedly long-dead mother, who has been kept locked up there for twenty years. In Lewis's Gothic play, *The Castle Spectre* (performed in 1797 and published in 1798), the heroine discovers that her father, long thought dead, is actually lying prisoner in the dungeons of his own castle. At other times, however, the tomb is empty or the search is transferred to a search for manuscripts, documents, or portraits— alternative representations of what has been lost. Scott's novels contain many accounts of portraits which stand in for lost people, as the portrait of Malisius de Ravenswood does at the end of *The Bride of Lammermoor*; or which, as in *Woodstock*, conceal the entrance to secret passageways and chambers. Similar processes of discovery and substitution are at work in many Gothic novels. In Radcliffe's *The Romance of the Forest* (1791), for example, the heroine explores—first in a dream, then in reality—a concealed passageway which leads to a chamber which, the narrative emphasizes, forms 'an interior part of the original building'.[7] In this authentically ancient secret chamber she dreams she discovers an imprisoned man. When she explores it in reality, however, she finds neither a dead body nor a living man, but a written record,

---

[7] *Romance of Forest*, ii. 12: see also ii. 10.

the manuscript journal of the man who turns out to have been her father. The passage leads her to the secret of her own identity and to her family's past, but it also allows her to substitute a narrative for the father who was available to her in her dreams. The substitutions at work in this section of *The Romance of the Forest* are complex. In some Gothic novels, however, they are crude to the point of parody. In John Palmer's *The Haunted Cavern* (1796), the manuscript which recounts the story of the lost father (in this novel not dead after all, but imprisoned) falls abruptly on the head of the questing hero. On the evidence of these novels, however, it is clear that one of the 'nothings' to which the passages of Gothic lead is an authoritative and authentic narrative of the past.

Sophia Lee's novel *The Recess* (1785) is not concerned directly with substituting manuscripts for people, but it develops its own ways of negotiating a complex symbolic relationship between the present and the dead or absent past. In this novel, however, the personal past also has strong cultural implications, for the absent mother (Mary, Queen of Scots) is also a symbol of a lost religio-political system. The two heroines of *The Recess*, Matilda and Ellinor, are twin daughters of Queen Mary by a secret marriage to the Duke of Norfolk. Their quest to be reunited with her is doomed to failure, although they are able to glimpse her through the bars of her prison. (This is fitting, for the historical Queen of Scots is always lost, the fantasy of her revival being one of the most powerful to entice fiction in this period. Marie Antoinette is the Gothic heroine of post-revolutionary narrative, while Mary of Scotland is both her (historical) anticipation and her (fictional) echo.) The history of the Recess itself, once inhabited by nuns but deserted before the Reformation, and during that time used as a hiding-place for monks, draws attention to the larger cultural oppression of Roman Catholics, and establishes a context in which the novel can examine at several imaginative removes the historical persecution of Mary.

Like Adeline in *The Romance of the Forest*, the two heroines of *The Recess* suffer not because of their sins but because of their parentage. Matilda identifies herself from the start as 'a solitary victim to the crimes of my progenitors'.[8] Their parents are represented by two imposing portraits which dominate their secret

---

[8] *Recess*, i. 2.

retreat, the Recess. This retreat is connected with the outside world by a passage which opens up behind the portrait of their father, a detail which anticipates the secret passageways concealed by Victor Lee's portrait in Scott's *Woodstock*. Matilda notes that the pictures in the Recess have almost a living presence, an observation which takes on new force when Mrs Marlow, relating the history of the sisters, announces: 'I would describe the Queen of Scotland to you, my dear children, had not nature drawn a truer picture of her than I can give.—Look in the glass, Matilda, and you will see her perfect image.'[9] As this remark suggests, *The Recess* displaces the persecution of Mary on to the sufferings of her two imaginary daughters, giving the events of the plot a symbolic significance while avoiding overt political comment. Lee rewrites Mary's history, which is political, as a sentimental tale complete with bandits, faintings, and extravagant regrets. One daughter, Ellinor, is subject to fits of insanity brought on by disappointment in love and persecution in marriage. The other, Matilda, also suffers betrayal in love and develops a marked death-wish.[10] *The Recess* is a peculiarly death-obsessed novel, dominated by a secret place of refuge which is at once protecting and stifling. Each of Lee's three volumes ends with the dissolution of the heroines' identities in a death-like insensibility. At the end of the third volume, Ellinor has relapsed into insanity, while Matilda looks forward to a release in death. Their histories also include mock-deaths and the actual deaths of the men they love,

---

[9] *Recess*, i. 57. For Matilda's earlier comment, see i. 10. See the framed effect of the sisters' only glimpse of Queen Mary, i. 195–7. A recognition-formula very similar to that of the *Recess* looking-glass is to be found in the scene by Laurentini's deathbed at the end of *Udolpho*, when Emily is asked to see her own image in the portrait of the dead Marchioness de Villeroi.

[10] In her analysis of *Recess* as 'romance's revenge on recorded history', Jane Spencer emphasizes the Recess as both refuge and prison, and the novel as a whole as a protest against the marginalization of women in history (history rewritten as a series of love entanglements in Elizabeth's 'reign of romance'), in *The Rise of the Woman Novelist from Aphra Behn to Jane Austen* (Oxford, 1986), 195–201. Continuing this line of analysis, Kate Ferguson Ellis, in *The Contested Castle: Gothic Novels and the Subversion of Domestic Ideology* (Urbana, Ill., 1989), 68–75, focuses on the treatment of women and domestic imprisonment. According to Ellis, Lee 'unabashedly recasts history in such a way as to make passion its motivating force' (p. 69). My view is that *The Recess* is political in a broader sense than is suggested by Ellis's account of it as a 'radical critique of familial domination' (p. 70). Lee views through domesticity and the passions the national (political and religious) implications of Mary's story.

as well as the suicide of a secondary heroine, Rose Cecil, who kills herself to find release from the pressures of acute sensibility and disappointed love. In *The Recess*, therefore, Lee forges imaginative links between femininity, Catholicism, excess sensibility, and death. Although Scott's presentation of Mary Stewart in *The Abbot* dispenses with imaginary twin daughters on to which her sufferings may be displaced (and made blameless in the process), it makes its suggestions about cultural obsolescence by playing on exactly the same combination of ideas.

One general point about plotting arises out of this analysis of *The Recess* and its backdating of sin to the ancestral past. Gothic plots disrupt the reader's conventional expectations about the workings of cause and effect. All responsibility for sin in Gothic is typically referred back to the past, so that the evil effects suffered by protagonists in the present are clearly unrelated to any sins they themselves might have committed. This temporal displacement of sin persistently breaks up the logic of cause and effect in Gothic plots. Protagonists' sufferings come to resemble that disproportionate punishment which Coleridge describes in *Biographia Literaria*:

It sometimes happens that we are punished for our faults by incidents, in the causation of which these faults had no share; and this I have always felt the severest punishment. The wound indeed is of the same dimensions; but the edges are jagged, and there is a dull underpain that survives the smart which it had aggravated. For there is always a consolatory feeling that accompanies the sense of a proportion between antecedents and consequences.[11]

The lack of relationship in Gothic between suffering and crime dislocates its plotting as well as its moral and political implications.

Such descriptions of the ways in which the past is rediscovered in Gothic, often by means of symbolic substitution, do not, however, give any sense of the narrative structure of suspense and delay which makes them distinctive. It is frequently a simple matter of interruption. In Eliza Parsons's *Castle of Wolfenbach* (1793), the Countess mysteriously disappears just before she is

---

11 *Biographia Literaria: or Biographical Sketches of My Literary Life and Opinions* (1817), ed. James Engell and W. Jackson Bate, 2 vols., *The Collected Works of Samuel Taylor Coleridge*, vii, Bollingen Series lxxv, gen. ed. Kathleen Coburn (Princeton, NJ, 1983), ii. 234.

about to relate her life-story to the heroine. In *The Italian* (1797), the narration of essential details is repeatedly interrupted by the action. Paulo breaks off his account of the Black Penitents to Vivaldi to pursue the very monk who has aroused their curiosity, and Schedoni's guide tantalizingly hints at the story of the Barone di Cambrusca, a tale which he gradually unfolds. On a more extended scale, however, the narrative structure of Gothic is probably best illustrated in the most famous of all the novels it produced, *The Mysteries of Udolpho* (1794).

The most compelling and most celebrated mystery in Radcliffe's novel serves also as a model for its narrative structure. In his 'Life' of Radcliffe, Scott pays close attention to the mystery of the Black Veil, and uses it to suggest that Radcliffe's techniques of preserving mystery and suspense frequently leave the reader frustrated: 'We fear that some such feeling of disappointment and displeasure attends most readers, when they read for the first time the unsatisfactory solution of the mysteries of the black pall and the wax figure, which has been adjourned from chapter to chapter, like something suppressed, because too horrible for the ear.'[12] Scott devotes several paragraphs of the 'Life' to Radcliffe's techniques of deferral, in which he includes her habit of breaking off the narrative just as it is about to become most interesting, her way of suddenly extinguishing reading lamps, and her predilection for 'shadowy forms and half-heard sounds of woe'. The mystery of the Black Veil is in many ways paradigmatic of *The Mysteries of Udolpho* as a whole. Its significance as mystery is far greater than any possible significance as a clue to the plot or as evidence of a crime. It exists to be approached, to be misread, and therefore to shock to the point of insensibility: Emily lifts the veil, mistakes the waxwork for a corpse, and faints. Throughout *The Mysteries of Udolpho*, likewise, adventures are constantly posited, never enacted, and threats are made only to be responded to, then replaced by something yet more fearful. Even the castle of Udolpho is a displacement of the genuine mysteries of the novel. In one sense, Udolpho gives substance to Emily's persistent anxieties. The funeral of her aunt Madame Montoni, for example, completes an imaginative pattern of fear and loss initiated at the funeral of Emily's father in the first volume of the novel. Before leaving the

[12] *MPW* iii. 375.

convent of St Clair after her father's death, Emily visits his grave alone at midnight, and, in spite of warnings, almost stumbles upon an open grave. In the crypts of Udolpho she stands before another open grave which she once imagined to have been dug for herself. The pattern of Emily's seeing an object of horror, in all three scenes a corpse, extends from the incident in which she lifts the Black Veil (and faints), to the scene in the 'portal-chamber' in which she pulls aside a curtain to find the body of a murdered man (and faints again), to the scene at the Château Le Blanc in which she and Dorothée pull aside the curtains of the bed in which the Marchioness de Villeroi died. Around this bed, in a description which strongly allies it with the veiled picture in Udolpho, hangs 'a counterpane, or pall, of black velvet'. As Emily's mind flashes back to Madame Montoni's deathbed, Dorothée terrifies both of them by crying out that she thinks she sees the dying Marchioness de Villeroi still stretched on the bed, so vivid is her recollection of past sufferings.

In another sense, however, Udolpho is not the source of the mysteries which beset Emily, but a displacement characteristic of medieval and Renaissance romance. In *Sir Gawain and the Green Knight*, for example, Gawain's meeting with the Green Knight is a displacement of the social tests which have already taken place at Bertilak's castle. In Book II of *The Faerie Queene*, Guyon's encounter with Mammon and destruction of the Bower of Bliss are enactments of tests he has already undergone in spirit; while, in Book III, Amoret's imprisonment in the House of Busirane is the physical representation of problems which lie elsewhere. So, in Radcliffe's tale of a modern-day Amoret, there is much to be said for interpreting Udolpho as the castle of romance ordeal, a formal embodiment of conflict rather than its source or its explanation. The social round at Madame Cheron's home in Tholouse (*sic*) precipitates Montoni's ambitions for Emily's estates, while Emily's visit to Venice brings the added complication of Morano's schemes to seduce her. Finally, the château of Le Blanc, not Udolpho, conceals the mysteries of Emily's birthright, and the nearby convent of St Clair, not some hidden grave or veiled recess, conceals the nun Agnes (Signora Laurentini). Laurentini herself completes another pattern begun but not resolved at Udolpho, the punishment of the passionate woman who must, literally or figuratively, be buried alive. Madame Montoni's fate is a variant on this pattern. Each confrontation in the novel functions simultaneously as a displacement of something else. Hence the narrative structure of deferral which it shares with works like *The Faerie Queene*. One of the 'mysteries' of Udolpho is that it in itself is not mysterious. The key to its significance always lies elsewhere.

The Mysteries of Udolpho operates by breaking down the certainties of the social idyll with which it opens, and by close repetition and revisiting of situations and motifs. The first of these principles has been widely analysed. The perfect family group of the opening chapter is rapidly broken down as first Emily's mother, then her father, dies. Her new protector, Madame Cheron, is soon metamorphosed into Madame Montoni, and her potential protector, Valancourt, into a dissolute hanger-on of fashionable Parisian society. Spatially, Emily must exchange her secure room at La Vallée for the so-called 'double chamber' at Udolpho, which allows Morano access to her chamber while she sleeps. Even her certainty about her parentage is gradually broken down, first by the shock of the sentence glimpsed as she destroys the manuscript secreted in her father's chamber, and later by all the hints that she is a blood relation of the victimized Marchioness de Villeroi. Less widely recognized is the extent to which *The Mysteries of Udolpho* is patterned by return and repetition. The geographical patterning of the story is meticulous. All the scenes of early trial and suffering are ritually revisited and redeemed after the flight from Udolpho. The mystery of the Black Veil, similarly, is repeated symbolically at key points in the plot even though (as the experience of most first-time readers confirms) the narrator seems to have forgotten all about it. The mysterious object concealed by the Black Veil turns out not to be a picture, but it suggests that the other pictures and miniatures in which the novel abounds may on a symbolic level be comparable images of death. After the scene in the portal-chamber, when Emily's health and nerves at last give way, her death as the victim of Montoni's persecution is displaced on to Madame Montoni. As soon as her aunt has died, Emily takes over her role in the arguments with Montoni over the retention of her estates. In another shift of identity, the prisoner whom she expects to be Valancourt turns out instead to be the unknown suitor from the fishing-house at La Vallée (another deferral). Marking the beginning of her restoration, Emily next appears in the figurative disguise of Blanche, the daughter of the

Count de Villefort, who approaches with romantic feelings of delighted suspense the house which is to redeem Udolpho, the Château Le Blanc itself. Ludovico's disappearance from the haunted chamber at Le Blanc repeats in comic mode the insecurities of Emily's situation in the double chamber at Udolpho. *The Mysteries of Udolpho* therefore can be seen to be tightly patterned around key scenes and repeated images, most especially the scene of pulling back a veil to find a corpse or a waxwork or a picture which mirrors oneself, and the scene of avoiding an open grave, with which it is imaginatively associated.

Throughout Gothic, the narrative structure of suspense and evasion which governs *The Mysteries of Udolpho* is repeated on the more immediate level of narrative style. If the actions of Gothic are to remain mysterious, the narrator must either keep secrets (as Radcliffe's narrator does in relation to the Black Veil) or develop a style which suggests but does not describe. The process places a burden on descriptive language to which the narrators of Gothic (drawing on the conventions of sentimental fiction) frequently draw explicit attention. In *The Castle of Otranto*, as Isabella flees from Manfred, Walpole comments: 'Words cannot paint the horror of the princess's situation.'[13] By using the metaphor of painting, Walpole instinctively moves away from the problem of finding words to describe the scene. The burdens placed on language by the need to describe extreme states of emotion become a common subject of narratorial reflection in Gothic, and are also intermittently a topic of interest to eighteenth-century theorists of the sublime, whose work is closely connected with the aesthetics of Gothic fiction. In *A Philosophical Enquiry into the Origin of our Ideas of the Sublime and Beautiful* (1757), Burke describes how the sublime is experienced in a state of 'astonishment' ('that state of the soul, in which all its motions are suspended, with some degree of horror').[14] Fear, being an apprehension of pain or death, suspends physical powers. Burke provides no detailed discussion of the suspension of language or of the language used to express fear. Instead, like Longinus, he examines in Part Five of the *Philosophical Enquiry* the literary

---

[13] *Otranto*, 26.
[14] *A Philosophical Enquiry into the Origin of our Ideas of the Sublime and Beautiful* (1757), ed. and introd. J. T. Boulton (London, 1958), 57.

language used to excite fear in others. (Longinus had asserted 'that sublimity consists in a certain excellence and distinction in expression', and had emphasized 'the command of language' which is a pre-condition of the sublime in literature.[15]) In one evocative general comment, however, Burke proposes: 'All *general* privations are great, because they are terrible; *Vacuity, Darkness, Solitude* and *Silence*.'[16] Adapting Burke's emphasis on 'astonishment' in the aesthetics of sublimity to the stylistic devices of literature in particular, Beattie argues in his dissertation 'Illustrations on Sublimity' that the impression of the sublime can be reduced by an unskilful writer in several ways: 'First, by too minute description, and too many words. For, when we are engrossed by admiration or astonishment, it is not natural for us to speak much, or attend to the more diminutive qualities of that which we contemplate.'[17]

There are two issues in question here. One is the use of language to describe the sublime in literature. The other is the language available to those directly experiencing fearful and tremendous events or feelings. Gothic, as already suggested, marks the points at which its own narratorial language breaks down and is defeated by the enormity of what it attempts to describe (the 'words cannot paint the horror' formula). It also features prominently in its standard plots situations in which the language of individual characters is suspended by strong feeling. Anticipating the heroes of the Waverley Novels, characters in Gothic cannot speak out, fail to respond with the right words to accusations and interrogations, and have their powers of independent speech suspended by eloquent figures of power.[18] Going further than the conventional alliance between virtue and enforced silence, Gothic commonly denies the capacity of words to express the extremes of feeling. The process by which other experiences are obliterated, and the

---

[15] *Classical Literary Criticism: Aristotle: On the Art of Poetry; Horace: On the Art of Poetry; Longinus: On the Sublime*, trans. and introd. T. S. Dorsch (Harmondsworth, 1965), 100, 108.

[16] *Philosophical Enquiry*, 71.

[17] James Beattie, *Dissertations Moral and Critical* (London, 1783), 639.

[18] Sometimes the words of vindication are cruelly suppressed by astonishment and terror, as the schoolboy McGill discovers in *Confessions*, when he tries to deny a crime of which he is entirely innocent, 'and the words stuck in his throat as he feebly denied it' (*Confessions*, 166–7). Contrast Gil-Martin's 'mighty fluency', p. 131, and 'overpowering' eloquence, p. 203; the eloquence of the demonic preacher in the Auchtermuchty Preachment, p. 307.

individual loses power in the presence of an overwhelming object, closely resembles Burke's account of the 'suspended' state in which we experience the sublime, which 'hurries us on by an irresistible force'.[19] In matters of description, language itself is the medium suspended and weakened by the abuse of power.[20]

These different types of crisis facing language are found in a particularly concentrated form in *Melmoth the Wanderer* (1820), in which the deferred object of the quest is a series of words which must always remain 'unutterable'. *Melmoth the Wanderer* follows many of the patterns of the search for the personal and cultural past already analysed in *The Romance of the Forest* and *The Recess*, and its structure is a version of the structure of deferral and substitution analysed in *The Mysteries of Udolpho*. It is also peculiarly obsessed with the nature and the power structures of language.

In *Melmoth the Wanderer*, a series of interlinked adventures deal with a few central words, Melmoth's temptation to victims to sell their souls at the lowest point in their worldly fortunes, which must always remain 'unutterable'. The act of speaking, telling, itself becomes almost unbearably painful and difficult at some points of the story, as it is for Monçada when he is first rescued from the shipwreck by John Melmoth and must try to explain his reasons for travelling to Ireland: '"Senhor, I understand your name is——" He paused, shuddered, and with an effort that seemed like convulsion, disgorged the name of Melmoth.'[21] Monçada's plight is symptomatic of the whole narrative endeavour of *Melmoth the Wanderer*. The novel tells stories about, but does not record, the unutterable words of demonic temptation, and prepares for confrontations which, when described, are described only fitfully or unsatisfactorily, as in the final scenes between Melmoth, Monçada, and John Melmoth. Monçada concludes his tale arbitrarily, promising to tell of other victims, whose fates are 'still darker and more awful than those he had recited'. John Melmoth

---

[19] *Philosophical Enquiry*, 57.
[20] Particularly interesting work on Gothic's relation to the unspeakable has been done by Eve Kosofsky Sedgwick, *The Coherence of Gothic Conventions* (1980; repr. New York, 1986), ch. 3. Also of interest to this discussion are Punter's comments on language and taboo (*Literature of Terror*, 19–20), and Jackson's argument for the 'non-signification' of fantasy (*Fantasy*, 37–42).
[21] *Melmoth*, i. 177.

is tempted to gratify his 'dangerous curiosity' and still entertains 'the wild hope of seeing the original of that portrait he had destroyed, burst from the walls and take up the fearful tale himself':[22] the wild hope, that is, of breaking the frame of narrative, and the pact by which the agent of evil has been distanced from the reader and his direct representative in the role of listener, John Melmoth. The narrative structure exists to protect John and the reader from the horrific actualization to which it logically leads, of having Melmoth tempt them, of hearing the unspeakable condition spoken. Melmoth, when he appears, seems conscious that he is the ultimate authority for the narrative which attempts to describe him. He threatens to end John's 'wild and wretched curiosity', asking: 'Who can tell so well of Melmoth the Wanderer as himself?'[23] Throughout *Melmoth the Wanderer*, Maturin is fascinated by the possibility that the story will become real, the threat carried out, the approach become a confrontation. On every level, however, he denies the reader that moment of knowledge and confrontation.

This avoidance of direct contact with the source, the authority, is repeated on the level of narrative style. One tortuous sentence from the opening section of *Melmoth the Wanderer* is characteristic of the structures of authentication prompted by the regressive structures of Gothic, which gesture toward explanations which recede beyond the power of the narrative to fix or endorse. The sentence forms part of Maturin's reflections on the 'supernatural' powers of the peasant sibyl, Biddy Brannigan:

No one, in short, knew better how to torment or terrify her victims into a belief of that power which may and has reduced the strongest minds to the level of the weakest; and under the influence of which the cultivated sceptic, Lord Lyttleton, yelled and gnashed and writhed in his last hours, like the poor girl who, in the belief of the horrible visitation of the vampire, shrieked aloud, that her grandfather was sucking her vital blood while she slept, and expired under the influence of imaginary horror.[24]

This dizzying sentence begins in rational social observation and moves further and further back into the legendary and the bizarre.

[22] *Melmoth*, iv. 432.
[23] *Melmoth*, iv. 436.
[24] *Melmoth*, i. 12-13. The reference is to Thomas, 2nd Baron Lyttleton (1744-79).

As in the larger narrative of *Melmoth the Wanderer*, story is cited
to support story. The tale of the girl and vampire is introduced to
support the reference to Lord Lyttleton. Lyttleton is mentioned to
support Maturin's observations on the debilitating effect of superstitious fear, and these in turn have been offered to support the
presentation of Biddy Brannigan. Narratives verify each other,
stretching from the present and recent past, to the more distant
matter of the previous century, back to the elemental realm of
legendary good and evil.

Throughout *Melmoth the Wanderer*, Maturin develops a contrast between 'natural' and 'unnatural' communication, which he
extends throughout the novel in a series of reflections on the
governing principles of 'natural' and 'artificial' language. Monçada
notes that those who speak the truth become outcasts and objects
of terror, suspected of subversion and insanity: 'These words,
though uttered by a ragged demoniac, (as they thought me), made
them tremble. Truth is rarely heard in convents, and therefore
its language is equally emphatical and portentous.'[25] Issues of
personal, political, and spiritual conflict are explored on the level
of incompatible syntax and vocabulary. As in the linguistic games
in the tortured confrontations between Monçada and his spiritual
Director, systems of social oppression appropriate language. A
long section of *Melmoth the Wanderer* is devoted to a story in
which an innocent girl, Immalee, learns a language and a social
code from the demonic, eloquent Melmoth. Their early encounters
centre on Immalee's discovery of 'the world of voices', 'the world
of answers', and on the struggle between the corrupting eloquence
of Melmoth and the linguistic innocence of Immalee, who possesses
not just natural feeling but also an Edenic language which perfectly corresponds to the thoughts she wishes to express. Even after
her involvement with Melmoth, and in the midst of hypocritical
Spanish society, she retains something of this purity: even here,
rejecting the prescribed forms of established religion, 'she ventured
to address the image of the Virgin in language of her own'.[26] In
contrast to this, Melmoth is at once the perfect communicator and
a dealer in 'unutterable' words.

He is also, ironically, the perfect narrator of history. Melmoth,
who has lived through several troubled centuries, is an uncannily

---

[25] *Melmoth*, ii. 91–2.   [26] *Melmoth*, iii. 267.

accurate historian, narrating from the absolute authority of personal experience. This is a possibility implicit in many tales which tell of lives extended beyond the natural span (including Godwin's *St Leon*), but in Maturin's novel it becomes part of the compulsion to narrate. In one scene, Monçada realizes with horror that Melmoth has been present at the events he describes, and that sinister implications underlie Melmoth's 'anecdotical history', in which he speaks 'with the fidelity of an eye-witness'.[27] The 'minuteness and circumstantiality in his details' disturbs Monçada with a feeling which he finds hard to describe: 'I listened to him with an indefinable mixture of curiosity and terror.'[28]

It is appropriate that the perfect narrator of history, its most convincing authenticator, should turn out to be possessed of supernatural and unnatural powers. The narrators of Gothic, many of whom claim access to materials miraculously preserved and authoritatively interpreted, have rather more problems than Melmoth in creating for their work the authentic trappings of history and ancient provenance.

2. *Legitimate History and the Fantasy of Origins*

NOT being permitted to publish the means which enriched
me with the obsolete manuscript from whence the following
tale is extracted, its simplicity alone can authenticate it. . . .
The depredations of time have left chasms in the story, which
sometimes only heightens the pathetic. An inviolable respect
for truth would not permit me to attempt connecting these,
even where they appeared faulty.

(Advertisement to *The Recess*, 1785)

Wolfgang Iser, among others, has claimed that Scott's historical novels link past and present in an innovative way which decisively distinguishes them from the conventions of Gothic. Iser argues that 'for Scott the past can only take on historical reality if it is linked with the present, for the world portrayed in the Gothic novel remains unhistorical precisely because it lacks this link'.[29] If

---

[27] *Melmoth*, ii. 277, 278.
[28] *Melmoth*, ii. 280.
[29] *The Implied Reader: Patterns of Communication in Prose Fiction from Bunyan to Beckett* (1972), trans. anon. (Baltimore, 1974), 84.

'historical reality' is to be made dependent upon links with the narrative present, however, Gothic novels abound in it. In the very crudest sense, Gothic tales are commonly introduced as 'edited' by the author from manuscripts—often fragmentary, partially illegible, or in several languages—which supposedly authenticate them but which also draw attention to the need for the past to be translated, to be made accessible to interpretation in new ways.

Analysing the interplay between moments of experience and processes of description in Richardson's *Pamela*, Lennard J. Davis locates a 'fetishization of style and penmanship, the concern with the minutiae of sending and receiving, intercepting, forging, and the logophilia that demands every event be obsessively incarnated into the word'.[30] Gothic fiction has its version of this fetishization of the processes of narrative: a fascination with the origin and transmission of historical and pseudo-historical materials. As Scott reminds readers in his 'Essay on Romance' in 1824, 'modern authors were not the first who invented the popular mode of introducing their works to the world as the contents of a newly-discovered manuscript'.[31] Even so, the convention had become a staple of eighteenth-century fiction. Henry Mackenzie's *The Man of Feeling* (1771), one of the novels which Scott cites most often in his work, is a useful example, partly because it is not a novel which obviously invites elaborate fictions of authenticity. In the introduction to *The Man of Feeling*, the 'editor' sets out the circumstances in which he first heard about Harley's manuscript, ignobly used as wadding by the local curate during hunting expeditions. Mackenzie uses this frame to make modest remarks about the pretensions of the work, but also to claim, in a footnote to the first chapter, that he is to be held responsible only for scattered chapters and fragments in the disjointed series of reflections to follow. This is a characteristic use of a fantasy of origin to provide both literary definition and a measure of protection for the author. Although it is a commonplace of non-historical material in the eighteenth century, the tradition of the tale which is put together from ancient manuscripts, edited memoirs, and fragmentary records of a greater narrative now lost, is of par-

---

[30] Davis, 'A Social History of Fact and Fiction: Authorial Disavowal in the Early English Novel', in *Literature and Society: Selected Papers from the English Institute, 1978*, NS No. 3, ed. Edward W. Said (Baltimore, 1980), 143.

[31] *MPW* vi. 179, and examples of authentication given, 179–83.

ticular interest in Gothic fiction, with its complex and mannered relationship to the subject of the past.

In their prefaces, Walpole and Reeve set the voices of a present editor and antiquarian between the reader and the historically imperfect text. In *The Old English Baron* (first published as *The Champion of Virtue* in 1777 and renamed for the second edition in 1778), Reeve continues Walpole's pretence of editing from an original manuscript. Her use of the device of the incomplete manuscript serves a familiar fictional purpose, to pass over inessential aspects of the story, but the details of the editing process draw upon problems of contemporary scholarship in dealing with incomplete, inconsistent, and obscure manuscript materials, as evidenced in the controversies over the work of Macpherson and Chatterton. Critics also debated the likely authenticity of William Beckford's *Vathek*, which, with its weighty appendage of notes by Samuel Henley, was first published in England in 1786 as *An Arabian Tale, From an Unpublished Manuscript*.[32] *The Recess*, likewise, purports to be extracted from an 'obsolete manuscript', details of which the 'editor' is not permitted to divulge, although she admits that she has made some alterations to the language of the original. Again, the frame serves as artistic apology. Lee admits that there are 'chasms' in the story which she is unable to amend without tampering too heavily with the manuscript. The claims made in the Advertisement, however—that characters and events in the novel 'agree' with history—create a distinction between history and the present fiction which breaks down the pretence of authenticity.

As the contradictory claims put forward in Lee's Advertisement foretell, Gothic fiction was to develop a complicated relationship to historical knowledge. It was a common complaint that Radcliffe, for example, seemed to have forgotten to try to make her novels historically accurate. In the 1790s, a periodical article attacking 'Terrorist Novel Writing' derided the failures in historical understanding and information which her novels exposed; while Jane Porter complained in her introduction to the 1832 edition of *Thaddeus of Warsaw* (first published in 1803) that Radcliffe's

---

[32] *An Arabian Tale, From an Unpublished Manuscript: With Notes Critical and Explanatory* [by Samuel Henley], (London, 1786). In a letter to Byron, *Letters*, iv. 4, Scott remarks: 'I would give a great deal to know the originals from which it was drawn.'

'wildly interesting romances' had seduced the public away from real history, so that she feared *Thaddeus of Warsaw* itself would be received as only 'a dull union between real history and a matter-of-fact imagination'.[33] It is instructive, therefore, to find that her novels experiment persistently with different methods of historical authentication. With the exception of *The Castles of Athlin and Dunbayne* (1789), all Radcliffe's novels show an interest in the provenance and transmission of manuscript tales, especially *The Romance of the Forest*, in which the main adventure is the discovery and deciphering of a manuscript journal, and *The Italian*. In *The Romance of the Forest*, furthermore, Radcliffe makes a clear attempt to claim for one of her characters the authority of historical fact. Her portrayal of La Motte and the Marquis de Montalt is backed up by the cited authority of Gayot de Pitaval's records of seventeenth-century legal cases in Paris, *Causes célèbres et intéressantes*. This work, first published in 1734, had already been used as the basis of a shorter collection of tales by Charlotte Smith, *The Romance of Real Life* in 1787.[34] By the time she came to work on her final novel, *Gaston de Blondeville* (1826), Radcliffe was clearly interested in honouring the claims to historicity which her earlier works had made, however superficially. Some critics have ascribed the self-conscious historicity of this last novel to Scott's influence, and its story bears some coincidental resemblances to the ghostly joust-scene in *Marmion* and the death of Brian de Bois-Guilbert in *Ivanhoe*. Although it remained unpublished until 1826, however, it was written in 1802, and is clearly not the result of the educational impact of Scott's poems or novels. *Gaston de Blondeville* makes scrupulous use of its imagined provenance in a manuscript dating from the reign of Henry III and found by two English tourists on a visit to Kenilworth. Radcliffe even interrupts to question their dating of this source. Within the course of her work, therefore, the insistence on imagined manuscript sources becomes more

[33] 'Terrorist Novel Writing', *The Spirit of the Public Journals for 1797*, i, 3rd edn. (London, 1802), 227 n.; *Thaddeus of Warsaw: Revised, Corrected, and Illustrated with a New Introduction, Notes, Etc. By the Author*, Standard Novels, No. 4 (London, 1832), p. xi.

[34] Radcliffe seems to follow Smith in misspelling the author's name as 'Guyot de Pitaval'. The story told in *Romance of Forest* does not form part of either collection. See Clara F. McIntyre, *Ann Radcliffe in Relation to Her Time*, Yale Studies in English, No. 62 (New Haven, Conn., 1920), 57–8.

elaborate and more intense, the play on historical authenticity being particularly marked in her last two novels.

These instances of early Gothic usages of frames and authenticating interventions by editors and narrators suggest that Gothic was developing a complex and self-conscious relationship to its historical materials, and to different types and levels of authority within its narrative schema.

The pretence that their novels were based on manuscripts— fragmentary, indecipherable, or unreliable—allowed Gothic writers to develop a narrative form which could maintain suspense while also suggesting the incompleteness of historical evidence. Descriptions of the manuscripts' physical appearance also provided novelists with opportunities to comment on the organization of their own narratives. The extent to which they made use of these opportunities varied. In *The Old English Baron*, the written version of the past, although incomplete, nevertheless provides all the information the reader needs. By the time of Maturin's *Melmoth the Wanderer*, manuscripts are genuinely frustrating:

The stranger, slowly turning round, and disclosing a countenance which ——(Here the manuscript was illegible for a few lines), said in English ——(A long hiatus followed here, and the next passage that was legible, though it proved to be a continuation of the narrative, was but a fragment).[35]

In between Reeve and Maturin, *The Romance of the Forest* describes one manuscript which suggests in miniature the characteristics and organization of the novel's narrative as a whole. The manuscript journal which Adeline reads at interrupted intervals of her own history follows the principles of the novel's narrative organization, by which information is half-given, half-withheld, and the process of discovery becomes as important as the information discovered. The first description of the manuscript suggests its importance as a prototype and symbol:

It was a small roll of paper, tied with a string, and covered with dust. Adeline took it up, and on opening it perceived an handwriting. She attempted to read it, but the part of the manuscript she looked at was so much obliterated, that she found this difficult, though what few words were legible impressed her with curiosity and terror, and induced her to return with it immediately to her chamber.

[35] *Melmoth*, i. 67: see also iii. 311–12.

The manuscript contains many 'illegible' passages which contrive to keep from Adeline all the vital information about the identity of the author and his oppressor, while arousing her horror and compassion. Like *The Romance of the Forest* as a whole, it withholds information while soliciting emotional response. Peter's long-winded account of his information about the Marquis prevents his actually warning Adeline about the dangers which surround her. The Marquis himself avoids explicitly stipulating that La Motte must murder Adeline. Later, Du Bosse, the accomplice who initiates the revelations about Adeline's birth and her father's murder, tells La Motte, and the reader, just enough to awaken curiosity, and then withholds further communication until his appearance in court.[36] All three scenes work on the same principle of broken and withheld narrative. The failures and omissions of the process of explanation arouse the reader's curiosity, just as Adeline's curiosity is aroused by the manuscript's mysteries and silences.

In some fictions which draw on the conventions of Gothic, manuscripts not only stand in for lost people but also compete with them for authority. In *Caleb Williams* (1794), Caleb's greatest desire is to find in the mysterious chest an authoritative account of Falkland's past. He declares at the end of the novel: 'I am now persuaded that the secret it inclosed was a faithful narrative of that [the murder of Tyrrel] and its concomitant transactions.'[37] Caleb's interest in manuscript sources is taken further in the work of Godwin's follower and imitator, Charles Brockden Brown. In *Edgar Huntly* (1799), the fetishization of manuscripts, and a pervasive imagery linking them to the other quests and adventures of the novel, is developed in a particularly elaborate and interesting fashion. The labyrinthine natural wilderness of the Norwalk, through which Edgar first pursues Clithero, is described as a region of secrets, which the traveller and explorer must seek to unravel. In this, it is the natural version of the skilfully wrought boxes and chests which both Edgar and Clithero fashion as guardians of manuscripts precious to them. At linked crises in the plot, Edgar breaks open the chest of Clithero but fails to find the

[36] *Romance of Forest*, ii. 68–71, 87–100 (Peter); ii. 281–6, iii. 2–7 (Marquis); iii. 263–7 (Du Bosse).
[37] *Caleb Williams*, iii. 273.

manuscript of Eugenia Lorimer; then finds his own secret chest broken into and the letters of his murdered friend Waldegrave stolen. Edgar's description of this discovery strongly recalls the terms in which he has described his search for Clithero among the recesses of the Norwalk: 'I was lost in horror and amazement. I explored every nook a second and third time, but still it eluded my eye and my touch. I opened my closets and cases. I pryed every where, unfolded every article of cloathing, turned and scrutinized every instrument and tool, but nothing availed.'[38] The mysterious chests and precious manuscripts recall *Caleb Williams*. Brown fills the empty trunk which retains its mystery in Godwin's tale. More importantly, however, the quest for lost manuscripts buried by the elm and lost in the caves of the Norwalk parallels the quest for Clithero and later for Edgar himself. In the novel's most disorientating sequence, Edgar wakes to find himself mysteriously immured in a concealed cavern. Thinking that he must somehow have been buried alive, he finds that he has replaced both Clithero and the two sets of papers as the secret, the object of the quest. The secret mechanized boxes parallel the tricky passageways and caves of the natural world. Later, when Edgar rediscovers Clithero, Clithero tells him that only his repossession of Eugenia Lorimer's manuscript made it possible for him to live: 'while in possession of this manuscript I was reconciled to the means of life'.[39] The written word acquires a talismanic potency in the novel's search for a reliable version of disputed events.

Melmoth the Wanderer has already been analysed as a novel preoccupied with systems of communication. It also continues Gothic's fascination with the ways in which communicated tales are made authentic. The novel as a whole is centrally concerned with the origin and transmission of stories. Melmoth's appearance in Madrid is accompanied by a scene of reporting and conjecture, so concerned is Maturin with the gradual accumulation of fact and fantasy which creates narrative and biography. One narrator comments:

The person whom you saw ride by, is one of those beings after whom human curiosity pants in vain,—whose life is doomed to be recorded

[38] Charles Brockden Brown, *Edgar Huntly; or, Memoirs of a Sleep-Walker* (1799), ed. and introd. Norman S. Grabo (Harmondsworth, 1988), 128.
[39] *Edgar Huntly*, 262.

in incredible legends that moulder in the libraries of the curious. . . . who has become already the subject of written memoirs, and the theme of traditional history.[40]

The same speaker links the silence surrounding Melmoth with the taboo subject of his offer to his victims:

'There are other narratives,' continued the stranger, 'relating to this mysterious being, which I am in possession of, and which I have collected with much difficulty; for the unhappy, who are exposed to his temptations, consider their misfortunes as a crime, and conceal, with the most anxious secresy, every circumstance of this horrible visitation. . . .'[41]

Monçada, transcribing some other memoranda of Melmoth in Adonijah's cellar, turns storytelling into a scholarly and historical endeavour to recapture, preserve, and pass on the words of Melmoth's temptation. The series of interrelated tales which results is self-consciously contained within the most fragile of narrative frames. At times, Maturin, or an unnamed editor, deliberately breaks through the frame. One of his footnotes points out the incongruity of a passage in the manuscript of the Jew Adonijah, 'as savouring more of Christianity than Judaism'.[42] This highly self-conscious interpolation erodes the narrative consensus, drawing attention to the fragility of the novel's construction. Even the narrative authority of Donna Clara's letter to her husband is undermined by the dictation and interpolations of Fra Jose.

Later still in Gothic's development, Hogg's Confessions of a Justified Sinner (1824) persistently questions individual perception and the authority of the observer to explore the difficulties not just of approaching a traditional tale with the apparatus of historical enquiry, but also of any kind of narrative reconstruction. The Editor's narrative opens with a flourish of authenticity and authority, parodying the dry factual style of the historian who is hopelessly out of touch with the life of the tradition he records. Although he claims that he observes a historian's duty towards his source materials—and besides, the manuscript memoir which he edits obliges him to be accurate, 'there being a curse pronounced by the writer on him that should dare to alter or amend'[43]—the

---

[40] *Melmoth*, iv. 56.   [41] *Melmoth*, iv. 160.   [42] *Melmoth*, iv. 35.
[43] *Confessions*, 388. A fuller discussion of Hogg's *Confessions*, taking its cue from this account of the manuscript and its curse on inauthenticity, is given in ch. 6.

Editor is forced at every turn to speculate and to reconstruct. Speculation is in any case inseparable from the materials of his story. Even the Laird's bride is 'the sole heiress and reputed daughter of a Baillie Orde, of Glasgow'.[44] Robert Wringhim's own narratorial authority is open to question, and his attempts to have his manuscript journal published in his own lifetime make it clear that the publishing profession does not confer the authority he seeks; a recognition which ironically invalidates the claims of the Editor before he has even made them.[45]

Gothic, then, develops over the course of its first sixty years a complex relationship both to historical verisimilitude and to the accepted processes of authentication. The device of the discovered and edited manuscript seems at first sight absolutely standard in terms of eighteenth-century fictional practice. There are signs, however, that its special potential as a medium for both promoting and questioning a sense of history in fiction was recognized by at least some Gothic novelists, and that the use of the frame narrative and the editorial aside, already staples of non-historical fiction, was being adapted to meet the particular needs of a sub-genre which foregrounded both its historicity and a saving, self-conscious fictionality.

3. 'Sheltered Under the Cannon': The Anxieties of Not Being Influenced

The title-page of the first edition of *The Castle of Otranto* in 1764 announces it as a translation by 'William Marshal, Gent. From the Original Italian of Onuphrio Muralto, Canon of the Church of St Nicholas at Otranto'. In his preface to the second edition a year later, Walpole replaces the fantasy of the preservation of the 'original manuscript', providentially 'found in the library of an ancient catholic family in the north of England',[46] by an appeal to a different kind of precedent. His new precedent, the supposed occasion for his composition, is literary. More specifically, it is

---

[44] *Confessions*, 2.
[45] Publication planned, *Confessions*, 339; the critical presentation of the publishing establishment, 336–42; and the publisher's denunciation of the journal as 'a medley of lies and blasphemy', 341.
[46] *Otranto*, 3.

Shakespearian. Walpole now appeals to Shakespeare's example 'to shelter my own daring under the cannon of the brightest genius this country, at least, has produced'.[47] If the device of the discovered manuscript offered Gothic writers one way of authenticating, and simultaneously distancing, material which might be farfetched or personally revealing, the habit of citing prestigious forebears for what was essentially, and self-consciously, a new style of prose fiction, could also offer a kind of shelter and justification. How far Gothic writers wished to be so indebted, however, was more problematic. The question leads into much more general problems about originality and individual inspiration as they affected Gothic experiment.

Eighteenth-century commentators commonly characterized the literature and architecture of Gothic times in terms of inspired imagination and creative individualism, associating the irregularity of Gothic with 'free' genius, untrammelled by convention. So, Hurd's *Letters on Chivalry and Romance* (1762) urges the '*poetical truth*' of Gothic romance as typified by Tasso, and claims that although Spenser and Milton made use of tales from classical literature, 'when most inflamed' they were 'rapt' with Gothic.[48] Five years later, William Duff praises the 'untutored imaginations' of Gothic architects, arguing that they produce sublime effects through 'that awful, though irregular grandeur, which elevates the mind, and produces the most pleasing astonishment'. Duff claims that these Gothic buildings 'shew the inventive power of the human mind in a striking light'.[49] For Nathan Drake, similarly, in 1798, Gothic is the highest form of artistic expression 'in point of sublimity and imagination'.[50] These celebrations of artistic liberation and inspiration stand in marked contrast to contemporary discussions of the stylistic qualities of literary Gothic as typified by

---

[47] *Otranto*, 12.

[48] *Hurd's Letters on Chivalry and Romance: With the Third Elizabethan Dialogue*, ed. and introd. Edith J. Morley (London, 1911), 114. A useful recent discussion of Hurd and other early theorists of Gothic, drawing on a much wider range of reference than is possible here and paying particular attention to questions of gender, is provided by Harriet Guest in 'The Wanton Muse: Politics and Gender in Gothic Theory after 1760', in *Beyond Romanticism*, ed. Stephen Copley and John Whale (London, 1992), 118–39.

[49] *An Essay on Original Genius; and its Various Modes of Exertion in Philosophy and the Fine Arts, Particularly in Poetry* (London, 1767), 257.

[50] *Literary Hours: or Sketches Critical and Narrative* (London, 1798), 90.

Lewis, Radcliffe, and their imitators. Reviewers were consistently scathing about novelists' strivings after sublimity, and, as part of a more general criticism of the novel itself as literary genre, about the lack of artistic discipline which modern fiction seemed to require. One hostile article in the *Aberdeen Magazine* in 1798 likens the decline of modern literature to the decline of the Roman empire, caused by 'an enormous increase of luxury, and the repeated inroads of Gothic barbarians'.[51] Critics regularly complained about the aesthetic as well as the moral degeneracy of such modern fiction, as Coleridge's review of *The Monk* exemplifies.[52] The problem is put most succinctly in a survey of recent romances in *The Miniature* in 1804: 'We are indeed much at a loss which to admire most, the total want of fire and imagination, or the systematic contempt of judgment and sense.'[53] There was obviously a considerable distance between the aesthetic appreciation of literary and architectural forms accepted as finished and achieved, and the reception of those new forms of literature which claimed to be inspired by them.

Placing the experiments of recent novelists in relation to previous literary tradition, and especially in relation to the traditions of Gothic and romance which their title-pages most frequently invoked, obviously caused problems for many commentators. As used by novelists themselves, there are signs that the term 'Gothic' retained more firmly geographical than historical connotations, signalled by the proliferation of tales with such titles as John Palmer Jr.'s *The Haunted Cavern: A Caledonian Tale* (1796) and *The Mystic Sepulchre; or, Such Things Have Been: A Spanish Romance* (1807), and Mrs Harley's *St Bernard's Priory: An Old English Tale* (1786). Reviewers of the time rarely referred to 'Gothic' novels, although they recognized a distinctive, even for-

---

[51] 'Modern Literature', *Aberdeen Magazine*, iii (July 1798), 338–40 (339). The author mocks the reception of Gothic by reporting an imaginary conversation about 'The Animated Skeleton' between two young ladies in the circulating library.

[52] Coleridge, *Misc. Crit.* 370–8 (on style, 373). Among complaints of the immoral tendencies of Gothic, see Hugh Murray, *Morality of Fiction; or, An Inquiry into the Tendency of Fictitious Narratives, with Observations on Some of the Most Eminent* (Edinburgh, 1805), on historical fiction (pp. 38–9), on Radcliffe (pp. 126–8). Fiction which conjures up horror, states Murray, weakens the mind and makes it 'liable to superstitious apprehensions' (p. 127).

[53] 'Solomon Grildrig' (pseud.), 'Remarks on Novels and Romances.—Receipt for a Modern Romance', *The Miniature: A Periodical Paper*, No. 2 (30 Apr. 1804) (Windsor, 1805), 21.

mulaic, literary style, which they traced to the influence of *The Castle of Otranto* and characterized by referring to the schools of Radcliffe and Lewis, 'terrorist' writing, the conventions of Lane's Minerva Press, or the 'German' style. The insistence on the 'German' label is in itself a significant move away from allowing these works a history and legitimacy within whatever might be defined as a 'pure' native British tradition. The immediate origins of the form were not questioned, for, as Hazlitt remarks in 1819, *The Castle of Otranto* was 'supposed to have led the way to this style of writing'.[54] Reeve's preface to the second edition of *The Old English Baron* explicitly presents the work as the 'literary offspring' of *The Castle of Otranto* and continues Walpole's musings about the union of romance and novel even though it sets out to correct defects in Walpole's plan. The origins of Walpole's work itself, however, were more puzzling. John Dunlop ponders:

> The work is declared by Mr Walpole to be an attempt to blend the ancient romance and modern novel; but, if by the ancient romance be meant the tales of chivalry, the extravagance of the Castle of Otranto has no resemblance to their machinery. What analogy have skulls or skeletons—sliding pannels—damp vaults—trap-doors—and dismal apartments, to the tented fields of chivalry and its airy enchantments?[55]

As Dunlop recognizes, the form of Walpolean romance bears no obvious relation to the antecedents it claims for itself; yet it is also clearly designed to intervene in literary tradition. *The Castle of Otranto* was based on an ideal of novelistic reformation, the premisses of which were in turn challenged by Clara Reeve. However formulaic certain branches of it were to become, Gothic never lost the sense of literary challenge. In 1820, one reviewer of *Melmoth the Wanderer* could still present Maturin as 'a sort of applauded rebel against all the constituted authorities of the literary judgment-seat'.[56]

Judith Wilt has found modern theories of literary influence so closely bound up with patterns of psychology familiar from Gothic that she declares Harold Bloom's entire poetics of the 'anxiety of influence' and misprision to be 'classic Gothic in plot

---

[54] Hazlitt, *Works*, vi. 127.
[55] *History of Fiction*, iii. 382.
[56] Review of *Melmoth*, *Blackwood's Edinburgh Magazine*, viii (Nov. 1820), 161–8 (161).

and space', figuring the way in which 'pre-empting' older figures block the creativity of their heirs.[57] For reasons which include the intrusiveness of competing voices and discourses, lower literary status, an emphasis on stories not invented but retold from 'real life', it is generally accepted that the application of any Bloomian model of influence or authorial anxiety to prose fiction in the eighteenth and early nineteenth centuries is unrewarding. Roger Sale has argued: 'Instead of embattled heirs, for more than a century after its inception in English, the novel and novelists seemed able not to have or need much sense of tradition, and there were no novelistic heirs of great importance.'[58] In fact, however, novelists and commentators on novels were busily concerned throughout the eighteenth century with establishing a genesis and an identity, pondering points of separation from epic, romance, and drama, discussing the validity of the marvellous and the fantastic in modern fiction, and preparing for the establishment of a generic tradition in such later works as *Ballantyne's Novelist's Library* (1821–4).

In spite of this emergent sense of a tradition, there is something like a rhetoric of anxiety to be detected in the authorial commentaries of many Gothic works. In a letter, Walpole describes himself writing *The Castle of Otranto* after a dream, 'without knowing in the least what I intended to say or relate'.[59] In his Advertisement to *The Monk*, Lewis makes a conscientious display of sources and precedents, appealing to oral and written authority in mitigation of his personal authorial responsibility. In turn, Lewis himself becomes a literary authority for other writers. After enthusiastically dedicating *Confessions of the Nun of St Omer* (1805) to him, Charlotte Dacre explains in her 'Apostrophe to the Critics' and introduction that both novel and dedication were written when she was only 18 years old, and that she has since thought better of her extravagances. Another of her works, *Zofloya, or the Moor* (1806), which features a sort of female Ambrosio as its central character, insists that it is not in any way an endorsement of sexual indulgence but instead a moral tale about good and bad examples in childhood. More generally, Gothic writers

---

[57] *Ghosts of the Gothic*, 11.
[58] Roger Sale, *Literary Inheritance* (Amherst, Mass., 1984), 3–4.
[59] *The Yale Edition of Horace Walpole's Correspondence*, ed. W. S. Lewis *et al.*, 48 vols. (New Haven, Conn., 1937–83), i. 88.

can frequently be seen negotiating a relationship back to the authority and the assumed superiority of fiction based on 'real life', as is clear from the subtitles of Francis Lathom's *The Midnight Bell: A German Story, Founded on Incidents in Real Life* (1798) and Eliza Parsons's *The Mysterious Visit: A Novel, Founded on Facts* (1802).

Maturin is a particularly good example of a novelist who works within sensationalist traditions while repeatedly complaining about them and striving to dissociate from them his 'genuine' impulses as a creative artist. In his letters, Maturin writes disparagingly of the 'wild tales' which he thought so unworthy of his talents, and the prefaces of his novels become opportunities to lament his situation as a neglected man driven to fiction by poverty. The repining preface serves (unsuccessfully) as a plea for preferment. In the preface to his second novel, *The Wild Irish Boy* (1808), Maturin laments having to restrain himself on the subject of Ireland in order to satisfy public taste for tales of fashionable life: 'He who would prostitute his morals, is a monster, he who sacrifices his inclination and habits of writing, is—an author.' A sentence later, the preface concludes with the woeful moral: 'He who is capable of writing a good novel, ought to feel that he was born for a higher purpose than writing novels.'[60] In the preface to *Women; or, Pour et Contre* (1818), Maturin looks back on his earlier works as failures, says why he thinks he may have done better this time but promises that, if not, 'it is the *last time* I ever shall trespass in *this way* on the indulgence of the public'.[61] He returns with *Melmoth the Wanderer* in 1820, however, apologizing for another appearance 'in so unseemly a character as that of a writer of romances', and 'regretting the necessity that compels me to it'.[62]

Maturin's feelings about the nature and status of his fiction are clearly problematic. The stylistic registers of his uncertainty are scattered throughout his fiction, and, although his protestations of disengagement mark him out as something of a special case among Gothic novelists, they are a useful indication of crises of style in Gothic fiction as a whole. Throughout Gothic, narratorial

---

[60] *The Wild Irish Boy*, introd. Robert Lee Wolff, 3 vols. (New York, 1979): both passages quoted from p. xi.
[61] Preface, *Women*, i, p. v.
[62] Preface, *Melmoth*, i, pp. xi–xii.

styles are unstable and internally inconsistent. Narrators are ironic, self-parodic, and evasive, as well as awkwardly earnest and moralistic, and they frequently detach themselves from the cruder manifestations of the sensationalism they promote. Even among Gothic's profusion of exclamation marks and chopped, heavily hyphenated syntax, Maturin is particularly renowned for his hectic style. The details of this style, however, reveal an uneasy and self-conscious combination of narratorial tones and conventions, as can be seen in the passage from the shipwreck scene in *Melmoth the Wanderer* when John Melmoth is confronted by his demonic ancestor. As an introduction to a scene of psychological horror, it is detached and disconcertingly literary:

His mind, by its late intense and bewildering pursuits, at once heated and darkened, like the atmosphere under an incumbent thunder-cloud, had now no power of inquiry, of conjecture, or of calculation. He instantly began to climb the rock,—the figure was but a few feet above him,—the object of his daily and nightly dreams was at last within the reach of his mind and his arm,—was almost tangible. *Fang* and *Snare* themselves, in all the enthusiasm of professional zeal, never uttered, 'If I but once get him within my vice,' with more eagerness than did Melmoth, as he scrambled up his steep and perilous path, to the ledge of the rock where the figure stood so calm and dark.[63]

Oddly recalled at this crisis of demonic confrontation, Fang and Snare establish an unmistakable, though disconcerting, note of comedy. Maturin seems, recklessly, to abandon this crisis of horror just when his prose is disintegrating with excitement. The strikingly inappropriate reference to 2 *Henry IV* can only disrupt the reader's interest in John Melmoth's predicament and draw attention to the leisured self-indulgence of the narrator. The whole movement of the previous sentence is towards confrontation, realization, and the reference—frustratingly, but functionally—throws the reader back into the improbable, the obstructively literary. The beginning of the passage emphasizes the unreliability of John's perceptions (his mind 'heated and darkened' by exertion and confusion), and the educated voice of the narrator interposes to set John's experiences at an additional literary remove from the reader. After the extract quoted, the style shifts again into a series of terse sentences, building to a climax at which John Melmoth

[63] *Melmoth*, i. 165. Maturin misquotes 2 *Henry IV*, II. i. 21.

falls into the sea and loses consciousness. He awakes to think it has all been a bad dream. The passage forces the reader through a process of expectation and frustration, excitement and deferral, which is repeated in the larger plan of *Melmoth the Wanderer*'s interlinked tales. This coincidence between the feelings of the reader and the feelings of the suffering narrator, hero, or heroine, is finally one of the most disturbing of all Gothic's narrative effects. All tales of suspense are in some sense celebrations of narratorial power, demonstrations of superior knowledge. Few, however, place readers in quite such conflicting and self-defeating roles as does *Melmoth the Wanderer*.

The proposals put forward in this section of the chapter are particularly important for an understanding of Scott's negotiation of Gothic conventions. The preface to the second edition of *The Castle of Otranto* establishes Gothic as a way of engaging with literary tradition and sets for it a conscious challenge, to unite the forms of modern novel and ancient romance. As the reception of the author of *Melmoth the Wanderer* as 'a sort of applauded rebel against all the constituted authorities of the literary judgment-seat' suggests, Gothic never entirely lost, in Scott's time at least, the stigma of being beyond the literary pale. Its continued notoriety is all the more remarkable given how adaptable Gothic had been to the tastes of readers and how formulaic it had become. The consciousness of originality, however, produces both a rhetoric of anxiety in the personal communications (in prefaces, letters, footnotes) of some Gothic writers, and a parading of certain types of literary and artistic authority. Shakespeare, Domenichino, and Salvator Rosa prop up Radcliffe's experiments. Marlowe's *Dr Faustus* suggests to Lewis a plan of escape from *The Monk*. Maturin hints darkly at the literary models which would, in a better world, inspire him to produce more than degenerate popular fiction. By deciding to label all these types of fiction 'Gothic', the critics of the 1920s actually smoothed over a problem of inspiration and legitimacy which was acute for practitioners of Scott's time. The label solves a problem which, as a result, has tended to become invisible. In granting Gothic both a name and an increasingly assured place in literary tradition, critics have implicitly answered the question posed most perceptively by Dunlop ('What analogy have skulls or skeletons—sliding pannels—damp vaults—trap-doors—and dismal apartments, to the tented fields of chivalry and its airy enchantments?'). If Gothic is to be seen as a developing and various form in Scott's time, however, it is important not to suppress the questions of origin and identity it asks itself.

4. The Implicated Reader in the Drama of Terror

Many recent readings of Gothic have concentrated on its political significance or its political indeterminacy.[64] In the most comprehensive of them, Ronald Paulson's argument in *Representations of Revolution (1789–1820)* that Gothic served 'as a metaphor with which some contemporaries in England tried to understand what was happening across the channel in the 1790s', there is an important though underdeveloped awareness of possible links between subject-matter and narrative form: the 'sense of unresolved mystery', Paulson argues, 'also fitted the way many contemporaries read the Revolution'.[65] The link between subject and style was made at the time, of course, most wittily in the letter from 'A Jacobin Novelist' in the late 1790s, which complains: 'we have exactly and faithfully copied the SYSTEM OF TERROR, if not in our streets, and in our fields, at least in our circulating libraries, and in our closets'.[66] Recent critical insistence on a definable political identity for Gothic, however, has not taken sufficiently into

---

[64] Readings of Gothic as an inversion of social standards begin in earnest with Northrop Frye's statement in his essay on Byron in *Fables of Identity: Studies in Poetic Mythology* (New York, 1963), 177: 'These thrillers were intended for an English Protestant middle-class reading public: consequently their horrid surroundings were normally Continental, Catholic and upper class, though Oriental settings also had a vogue.' The fullest exploration of Gothic as a literature of the taboo is Punter's *Literature of Terror*. The best recent discussion of Gothic as a way of understanding violent change is by Ronald H. Paulson in *Representations of Revolution (1789–1820)* (New Haven, Conn., 1983), ch. 7. It is striking, however, that over the course of Paulson's important study Scott features only in a footnote as a writer who 'displaces the experience of the French Revolution back to the English revolution/civil war of the seventeenth century and makes this the situation of a social revolution' (p. 252 n.). Among the many arguments for political readings of Gothic, especially pertinent to the following discussion are Baldick, *In Frankenstein's Shadow*, ch. 1; Guest, 'Wanton Muse', 119–20; Fred Botting, *Making Monstrous: 'Frankenstein', Criticism, Theory* (Manchester, 1991), ch. 9.

[65] Paulson, *Representations of Revolution*, 216, 224.

[66] 'Terrorist Novel Writing', 102.

account the evasiveness of its narrative form—Dunlop's *'passages that lead to nothing'*—and its insecure place in literary tradition.

The governing political fantasy of Gothic is that individual freedom can triumph over organized authority. This ideology is so pervasive and so concealed, however, that Gothic was read in its own time as if it had no bearing on social and political conditions, except in so far as these reflected the moral vitiation of its readers. Nothing, perhaps, makes the manipulation of self-conscious fantasy in Gothic more obvious than the lack of anxiety about its political implications which one finds in contemporary reviews. The 1790s are marked by politically conscious readings of popular literary forms. The *Anti-Jacobin*'s parody of German drama, 'The Rovers; or, The Double Arrangement' (1799), for example, explicitly links the moral and the political subversiveness of its target form. Criticisms of Gothic fiction, however, focus on the threats it poses for personal morality (especially female morality) rather than on any possible political content. This is understandable. Some Gothic fictions, notably those of Mary Robinson and Charlotte Smith, bring contemporary political concerns very close to the surface. Many more, in the manner of Mrs Harley's *St Bernard's Priory* (1786), which deals with civil war and political crisis in the reign of Henry II, seize upon historical situations which might with a little elaboration serve as commentary upon contemporary events. In general, however, Gothic novelists signally omit to provide such elaboration, allowing their readers free licence to connect, or not to connect, fantasy worlds and contemporary social anxieties.

Although it is especially difficult in this period to separate the political from the intellectual, Gothic's engagement with intellectual issues at least seems more sustained than its overt political significance. This is demonstrable from its most notorious product, *The Monk* (1796), which, with *Frankenstein*, has proved the text most amenable to recent politically conscious interpretation. As Paulson has pointed out, the scene of mob violence towards the end of the novel, in which an enraged crowd takes vengeance upon the Prioress of St Clare for the crimes committed in her convent, and ends by sacking the convent itself, hurting the rioters in the process, is a model of revolutionary violence, a scene shot through with memories of Paris in 1789. Such striking scenes do not work in isolation, however, but are part of a much more thoroughgoing engagement with 1790s debate than critics have always allowed.[67] Lewis was closely involved in political activity and debate (his status as a Member of Parliament being one of the most shocking of all the novel's revelations for his contemporary readers), and his wider humanitarian concerns are strongly advanced in works such as his *Journal of a West India Proprietor*, published in 1834.[68]

Although it has been suggested on the strength of the morally subversive content of *The Monk* alone that Lewis was writing against the current social and political establishment, his novel is more striking as a series of interlinked but diverse reflections on key intellectual topics of the day. Lewis conspicuously addresses the problems of education (for both Ambrosio and his sister, Antonia) and the 'natural' rather than cultural disposition of the individual. Among the many Rousseau-influenced educational novels of the 1790s, the same issue is most insistently raised in Inchbald's *Nature and Art* and Bage's *Hermsprong*. Like several Gothic novels, *The Monk* considers the case of the exceptionally talented man whose superior abilities bring him into conflict with the society which he ought best to represent, a variant on the theme of educating the aristocracy, common in both radical and conservative writing of the time. Lewis also expresses entirely conventional misgivings about the corruptions of city life, and creates rural idylls which emphasize the responsibilities of individuals to each other in small communities. Even more central to contemporary debate is the question of individual self-determination. In his *Enquiry Concerning Political Justice* (1793), Godwin had considered the dangers of habitual obedience to a source of authority, which undermined 'the independence of our understanding', mak-

---

[67] In *Eros Revived: Erotica of the Enlightenment in England and America* (London, 1988), Peter Wagner follows Paulson in reading *Monk* as part of the 'revolutionary drive of libertine literature against the authority of Church and state, noticeable from the 1660s onward' (p. 247). For a detailed discussion of the links between Gothic and the thought and fiction of the 1790s, see David Morse, *Romanticism: A Structural Analysis* (London, 1982), pt. 1. More briefly, Gary Kelly points out in *English Fiction of the Romantic Period 1789–1830*, Longman Literature in English Series (London, 1989), 55, the shared concerns of *Monk* and 'modern novels' of the 1790s, especially Jacobin fiction.

[68] See Louis F. Peck on Lewis, the slave trade, and his own slaves, *A Life of Matthew G. Lewis* (Cambridge, Mass., 1961), 150–8, and Lewis's *Journal of a West India Proprietor, Kept During a Residence in the Island of Jamaica* (London, 1834), 62, 88–90, 100–1, 118–20.

ing a special case for the dangers of obedience in a religious organization.[69] Such considerations reappear in Lewis's condemnation of monastic institutions: 'The nuns believed whatever the prioress chose to assert: though contradicted by reason and charity, they hesitated not to admit the truth of her arguments.'[70] On the more general subject of religious debate, Lewis's criticisms of religious hypocrisy, which extend beyond their ostensible target, Roman Catholicism, link him to Holcroft's denunciation of an uncaring and corrupt Anglican clergy in *Hugh Trevor*, and to Bage's attack on established religion in his satirical characterization of the Reverend Doctor Blick in *Hermsprong*. Sexual politics are also highlighted in a way which suggests the intellectual topics of the time. When, at one stage in their fraught relationship, Ambrosio pleads with Matilda, 'Let us forget the distinctions of sex', to live in friendship, his idealism reads interestingly, if cynically, in the context of Wollstonecraft's plea for friendship between two rational creatures, man and woman.[71] The presence throughout the novel of these topics of contemporary intellectual debate is just as important as the few scenes which most openly and most dangerously allude to recent events in political life.

The influence of Lewis's engagement with issues of contemporary intellectual debate is evident in the work of his most enthusiastic imitator, Charlotte Dacre. The heroine of Dacre's *Confessions of the Nun of St Omer* is an experimenter not just in sexual freedom but also in its intellectual varieties, so that her punishment reads as a warning against free thinking as well as free love. Dacre's later novel, *The Passions* (1811), also features an intellectual heroine and a range of characters who eloquently express different philosophical convictions. Several critics have suggested that Gothic works from the late 1790s onwards abandon political comment, although they certainly do not abandon a style of intellectual debate which is open to political interpretation. In carrying forward the political theme, moreover, it is important to

[69] *Enquiry Concerning Political Justice and its Influence on Modern Morals and Happiness* (1793), 3rd edn. (1798) ed. and introd. Isaac Kramnick (Harmondsworth, 1976), 237–48 (241), and 'Of Religious Establishments', 569–73.

[70] *Monk*, iii. 259–60. See also iii. 124–5, 178, 224.

[71] *Monk*, i. 157; *Vindication of the Rights of Woman; With Strictures on Moral and Political Subjects* (1792), ed. and introd. Miriam Brody Kramnick (Harmondsworth, 1975, 1982), esp. 112–14, 167–8, and a plea for 'rational fellowship', 263.

allow political significance to events beyond the French revolution and its immediate impact on British intellectual life. To this end, a second gory crowd scene will perhaps suggest how flexible the political connotations of Gothic can be. It comes from the episode in *Melmoth the Wanderer* in which Monçada, escaping from the clutches of the Inquisition, witnesses the murder of his old demonic ally the Parricide at the hands (and feet) of an enraged mob. The scene clearly recalls the fate of Lewis's Prioress, and, again like *The Monk*, the crowd proceeds after one murder to attack a religious institution (this time the Inquisition). The complexity of Lewis's presentation of the rights and wrongs of the mob's action has been widely recognized by recent critics. Maturin's attitude towards the murder of the Parricide is equally difficult to evaluate, though for different reasons. In this case, the complication comes not just from the description of the scene itself and the uncomfortable complicity established by Maturin between the violent crowd and the would-be urbane reader, but also from the associations set up in Maturin's editorial annotations. Although Monçada has been treated almost as badly as Agnes in *The Monk*, Maturin considerably reduces any pleasure which the reader can take in vengeance by dwelling on Monçada's horrified, fascinated response to the death of the Parricide. Readers shrink from a macabre enjoyment of which Maturin ruthlessly makes them aware. To complicate this situation further, the underlying significance of the scene of mob vengeance in *Melmoth the Wanderer* is marked by two important footnotes. One is to the murder of Dr Hamilton in Ireland in 1797, from which Maturin takes details of his murder scene, while the other refers to the murder of Lord Kilwarden, Lord Chief Justice of Ireland, during Emmet's insurrection in Dublin, 1803.[72] Maturin's alertness to the rights and wrongs of popular uprising is shaped by his experience of Ireland, and he had already fictionalized Irish rebellion in *The Milesian Chief*. Maturin's footnotes at this crucial point in *Melmoth the Wanderer* ally the crowd's immediate object of resentment, the Inquisition, with the systems of government in his own country. This alliance brings the Inquisition symbolically into line with English authority over the Irish individual, an authority treacher-

---

[72] *Melmoth*, iii. 32 and 34 n. Kelly also notes the presence of these footnotes, *English Fiction of the Romantic Period*, 198.

ously supported by the Ascendancy families (as Monçada's parents support the Inquisition). *Melmoth the Wanderer* is not just concerned with spiritual oppression and alienation, although its weight of theological implication is inescapable. It deals with social and political evils and with a political as well as a spiritual helplessness, the helplessness of the individual caught in an oppressive and denying institution. For Maturin, this institution is the Anglican Church in Ireland, which repeatedly refused him advancement.[73] For Ireland, it was a detached and faceless English government. Maturin expresses feelings about his own Church in the guise of the Catholic Church he so strongly opposed, and feelings about his own country in the figure of the trapped, thwarted, Monçada, whose frustrated imagination is condemned for ever after to circle around the image of his oppressors.

Not only crowd scenes but also courtroom scenes and all the legal paraphernalia of imputed guilt, defended innocence, last-minute reprieves, and unreliable witnesses, acquire social and political significance in Gothic. Gothic novels tell of heroes and heroines who are persecuted by impeccably legal and recognized authorities, and who cannot speak up in their own defence. The sins for which protagonists are subjected to these dark versions of legal process are notoriously indeterminate. In Walpole's Gothic drama, *The Mysterious Mother* (1781), the 'secret sin' which is hinted at throughout the characters' speeches is eventually explained, is given a suitably dark source in the incest between the Countess of Narbonne and her son. Not all Gothic plots give their protagonists such good cause for their violent expressions of guilt. The treatment of secret sin becomes more rigorously and urgently interrogative in the philosophical fictions of Godwin and his follower Charles Brockden Brown. Developing Godwin's search in *Caleb Williams*, Brown has Edgar Huntly ask, as he tries to persuade Sarsefield to use his medical skills to save the wounded Clithero: 'But what is that guilt which no penitence can expiate?'[74] Gothic comes to specialize in guilts which are difficult to attribute and therefore difficult to subsume. The climax, perhaps, comes in

---

[73] *Scott–Maturin Correspondence*, 6–7, 9–10, Scott's opinion, p. 12, the explanation given to Scott by the Bishop of Meath, p. 17, and Douglas Kinnaird's response to a report in the *Morning Chronicle* that Maturin would lose his curateship after the performance of *Bertram*, pp. 61–2.

[74] *Edgar Huntly*, 258.

Confessions of a Justified Sinner, with Robert Wringhim's realization that he has committed crimes which he cannot remember,
but a sense of being blamed for crimes one cannot remember
committing, or of which one is convinced one is innocent, is
a common feature of Gothic, and particularly strong in *Caleb
Williams*, *Frankenstein*, and *Melmoth the Wanderer*. *Melmoth the
Wanderer* hints at terrible crimes, but expresses them only through
a language of allusion. When the Superior and four monks enter
his cell, they promise Monçada a luxury which Gothic rarely
offers its protagonists, 'plain words', 'a few plain questions', but
in fact withhold any explanation from him: 'I said, "My God!
what is all this terrible preparation for? Of what am I guilty? Why
am I summoned by this warning voice so often, whose warnings
are only so many mysterious threatenings? Why am I not told
of my offence?"'[75] The accusations made against Monçada by
the monks acquire overtones of betrayal, fratricide, and sacrifice,
combined with little logical (or biblical) consistency, but with
oppressive imaginative force: 'You are the Judas among the
brethren; a branded Cain amid a primitive family; a scape-goat
that struggles to burst from the hands of the congregation into the
wilderness.'[76] As in *The Mysteries of Udolpho*, descriptions which
allude to more dreadful histories than those of the ostensible
narrative become part of the imaginative framework of both
protagonist and reader.

In keeping with their indictment for crimes of which they know
nothing, Gothic heroes and heroines are defined by their passivity.
As Maturin's Monçada states: 'Give me something to suffer, to
undergo, to submit, and I became at once the *hero of submission*.'[77] Faced with situations which they cannot control, protagonists account for their actions in terms of compulsion which
resemble an appeal to the non-accountability of infancy. Typically,
Gothic traces the process by which heroes or heroines claiming
childlike immunity must accept the responsibilities and consequences of adult action or of ways of thinking which prove them
to be adult, committed, and culpable. Figures of authority address
their victims as children, and protagonists struggle to assert their

---

[75] *Melmoth*, ii. 12 (and the perfect withheld communication, '"Your crime
is—"').
[76] *Melmoth*, ii. 87: see also ii. 308.
[77] *Melmoth*, ii. 188.

own will in defiance of an authority which uses the parental language of their 'best interests'.[78]

Without claiming that the terrors of Gothic can in any sense be reduced to models of reading, it is noticeable that many of the fears just described have parallels in the situation of readers of Gothic fiction. Readers and protagonists alike are repeatedly admonished not to let their imaginations run away with them, only to find themselves trapped in situations which replicate their worst fears. In *The Mysteries of Udolpho*, the narrator chides 'those starts of imagination, which deceive the senses into what can be called nothing less than momentary madness',[79] while denying either heroine or reader any alternative context in which to evaluate such possible deceptions. In *The Romance of the Forest*, similarly, Radcliffe undertakes a lengthy contrast of states of reason, passion, and imagination, but encourages the reader's wildest imaginings; while in *The Italian* Schedoni mocks what he describes as Vivaldi's imaginative delusions.[80] Again like heroes and heroines, readers fear more than actually happens. They are implicated yet rescued, threatened with tragedy but comforted with happy endings. In contrast, narrators who claim, conventionally, to be inadequate, unimaginative, and commonplace, wield absolute tyrannical power over readers who are involuntarily identified with helpless, victimized protagonists. Fantasies of control and breakdown, authority and rebellion, are not just aspects of the plot and of characterization, but also aspects of the relationship between narrator and reader. This is a feature developed most strongly in detective fiction, in which readers actively seek to outdo narrators in discovering plots. If it is impossible to identify in Gothic an idiosyncratic set of political or social messages, therefore, its wide dissemination in the reading culture suggests that it is at least possible to associate with it a shift in the moral politics of reading. The implicated reader is one of the most interesting by-products of Gothic literary experiment.

The moral responsibility of the voyeuristic reader is a complication in the reader-politics of Gothic which became more acute

---

[78] *Melmoth*, i. 221: on fathers and sons, i. 308, iii. 5, and Melmoth's comments on fatherhood, iv. 369.

[79] *Udolpho*, i. 273.

[80] *Romance of Forest*, i. 115, ii. 25–7, 55–7, 60, 79–81, 209, iii. 112–17, 223–4; *Italian*, iii. 394.

as Gothic grew in popularity. When Walpole published *The Castle of Otranto*, he could explain it in letters to friends as a private fantasy about the trappings of medievalism. When the circulating libraries could flood the popular markets for fiction with blood-curdling tales, there was rather more interest in and anxiety about collective responsibility for this degraded taste. Increasingly, Gothic novels themselves incorporated unsettling comments on readerly voyeurism. *Melmoth the Wanderer*, for example, parades its relationship back to the conventions of earlier Gothic, and its sense of literary indulgence can be mischievous or macabre, or a disconcerting mixture of the two, as in the Parricide's remarks on his voyeuristic enjoyment of the death of the lovers: 'You will call this cruelty, I call it curiosity,—that curiosity that brings thousands to witness a tragedy, and makes the most delicate female feast on groans and agonies. I had an advantage over them,—the groan, the agony I feasted on, were real.'[81] The Parricide's sudden inclusion of the fashionable female reader in his 'curiosity' about extreme suffering is only one example of his terrifying ability to break down comfortable barriers.

The reader is also implicated in one striking characteristic of Gothic's presentation of the relationship between its protagonists and their experiences. This characteristic is the sudden reversal by which observers become the objects of observation.[82] Observers are accused, involved, forced out of their spectatorship, as when Monçada witnesses the execution of the heretic in *Melmoth the Wanderer*: 'I actually for a moment believed myself the object of their cruelty. The drama of terror has the irresistible power of converting its audience into its victims.'[83] During another crisis, Monçada realizes that he has become the object of his own deepest horror: 'Had I been told such a story of another, I would have

---

[81] *Melmoth*, ii. 229. Maturin specifically refers to the conventions of romance, ii. 245–6, iii. 356–7. Relevant to this discussion of the changing role of the reader in Gothic is David H. Richter's argument 'that the Gothic novel sits astride a major shift in the response of readers to literature', which he examines in Jaussian terms as a move from *catharsis* to *aisthesis*, in 'The Reception of the Gothic Novel in the 1790s', in *The Idea of the Novel in the Eighteenth Century*, ed. Robert W. Uphaus (East Lansing, Mich., 1988), 117–37 (121).

[82] Thomas Weiskel's chapter on 'The Logic of Terror' in *The Romantic Sublime: Studies in the Structure and Psychology of Transcendence* (1976), foreword by Harold Bloom (Baltimore, 1986), touches briefly on the psychology of spectatorship in Burke's essay on the sublime: see pp. 89–90.

[83] *Melmoth*, iii. 34.

denounced him as the most reckless and desperate being on earth—
yet *I was the man*.'[84] This reversal is ominous enough for the
protagonists of Gothic, but it also threatens the assumptions on
which the leisured reader enjoys the spectacle of horror. This
question, in fact, is one of the most interesting of all those raised
in John Aikin's essays on terror-fiction in the 1790s, which strive
to place in a more consistently moral framework the implications
of Burke's aesthetic of the sublime. It is also an assumption of
Wordsworth's case in the Preface to the 1800 *Lyrical Ballads* that
habituation to objects of sensationalist fear vitiated the moral
imagination.

The implication of the reader in the construction of terrible
fantasies is something which is developed gradually over the course
of Gothic's history, primarily because Gothic becomes so highly
formulaic a brand of fiction that its style and situations can rely
heavily on the reader's prior expectations. Titles are a revealing
indicator of this. T. J. Horsley Curties's *The Monk of Udolpho*
(1807) promises (falsely) to be a combination of all that is most
horrid in Lewis and Radcliffe, and promises this even though its
own contents are in some ways unusual and innovative within the
conventions of Gothic. Less unusual or innovative, Mary Meeke's
The Veiled Protectress; or, The Mysterious Mother (1819) depends
upon the reputation of Walpole's play to give dark hints of incestuous relationships from which it eventually exculpates its main
characters. In terms of narrative style, however, several Gothic
novels develop a manner of referring readers beyond the present
moment of horror to still more frightful possibilities, suggesting
that the patterns it leaves suggestively incomplete may be extended
into other works of art, both literary and non-literary. Within the
most famous Gothic novels, narrators hint repeatedly at terrible
patterns completed elsewhere in literature and art, though left
incomplete in their own work. In *The Mysteries of Udolpho*, both
heroine and narrator indulge frequently in this kind of intensification, evoking a world of darker horror which lies just beyond

---

[84] *Melmoth*, ii. 170. See also *Edgar Huntly*, 87, when the hero tries to describe
his reaction to Clithero's all-too-involving story: 'My reading had furnished me
with no instance, in any degree, parallel to this, and I found that to be a distant
and second-hand spectator of events was widely different from witnessing them
myself and partaking in their consequences. My judgement was, for a time, sunk
into imbecility and confusion.'

the range of the narrative. Emily is never sure whether her terrible experiences are actual or imagined: 'Her present life appeared like the dream of a distempered imagination, or like one of those frightful fictions, in which the wild genius of the poets some-times delighted.'[85] Radcliffe, in her turn, assimilates her scenes to literary and artistic convention, hinting through allusion at darker possibilities than any her plots realize. During her description of the funeral of Madame Montoni, for example, she refers to Domenichino, inviting the reader to be aware of 'scenes more horrible, than even that, which was pictured at the grave of the misguided and unfortunate Madame Montoni'.[86]

If this process is clearly at work in Radcliffe's novels, it is even more important in those works of second- and third-generation Gothic which situate themselves most consciously in relation to the traditions of horror. Again, Maturin's work contains many of the best examples. The opening chapter of *Melmoth the Wanderer* adapts the narrative convention by which a mystery about the past is confronted in the secret chamber of an old mansion, by the family heir. As used in *The Old English Baron* and *The Romance of the Forest*, the motif of the secret chamber was already associ-ated with the discovery of dark crimes surrounding and threaten-ing a new inheritance. At first, Maturin makes the details of the convention noticeably more naturalistic and more domestic. His young heir, John Melmoth, enters the secret closet in search of wine for his dying uncle. Unlike the protagonists of Reeve and Radcliffe, he is prompted by compassion and duty, not by super-natural visitation or by irresistible psychological compulsion. Once in the secret closet, he is confronted by the portrait of his demonic ancestor. Maturin pauses over the comic and pathetic aspects of the miserly uncle's death, while the informed reader anticipates by literary association the kind of discovery which follows:

He could not but remark his uncle's extraordinary look, that had the ghastliness of fear superadded to that of death, as he gave him permission to enter his closet. He could not but see the looks of horror which the women exchanged as he approached it. And, finally, when he was in it, his memory was malicious enough to suggest some faint traces of a story, too horrible for imagination, connected with it.[87]

[85] *Udolpho*, ii. 359.
[86] *Udolpho*, iii. 101–2 (102).
[87] *Melmoth*, i. 29.

At the back of the contemporary reader's mind, the description of the 'story, too horrible for imagination,' might recall secrets like that of the Black Veil in *The Mysteries of Udolpho*. This particular recollection is invited again later in *Melmoth the Wanderer* when the young Monçada stumbles upon his grandfather's death-scene: 'I was neglected by my attendants, and wandered through the spacious rooms, till I by chance lifted up a curtain of black velvet, and saw a sight which, young as I was, paralyzed me.'[88] In both passages, Maturin exploits the reader's familiarity with a previous narrative pattern, while usefully detaching himself as authority for his reader's, and his hero's, fears.

As Gothic motifs and narrative conventions became associated with particular kinds or combinations of emotion, they became useful to other writers, either to intensify certain effects of plot and characterization, or to act as a form of imaginative shorthand by which the author could qualify the main effect and purpose of the narrative, while remaining uncommitted to the full effects of Gothic. Most writers of the period had read Gothic works, and could assume that their readers were familiar with Gothic conventions. Writers exploited through Gothic a conventional scheme of imaginative reference, aided by the extreme stylization of so many scenes, plot motifs, and characters. In other words, Gothic was important as a series of reading conventions on which other writers could elaborate.

The novels of William Godwin are full of interesting examples of this process. In *Caleb Williams*, Godwin defines the terrors and betrayals of the present by denying the simplified literary model which had seemed to banish them to a romanticized past. He explicitly politicizes the patterns of disproportionate anxiety and the sense of persecution found, variously, in *The Castle of Otranto*, *The Recess*, and *The Mysteries of Udolpho*, and he gives Gothic's vague legalistic threats the specific shape of English courtrooms and lawyers. Falkland taunts Caleb with the inefficacy of innocence in a legal system which merely reinforces social hierarchies: 'prepare a tale ever so plausible, or ever so true, the whole world shall execrate you as an impostor. Your innocence shall be of no service to you; I laugh at so feeble a defence.'[89] At the same time, and anticipating many a hero from the Waverley

[88] *Melmoth*, i. 188.   [89] *Caleb Williams*, ii. 140.

Novels, Caleb shares the Gothic child-protagonist's protestation of innocence, being unable 'to believe that, when things were brought to the test, any one could be seriously angry with me'.[90] In its fascination with secrets, also, *Caleb Williams* has a basic strategy in common with Gothic. Collins's apparently coherent story of Falkland's early life is, for a time, sufficient to quell Caleb's spirit of curiosity. As he thinks about it, however, its simple conclusions become less convincing:

> At first I was satisfied with thus considering every incident in its obvious sense. But the story I had heard was for ever in my thoughts, and I was peculiarly interested to comprehend its full import. I turned it a thousand ways, and examined it in every point of view. In the original communication it appeared sufficiently distinct and satisfactory; but, as I brooded over it, it gradually became mysterious.[91]

The clear tale turns out to be opaque. The explanation of mystery becomes itself mysterious.

In his novels after *Caleb Williams*, Gothic conventions, taken to their logical extremes and re-examined from a consciously radical and sceptical position, continue to be useful for Godwin. In *St Leon* in 1799 he extends the implications of the alienated outcast and the consequences of a magical pact, and unites them with an ambitious element of historicism. In *Cloudesley* in 1830 Gothic convention is a constant source of imaginative reference used to highlight the extremes of misanthropy, guilt, and alienation, and to reinforce a plea for social harmony which may be seen as his final solution to the problems raised in *Caleb Williams*. In *Fleetwood*, published in 1805 in the middle of his writing career, Gothic elements are concentrated in an inset tale, the history of Mrs Macneil. The conventionality of these elements perhaps explains why they have attracted no attention from critics, but they are at the very least a curiosity in the novel. Mrs Macneil is, after all, a key figure in the novel's critique of socially constructed gender roles, and has been recognized as a part-portrait of Mary Wollstonecraft ever since its first publication.

The history of Mrs Macneil is brief and sensational. At the age of 15 she is persuaded to elope with her unscrupulous and unprepossessing music teacher, and kept 'a prisoner in a dismantled and

---

[90] *Caleb Williams*, ii. 7. See also ii. 79–80.
[91] *Caleb Williams*, ii. 3–4.

unwholesome castle'. From this classic Gothic fate she is rescued by Macneil 'like a true knight-errant', her first marriage is dissolved, and she begins a new and exemplary married life.[92] The Gothic monstrosities of Mrs Macneil's seducer are set against the enlightened Rousseau-like character of Macneil.[93] In his review of the novel, Scott registers the conventionality of Mrs Macneil's story with a simple, expressive, exclamation mark.[94] Yet the story has its purpose in the social critique advanced in *Fleetwood*. Godwin uses the situation of Mrs Macneil to debate the values of female experience over innocence, and the difference between virtue and ignorance.[95] Mrs Macneil is banished from the society of 'respectable' women, but educates three exemplary daughters, one of whom Fleetwood marries. Fleetwood has been in his youth notorious for his philanderings with married Parisian women, and Godwin adroitly exposes the inequity of society's harsh judgement of Mrs Macneil in contrast to its indulgence of Fleetwood. The prejudices of Fleetwood himself are a constant source of irony throughout the novel and a primary vehicle for Godwin's implied criticisms of the hypocrisies lurking in the social institution of marriage. For Godwin, the Gothic element in Mrs Macneil's early history serves two functions. It reduces Mrs Macneil's moral responsibility for what is seen as her loss of virtue and engages the reader's sympathy on her behalf. More subtly, and potentially disruptively, it suggests the reader's complicity in the wrongs of this society by drawing attention to literary conventions which allowed sexual indiscretion to be a source of forbidden pleasure to readers. Mrs Macneil is shunned in society by those who might well weep over her misfortunes if she were to appear to them in fiction as a heroine of seduction-romance. The Gothic extravagance also has implications for the literary form of Godwin's novel. In his preface, Godwin presents *Fleetwood* as a 'commonplace' fiction of everyday occurrences, but indicates in its subtitle, 'The New Man of Feeling', that it is to contain an important element of literary exploration and reinterpretation. By including

---

[92] Both quotations are taken from *Fleetwood; or, The New Man of Feeling*, 3 vols. (London, 1805), ii. 158.

[93] For Macneil and Rousseau, see *Fleetwood*, ii. 155, 178–82, 190–201.

[94] *MPW* xviii. 126.

[95] The ideological significance of Mrs Macneil in the scheme of *Fleetwood* is particularly clear, ii. 162–8. For the association with Mary Wollstonecraft, see B. J. Tysdahl, *William Godwin as Novelist* (London, 1981), 111.

the literary extravagance of Mrs Macneil's marriage, Godwin implies the necessary subjection of the author to the literary expectations of his public. He emphasizes the kind of fiction his public will genuinely find instructive by contrasting it with a sample of the fiction the public commonly demands. At the same time, his shift into Gothic convention, by its very tendency to simplify the moral issues raised, suggests some uncertainty in approaching this controversial material. The temptation to use Gothic exaggeration as part of a plea for the sympathies of the reader creates comparable complications in the moral schemes of Elizabeth Inchbald's *A Simple Story* (volumes iii and iv), and Mary Wollstonecraft's own *The Wrongs of Woman; or Maria*.

As the details necessary in this type of discussion must already have suggested, Gothic interventions in different types of novel are used for a wide range of purposes and are certainly not assimilable to a single central message or ideology. Gothic conventions of setting, plot, and character-type caused problems for writers who wished to incorporate them, problems which sometimes show themselves as stylistic inconsistencies and uncertainties of tone, but which sometimes amount to implicit subversion of the moral messages of the new work. Although Gothic conventions were popular and widely imitated, therefore, they were never an automatic requirement for fiction which aimed at a large readership, and never a neutral presence. As already demonstrated in the final section of Chapter 1, writers' decisions to include Gothic elements in fiction of this period should never be regarded as a simple sacrifice to the tastes of the times.

This chapter began by citing Cixous' analysis of the self-referential and self-questioning patterns of authority and artifice in Freud's *Das Unheimliche* and her description of the 'sovereign but capricious stage-setter' who manipulates each scene. By making questions of authority and origin rather than the supernatural and the exotic central to this discussion of Gothic I have tried to avoid the simple categorizations which have separated the fake-histories of Gothic from the authentic reconstructions of the Waverley Novels. Each of the more detailed discussions of Scott which follow takes up a key concern from this chapter. Chapter 4 returns to the question of the narrative organization of Gothic, analysed here as a series of devices of delay and evasion, and a style which hesitates between expressing and concealing what it considers to

be 'unutterable'. Chapter 5 extends this by examining the complications caused by Gothic for political readings of the Waverley
Novels, while Chapter 6 looks at one novel's claims to be both
authentic history and convincing Gothic. All carry forward the
questions of generic identity which I have shown to be a focus of
internal debate in Gothic. I begin, however, with another 'sovereign
but capricious stage-setter' and his increasingly complex strategies
of historical and authorial authentication. Gothic's fascination
with origins and its elaborate contextual fantasies make it in turn
an appropriate context for the 'puppet theater' of the 'Author of
Waverley'.

3
Fictions of Authenticity:
The Frame Narratives and Notes of the
Waverley Novels

We do not know that Scott was *the* author of *Waverley*;
what we know is that he was *an* author of *Waverley*. To
prove that Scott was *the* author, we should have to survey the
universe and find that everything in it either did not write
Waverley or was Scott. This is beyond our powers.[1]

THERE has always been an inbuilt plurality in the identity of the
'Author of *Waverley*'. In philosophical analysis it made Scott one
of Bertrand Russell's favourite exempla of the problems of naming
and identity. In recent Bakhtin-inspired interpretation it has made
the Waverley Novels model instances of dialogism, setting out as
competing discourses the (several) official voices of authoritative
narrators and the unofficial voices of local gossips, incompetent
antiquarians, minstrels, poetic or prophetic amateurs. The most
fully dramatized version of this struggle comes at the climax of the
introduction to *Tales of the Crusaders* in 1825, when the Author,
having failed to silence the complaints of the shareholders in his
joint-stock company, declares in pique that he will turn his attention from fiction to 'real' history and write a *Life* of Napoleon:

'...—I will lay my foundations better than on quicksands—I will rear
my structure of better materials than painted cards; in a word, I will write
HISTORY!'
    There was a tumult of surprise, amid which our reporter detected the
following expressions:—'The devil you will!'—'You, my dear sir, *you*?'
—'The old gentleman forgets that he is the greatest liar since Sir John
Mandeville.'
    'Not the worse historian for that,' said Oldbuck, 'since history, you
know, is half fiction.'[2]

---

[1] Bertrand Russell's choice of example to illustrate the argument: 'No prop-
osition containing *the* (in the singular) can be strictly proved by empirical evidence.'
Ch. 2, 'Sentences, Syntax, and Parts of Speech', in *An Inquiry into Meaning and
Truth: The William James Lectures for 1940* (1950; repr. London, 1980), 47.
[2] WN xxxvii, pp. xxxix–xl.

This crisis of personal and generic identity is appropriately situated, for although discordant voices are noticeable enough in the central narratives of Scott's novels—belonging to such characters as the Glee Maiden in *The Fair Maid of Perth*, Willie Steenson in *Redgauntlet*, and Claud Halcro in *The Pirate*—they are particularly intrusive and disruptive in the proliferating narrative frames which Scott created for his novels on their first publication. The situation becomes more complicated, as I hope to show in this chapter, when, for classic economic reasons, the 'Author of *Waverley*' re-entered the fray in the introductions and notes of the Magnum Opus edition, in the best and most lastingly persuasive of all his disguises, 'Walter Scott'.

Frame narratives and other formal paratexts (including editorial introductions and explanatory notes) are exercises of authorial control and tests of competing narratorial and historiographical authorities. Like Wordsworth's note to 'The Thorn', they invite readers to project a narratorial identity for the work which detracts from the personal responsibility of the author. Like Byron's preface to Cantos I and II of *Don Juan*, which parodies the note to 'The Thorn', they also draw attention to the fact that no declaration of intent by the author can fully (or perhaps even appropriately) determine the response of the reader. Like the marginal glosses which Coleridge added to 'The Ancient Mariner' for *Sibylline Leaves*, they constitute an alternative but not a definitive reading of events in the fiction, making the imaginative material which they support in one sense more, in another sense less, accessible. The presence of an external editorial voice does not overrule the authority of the readings it encloses. Instead, it sets them even more sharply aside, drawing attention not to their explicability, but to their mystery.[3] Sometimes, indeed, as is the

[3] Among previous discussions of the function of frame narratives I am particularly indebted to Edward W. Said, *Beginnings: Intention and Method* (1975; repr. New York, 1985); Mary Ann Caws, *Reading Frames in Modern Fiction* (Princeton, NJ, 1985); and Elizabeth Deeds Ermarth, *Realism and Consensus in the English Novel* (Princeton, NJ, 1983). This chapter's discussion of the two different types of frame in Scott's novels draws on Genette's discrimination between categories of Kristevan intertextuality, first in *Introduction à l'architexte* (1979), which proposes the category of metatextuality or the relationship between a text and its commentary, as a sub-category of transtextuality (his proposed revision of Kristeva's term 'intertextuality'), and later in *Palimpsestes* (1982), where 'paratextuality' is redefined as the relationship between a text and its early drafts, titles, epigraphs,

case in Mary Shelley's 1831 introduction to *Frankenstein*, the mystery of the original creation may be the new subject-matter of the frame, so that the supposedly final level of authorial explanation becomes, as Fred Botting has recently described it, 'as frictional and fictional as the fractured and interimplicated narratives that it attempts to frame'.[4] Scott's own critical language sits oddly beside such descriptions, but it is clear that he was aware of the importance of introductions and frames in theory as well as in practice. Appropriately, the most explicit indication of this is to be found in his discussion of the frame narrative of *The Italian* in his 'Life' of Radcliffe, where he reflects: 'Most writers of romance have been desirous to introduce their narrative to the reader, in some manner which might at once excite interest, and prepare his mind for the species of excitation which it was the author's object to produce.'[5] The comment recalls his insistence on the importance of contracts of understanding between authors and readers, while also registering his awareness of fictional conventions as persuasive devices, ways of submitting the reader's expectations and personal associations to 'the author's object'.

There are two distinct types of paratext in the Waverley Novels: the frame narratives found in the prefatory materials and opening

illustrations, and explanatory notes. It also makes use of Erving Goffman's questioning of the distinction between 'reality' and 'fiction' in his sociological analysis of frames, which suggests that there may be no sustainable distinction between (in Genette's terms) text and paratext. Goffman's reminder of the hidden agenda of annotation is especially relevant to my discussion of Magnum Opus notes. The 'convention of print' is that 'howsoever doubtful the body of a text is, and whatsoever its realm status—whether biography, documentary, avowed make-believe, poetry—the footnoted editorial comments will be impeccable in regard to literalness and reliability'. Just as editorial prefaces 'can be used to induce temporary deception', Goffman goes on to claim, 'so editorial comments in passing can serve the same function' (*Frame Analysis: An Essay on the Organization of Experience* (1974; repr. Harmondsworth, 1975), 413). As Lionel Gossman has remarked of conventions of annotation in historical scholarship, 'those historians who have wished to create the greatest impression of continuity between their text and reality have in fact taken care to eliminate the telltale scar separating the two parts of the page' ('History and Literature: Reproduction or Signification', in *The Writing of History: Literary Form and Historical Understanding*, ed. Robert H. Canary and Henry Kozicki (Madison, Wis., 1978), 3–39 (32)). The Magnum Opus rarely splits its pages into two, but it regularly inserts long notes between chapters, allocating them the small dense type of secondary authority.

[4] *Making Monstrous*, 53.
[5] *MPW* iii. 348.

chapters of the first editions of his novels, which are designed
to preserve Scott's somewhat fragile anonymity; and the new
introductions and notes written for the Magnum Opus edition
from 1826 until the year of his death. These two categories of
frame have much in common as rhetorical and structuring devices,
but the attention paid to them by critics has been noticeably unequal. The playful, sometimes facetious, and immediately engaging
frames which Scott composed for the first editions of his novels
have received far more attention than the more sober antiquarian
and autobiographical introductions of the Magnum Opus, which
are still commonly regarded as a triumph of 'truth', or at least
of antiquarian authority, over fiction.[6] This chapter sets out to
redress the balance. The new frames of the Magnum Opus, secure
of the audience for the novels, are at liberty to disarm criticism by
avowing faults; to smooth over anything clumsy or contentious by
presenting it as part of a traditional tale heard in childhood; and
to gather the works into a temporary narrative harmony and a
new market. They are just as directive as the frames of the first
editions. Their notes, also, are not closures of fiction but new
beginnings. In Scott's notably fluid stratagems of authenticity
and fictionality, source becomes story just as surely as, in the
increasingly self-referential world of the first-edition frames, story
becomes source.

This outline of two quite distinct varieties of paratext may be
given a little more substance by a brief consideration of the functions of two types of frame in two very different novels. The

---

[6] The most important discussions of the various types of Scott frame are:
Richard Waswo, 'Story as Historiography in the Waverley Novels', *ELH* xlvii
(1980), 304–30; Jane Millgate, *Scott's Last Edition: A Study in Publishing History*
(Edinburgh, 1987); Steven F. Klepetar, 'Levels of Narration in *Old Mortality*',
Wordsworth Circle, xiii/1 (Winter 1982), 38–45; Frank Jordan, 'Scott, Chatterton,
Byron, and the Wearing of Masks', *Scott and His Influence*, 279–89; Judith Wilt,
Secret Leaves, 185–203; Mark A. Weinstein, ed., *The Prefaces to the Waverley
Novels* (Lincoln, Nebr., 1978); Marilyn Orr, 'Voices and Text: Scott the Storyteller,
Scott the Novelist', *Scottish Literary Journal*, xvi/2 (Nov. 1989), 41–59; Patricia
S. Gaston, *Prefacing the Waverley Prefaces: A Reading of Sir Walter Scott's
Prefaces to the Waverley Novels*, American University Studies, Series IV, English
Language and Literature, vol. cxxx (New York, 1991). Of these, Millgate's
is the only extensive analysis of the Magnum Opus, and its emphasis falls on
composition and publication history rather than on the construction of authority.
Gaston's full-length study of Scott's prefaces offers little detailed interpretation of
the Magnum Opus frames, but emphasizes the importance of the edition as a
whole in recasting the novels as one series.

novels are *The Castle of Otranto* and Nabokov's *Lolita*, not the
most obviously linked of fictions in subject or style. Each of
these novels, however, surrounds itself with two distinct types of
paratext, one 'fictitious' and one 'truthful', and in this way they
help to focus some of the issues at stake in the multiplying
frames of the Waverley Novels. The preface to the anonymous
first edition of *The Castle of Otranto* details an extravagant fantasy
about an old Italian black-letter text, by which the tale which is to
follow may be read as a genuine survivor of a lost culture. The
preface to the second edition presents the 'true' figure of the
author. One might expect the first edition to be the more tightly
explanatory of the work's origins, the more carefully detailed.
However, the preface to the second edition is equally careful to set
up a system of interpretation. First it declares that this is a literary
experiment, a way of fusing the ancient romance and the modern
novel. It then gives precedents for everything which might be
thought most disruptive to this plan, especially the intrusion of
ludicrously comic and 'low' characters. It suggests a precedent for
its experiment in the plays of Shakespeare, and elevates these
as the most illustrious examples of English genius. The second
edition, therefore, offers an alternative way of understanding
The Castle of Otranto, not as an outlandish product of ancient
monkish culture but as a natural product of English inspiration
and new literary enterprise. The first preface acts as interpretative
defence for the problem of the supernatural; the second, as interpretative defence for the mixed form, the impure combination of
serious and comic elements.

Two hundred years later, Nabokov's *Lolita* is introduced by a
letter from 'John Ray, Jr., Ph.D.', a lawyer who has been asked by
his friend Clarence Choate Clark to prepare for the press the
manuscript left by Humbert Humbert. Nabokov originally hoped
to publish *Lolita* anonymously, but found, as he describes in his
Postscript, that Humbert Humbert was rather too convincing a
narrator to find a publisher in this form.[7] The frame device of the
fake editor contains key pointers about the interpretation of the
novel. Slyly using the introductory letter to publicize a work of his
own, John Ray offers sententious comments on 'the ethical impact
the book should have on the serious reader', attempting to control

[7] *Lolita* (1959; repr. Harmondsworth, 1980), 5–7, 311–12.

the reader's response to *Lolita* by suggesting that Humbert's narrative points a moral about society.[8] As a result, the reader expects to find a story which can be reduced to a moral message. The frame sets up expectations which the fiction thwarts, and creates an editor whose incomprehension challenges any preconceptions about morality and psychology which would simplify the problems of *Lolita*. Nabokov's editor, an insignificant man elevated to public attention by his involvement in a narrative which his own conventional brain could not have conceived, is a modern Jedediah Cleishbotham—meretricious, self-seeking, morally complacent, spiritually obtuse. Nabokov's own Postscript, finally, introduces another commenting voice with which the reader of *Lolita* must engage in deciding on an interpretation. Different conventions of authorial address, as well as in the status of fiction, make the Magnum Opus more reticent and more unassuming than the voice which announces itself as Nabokov, but both forms of postscript direct the reader towards certain goals of interpretation which may or may not fit the requirements of the novel. Just as Nabokov's Postscript revises and historicizes John Ray, and Walpole's preface to the second edition of *The Castle of Otranto* revises and historicizes the preface to the first, so Scott's introductions and notes for the Magnum Opus set themselves up in competition with the voices and jokes of the introductions and frames to the first editions.

The discussion which follows is organized in a way which highlights the differences between the two main types of paratextual activity at work in the Waverley Novels, but it also aims to suggest formal and rhetorical similarities between them. It first traces in a broadly chronological manner the development of Scott's frame narratives in the first editions of his works, paying particular attention to the first-edition frames of two novels, *The Monastery* and *The Fair Maid of Perth*. Next, it focuses on the new opportunities for legitimizing and authenticating fiction which Scott created in the Magnum Opus edition, and argues that these deserve just as much attention as the first-edition frames have already secured in recent criticism. There is an agenda, in fact, to which the chapter does not have space to attend, but which

[8] Ibid. 7. Nabokov's Postscript explicitly denies the moral, p. 313 ('despite John Ray's assertion, *Lolita* has no moral in tow').

deserves some acknowledgement here: that the Magnum Opus is a fittingly complex conclusion to Scott's lifetime of inventing stories, and stories in support of stories. Beginning with the disguises and bluffs of the first-edition frames, and ending with the framing by personal history in the Magnum Opus, Scott defines, protects, and controls his fiction. The frames of the first editions facetiously ask why the reader bothers to read the Waverley Novels at all. In fact, Scott closely involves himself not just with whether, but also with precisely how, his work is read.

1. Scott's First Editions: The Author in Disguise

Comfortable among narrative conventions, unalarmed by confusions between fiction and fact, Scott feels no need to push these games to their logical or illogical conclusions. Once we know that the narrative is fictitious, we need not seek revelatory truth behind the narrative, or explore (as in *Wuthering Heights* or *Under Western Eyes*) the complexities of narrative perspective for their influence on the substance of the story.[9]

The most liberating feature of any game is the collective decision to regard it as a game. In Scott's case, however, the insistence that he is only playing (or only dressing up) has sometimes proved more limiting than liberating. Although the puzzle of Scott's anonymity has been the most frequently discussed of the issues addressed in this chapter, it is important to register the devices by which Scott preserved (while mocking) his imaginative privacy, and their cumulative impact on the reception of his novels. This impact was both considerable and subtle. The Waverley Novels became so closely identified with the mystique of their production that parodies of the craze for romantic Scottishness, like Sarah Green's *Scotch Novel Reading* in 1824, made a comic feature of the uncertainty over 'who the deuce it is that scribbles away so fast'.[10] In this novel, the despairing father of the tartan-infatuated heroine drily favours the theory that a Scottish literary conspiracy has

---

[9] Levine, *Realistic Imagination*, 90.
[10] *Scotch Novel Reading; or, Modern Quackery: A Novel Really Founded on Facts*, 3 vols. (London, 1824), i. 5. The discussion takes place in the opening chapter, 'Caledonian Mania'.

been organized to monopolize the book market and to spirit English money north. It is not, in his opinion, safe to assume the independent identity of any Scottish writer. 'James Hogg', he warns, is in all probability just another pseudonym of the 'Author of *Waverley*'. *Scotch Novel Reading* neatly explodes the received wisdom that Scott's anonymity was a mark of modesty. Instead it quietly notes the expansionist potential of namelessness.

Scott found it difficult to explain the reasons for his anonymity, although he suggested several times that writing incognito gave him courage (to carry on after the supposed failure of *The Monastery*, for example).[11] Critics have put forward several more thoroughgoing psychological explanations, including arguments based on Scott's supposed defensiveness and habits of self-deprecation, his unease in the role of narrator, his addiction to the tones of gentlemanly ease, to secrecy, and even to 'truthfulness', by which the frames and notes are said to offer readers 'honest revelations of the fictionality of the fictions'.[12] (If Scott was not being honest about himself, the argument goes, he was at least being honest about his art.) Some of the most recent discussions of frame narratives in the Waverley Novels continue to emphasize Scott's 'distrust of the authorial role and of narrative form itself'.[13] Scott's anonymity often features in the list of his virtues, as a modest and noble desire to distance himself from too much public notice and to keep his readers alert at all times to the deceptions being practised on them. Not surprisingly, this diffidence is the explanation most frequently hinted at by Scott himself. In a more

---

[11] *WN* i, pp. xx–xxxvii; xli, pp. viii–xxx. On *The Monastery*, see the Magnum Opus introduction to *The Abbot*, in which that novel is skilfully presented as putting right the misjudgements of its predecessor, *WN* xx, p. ix.

[12] Quoted from J. M. Rignall, 'The Historical Double: *Waverley*, *Sylvia's Lovers*, *The Trumpet-Major*', *Essays in Criticism*, xxxiv (1984), 14–32 (19). See also Levine, *Realistic Imagination*, 88, and Frederick A. Pottle's remark on Scott's compulsion to 'deflate' his romances with 'parallel columns of history', 'The Power of Memory in Boswell and Scott' (1945), in *Scott's Mind and Art*, ed. A. Norman Jeffares (Edinburgh, 1969), 230–53 (251). Lockhart comments on Scott's prolonged anonymity, the effect of habit, and the opportunity to escape from any sense of financial danger, x. 232–6; his love of role-playing and masks, ii. 212; and dislike of being the subject of literary discussion, iv. 403. Alexander Cargill notes 'the innate nobility' of Scott's character as revealed by his keeping himself in the background of his fictions, 'Sir Walter Scott and his "Anonymous" Quotations', *The Scotsman*, No. 24175 (20 Nov. 1920), 9.

[13] Orr, 'Voices and Text', 42.

negative spirit, Scott's fictions of anonymity, and the extravagant false identities to which they led, have sometimes been ascribed to his carelessness and indifference, his fatal inability to believe absolutely in the quality and importance of his art. What these accounts of Scott's anonymity have in common is a conviction that questions of personal psychology are central to the debate. Even Judith Wilt's interpretation of the prefaces is based on a reading of Scott's psychology, discovering there unacknowledged motivations and desires such as ambition, wrath, and rivalry. Scott might not have chosen to admit to these particular desires, but such interpretations preserve the strategic principles underlying his decision to present his anonymity as a quirk of personality rather than a question of technique.

The consequences of Scott's anonymity and fondness for narratorial disguise are far more technical than personal, however. The complicated disguises of the first editions attempt to establish new, unrestricted personalities, so as at once to avoid the constraints, and to secure the specialized function, of the rational voice of the narrator. On the subject of personal motivation, the only relevant factor for the present argument is the obvious point that Scott associated disguise with artistic liberation. As his 'Eidolon' declares in the Introductory Epistle of *The Fortunes of Nigel*: 'Let Fame follow those who have a substantial shape. A shadow—and an impersonal author is nothing better—can cast no shade.'[14] Impersonality, however, was a difficult state to preserve: it is significant that this remark is made by an author who has already become a ghostly emanation of himself.

At first, the image of the 'Author of *Waverley*' brought Scott a kind of liberty, but, as his career progressed, that image came in turn to be restrictive. A clear example of this occurs in a letter written to the actor-manager Daniel Terry while he was at work on *The Doom of Devorgoil*. He planned that Terry should claim the play as his own, and liked to think he was writing in a style appropriate to the occasion. The letter makes clear the half-guilty but attractive liberation of avoiding the reputation and role of the 'Author of *Waverley*':

---

[14] *WN* xxvi, p. xxxiv, and already a favourite image (see e.g. the frame of *The Abbot*, *WN* xx, p. viii). Contrast his use of the same metaphor when discussing Thomas Campbell with Washington Irving in 1817: '*He is afraid of the shadow that his own fame casts before him*' (Lockhart, v. 250).

I should never have dreamed of making such an attempt in my own proper person; and if I had such a vision, I should have been anxious to have made it something of a legitimate drama, such as a literary man, uncalled upon by any circumstance to connect himself with the stage, might have been expected to produce. Now this is just what any gentleman in your situation might run off...[15]

The role of the literary man is described with a significant mixture of pride, distaste, and insecurity. The chance to escape the restrictions of his self-imposed authorial role offers him the opportunity to break rules (here, the rules of drama). The letter to Terry provides a useful context in which to set more familiar comments on the role of the 'Author of *Waverley*'. It clarifies, for example, the combination of embarrassment and conscious restriction with which he surveys the extravagances of the first-edition frame in the introduction to *The Fortunes of Nigel* in the Magnum Opus:

As it is the privilege of a masque or incognito to speak in a feigned voice and assumed character, the author attempted, while in disguise, some liberties of the same sort; and while he continues to plead upon the various excuses which the introduction contains, the present acknowledgment must serve as an apology for a species of 'hoity toity, whisky frisky' pertness of manner, which, in his avowed character, the author should have considered as a departure from the rules of civility and good taste.[16]

Scott's disguises enable him to avoid this 'avowed character'. Yet the attractive 'liberties' offered by the 'hoity toity, whisky frisky' manner are amply registered by the vocabulary and style of this sentence alone.

Scott's experimentation with frame narratives and competing narratorial authorities started long before he turned his full attention to prose fiction in 1814. In his first venture into prose fiction, he made use of the convention of the damaged, illegible manuscript to bring to a close Joseph Strutt's *Queen-Hoo Hall*. In his work as editor of *Sir Tristrem*, Dryden, and Swift, and in his many comments on authentication of materials from the past, he demonstrated his sensitivity to the authority conveyed by manuscript evidence.[17] He experimented in his long poems with

---

[15] *Letters*, v. 77 (8 Feb. 1818): see also v. 87–90, and on the play's claim to be exempt from dramatic rules, v. 61.

[16] *WN* xxvi, pp. xvi–xvii.

[17] Lockhart discusses several times Scott's views on antiquarian editing and editors: see e.g. ii. 62 (Ritson and Ellis), ii. 131 (*Minstrelsy*), iii. 1 (Dryden), iii.

frame narratives and intervening narrators which deflect authority
from a single accountable narrative voice. Especially complex is
the layering of narrative voices and points of view over several
centuries in his poem *The Bridal of Triermain*, published anonymously in 1813. Anonymity also, as this suggests, was nothing
new either for him or for others in his immediate literary circle.
Among his immediate associates, there was an interest in anonymous and mock-antiquarian publications (the 'Translation from
an Ancient Chaldee Manuscript' for *Blackwood's* is an example).
Later, Scott made appearances in print as 'L. T.' (Templeton),
'Paul', 'Somnambulus', and 'Malachi Malagrowther' when he
wished to comment upon politics, and wrote letters in the character of his fake editors. An example is his letter to Charles
Mackay, creator of the stage role of Bailie Nicol Jarvie in *Rob
Roy*, a novel outside the *Tales of My Landlord* but claimed as a
'near relation' by Cleishbotham.[18]

He also liked to cite the example of Junius as a precedent. This
still-mysterious figure may have been a more attractive model
than the potentially embarrassing, and more contentious, masks
of 'Rowley' and 'Ossian', to which there are many studiedly
irreverent references in Scott's work. In *A Legend of Montrose*,
potentially the most Ossianic of all Scott's novels (hence the refuge-
character of Dalgetty), he jokes about 'Secundus M'Pherson, Esq.
of Glenforgen', while in the frame narrative of *Ivanhoe* Laurence
Templeton refers to Dr Dryasdust's opinion that the charm of the
Waverley Novels 'lay entirely in the art with which the unknown
author had availed himself, like a second McPherson, of the antiquarian stores which lay scattered around him',[19] an ominous hint
that the Author is not to be trusted with the material he passes off
as authentic. Macpherson's is not a neutral name to conjure up in
the reader's mind at the beginning of a historical novel. In his
reply to Clutterbuck at the beginning of *The Monastery*, the
Author draws attention to the fact that 'many of the most estim-

2–3 (notes on memoirs of the Civil Wars), iv. 162–3 (Swift), vi. 407–8 ('Private
Letters of the Seventeenth Century'). Scott gives a critique of Chatterton (1804),
MPW xvii. 215–41. He also wrote an essay 'On the Authenticity of Ossian's
Poems' for the Speculative Society in 1791, and comments directly on the authenticity debate, *Letters*, i. 320–4, xii. 24, as well as indirectly through the discussions
of Oldbuck and McIntyre in *The Antiquary* (*WN* vi. 121–6)
[18] *Letters*, v. 305–7.
[19] *WN* xvi, p. xxv.

able of them [imaginary authors], such as an old Highland gentleman called Ossian, a monk of Bristol called Rowley, and others,
are inclined to pass themselves off as denizens of the land of
reality'.[20] Junius, by contrast, was a mask but not a fake.

The ongoing story of the frames, and the expectation that in
each novel the author would give new clues to his identity, also
served commercial functions: as invitation, 'salesmanship', and
spur to competition. Kathryn Sutherland has recently argued
that Scott's many authorial personae act as salesmen, mediating
between producer and consumer and, on the model of Adam
Smith's economics, increasing productivity by subdividing authorial labour.[21] Quite apart from their internal status as 'an
economics of the imagination', Scott's devices of anonymity established the 'Author of *Waverley*' as an enticing mystery for the
reading public. As Byron remarks of the unforthcoming hero of
Lara:

> Opinion varying o'er his hidden lot,
> In praise or railing ne'er his name forgot;
> His silence formed a theme for others' prate ... [22]

Extended games of anonymity guaranteed attention even as they
began to construct the image of the Author as 'some living mythological personage', as he was later described by Carlyle.[23] The
disclosure of identity was repeatedly postponed, always forthcoming in some new production, and was sufficiently suspenseful
to prompt Adolphus's painstaking scholarly investigation (*Letters
to Richard Heber, Esq. Containing Critical Remarks on the Series
of Novels Beginning with 'Waverley,' and an Attempt to Ascertain
their Author*, 1821). Meanwhile, Scott himself fuelled the debate
about plural authorship, referring in the Introductory Epistle
to *The Fortunes of Nigel* to attempts 'to prove the Author of
Waverley to be two ladies of talent'.[24] Twenty years after his
death, scholars were still publishing pamphlets to prove that he

[20] *WN* xviii, pp. xc–xci.
[21] 'Fictional Economies: Adam Smith, Walter Scott and the Nineteenth-Century
Novel', *ELH* liv (1987), 97–127 (104–6).
[22] *The Complete Poetical Works*, ed. Jerome J. McGann (Oxford, 1980–), iii.
224, lines 291–3.
[23] Carlyle, *Works*, xxix. 61.
[24] *WN* xxvi, p. xxvi.

had shared authorship with his brother Thomas and Mrs Thomas Scott.

In addition to the spur they gave to readerly curiosity, Scott's disguises also made a more immediate commercial impact on individual publishing houses. They were often directly prompted by financial battles and private jealousies in the publishing world.[25] Sometimes, Scott's anonymity caused problems for Scott and his publishers, including the crises over the threatened publication of *Pontefract Castle*, which was to appear under the name of Jedediah Cleishbotham, and the German forgery *Walladmor*. Scott intervened directly to discredit the impostor 'Tales of My Landlord' in the frame narrative of *The Monastery*, making apposite comments on the 'wrathful trade' of bookselling.[26] In another sense of the commercial spirit, the frames gave Scott an opportunity to canvass opinion on projected works (as in Josiah Cargill's project at the end of *St Ronan's Well*, which anticipates *Tales of the Crusaders*), and to advertise forthcoming works (as the frame of *The Betrothed* advertises *The Life of Napoleon*).

Although the decision to publish his first novel anonymously was not in itelf strange, Scott continued his anonymity well beyond the expectations of friends and reviewers, and wrote a commentary for the third edition which defends and explains his working practices for some details in the novel.[27] This introduction also flirts with the reasons for his publishing anonymously, 'leaving it to the candour of the public to choose among the many circumstances of life, such as may induce him to suppress his name on the present occasion', and with the notion that the author may

[25] For further information see Peter Garside, 'Rob's Last Raid: Scott and the Publication of the Waverley Novels', in *Author/Publisher Relations During the Eighteenth and Nineteenth Centuries*, ed. Robin Myers and Michael Harris (Oxford, 1983), 88–118; Johnson, 547–51; Jane Millgate's discussions at the beginnings of each chapter in *Walter Scott: The Making of the Novelist* (Edinburgh, 1984); Lockhart on Scott's independence and publishing deals, iii. 3–4.

[26] WN xviii, pp. xcvii–c.

[27] For reactions to the continued anonymity of *Waverley* see Johnson, 456 (quoting Hume, Clephane, and Morritt). Scott defends himself, *Letters*, iii. 480–1. Suggestions that Scott was the author are made in reviews in *Antijacobin Review*, xlvii (Sept. 1814), 217–47; *British Critic*, NS ii. 189–211; *The Champion* (24 July 1814), 238–9; *Monthly Review*, NS lxxv (Nov. 1814), 275–89; *Scots Magazine*, lxxvi (July 1814), 524–33. Decisively opposed to the theory was *The Port Folio*, 3rd ser. v (Apr. 1815), 326–33. Ina Ferris contrasts the first chapter and the postscript of *Waverley* in terms of narrative voice, *Achievement of Literary Authority*, 109–11.

be 'like Cerberus—three gentlemen at once'.[28] This anonymous address, notably, enables Scott to fend off criticisms of *Waverley* which question his reliability as an observer of national character and interpreter of historical fact. By the time he came to announce in the Advertisement to his third novel, *The Antiquary*, that this was the final instalment of a tripartite illustration of Scottish life at different periods of history, he had already begun to construct a frame for each fiction which would allow it to draw strengths from its predecessors. (The plan perhaps reflects Richardson's announcement in *Sir Charles Grandison* of three complementary but contrasting tales of moral life.) This Advertisement immediately validates *The Antiquary* as the conclusion of a popular sequence. It also works to protect the novel from the charge of piecemeal construction which has so often been levelled against it, and to which Scott himself draws the reader's attention.

After this, and using different publishers (Murray and Blackwood), Scott went on to develop an entirely new frame for *Tales of My Landlord*, in which a pompous editor, Jedediah Cleishbotham, introduces the narratives of a dead schoolmaster and collector of local stories, Peter Pattieson. Gilbert J. French argues in his mid-Victorian case for the plural identity of the 'Author of *Waverley*' that this shift was designed to distinguish works genuinely written by Scott from those in which 'he had little more than an editor's interest'.[29] There certainly is a shift in interest and emphasis, although French interprets it too literally. Although the first three Waverley Novels contain several local storytellers and competing stories, *Tales of My Landlord* takes its entire form from the transmission and authentication of stories. Pattieson describes his methods of research, emphasizing the role of the scrupulous seeker after fact in contrast with superstition, a role adopted by 'editors' in Gothic:

After my usual manner, I made farther enquiries of other persons connected with the wild and pastoral district in which the scene of the following narrative is placed, and I was fortunate enough to recover many links of the story, not generally known, and which account, at least in

[28] WN i. 3–4. Scott suggests a variety of reasons for anonymous publication, all of which, excepting those of extreme youth or age, are partly applicable to his own situation.
[29] *An Enquiry Into the Origin of the Authorship of Some of the Earlier Waverley Novels* (Bolton, 1856), 35.

some degree, for the circumstances of exaggerated marvel with which superstition has attired it in the more vulgar traditions.[30]

Pattieson, in turn, derives his authority from the eyewitness accounts of those he consults. In the Third Series of *Tales*, for example, his account of Sergeant More McAlpine and his day-to-day life in Gandercleugh persuades the reader 'to give implicit credit to the natural events of the story, which, like all those which I have had the honour to put under his notice, actually rest upon a basis of truth'.[31] The seriousness of Pattieson's working methods, and his insistence on truthfulness, contends with the ludicrous claims and stylistic self-indulgence of Cleishbotham. To complicate the frame and its competing authorities still further, an additional unnamed editor draws attention in footnotes to alleged textual interpolations by Cleishbotham, and the publisher whom Cleishbotham enlists to deal with Pattieson's manuscripts himself turns out to be 'cunning in the counterfeiting of voices, and in making facetious tales and responses'.[32]

As well as foregrounding complications of historical authenticity and personalized authorship, Scott's frames set a subtle and ambitious literary agenda. In the introductory chapter of *The Heart of Midlothian*, two young lawyers propose to publish stories of prisoners in the Tolbooth, with a side-sweep at this being enough 'to gorge even the public's all-devouring appetite for the wonderful and horrible'.[33] They debate the status of novels as idle entertainment and posit that the truest stories are always the best. The reader's appetite is whetted with promises that from these prison-tales 'the blood of each reader shall be curdled, and his epidermis crisped into goose skin'; to be followed by a novel which half-satisfies and half-frustrates such expectations. Scott indulges himself with another in-joke, the rumour that some senior lawyers read and maybe even write novels. But through this indulgence Scott considers the form of fiction he is writing, and how best (again in tune with Wordsworth) to provide excitement of a

---

[30] *WN* ix. 7–8; and see Pattieson's account of his mediating task as editor of *Old Mortality*, *WN* ix. 253–6. Klepetar provides the most succinct account of the use of the Pattieson frame as a guide to interpretation. See also Orr, 'Voices and Text', 44–6.

[31] *WN* xv, p. xliii.

[32] *WN* ix. 2–3 n.

[33] *WN* xi. 177.

permanently interesting nature. In this introduction, the historical and the blood-curdling interact and begin to redefine each other, just as they do in the novel itself, with its odd perspectives on the historical-demonological characters of George Staunton and Meg Murdockson. In *The Bride of Lammermoor*, even more explicitly, Peter Pattieson and the painter Dick Tinto spend the introductory chapter debating Pattieson's preference for dialogue over description in his previous works, debating not just what but also how to narrate. Increasingly, the frames of the first editions become highly conscious of readers and markets for fiction. The fairly mild disagreements between Tinto and Pattieson become heated exchanges in the later frames involving Dryasdust, Clutterbuck, and the 'Eidolon' of the Author. The tales told by Pattieson are the product of amateur enthusiasm, labours of love by an obscure schoolmaster who has died before his tales come to public attention. In contrast, the 'Eidolon' of the Author, in the frames of the early 1820s, is an embattled professional, fighting off demands that he write plays, that he attend more carefully to historical accuracy, that he be less dull, that he resist the temptation to turn books into commodities.

After three series of *Tales of My Landlord*, and another appearance of the 'Author of *Waverley*' in *Rob Roy* (this time as editor of a manuscript sent to him by an unknown correspondent), the frames diversify further, with the appearance of antiquarians like Dr Jonas Dryasdust (a name which recalls Smollett's Jonathan Dustwich in the frame-narrative of *Humphry Clinker*), Captain Clutterbuck, and Laurence Templeton. These antiquaries take over the frame devices of the Waverley Novels after *Ivanhoe*, demonstrating the increasingly close relationship between text and paratext. A sceptical and pedantic group, they debate with the Author the shortcomings and occasionally the merits of his work, and are eventually seen in colloquy with the 'Eidolon' of the Author in the frame narratives for *The Fortunes of Nigel* and *Peveril of the Peak*. In the frame of *Quentin Durward*, the Author specifically denies being Walter Scott, and discusses with a sceptical French aristocrat the literary value of 'The Bridle of Lammermore'. As the particularly exuberant frame of *Tales of the Crusaders* shows, the habit of reference between novels develops into an awareness of the whole series of novels as an internally consistent system. The novels become increasingly self-referential,

citing fiction in support of fiction. *Ivanhoe*, for example, is auth-
enticated by a manuscript supposedly owned by *The Antiquary*'s
Sir Arthur Wardour, and Dr Dryasdust's watch turns out to be the
work of 'Vincent and Tunstall', the two apprentices from *The
Fortunes of Nigel*.

Among Scott's antiquarian interlocutors, Captain Clutterbuck,
who tells his life-story in a letter to the Author prefacing *The
Monastery*, is especially interesting. In his letter to the renowned
'Author of *Waverley*', Clutterbuck encloses a bulky manuscript
passed on to him by a Benedictine monk who has visited the ruined
monastery of St Mary at Kennaquhair (based on Melrose). In his
reply, the Author wryly comments on Clutterbuck's 'Utopian'
status, while, ironically, a footnote suggests that the Author's
letter has itself been edited by Clutterbuck. The narrative frame
of *The Monastery*, with its competing levels of authority more
sharply discriminated than in *Tales of My Landlord*, both celebrates and questions fictionality. The Author mockingly exposes
the spectral imaginative status of both Clutterbuck and his authentic manuscripts, while Clutterbuck tells a strange story of the
exchange (and symbolic interchangeability) of two treasures:
the mouldered heart of the last Abbot of St Mary's, dug up by the
Benedictine from an obscure recess in the monastery, and the
manuscript history of his life, completed by the Benedictine but
begun by his uncle, and including some original materials. Already
interpreted, modernized, and (improbably enough) adapted to
Protestant tastes by the Benedictine, who turns out to be unusually
sensitive to his potential audience, this account is then offered for
further revision and 'correction' by the 'Author of *Waverley*'. In
his reply to Clutterbuck, the Author, echoing Swift, mocks the
miraculous discovery of authentic manuscripts by the 'editors of
the land of Utopia'.[34] In fact, however, he has offered in this tale
of the Benedictine and the buried heart a different way of looking
at the tale for which that heart is exchanged—one which far
exceeds in imaginative and symbolic force any of the run-of-

[34] The source is the opening letter from Gulliver to Sympson, in *Gulliver's
Travels and Other Writings*, ed. Louis A. Landa (Oxford, 1976), 5: 'If the censure
of yahoos could any way affect me, I should have great reason to complain that
some of them are so bold as to think my book of travels a mere fiction out of my
own brain; and have gone so far as to drop hints that the Houyhnhnms and
yahoos have no more existence than the inhabitants of Utopia.'

the-mill accounts of manuscripts discovered in antique bureaux, waste-paper bins, or caskets cast up by the sea, which are the miraculous circumstances alluded to by the Author. The mouldered and forgotten heart of the Abbot Ambrosius, in its porphyry case, is exchanged for narrative. The heart is rescued, taken to a more sympathetic spiritual refuge by the Benedictine, and the legend is modernized and Protestantized to suit contemporary taste. The grave-robbing of The Monastery produces a heart, not a narrative, but the words used by the Benedictine to describe the heart make it clear that on a symbolic level the two can be equated. The heart is 'an inestimable treasure, for those who know how to use it rightly'.[35] Interestingly, when Scott came, in the Magnum Opus introduction to The Abbot, to review the use or non-use made of the story of the heart in the two novels, he likened this absent subject to the contents of the mysterious chest in Godwin's Caleb Williams, in terms which recall the empty secrets of Gothic convention:

Thus, the incident of the discovery of the heart, which occupies the greater part of the Introduction to the Monastery, is a mystery unnecessarily introduced, and which remains at last very imperfectly explained. In this particular, I was happy to shroud myself by the example of the author of 'Caleb Williams,' who never condescends to inform us of the actual contents of that Iron Chest which makes such a figure in his interesting work, and gives the name to Mr Colman's drama.[36]

The frame narrative of The Monastery in its first-edition form also includes the usual flourishes of contempt for 'trashy novels' (and milliner's-miss readers), this time attributed to Clutterbuck, who confesses himself bored to tears by the manuscript providentially entrusted to his care. The Author, in return, can spring to the defence, redefining the value of fiction by redefining its readership. Clutterbuck cites the milliner's miss; the Author retaliates by citing Sir Isaac Watt. The frame also bolsters others in the series, both Clutterbuck and the Author referring to Jedediah Cleishbotham. At the end of The Monastery, the Author intervenes again to throw doubt over the dates of the events alluded to, and to draw attention to the historical flaws of his last work, Ivanhoe. This is the kind of ploy often thought defensive by Scott's critics, yet by pointing out historical inaccuracy Scott manages simul-

[35] WN xviii, p. lxviii.   [36] WN xx, pp. x–xi.

taneously to elevate the new syntheses possible in fiction. The move from the milliner's miss to Sir Isaac Watt, likewise, is a clear statement of the potential worth, in intellectual and moral as well as aesthetic terms, of the new genre in which he is writing.

The first-edition frame narratives can also be used to support hypotheses about phases of enthusiasm and doubt in Scott's writing career. After the unpopularity of *The Monastery* the frames are subdued for a while. *The Abbot* is prefaced by a very short continuation of the *Monastery* frame, a letter from the Author to Clutterbuck noting his correspondent's disapproval of the changes made to the Benedictine's manuscript, and explaining his reasons for removing further allusions to the White Lady and further passages sympathetic to Catholicism. *Kenilworth*, immediately following *The Abbot*, plays safe by continuing the use of popular historical figures. It also continues to marginalize *The Monastery* by moving from Queen Mary to Queen Elizabeth, as if *The Abbot* and *Kenilworth* were the true sequence, not *The Monastery* and *The Abbot*. *Kenilworth* has no frame at all, and the Advertisement to *The Pirate* is comparatively direct, earnestly setting out that the novel's purpose is 'to give a detailed and accurate account of certain remarkable incidents which took place in the Orkney Islands', although it closes with a hint of the old swagger about 'the following veracious narrative, compiled from materials to which he himself alone has had access'.[37] One measure of Scott's purposefulness in using frames is that the exercise is never allowed to become uniform or automatic. For all his exuberance, he observes discernible guidelines of relevance, convention, and plausibility. *St Ronan's Well* and *Redgauntlet* have no frame, for example, although *Redgauntlet* is formally concluded by Dr Dryasdust. *St Ronan's Well* is a venture into new territory, an attempt to describe modern fashionable society, to which an antiquarian frame would have little to contribute. *Redgauntlet* opens as an epistolary novel and goes on to contain so many narratorial perspectives and voices that another layer of editorializing would seem both unnecessary and confusing. Even when the frames are in comparative abeyance, however, they inspire and advertise new

---

[37] WN xxiv, p. xix. Despite its modest claim that *The Pirate* aims to complete extant accounts of the arrival of the pirate ship, even this restrained introduction provides an alternative ending to the events described in the novel.

productions. *Tales of the Crusaders* develops out of the mock-advertisement at the end of *St Ronan's Well* for Josiah Cargill's projected 'Siege of Ptolemais', planned to form part of a 'General History of the Crusaders'.

The new exuberance which enters the frames of *The Fortunes of Nigel* and *Peveril of the Peak* is accompanied by a restless spirit of self-examination. The 'Eidolon' of the Author, whose solid bulk and robust pragmatism, Fitz-Fulke-like, contrasts comically with his spectral accoutrements, energetically debates with Clutterbuck and Dryasdust such issues as the organization of plot, historical accuracy, the commoditization of literature, and dramatizations of his work. The self-reflexive jokes now include one on the practice of writing introductions.

Manuscripts, and an entirely new antiquarian editor, revive with a vengeance in the frame for *Woodstock*. In the preface to the first edition of *The Castle of Otranto*, Walpole had suggested that his manuscript might once have been in the possession of a Catholic family in the North of England. Scott tells of a more meddlesome family, for parts of the manuscript on which *Woodstock* purports to be based seem to be interpolations made by an unidentified Presbyterian commentator. When he comes to edit this very detailed frame narrative for the Magnum Opus, Scott remarks in a footnote: 'It is hardly necessary to say, unless to some readers of very literal capacity, that Doctor Rochecliffe and his manuscripts are alike apocryphal.'[38] The very presence of this comment, however, testifies to the conceivable credibility of the frame. A comparable case is the Advertisement to the first edition of *Rob Roy*, which presents that novel as substantially the work of an unnamed correspondent. In the Magnum Opus, a footnote explains: 'As it may be necessary, in the present Edition, to speak upon the square, the Author thinks it proper to own, that the communication alluded to is entirely imaginary.'[39]

By the time he published his next novel, Scott unexpectedly found himself publicly declared the 'Author of *Waverley*', and obliged to conduct himself accordingly. Ironically, however, some of Scott's most sustained experiments with mutually supporting

[38] WN xxxix, p. lxix n. A similar disclaimer appears in the Magnum Opus edition of *Quentin Durward*, WN xxxi, p. xxv.
[39] WN vii, p. iv.

frames and tales were conducted after the declaration of his authorship, in the extensive frames for the two series of *Chronicles of the Canongate* with their communicative narrator, the debtor and solitary Chrystal Croftangry. For 'The Highland Widow' in the first series of *Chronicles*, Chrystal Croftangry draws on material from the manuscript resources left to him by Mrs Bethune Baliol. In turn, her account is derived from the oral tale of her Highland guide, Donald MacLeish. Chrystal Croftangry partly echoes Scott's new interest in detailing the sources and processes of his composition for the Magnum Opus. So, for example, Croftangry draws the reader into his confidence as he describes the preparation of the tales. This is particularly clear in the first chapter of *The Surgeon's Daughter*, again part of the first series of *Chronicles*, with its inclusion of comments by Croftangry's man of business, Fairscribe. Croftangry is a more extended portrait of the artist than Peter Pattieson, and, because he speaks independently of some more ludicrous figure (the role of Cleishbotham), he is a much more immediate authority. Although Croftangry is closer to his author than most of Scott's partial self-portraits, the protective disguise remains functional; so that Scott can, for example, direct through Croftangry a few blows at his competitors, Anne Grant of Laggan and General Stewart of Garth.[40] Of the later novels, *Anne of Geierstein* has no frame, and when Jedediah Cleishbotham re-emerges to introduce the Fourth Series of *Tales of My Landlord*, he has lost confidence in the skills of Peter Pattieson and employs Peter's brother, Paul, to revise his papers and remove their irritating inconsistencies. Paul, however, absconds to America and publishes the tales there, forcing Cleishbotham to present them in their unsatisfactory state after all. He begs the reader's indulgence. Even in this more straightforward use of the frame as apology, however, there is an expressive evocation of the loss both of imaginative power and of imaginative control.

Among the many incidental stories told in the course of Chrystal

---

[40] *WN* xli. 240–2 (on Grant and Stewart). Lockhart points out the resemblances between Scott and Croftangry, ix. 173–4. For an extended reading see Frank Jordan, 'Chrystal Croftangry, Scott's Last and Best Mask', *Scottish Literary Journal*, vii/1 (May 1980), 185–92. An example of the way in which the Croftangry persona was received by Scott's contemporaries can be found in the review of *Chronicles of the Canongate*, 1st ser., *The Scotsman*, xi, No. 816 (3 Nov. 1827), 697.

Croftangry's autobiographical reflections over the two series of
Chronicles of the Canongate, one is particularly interesting in
relation to the novel which it introduces, although the relationship
is far from obvious. The second series of *Chronicles*, *The Fair
Maid of Perth* (1828), a novel about a fourteenth-century Highland feud, is introduced by Chrystal Croftangry's comic anecdote
about a cockney salesman who attempts to remove the centuries-
old bloodstains, traditionally traced to the murder of David Rizzio,
in Queen Mary's apartments in Holyrood Palace. Superficially,
nothing could be farther from the tone and preoccupations of
the novel to follow. Croftangry, taking his usual walk through the
gallery adjoining the Queen's apartments, and wondering why 'the
Kings of Scotland, who hung around me, should be each and
every one painted with a nose like the knocker of a door', is called
by the shrieks of the housekeeper to the rescue of the stains, which
are about to fall victim to the salesman's wonder-detergent. The
salesman is literally at work to clean up the past, to obliterate the
evidence of its bloodiness and violence. Croftangry heroically intervenes to protect this historical evidence against the well-meaning
innovations of modern science and commercial enterprise.

Although he does not make the connection, it is ironic that
Croftangry should be called to this heroic feat of preservation
from his sceptical viewing of the portraits of fake Stewart kings.
There is a complex interplay here between different degrees
of possible historical verification. Even the bloodstains are only
reputed to have been caused by Rizzio's murder. The eager salesman wishes to clean up the past, but so, in his way, did the
portrait-painter of the Stewarts. In the light of Croftangry's profession as publishing writer, for whom the past is a kind of com-
modity, there is an additional irony in his rather lofty explanation:

> It cost me some trouble to explain to the zealous purifier of silk-stockings,
> embroidered waistcoats, broad-cloth, and deal planks, that there were
> such things in the world as stains which ought to remain indelible, on
> account of the associations with which they are connected. Our good
> friend viewed every thing of the kind only as the means of displaying the
> virtue of his vaunted commodity.[41]

Comically, the salesman, who has so little interest in preserving
the integrity of tradition, is sharply alive to the importance of

41 *WN* xlii. 7.

authenticity in the potion he sells, that 'Infallible Detergent Elixir, prepared and sold by Messrs Scrub and Rub, in five shilling and ten shilling bottles, each bottle being marked with the initials of the inventor, to counterfeit which would be to incur the pains of forgery'.[42]

Croftangry goes on to relate this ludicrous tale to his friend Mrs Bethune Baliol, and to discuss at length whether the famous stains were indeed caused by the murder of Rizzio and ominously preserved from that time. Mrs Baliol concedes the probability of his case and makes the more general point that we must not reject tradition out of a false and lazy scepticism:

We talk of a credulous vulgar, without always recollecting that there is a vulgar incredulity, which, in historical matters, as well as in those of religion, finds it easier to doubt than to examine, and endeavours to assume the credit of an *esprit fort*, by denying whatever happens to be a little beyond the very limited comprehension of the sceptic.[43]

It is no doubt useful for the historian to hold his reader under suspicion of vulgarity. Mrs Baliol goes on, however, to persuade Croftangry to continue his work as historical romancer, and encourages him in his intention to write on those obscure parts of the Scottish past which readers know little about.

This introductory chapter also contains two passages which mock the Gothic conventions of the discovered manuscript and the night spent in the haunted chamber. Croftangry wishes that he could, 'with the good-luck of most editors of romantic narrative, light upon some hidden crypt or massive antique cabinet, which should yield to my researches an almost illegible manuscript, containing the authentic particulars of some of the strange deeds of those wild days of the unhappy Mary'.[44] Continuing the type of joke about literary miracles which has already been noted in the frame-narrative of *The Monastery*, Mrs Baliol agrees that 'all god-

---

[42] WN xlii. 8. In a brief account of the first-edition frame of *The Fair Maid of Perth* in *Prefacing the Waverley Prefaces*, 137–8, Patricia S. Gaston draws a parallel between literary speculation and selling the past for profit, and suggests that the stained floor is a type of historical narrative which the salesman attempts to 'edit'. Although her account implicitly separates the concerns of the frame from those of the novel, they are pressingly relevant to each other, as I hope to demonstrate.

[43] WN xlii. 12.

[44] WN xlii. 8–9.

sends of this nature had ceased to occur, and that an author ...
might break his shins in stumbling through a hundred vaults,
without finding any thing but rats and mice, and become the
tenant of a dozen sets of shabby tenements, without finding that
they contained any manuscript but the weekly bill for board and
lodging'.[45] If the miraculous provenance of many historical tales
is to be discarded, so is the appearance of ghosts in haunted
chambers. Separating historical imagination from the terrors of
ghostly presences, Croftangry and Baliol produce between them a
vivid imaginative reconstruction of the scene of Rizzio's murder,
the expressions and motives of those who took part in it. At the
end of this virtuoso display, however, Croftangry disclaims any
intention to 'novelize' the story of Rizzio, insisting that it is too
well known, and that nothing he might write could possibly compete with William Robertson's account (in his *History of Scotland
during the Reigns of Mary and James VI*, 1759). He admits that
he hates being detected in such lies, and therefore prefers to write
about subjects with which readers are unfamiliar.

The agenda set by this frame is both thematic and technical. It is
possible to read Croftangry's leisurely anecdotal introduction in
various valid but technically reductive ways—as typical of Scott's
humour, or of his sense of a lost heroism in modern life, or as a
chance to display historical knowledge and appeal to nationalistic
sympathies—but the tone which it establishes for the opening of
The Fair Maid of Perth is unsettling and sceptical. It at once
introduces readers and cautions them, inviting both familiarity
and informed judgement. Thematically, it alludes through Mary
and Rizzio to a violent period of Scottish history, to treachery and
assassination, and to unstable monarchy, all of which are to be
key concerns of *The Fair Maid of Perth*. After the introductory
chapter, for example, the first chapter of the novel proper tells
the story of other violent incidents in the past of the Scottish
monarchy, the murder of James I, like Rizzio 'a victim to the
jealousy of the vengeful aristocracy', and the mysterious Gowrie
affair of 1600. The stage is set for a tale of violence and terror,
jealousy and revenge. The mock-chivalry of Croftangry's and
Baliol's reflections on his battle against the salesman ('you, the
Knight of Croftangry, who braved the fury of the "London pren-

tice bold," in behalf of the fair Dame Policy, and the memorial of Rizzio's slaughter!')[46] is also an apposite introduction for a tale which highlights and problematizes mercantile redefinitions of the codes of chivalry and heroic intervention.

In terms of narrative and historical technique, the introduction to this first edition of *The Fair Maid of Perth* is highly prescriptive. Croftangry sets out precisely the kind of historical fiction which can be expected of him, and dissuades the reader from any expectations of scholarly accuracy. (This is an issue to be taken up again three years later when Scott writes a new introduction for the Magnum Opus version of the novel.) Although Croftangry is not to measure himself against Robertson's history, he may be encouraged by Mrs Baliol's timely distinction between the responsibilities of historians and the colourful licence permissible in historical romance: 'What is the classic Robertson to you? The light which he carried was that of a lamp to illuminate the dark events of antiquity; yours is a magic lantern to raise up wonders which never existed. No reader of sense wonders at your historical inaccuracies.'[47] This discussion returns to the themes of the introductory epistles of *The Fortunes of Nigel* and *Peveril of the Peak*, with their reflections on the process of writing fictitious history, its possible educational function, the relationship between it (the sweetener) and scholarly history (the pill of knowledge). Technically, this introduction prepares readers for a method of treatment while alerting them to its inherent misrepresentations. It also absolves Croftangry from any attempt to reproduce the dialect in which the characters might be expected to speak. 'Those who wish to investigate the subject,' he adds, 'may consult the Chronicles of Winton, and the History of Bruce, by Archdeacon Barbour.'[48]

By the time Scott was working on this first-edition frame narrative for *The Fair Maid of Perth* he was also engaged in the very different project of creating new historical and autobiographical frames for earlier novels. Throughout the publication of the first-edition states of his texts, anonymity had given Scott a faceless authority which merged in the imagination with limitless personal wisdom and information. The new introductions and notes written for the Magnum Opus restored his personality and uncovered the anecdotes and casual remarks which inspired, and

[46] WN xlii. 9.   [47] WN xlii. 15–16.   [48] WN xlii. 17.

contradicted, his fictions. Some preoccupations remain constant over the two enterprises, as the next section of this argument will go on to show. One of them is a complex and shifting attitude towards narratorial authority (not merely an 'anxiety' or a 'distrust', as some critics have suggested, but a shrewd technical appreciation of its opportunities, dangers, and contradictions). Another is a sense of origins which perpetually recede as they are explained, of stories which call for previous stories *ad infinitum*. If one is seeking a means of contrasting the paratexts of the Magnum Opus with those of the first editions, however, a loosely Bakhtinian analogy has certain advantages (and limits which will become clearer in the next section). The first editions of the Waverley Novels, taken as a series, are emphatically dialogic productions. What then happens when the author and his publisher decide to impose on them a new degree of uniformity, a new monologic frame for a diversely dialogic collection of works? In their Magnum Opus format the Waverley Novels at last find their single author, but they also find a whole new range of voices to add to their existing medley. Their readers, meanwhile, discover that the end of the search for the 'Author of *Waverley*' merely leads into an increasingly complex search for the nature of authority.

2. *Notes and the Magnum Opus: 'The Mask of Veracity'*[49]

> And if it serves for no other purpose, at least that long catalogue of authors will be useful to lend authority to your book at the outset. Besides, nobody will take the trouble to examine whether you follow your authorities or not, having nothing to gain by it.
>
> (Prologue, *The Adventures of Don Quixote*, Part I)[50]

> Right well I wote most mighty Soueraine,
> That all this famous antique history,
> Of some th'aboundance of an idle braine
> Will iudged be, and painted forgery,
> Rather then matter of iust memory,

[49] A phrase from Scott's discussion of the common origin of romance and 'real history' in his 'Essay on Romance' (1824), *MPW* vi. 134.
[50] Miguel de Cervantes Saavedra, *The Adventures of Don Quixote* (1605, 1615), trans. J. M. Cohen (Harmondsworth, 1950, 1988), 29.

> Sith none, that breatheth liuing aire, does know,
> Where is that happy land of Faery,
> Which I so much do vaunt, yet no where show,
> But vouch antiquities, which no body can know.[51]

Writing in his *Journal* in April 1828, Scott joked about his talent for writing voluminous antiquarian notes, debating whether he should produce a Poetical Works of Hume, in which Hume's four lines of verse would be supported by notes to form a quarto volume: 'Gad, the booksellers would give me five hundred for it—I have a mind to print it for the Bannatynians.'[52] After the financial crash of 1825–6, when Scott was anxious to find ways of maximizing the earning potential of his existing publications, he took up the plan first suggested by Constable, of producing historical and biographical notes for the novels and reissuing them in an authoritative collected format. So began the Magnum Opus, first envisaged as 'light work' and now recognized as one of the most significant publishing ventures of the nineteenth century.[53] Having resumed 'a sort of parental control' over his earlier work, Scott proceeded to prepare accounts of the circumstances in which his novels had been composed, their sources in legend, family tradition, or obscure historical fact, and to provide a glossary and notes on customs and local superstitions.[54] The new venture was shaped in part by the exigencies of publishing, and it continues Scott's artistic preoccupation with the relationship between artistic products and their markets. When revising *Peveril of the Peak* for its expanded Magnum Opus format of three volumes, for example, he chose to add long notes rather than interfere too much with the text itself. He also developed the practice of creating 'pegs' in the text on which to hang notes, as demonstrated by additions to both *The Pirate* and *Peveril of the Peak*.[55] Yet the

[51] Edmund Spenser, *The Faerie Queene* (1590, 1596), II, Proem, i, ed. A. C. Hamilton, Longman Annotated English Poets (1977; corr. edn. London, 1980), 169.
[52] *Journal*, 452. In *The Antiquary*, Oldbuck proposes to provide notes for a work, 'The Caledoniad', without any text at all, *WN* v. 195–9, vi. 337.
[53] *Journal*, 48. For Constable's scheme, see also *Letters*, vii. 353, 354, 360.
[54] Quoted from Advertisement, *WN* i, p. i (Advertisement is separately paginated). See the general scheme of the Advertisement, i, pp. i–iv: and Scott's attitude to the compilation of notes, *Journal*, 62, 423, 566, 634.
[55] On *Peveril*, see Jane Millgate, 'Adding More Buckram: Scott and the Amplification of *Peveril of the Peak*', *English Studies in Canada*, xiii (1987), 174–81.

process of authoritative annotation was more than a lucrative publishing venture and a chance to revise his texts. It involved putting his life's work in order, making the Waverley Novels coherent as an interrelated series, and constructing around them his most ambitious system of support and defence; a complex historical, autobiographical, and scholarly frame.

One would think that the process by which a faceless author transformed himself into a coherent final authority and his works into the ultimate Standard Edition would have been the subject of sustained critical discussion. By any standards it is a striking metamorphosis. Like so many of Scott's oddities, however, it has been concealed partly by its effectiveness in influencing subsequent novelistic practice. Scott's authoritative re-possession of his works was so successful that it quickly came to seem entirely natural. The story of Jane Porter and the later editions of her novels (of which more soon) is a particularly clear instance of this. The oddity is worth emphasizing, however. No series of works before the Waverley Novels had been reissued by their author with a User's Guide. Critics sometimes assume that Scott expanded at such length on his life in order to fulfil a frustrated autobiographical bent. This is not autobiography told for its own sake, however, but a life appended to a work—a life re-created in the service of a work. Scott's autobiographical details serve as an explanatory structure for a series of novels, a process validated for literary criticism by Johnson's *Lives of the Poets* (a scheme which Scott had adapted in *Ballantyne's Novelist's Library*), but quite different when conducted by the author himself over forty-eight volumes of prose. *Biographia Literaria* and *The Prelude*, which aim to support philosophical and critical reflection by accounts of life and personality, offer the most appropriate parallels for Scott's system of self-presentation in the Magnum Opus. Yet there is an obvious difference between the kinds of criticism believed to be appropriate to the defensive strategies and elusiveness of Coleridge

The process of 'pegging' is further analysed by Millgate in *Scott's Last Edition* and illustrated by Iain Gordon Brown in *Scott's Interleaved Waverley Novels (The 'Magnum Opus': National Library of Scotland MSS. 23001–41): An Introduction and Commentary* (Aberdeen, 1987), 103. More generally, the entire venture of adding new notes and introductions has been regarded as a 'value-adding' exercise by Martin Green in *Dreams of Adventure, Deeds of Empire* (London, 1980), ch. 4, esp. p. 127.

or the Miltonic parallels which elevate and protect Wordsworth, and the approach which is assumed to be appropriate for Scott. Many critics have documented Coleridge's autobiographical strategies of defence and deferral. Few have paid much attention to Scott's.

For this reason, most of the space available in this section is necessarily devoted to the ways in which the re-marketing exercise of the Magnum Opus affects literary interpretations of Scott's novels. It is a neglected topic and one which requires careful attention to tone and detail. It also, however, requires some exploration of the contexts of literary fashion, for, like the more celebrated frames of the first editions, the introductions and notes of the Magnum Opus depend upon certain types of reader expectation and mingle innovation with established practice. Scott's new edition reflected as well as encouraged a growing taste for factual annotations which can clearly be seen in the works of some of the writers with whom Scott was most involved in the early stages of his writing career. The most immediate influence was the extensive annotation in the ballad and romance editing of Percy, Warton, and Ellis—a system of support and commentary normally associated, that is, with editions of other writers' works. Scott himself produced detailed notes to his contributions to Lewis's *Tales of Wonder*, as did Southey. Lewis's own sporadic and usually brief notes to *Tales of Wonder* include quotations of a paragraph or more from some major sources: they demonstrate, if not a painstaking determination to credit and explain, at least a desire to transfer such information as was immediately available from the personal knowledge of the author.[56] Closer approximation to Scott's practice is found in Southey's epic poems, which are heavily and precisely annotated. Their frame material does not work to establish Southey as a literary personality, however. Instead, it depersonalizes him, while emphasizing his scholarly authority. The title-page of *Roderick, the Last of the Goths* (1814),

---

[56] For his own contributions to *Tales of Wonder* Lewis provides notes on local tradition ('Bothwell's Bonny Jane', i. 5, 6); acknowledges sources and translations (to Herder's version of the 'Kiampe-Viiser', i. 31; Goethe, i. 51); comments on literary parallels ('Osric the Lion', i. 11); acknowledges alterations to the original version ('The Water-King', i. 60–1); chooses between versions ('Laidley Worm of Spindlestone Heughs', ii. 434); appends extracts from historical records ('Tam Lin', ii. 459): but there is no serious attempt at scholarship, as can be seen in the note to 'The Gay Gold Ring', i. 99–100.

for example, announces him as 'Poet Laureate, and Member of the Royal Spanish Academy'. The preface to *The Curse of Kehama* (1810) notes the unfamiliarity of Hindoo custom, and promises to make it intelligible for non-Orientalists. Southey then provides a table of the mythological names which the reader is required to recognize. With similar intentions, the prefaces of *Thalaba the Destroyer* (1801) and *Madoc* (1805) provide an outline of the main events or background of the tales. As a general rule, Southey makes little attempt to establish a personal anecdotal voice in these prefaces. Equally impersonal are Thomas Campbell's notes to the customs and history of American frontier settlements and the course of the War of Independence in *Gertrude of Wyoming* (1809), although, like Southey's, they rely for their effect on the assumption that they are a personal selection from a much wider preparatory reading.

In the early years of the nineteenth century, therefore, the tradition of annotation was used most frequently by *poets*, particularly those eager to present themselves as collectors and adaptors of ancient or esoteric traditions rather than to make direct claims for their own creativity. Even so, processes of authentication were varied but well-established in fictional and non-fictional prose writing of Scott's time. Important examples include Maria Edgeworth's *Castle Rackrent* and Lady Morgan's *The Wild Irish Girl*, but the instances chosen here are intended to give some sense of the specifically Scottish context which was available to Scott. Introducing *The Cottagers of Glenburnie* in 1808, Elizabeth Hamilton focuses her attention not on texts or sources but on readers and reactions, a tendency anticipated in her Burnsian subtitle, 'A Tale for the Farmer's Ingle-Nook'. Her 'Address to Hector MacNeill', which acts as preface, anticipates the disdain which her work will arouse in the wrong kind of reader. In a form of definition by reader, it works by suggesting that any failure to appreciate the novel is not the fault of the author. In her introduction to *Essays on the Superstitions of the Highlanders of Scotland* (1811), Anne Grant of Laggan specifically lays aside the pretence of scholarship to adopt a pose of deliberate amateurism, transformed by personal passion for her subject. Her authority is the result not of learning but of personal observation.[57] Colonel

---

[57] *Essays on the Superstitions of the Highlanders of Scotland: To which are added, Translations from the Gaelic; and Letters connected with those formerly published*, 2 vols. (London, 1811), 'To the Reader', i, pp. iii–iv.

Stewart of Garth's *Sketches of the Character, Manners, and Present State of the Highlanders of Scotland* (1822) contains a map of the clan territories, explanatory notes, and long appendices, yet in a brief preface outlining the circumstances under which the work had been undertaken, Stewart describes himself as 'a writer whose only qualification is a long and intimate knowledge of the subject, and of facts connected with it, conjoined with a great and earnest desire to do it justice'.[58] The preface noticeably plays down any pretensions to literary skill or imagination.

The most telling context of all for a study of Scott's work on the Magnum Opus is the career of Jane Porter, which interacts so interestingly with his in many ways. Porter was the inventor of the historical form adopted by Scott, in her eyes; and the literary betrayer of William Wallace, in his. The aspect of her work which is of significance here is the difference between the support-structures created for the early editions of her novels *Thaddeus of Warsaw* (1803) and *The Scottish Chiefs* (1810) and those created for later editions inspired in part by the Magnum Opus. Scott's example suggested to Porter a way of constructing a personal authority for fictionalizing history.

In contrast to the moralizing tone of the introduction to the first edition of *Thaddeus of Warsaw*, in which Porter presents her hero, the Polish general Kosciuszko, as a modern type of 'Magnanimity', the introduction to the edition printed in Bentley's Standard Novels in 1832, 'The Author to Her Friendly Readers', was planned to capitalize on the success of the Magnum Opus.[59] The plan was formed by Porter's publisher, but shaped the way in which she presented herself and her work. Porter takes every advantage of her work's established reputation, lauding its authenticity by quoting the approval of Kosciuszko himself, and reporting that another reliable authority had been convinced that she must have been an eyewitness of the events the novel describes. In a republication of this kind, Porter states, it is appropriate for the author to add introductory comments and notes 'illustrative of the

[58] *Sketches of the Character, Manners, and Present State of the Highlanders of Scotland: With Details of the Military Service of the Highland Regiments*, 2 vols. (Edinburgh, 1822), i, p. ix.
[59] *Thaddeus of Warsaw*, Standard Novels, No. 4, pp. xxiii–xxiv ('Preface to the First Edition of this Work'); pp. v–xvi ('The Author to Her Friendly Readers'), see esp. pp. v–vi. Millgate notes the special influence of the Magnum Opus on Bentley's Standard Novels in *Scott's Last Edition*, 98–9.

origin of the tale, of the historical events referred to in it, and of the actually living characters who constitute its personages'.[60] If this plan sounds just like the Magnum Opus, Porter goes on to strengthen the link, citing Scott's new edition as her model and commenting that by doing so she was repaying the compliment which he had paid her by writing in the genre of fictionalized historical biography.[61]

The first edition of *The Scottish Chiefs*, with its epigraph from Ossian, contains detailed annotation, mainly on historical information, but ranging fairly broadly over topography, local history, legend, and custom. In her introduction to this first edition, Porter emphasizes her thorough preparation, stating that she has 'spared no pains in consulting almost every writing extant which treats of the sister kingdoms during the period of my narrative'. Explaining that lack of space prevents her from annotating all that is worthy of annotation, she concludes with a direct appeal to personal effort: 'in one word I assure the reader that I seldom lead him to any spot in Scotland whither some written or oral testimony respecting my hero had not previously conducted myself'.[62] Porter insists that she has not added to her historical sources except in the interests of coherence and unity. She draws attention to the liberties taken with time and circumstance after Wallace's return from France, and in the management of the catastrophe.

The move towards a more strongly personalized system of historical verification is clear in the new preface written for the 1828 edition of *The Scottish Chiefs*, which offers, for example, her personal recollections of the discovery that Napoleon had placed a ban on her novel.[63] Later, Porter produced another new account of herself, the 'Retrospective Introduction' to the Standard Novels edition of *The Scottish Chiefs* in 1831, in which

---

[60] *Thaddeus of Warsaw*, Standard Novels, No. 4, p. v.

[61] Ibid., p. vi. Porter claims to have invented this form of historical fiction in *Thaddeus of Warsaw* (see p. vi). Porter's claim is ridiculed in a satirical piece, 'Letters to Certain Persons. Epistle I. To Miss Jane Porter', signed 'Peter Puff', *Aberdeen Magazine*, i (Oct. 1831), 552–7 (553): 'Believe us, Miss Porter, when we read this fine passage, we blushed as red as our morocco slippers at our disgraceful ignorance.'

[62] *The Scottish Chiefs: A Romance*, 5 vols. (London, 1810), i, pp. v–vi, x.

[63] The preface of the 1828 edn. is included in *The Scottish Chiefs: Revised, Corrected, and Illustrated with A New Retrospective Introduction, Notes, &c., By the Author* (London, 1840), 8–11.

she recalls hearing the tales on which the novel is based. Later still, for the more lavish 'Illustrated Edition' of 1840, she gave a much more ambitious and inclusive account, a 'Retrospective Preface' describing her friends, literary interests, and historical enthusiasms, including a description of her meeting with Scott and gratitude for his approval.[64] Again, this rush of authorial communicativeness is ascribed to the wishes of her new publisher, George Virtue, and to the wishes of readers who had expressed interest in how a lady came to write a tale of war (the 'where and when' of her inspiration, as she terms it).[65] The later introductions to Porter's novels suggest the direct influence of the Magnum Opus on the system of authentication through authorial reminiscence which, as Scott had shown, could anchor the authority of the historical novelist.

With the practices of other annotators in mind, one turns to the extensive re-modelling of the Magnum Opus and to the notes which one critic has seen as 'sensibly Johnsonian' exercises in self-defence.[66] As will already be apparent, annotation and scholarly introductory materials may serve political, didactic, and socially normative functions. They may persuade the reader, for example, that a bizarre fictional incident is true to the reality of history, or that seemingly unimportant events or people had an impact on the development of nations. They may help to construct a culture and its history. They may be directly combative, arguing that the version of events given by another writer is false or partisan. Significant exchanges between writers take place in footnotes and introductions, and Scott's work, from the *Minstrelsy* to the Magnum Opus, is no exception. In the following discussion, however, the explanatory and introductory material for the Magnum Opus is considered in terms of its literary impact, its persuasiveness in supporting particular interpretations of individual novels, and in creating a main direction for Scott's work as a whole. Once again, Scott's unwillingness to commit himself to any single

[64] *The Scottish Chiefs* (1840 edn.), 12–50, esp. 38–9 (on Scott).
[65] Ibid. 12.
[66] In *Realistic Imagination*, 8, Levine comments: 'Scott defensively bolsters his fictions with footnotes and lexicons, urging the possibility of even the most fantastic elements of his narrative, the historical sources for each major incident, the rightness of the decor and the everyday objects that fill his pages.' Levine takes the frames, with Scott's anonymity and fondness for writing in disguise, as evidence of the defensiveness 'reenacted everywhere in his novels' (p. 81).

version of facts stimulates his need to tell stories. The Magnum Opus introductions and notes are more accurately viewed as corollary fictions than as a straitjacket of information.

The opening gambit of the Magnum Opus is the creation of a narrating and authenticating personality, a sober presence who, as already noted, feels the need to regret the 'hoity toity, whisky frisky' pertness of his earlier manner. Personality comes to dominate the Magnum Opus just as much as anonymity had dominated the first editions. The new persona of the Author is deceptive because one of its most immediate characteristics is a tone of personal communicativeness, self-consciously dramatized in his shift from the third person to the first person in the first two paragraphs of the General Preface. Scott describes specific personal memories—of his meetings with David Ritchie and Robert Paterson, of his friendship with Mrs Murray Keith, of his childhood impressions of Jean Gordon and Andrew Gemmells, of the family servant Dumb Lizzie who parallels the feigned muteness of Fenella—which are introduced casually, 'considering these illustrations as a sort of gallery, open to the reception of any thing which may elucidate former manners, or amuse the reader'.[67] This ease, however, conceals important redefinition, both of himself and of the novels. Scott's persona of unpretentious, plain, tolerant, modest man of letters with a predilection for antiquarian obscurantism directs his public towards certain aspects of his writing and away from others. The introductions of the Magnum Opus lay down the way in which Scott now wanted his novels to be read: as historical yet romantic, thoroughly researched but carelessly written. To adapt Robert Shortreed's famous remark, Scott might be said to have been re-'makin' himsell a' the time' in the introductions, transforming his life, reading, opinions, and antiquarian possessions into a supportive structure for his fictions. In the footnotes which back up his account of the Porteous riots in *The Heart of Midlothian*, for example, Scott offers personal memories in reinforcement of his fiction. In the first edition of the novel, one passage from the riot scenes emphasizes: 'Persons are yet living who remember to have heard from the mouths of ladies thus

<hr/>

[67] *WN* v, pp. xvi–xvii. Some sense of the effect of Scott's personal recollections in the Magnum Opus frames can be found by contrasting them with the collection of source material given as introduction to *Count Robert of Paris* by Lockhart during Scott's illness.

interrupted on their journey in the manner we have described.'[68] For the Magnum Opus, Scott adds a footnote which begins: 'A near relation of the author's used to tell of having been stopped by the rioters, and escorted home in the manner described.'[69] In the same novel, he wryly breaks off another note tracing the links between his family and the Quakers, 'lest the reader should remonstrate that his desire to know the Author of Waverley never included a wish to be acquainted with his whole ancestry'.[70] The humorous exit is disarming and the autobiographical detail shrugged off, but Scott has quietly made the point that he can be trusted with Quaker tradition.

However soothing or self-mocking their narratorial tones, the notes included in the Magnum Opus edition can unsettle reader expectations and sometimes openly disrupt the compact between narrator and reader which Scott is so fond of citing. The desire for certainty is continually deflected by the narrative and its support-ing wealth of annotation. The impression of solidity which it creates is false: the whole structure is flimsy, and each part is set against others which at the same time it contributes to support. For example, Scott presents Charles Edward Stewart in the fiction of *Waverley* or *Redgauntlet*, then mutinies by citing contradictory interpretations in the notes and introductions. While insisting that he personally has no high opinion of the worth of his fiction, he manages to persuade the reader that, after a cool perusal of the evidence, his own interpretation is after all the fairest and most probable. It is difficult for a reader either to resist this persuasiveness or to isolate anything which might incrimi-nate Scott's knowledge, judgement, or sensibility. Like Pattieson's account of his impartial ordering of *The Black Dwarf* and *Old Mortality*, this impression of presenting all the facts encourages readers to trust him, all the more so because they believe that Scott is not denying their right to disagree. As Punter remarks in his analysis of the appearance of Alice's ghost in *The Bride of Lammermoor*, they feel that Scott has nothing to gain by deceit. In fact, Scott undermines these tactics every time he gives as

---

[68] *Tales of My Landlord, Second Series, Collected and Arranged by Jedediah Cleishbotham, Schoolmaster and Parish-Clerk of Gandercleugh*, 4 vols. (Edinburgh, 1818), i. 147–8.
[69] WN xi. 251 n.
[70] WN xi. 161.

authority 'Old Play', or a misquotation from an author. This penchant for false authentication (which he derives ultimately from Cervantes) can be interpreted harshly, and Scott has been accused on the evidence of the chapter-mottoes alone of 'intentionally fooling his readers, treating them as blockheads and being "entertained" by their bewilderment'.[71] The sense of personal betrayal in this accusation suggests how important the illusion of Scott's reliability has come to seem. In fact, the Magnum Opus is full of warnings about the historical novelist's trustworthiness.

Another way of highlighting the construction of personality and its artistic purposes is to examine Scott's gradual assembling of the authority of his ancestors. It is a commonplace that Scott was proud of his ancestry and connections. In the introductions and notes of the Magnum Opus he lends weight and dignity to their history, according it a central place in the broader Scottish history depicted in his novels, and giving himself a right to comment on the politics, religious crises, and manners of the Scottish past. He names ancestors whose fortunes were caught up in Jacobitism, in Covenanting times, in the Douglas wars, and in the Reformation; and in doing so he confers on himself a kind of authority in discussing them. '[T]here are few in Scotland, under the titled nobility, who could trace their blood to so many stocks of historical distinction', writes Lockhart in his *Life of Scott*, taking up these hints.[72] References to his reading and legal training serve a similar function. In the context of the Magnum Opus, Scott's descriptions of himself as a boy, wrapped up in his own imaginative world and avidly reading Spenser, Percy's *Reliques of Ancient English Poetry*, Froissart, and histories of Scotland, are functional rather than incidental. They also have a way of making fiction and fact interdependent, for Scott anchors the description of his boyhood reading by likening himself to his own fictional creation, Edward Waverley. When appended to a collection of novels, such descriptions are more than merely an exercise in personal taste. The personality of the author is set up as a unifying device as thoroughly as had been the evasion of personality between 1814 and 1826.

---

[71] Dieter A. Berger, '"Damn the Mottoe": Scott and the Epigraph', *Anglia*, c (1982), 373–96 (397, where the charge is linked to Scott's contempt for his craft). On the false attributions and inventions, see also Tom B. Haber, 'The Chapter Tags in the Waverley Novels', *PMLA* xlv (1930), 1140–9.

[72] Lockhart, i. 85.

In effect, the system of aesthetic definition and personal defence developed in the first editions was replaced in the Magnum Opus by one which it is even more difficult for readers to refute or dismiss. This throws into doubt recent critical characterizations of the edition as (variously) a public-spirited or a self-fulfilling enterprise. Jane Millgate's study of the Magnum Opus suggests that it repaid a debt to the public as well as being a 'repossession' of the work of the 'Author of Waverley'; and despite her sharp insight into the guises of the first editions, Judith Wilt argues: 'The prefaces of the magnum opus edition, so disarmingly revelatory of the history of the stories, so sweetly candid about the history of their composition by Walter Scott, finally allow him to claim his property.'[73] The Magnum Opus is certainly 'revelatory', and certainly a type of 'repossession' or claiming of property. If we are to consider its 'disarming' qualities, however, it is worth considering what exactly is being disarmed, and why.

The introductions and notes written for the Magnum Opus develop a series of defensive strategies for the fictions by appealing to various forms of literary, historical, and biographical authority. Literary defences of The Monastery, for example, include appeals to de la Motte Fouqué in defence of the White Lady and to Shakespeare in defence of the Euphuist. Some introductions are devoted to defence of one serious historical inaccuracy, as are Peveril of the Peak, which has to explain why it makes the Countess of Derby a Roman Catholic, and Anne of Geierstein, with its lengthy extracts from Palgrave on the practices and history of the Vehme Gericht. The Heart of Midlothian quotes not only the information given in a letter from Helen Goldie, but also further correspondence between Scott and her daughter on Goldie's later enquiries, and John McDiarmid's Sketches from Nature on the original case of Helen Walker. Scott states that these details are given so that the reader may judge the extent and success of his alterations, being careful, as one might now expect, to claim that he has marred the simplicity of Goldie's account. Scott has a habit of assuring the reader that his is an inferior version of a really good story, which others have told well. In this way, he describes

---

[73] Millgate, Scott's Last Edition, ch. 8 (p. 114), in an excellent discussion of the function of the Magnum Opus edition as a final testament to Scott's career; Wilt, Secret Leaves, 186. Also pertinent are Robert Mayer's comments in 'The Internal Machinery Displayed: The Heart of Midlothian and Scott's Apparatus for the Waverley Novels', Clio, xvii (1987), 1–20.

how his aunt Margaret Rutherford narrated 'My Aunt Margaret's Mirror', and how Anna Seward narrated 'The Tapestried Chamber'. This tendency, apparently so modest, disarms criticism, for, amid the flaws of Scott's narration, the story itself is preserved as genuinely interesting.

Sometimes, the very different introductions provided for the first edition and the Magnum Opus perform comparable functions in directing literary interpretation. As already stated, the Advertisement to the first edition of *Rob Roy* explains that the Author has received through his publishers a parcel of papers with the request that he prepare them for publication. His revisions have been so extensive, however, that 'the work may in a great measure be said to be new written'.[74] For the Magnum Opus, Scott replaces the pretence of editing a manuscript with one of the longest of his historical authentications, the history of Rob Roy and the fortunes of the Macgregors. However, both frames (memoirs of a banker and memoirs of a thief) give the narrative the effect of pre-arranged structure which is beyond the author's jurisdiction.[75] Each frame, moreover, privileges a different aspect of the novel. The Advertisement to the first edition, however conventional it may be thought as a ploy of authorial evasion, is entirely appropriate to the special experiment of *Rob Roy*, the experiment in first-person narration. Scott writes the novel in the form of a personal memoir, and invents in his frame a correspondent who sends it, via his publishers, to be edited. The frame, slight though it may be, reinforces the sense of Frank Osbaldistone's memoirs as *private*, penned for Will Tresham alone and submitted after his death for the attention of a suitable editor. In the Magnum Opus, Scott writes in the historical introduction the account of Rob Roy which he had not originally chosen to include in the novel, and which had been thought conspicuous by its absence. Significantly,

---

[74] *WN* vii, p. iv. Gilbert J. French and W. J. Fitzpatrick believed in the frame of *Rob Roy*, and cite it as evidence that in some of the novels Scott was merely an editor of other men's work. See French, *Enquiry*, 39–44; Fitzpatrick, *Who Wrote the Waverley Novels? Being an Investigation into Certain Mysterious Circumstances Attending their Production, and an Inquiry into the Literary Aid which Sir Walter Scott may have Received from Other Persons* (London, 1856), 51.

[75] See the important assumption in the Macgregor history that 'No introduction can be more appropriate to the work', *WN* vii, p. vii. My interpretation concurs with Millgate's argument that the details about Rob Roy were given in order to justify in retrospect the choice of the title (*Scott's Last Edition*, 82–3).

Scott begins by telling how he came to choose *Rob Roy* as his title, justifying it as essentially a good marketing tactic ('The title ... was suggested by the late Mr Constable, whose sagacity and experience foresaw the germ of popularity which it included').[76] This marketable title, however, creates certain expectations which are not entirely fulfilled by the memoirs of Frank Osbaldistone. As if aware of a contract unfulfilled, Scott now tells the 'true story', as far as it may be ascertained, of his peculiarly marginal central character. Scott never missed an opportunity to expand on historical evidence, of course. What matters here, however, is the effect his new editorial direction has on the novel. The decision to highlight Rob Roy has a double effect. It refocuses the tale, away from the psychology of its anxious narrator and towards the more public social significance of Rob Roy's way of life. At the same time, this decision liberates the novel, defusing from the start any mounting irritations that a work so enticingly titled should make so little for so long of its star attraction. Paradoxically, the Magnum Opus introduction clears the way for a private narrative which it simultaneously marginalizes.

The introductions also, like the first-edition frames, set literary agenda. Many defend or explain Scott's choice of subject or characterization. He defends himself against the charge that Norna of the Fitful Head is merely an inferior copy of Meg Merrilies, for example. More generally, they emphasize particular aspects of the novel. In his reflections on *Guy Mannering*, Gilbert French accuses Scott of deliberately concealing major debts to the Annesley case (*Memoirs of an Unfortunate Young Nobleman*, published in the *Gentleman's Magazine* in 1743).[77] Scott's introduction concentrates upon the tale of the astrologer, as related by an old Highland servant of his father. The tale of John MacKinlay

---

[76] *WN* vii, p. vii. The advantages and disadvantages of the 'taking title' are further discussed in the context of Mary, Queen of Scots as subject in the Magnum Opus introduction to *The Abbot*, *WN* xx, pp. xii–xiii.

[77] *Parallel Passages from Two Tales Elucidating the Origin of the Plot of Guy Mannering*, ed. G. J. French (Manchester, 1855), pp. iii–ix. French's pamphlet provoked furious reviews, but W. J. Fitzpatrick insisted that Lockhart was unable to refute the case it made. When reporting the story about Galloway gipsies and an astrologer, passed on to Scott by Joseph Train, Lockhart suggests that these two sources of *Guy Mannering* (Scott's own memories of MacKinlay and Train's anecdote) may have been strengthened by a third, a recollection of a Durham ballad (Lockhart, v. 4–5).

emphasizes the legendary and wonderful rather than the social and legal aspects of the story. It also adds the important new suggestion of spiritual struggle, which Scott then qualifies by providing a sociological account of gypsies and a personal account of his childhood memories of them. The introduction chooses to tell a modern fairytale instead of a modern legal case, with the result that the reader approaches the story of *Guy Mannering* with a sense of the marvellous and the providential, a suitable preparation for the mysterious opening sequence of the novel. In contrast, the introduction to *The Antiquary* provides facts and figures about the status of Bedesmen. It seems obvious that Scott should have wanted to write at length about Bedesmen. Given the enthusiastic critical reception of the Mucklebackit scenes, however, an account of the social station of fishing families would have been equally appropriate. For all its apparent ease and eclecticism, the introduction to *The Antiquary* makes the role of Edie Ochiltree central to the novel, emphasizes his classlessness, and elevates him into a source of moral and historical authority. He has performed this role ever since. The detailed account of Robert Paterson in the introduction to *Old Mortality*, which extends to a list of expenses found in his pocket book, serves a comparable function.

The two novels which make up the Third Series of *Tales of My Landlord* (*The Bride of Lammermoor* and *A Legend of Montrose*) are given significantly different types of historical introduction in 1830. In the Magnum Opus version of *The Bride of Lammermoor*, the gossip's tale given as inspiration for Dick Tinto's sketch in chapter 1 is supplemented in the introduction by several different versions of the Dalrymple story in contemporary and near-contemporary accounts. The primary implication of these different versions is that the death of a Lord President's daughter may be domestic, but the story telling it must be political. In contrast, the introduction to *A Legend of Montrose* traces with historical precision the deadly feud between Lord Kilpont and James Stewart of Ardvoirlich. Scott quotes Monro and Turner, whose memoirs were published by the Bannatyne Club, as authority for Dalgetty. Two appendices quote from Alexander Boswell's 'Clan Alpin's Vow' (1811) and from the Act of the Privy Council, 1589, on the heritage of the 'Children of the Mist'. A postscript scrupulously records a letter to Scott from Robert Stewart of Ardvoirlich, differing from Bishop Wishart's account of Kilpont's death. The accumulation of evidence from several points of view tends to implicate Scott only in the historical parts of *A Legend of Montrose*, rather than in the marvellous and doom-laden associations of Allan McAulay's character. *The Bride of Lammermoor* and *A Legend of Montrose* demonstrate that the topics raised in the introductions to the Magnum Opus can be as thoughtfully tailored to the requirements of the individual novels as were those of the first editions.

The first epigraph to this section of the chapter quoted part of the advice given to Cervantes by his friend in the Prologue to *Don Quixote*, Part 1. Cervantes is advised that he can cite whatever authorities he likes because no reader will go to the trouble of consulting them. Scott sometimes works on a similar principle. In the introduction to the Magnum Opus version of *The Betrothed*, he explains that he chose the wars between the Welsh and the Norman lords of the Marches 'as a period when all freedoms might be taken with the strict truth of history without encountering any well-known fact, which might render the narrative improbable'.[78] He then quotes from a Haighhall manuscript citing the 'Noble Moringer' and refers the reader for further details to Roby's *Traditions of Lancashire*. This has a perfunctory air, and it is clear that historical learning is not strictly necessary for enjoyment of the story. The introductions of the Magnum Opus are full of such feints, which rather incline the reader to accept the novels as he or she finds them than to check their details meticulously against a wealth of historical documentation. As Scott states in *Marmion*, there comes a point at which the reader must leave documentation aside:

> Such acts to chronicles I yield;
>   Go seek them there, and see:
> Mine is a tale of Flodden Field,
>   And not a history.—[79]

Similarly, the historical documentation in the notes and introduction to *Woodstock* (so full that the introduction has an appendix of two pamphlets which has its own separate preface) seems curiously detached from the fiction it introduces. In the introduction, Scott explains that, after renewed research, he now

---

[78] *WN* xxxvii, p. xvi.   [79] *PW* vii. 287.

knows more about the incidents of 1649 described in the novel than he did when he wrote it, yet he uses this new information not to revise the fiction but to provide scholarly additions about historical documents.[80] Such introductions support the fictions in a way which affects to make them more believable but which also rarefies and elevates them as art. They at once limit the imagination by surrounding it with physical and historical details, and increase the mystery of artistic inspiration, the process by which the details can be seen to have been combined to make the very different fiction which the reader encounters in the novel. Scott at once controls the reader's imagination and elevates his own, since so full a display of the raw materials of fiction cannot but remind the reader of the creative power which has so transformed them.

At this point it is instructive to return to *The Fair Maid of Perth* and to see what Scott chose to add to that novel's highly evocative though tangential first-edition frame. Only three years separate the salesman of the Infallible Detergent Elixir (1828) from the new frame of the Magnum Opus (the introduction is dated 15 August 1831), yet the interpretative parameters set by the two frames are interestingly different. In the first edition of *The Fair Maid of Perth*, Croftangry sets himself up in mock-heroic fashion as the preserver of the past against the encroachments of insensitive innovation, while also distinguishing himself as historical romancer from historians whose main concerns must be evidence and accuracy. In Mrs Baliol's phrase, he is not a lamp but a magic lantern, conjuring rather than illuminating the past. The much briefer introduction to the Magnum Opus also marks out territory for its author. Scott notes that 'although the press had of late years teemed with various descriptions concerning the Scottish Gael', no one had yet intruded on the specific territory of this novel. Moreover, he claims, the central incident of the battle of the clans on the Inch of Perth in 1396 is well attested, forming a suitable subject on which to 'hinge' a romantic tale. Scott also takes the opportunity to engage with dissertations on the identity of the clans published in the wake of his novel. The concentration

---

[80] *WN* xxxix, pp. iv, xvii–xxi. The introd. and notes to *Woodstock*, the last novel to be republished in the Magnum Opus format during Scott's lifetime, were written in illness and some confusion. This may, in part, explain the reluctance to revise in accordance with the material discovered in the British Museum. See Iain Gordon Brown's comments, *Interleaved Waverley Novels*, 126.

on sources of the tale of the battle of the clans, which brings Wyntoun, Boece, Buchanan, and others into play, makes this climactic incident much more the centrepiece of the novel than it might have seemed in the first edition. There, the emphasis, rather disturbingly for Scott, falls on the consequences of unstable monarchy. Here, the confrontation becomes more specific, less threateningly generic. As in *The Betrothed*, however, the plethora of supporting references and cited authorities finally works to excuse readers any further investigation: 'Out of this jumble what Sassenach can pretend *dare lucem*?'[81] Scott also notes, though in a typically understated manner, the mingling of history and literary convention in the written sources of his tale. After quoting at length from the account of the battle of the clans in the *Scotichronicon*, he notes: 'The scene is heightened with many florid additions by Boece and Leslie, and the contending savages in Buchanan utter speeches after the most approved pattern of Livy.'[82] This is a timely reminder that the historical sources he has so lavishly quoted themselves follow literary rules. While seeming to subordinate his own romantic tale to more weighty historical accounts, he simultaneously questions any such simple division between true source and romantic elaboration. Also of interest is the new direction suggested for interpretation of the novel by Scott's expansion on the psychology of his central characters, especially the cowardice displayed by Conachar. Citing Joanna Baillie as authority and inspiration, Scott makes the novel into less of a romantic history and more of a study in psychology.[83]

Systems of annotation were common before Scott, especially in the genre of epic romance typified by Southey, and the system of defence through autobiographical annotation became increasingly common after the publication of the Magnum Opus. Scott's special contribution lay in his ability to fuse a fact with an interesting moment of reading, to personalize an impersonal tradition. After the Magnum Opus, historical novelists rapidly began

[81] *WN* xlii, p. vii.

[82] *WN* xlii, p. xi.

[83] Lockhart was involved in revising Scott's new materials for the last eight volumes of the Magnum Opus. The manuscript of the introduction to *The Fair Maid of Perth* (in the National Library of Scotland) suggests extensive redrafting by Lockhart before the published version, but the material included was Scott's choice. See Millgate, *Scott's Last Edition*, 59.

to record the links between their own lives and personalities and the historical material they had gathered, and the combination has come to seem obvious and natural. The reader re-creates a personality as authority and explanation for a group of novels, and Scott is still discussed primarily within the terms which he established in the Magnum Opus. For this reason it is vital to recognize the specialized nature of this re-created image, the significance of its positioning (as described earlier, a Life appended to a Works, a User's Guide for the all-important standard edition), and the types of literary interpretation which it implicitly (and sometimes explicitly) endorses.

As persuasive devices and guides to interpretation, therefore, the paratexts of the Magnum Opus continue rather than expiate the 'liberties' taken under the guise of anonymity in the first editions. Reviewing Godwin's novel *Cloudesley* for the *Edinburgh Review* in April 1830, Hazlitt contrives to implicate both Scott and Godwin in a contrast ostensibly introduced to expose Godwin's short-comings as a novelist: 'Mr. Godwin has unfortunately no resources but his genius. He has no Edie Ochiltree at his elbow.'[84] Five years earlier, in *The Spirit of the Age*, he had declared that Scott was 'only the amanuensis of truth and history'. At least, in the review of *Cloudesley*, Scott manages to achieve something like equality with Ochiltree as the source of his work. In both comments, however, Scott is denied, and protected from, absolute responsibility for what he writes. The move from the first editions of the Waverley Novels before the acknowledgement of authorship in 1827 to the personalized voice of the Magnum Opus may be compared to the move from Hazlitt's view of Scott in 1825 as only an amanuensis to his image of Scott in 1830, writing with the voice of folk tradition (and folk common sense) at his elbow. As the discussions of individual Waverley Novels in the following three chapters will show, however, Scott's work contains many more voices and styles than would be approved by Edie Ochiltree, and a strain of conscious literariness which is never quite accounted for in the Magnum Opus's personalized and naturalized portrait of the artist.

---

[84] Repr. as 'Mr. Godwin' in *Works*, xvi. 393–408 (407). On p. 401 Hazlitt repeats the idea that Scott is an amanuensis of reality, and expands it with the suggestion that truth and nature shine through him as though he were transparent.

4
Secrecy, Silence, and Anxiety: Gothic Narratology and the Waverley Novels

What is this secret sin; this untold tale,
That art cannot extract, nor penance cleanse?[1]

They dare not murder me,—they dare not incarcerate me;—
they are answerable to the court to which I have appealed for
my forthcoming,—they dare not be guilty of any violence.

(Monçada, *Melmoth the Wanderer*)[2]

WHEN Edie Ochiltree is not sitting at his elbow Scott writes stories structured by loss, anxiety, and what is called in *Peveril of the Peak* 'the influence of undefinable apprehension'.[3] It would be easy, given the common critical association of Gothic, repression, and the unconscious, to make these stories into subtexts of the Waverley Novels, 'buried letters' of the type Mary Jacobus has proposed for the workings of Gothic in *Villette*.[4] This chapter and the two which follow propose instead to interpret individual Waverley Novels in some detail without presupposing any such aesthetic ranking or blurring the distinction between the claims that Scott uses Gothic devices to represent anxiety and that Gothic can in any way be equated with Scott's personal fears. Before turning in Chapter 5 to a consideration of the political implications of Scott's use of Gothic, the argument aims first to establish that imitation, parody, and extension of Gothic conventions in the Waverley Novels help Scott to construct some of the non-authorial and even anti-authorial voices described in the previous chapter. The discussion of *The Pirate*, *Rob Roy*, and *Peveril of the Peak* in this chapter focuses on the techniques (not lapses) of tone, narrative structure, description, and interior monologue by which

[1] Horace Walpole, *The Mysterious Mother: A Tragedy* (London, 1781), I. iii. 8.
[2] *Melmoth*, ii. 31.
[3] WN xxix. 186.
[4] 'The Buried Letter: *Villette*' (1979), repr. in *Reading Woman: Essays in Feminist Criticism* (London, 1986), 41–61.

Scott both raises and controls interpretations of the social world which sharply contradict the interpretations endorsed by his rational authorial voice. From this discussion two points emerge most strongly. One is that Scott's narrative techniques of deferral and denial have much in common with Gothic, and are used with a complex alertness to their literary signification. This is particularly true of the manipulation of secrets and narratorial secrecy, and it reinforces the argument that when looking for the impact made by Gothic on the Waverley Novels critics must attend to technique and tone as well as to events and settings. All Scott's plots depend upon the preservation then unravelling of secrets, although few go so far as *Kenilworth*, which can be read as an allegory of secrecy, as a cautionary tale about what happens when a man compromises with truth and plain-dealing, and when the secret (Amy) to which he rashly commits himself bursts out of his control. The second main point is that Scott, so often censured for a supposed shallowness in psychological representation, is much more versatile and resourceful as an analyst of states of mind than he first appears.

The first section of Chapter 2 analysed the methods developed in Gothic fiction to ritualize 'not secrets . . . but Secrecy', in Kermode's formulation. This process in Gothic is self-consciously literary, bolstered by close reference to other texts. The first epigraph to this chapter, the plea for explanation in Walpole's play about incest, *The Mysterious Mother* (1781), became a favourite point of reference in later Gothic fiction, used to suggest both the fearfulness and the inexpressibility of the secrets around which literary Gothic is plotted. A constant point of reference in Radcliffe's *The Romance of the Forest* and *The Italian*, the 'untold tale' of 'secret sin' hints at the forbidden subject of incest (between Montalt and Adeline, Schedoni and Ellena) with which both novels flirt, but which they finally evade.[5] More generally, novelists used the promise of the 'untold tale' both as a stimulus to readers' curiosity and as an acknowledgement of the limits of the fictional 'art' which could never hope to satisfy it. Although all narratives depend upon a degree of secrecy, Gothic novels are particularly dominated by the sense of 'secret sin', the unutterable or unnar-

---

[5] *Italian*, chs. 1, 4, 9; *Romance of Forest*, ch. 2.

ratable source of mystery which must remain safely beyond the bounds of fiction.

The Waverley Novels, likewise, hint repeatedly at horrors which they do not enact, and build mysterious plots around the silence (willed or enforced) of key characters. In order to do this they employ techniques of deferral and delay which owe much to the example of Gothic; and they also develop ways of suggesting forms of free-floating anxiety, best analysed by Alexander Welsh in his discussion of *Rob Roy*, which again have much in common with the construction of fear in Radcliffean Gothic. Secret sins and unvoiced (what *Melmoth the Wanderer* terms 'unutterable') fears are traceable to many of the same narratorial ploys and habits of imaginative reference. A simple and striking instance may be found in the passage in *The Fortunes of Nigel* in which the Lady Hermione relates her life-story to Margaret Ramsay and delays its crisis by lingering over insignificant details:

'It is only,' said the Lady Hermione, 'because I linger like a criminal on the scaffold, and would fain protract the time that must inevitably bring on the final catastrophe. Yes, dearest Margaret, I rest and dwell on the events of that journey, marked as it was by fatigue and danger, though the road lay through the wildest and most desolate deserts and mountains, and though our companions, both men and women, were fierce and lawless themselves, and exposed to the most merciless retaliation from those with whom they were constantly engaged—yet would I rather dwell on these hazardous events than tell that which awaited me at Saint Jean de Luz.'[6]

The long sentence, elaborating on details of the journey, delays the moment when Hermione must instantiate Dalgarno's villainy. When, anticipating many other readers, Maria Edgeworth complained of Scott's tendency to 'huddle the cards together in such a shameless manner' at the end of his novels, she responded to a structural pattern characteristic of fictions based on secrets, seen here in miniature in Hermione's effort to expand on every detail except the one her listener wants to hear.[7]

There are close technical links, therefore, between narratorial delay (the 'huddled' structure), secrecy-driven plotting, and the

---

[6] *WN* xxvii. 50–1.
[7] In a letter of Jan. 1824 about *St Ronan's Well*, quoted in *Letters*, viii. 142 n.

suggestion, but not explication, of anxiety. By bringing these closer together in the following discussion I hope also to question one of the most common and most damaging of all complaints about Scott: that is, that he did not understand, or did not care to investigate, the workings of the mind in states of anger, obsession, neurosis, or desire. Lukács, as usual, pronounces decisively on the matter: 'Scott does not command the magnificent, profound psychological dialectics of character which distinguishes the novel of the last great period of bourgeois development.'[8] A belief in Scott's 'sunny' disposition may have been useful for writers who, like Carlyle, wished to attack the morbid tendencies of modern literature. For twentieth-century critics, however, accustomed to praise different (and equally conventional) methods of psychological examination in fiction, Scott has sometimes seemed embarrassingly inadequate. Even for Carlyle, the conviction that Scott was 'a genius *in extenso*, as we may say, not *in intenso*' limited his artistic standing.[9] Virginia Woolf, reappraising Scott at a time when his work was out of fashion among critics, had to conclude that he was 'not among the great observers of the intricacies of the heart'.[10] David Cecil agreed: 'Scott was no analyst.'[11] Scott himself made coy asides referring to this supposed deficiency. 'I like so little to analyze the complication of the causes which influence actions', he demurs (thinking of Fielding) in the first chapter of *The Antiquary*.[12] The aside in *The Antiquary* is clearly misleading, however. Scott does deal with the darker aspects of psychology, but in order to preserve the usefulness of his rational narrative persona he is obliged to find alternative, extra-narratorial ways of exploring them. If one leaves aside for a moment the complications introduced by fictional contexts, the technique can be seen quite clearly at work in Scott's private writings. When obliged to describe distressing experiences in his own life in his letters and *Journal* he uses a distinctive language of literary refer-

---

[8] Lukács, *Historical Novel*, 34.
[9] Carlyle, *Works*, xxix. 35.
[10] Woolf, *Collected Essays*, 4 vols. (London, 1966–7), i. 142.
[11] Cecil, *Scott*, 36.
[12] *WN* v. 13. David Craig links this to Scott's supposed unwillingness to examine his own psychology, in *Scottish Literature and the Scottish People*, 311. Kurt Wittig notes that Scott does not pry into 'the dark abysses of its deepest passions', *The Scottish Tradition in Literature* (Edinburgh, 1958), 221.

ence and suggestion, overstatement and cliché. A friend's disgrace leads him to reflect in the *Journal*:

It is a mercy our thoughts are conceald from each other. O if at our social table we could see what passes in each bosom around we would seek dens and caverns to shun human society. To see the projector trembling for his falling speculations, the voluptuary ruing the event of his debauchery, the miser wearing out his soul for the loss of a guinea—all—all bent upon vain hopes and vainer regrets—we should not need to go to the hall of the Caliph Vathek to see men's hearts broiling under their black veils.[13]

In this passage, Scott progressively distances himself from the immediate cause of his abhorrence by making it increasingly figurative and literary. He first imagines other examples which elaborate his friend's disgrace but which also place it in a more general moral context. Here he is close to the practice of eighteenth-century moralists and ultimately to the evocative style of the pulpit. Then he uses literary precedent (*Vathek*) and exaggerated literary language ('hearts broiling under their black veils') as a form of protection by exaggeration. Elsewhere in his personal writings, Scott imagines the conflicts between abstracted qualities of the mind in strikingly literary ways, some of which resemble the common elements of his own novels. Trying to express his feelings about the suicide of his friend Huxley, for example, he writes in his *Journal* in December 1826:

A thousand fearful images and dire suggestions glance along the mind when it is moody and discontented with itself. Command them to stand and shew themselves and you presently assert the power of reason over imagination. But if by any strange alterations in one's nervous system you lost for a moment the talisman which controuls these fiends? Would they not terrify into obedience with their mandates rather [than] we would dare longer to endure their presence?[14]

This passage, sparked by the experience of a vivid nightmare, echoes a passage from the fictional journal of Darsie Latimer in *Redgauntlet*, written eighteen months earlier. In turn, both

---

[13] *Journal*, 236–7. Scott was probably reacting to the Heber scandal, which he reports, *Journal*, 162.
[14] *Journal*, 253 (Scott's attempt to deal with his thoughts of Huxley's suicide, which he describes in terms of macabre compulsion: see his nightmares about Huxley, pp. 247–8). For Scott's growing fear of madness and loss of control, see also pp. 615, 621, 632.

passages recall Clarence's account of his dream in the first act of *Richard III* ('Methoughts I saw a thousand fearful wracks ...').[15]

Scott uses comparable techniques of detachment followed by literary exaggeration at emotional crisis-points in his fiction. Faced simultaneously with emotional and linguistic collapse, characters search, like Scott in his *Journal*, for a 'talisman' by which to control the fiends of imagination. This talisman is as much linguistic as rational. Their passivity being strongly linked to an inability to speak effectively, they are reduced, like *Rob Roy*'s Frank Osbaldistone, to outbursts of childish passion rendered in self-consciously literary terms:

> Heaven knows, it was not apathy which loaded my frame and my tongue so much, that I could neither return Miss Vernon's half embrace, nor even answer her farewell. The word, though it rose to my tongue, seemed to choke in my throat like the fatal *guilty*, which the delinquent who makes it his plea knows must be followed by the doom of death.... I felt the tightening of the throat and breast, the *hysterica passio* of poor Lear; and, sitting down by the wayside, I shed a flood of the first and most bitter tears which had flowed from my eyes since childhood.[16]

Frank Osbaldistone's inability to grasp the reality of his youthful experiences is to some extent a special feature of his individual personality.[17] Even so, the way in which Frank describes his outburst of emotion, veering away from the uncomfortably personal to the safely literary (*King Lear*), has much in common with distinctive habits of Scott's narrative technique throughout the Waverley Novels. The intrusion of possibly incongruous literary references does not always work so abruptly to defuse moments of horror as does the sudden appearance of Fang and Snare in the climactic confrontation from *Melmoth the Wanderer* described in Chapter 2, but it works on the same principle of literary transgression.

Frank Osbaldistone's description of a baffling and complex paralysis—physical, emotional, and linguistic—holds true for the experiences of many characters in Scott's novels. Like many Gothic fictions, the Waverley Novels trace the consequences of the sins of curiosity, a movement out of the unaccountability of child-

---

[15] WN xxxvi. 47; *Richard III*, I. iv. 24.
[16] WN viii. 271–2.
[17] The argument proposed by Millgate, *Making of the Novelist*, ch. 7.

hood not into adult power but into adult responsibility, often detached from power. Julia Mannering, the heroine of Scott's second novel, gives a memorable account of this process:

I feel the terrors of a child, who has, in needless sport, put in motion some powerful piece of machinery; and, while he beholds wheels revolving, chains clashing, cylinders rolling around him, is equally astonished at the tremendous powers which his weak agency has called into action, and terrified for the consequences which he is compelled to await, without the possibility of averting them.[18]

Such a perception of the world is very close to that lack of control so vividly described by Maturin's Monçada in *Melmoth the Wanderer*, where human beings, in a kind of parody of the Newtonian universe, set machines moving which they are then unable to halt:

Every thing passed before me as in a dream. I saw the pageant move on, without a thought of who was to be the victim. I returned to the convent—I felt my destiny was fixed—I had no wish to avert or arrest it—I was like one who sees an enormous engine (whose operation is to crush him to atoms) put in motion, and, stupefied with horror, gazes on it with a calmness that might be mistaken for that of one who was coolly analysing the complication of its machinery, and calculating the resistless crush of its blow.[19]

This sense of physical paralysis extends, as many critics after Alexander Welsh have noted, to a breakdown of control and a rhetoric of anxiety and persecution. The rationalist commitments of the Waverley Novels are continually undermined by the terms in which Scott's protagonists perceive and describe their experiences. 'Undefinable apprehension', 'acute anxiety', and 'irrational dread' beset one protagonist after another. Even the redoubtable Hereward the Varangian of *Count Robert of Paris*, left alone in a chamber which leads to the palace dungeons, responds in the unmistakable tones of Waverley-Novel anxiety: ' "I have done nothing," he thought, "to merit being immured in one of these subterranean dens...." '[20] As Nigel Oliphant complains, the hero is placed in a situation 'where every fair construction of [his] actions and motives is refused [him]'.[21] Alternatively, as Scott

---

[18] *WN* iv. 18.   [19] *Melmoth*, i. 233–4.
[20] *WN* xlvi. 66.   [21] *WN* xxvii. 243.

describes the situation of Harry Bertram, in terms which already move his experiences one step away from actuality, he is confused by 'the mysteries which appeared to thicken around him, while he seemed alike to be persecuted and protected by secret enemies and friends'.[22]

The form of paralysis which is most rewardingly analysed in the context of Gothic, however, is the linguistic variety, recalling the many scenes in Gothic in which characters are implored to speak or to take decisive action to save loved ones (typified, perhaps, by Lorenzo's nightmare vision of Antonia's death near the beginning of *The Monk*). Scott's young heroes struggle for speech yet find themselves 'choked', struggle to declare their love or honour yet are laughed at as children, seek action but find paralysis, 'enchant-ment', and imprisonment. Ironically, the Waverley Novels built their reputation upon speech. In the opening chapter of *The Bride of Lammermoor*, Dick Tinto complains that Peter Pattieson's characters 'make too much use of the *gob box* ... there is nothing in whole pages but mere chat and dialogue'.[23] Yet despite the garrulousness of some characters many others undergo agonies of self-expression in which they are silent, inarticulate, and hesitant. The Waverley Novels repeatedly test the hero who cannot speak out, or who stifles his emotions, often in legal situations or crises which are described in the language of law. Two such narratives—*Rob Roy* and *Peveril of the Peak*—are analysed below. The focus of the first part of the chapter, how-ever, is one of Scott's most complex analyses of secrecy and the ideological implications of secrecy-driven plotting—*The Pirate*. It is chosen here partly because it is one of the Waverley Novels most frequently decreed to have been spoilt by inappropriate literary conventions, and partly because it seems to be such a clear endorsement of rational interpretations of life. David Brown is typical in linking the proliferation of supernatural and fantastic elements to a lack of basic historical understanding: 'With only a limited understanding of the period and setting concerned, Scott instinctively falls back on Gothic horrors, spurious romance, and antiquarian curiosities to sustain the novel for its four hun-dred pages.'[24] *The Pirate*, however, was the novel which irri-

[22] *WN* iv. 210.
[23] *WN* xiii. 271: see Woolf on Scott's 'chatterboxes', *Collected Essays*, i. 42.
[24] *Historical Imagination*, 187.

tated Coleridge into his marginal comments on the 'make-believe' supernatural in the Waverley Novels, already quoted in the Introduction. Throughout *The Pirate* Scott experiments with different literary forms with the apparent intention of sorting and ranking them, and it is not difficult to determine which form(s) win. Despite this, however, it is significant that Coleridge registers such tensions and difficulties in the novel. *The Pirate* seems to offer supporters of a pro-rationalist, anti-Gothic Scott their ideal text. Yet the contest actively foregrounds the complexity of the forces at work.

1. The Pirate: 'The Interest of a Riddle'

I must remain the dreaded—the mystical—the Reimkennar —the controller of the elements, or I must be no more! I have no alternative, no middle station.... The parricide shall never also be denounced as the impostor!

(Norna of the Fitful Head)[25]

In *The Pirate*, Scott takes up the social and literary challenges presented by piratical heroes from Byron's Conrad to Maturin's Bertram, firmly rejecting the charismatic misanthropy which they had substituted for heroism. Although some of this rejection stems from the ironic depiction of the pirate, Clement Cleveland, much is conducted on the level of plot. *The Pirate* is a deconstruction of mystery and its alliance with anti-social imagination. In spite of all Norna's misgivings, it systematically denounces the parricide as the impostor, the rebel against society as the victim of delusive visions.

In *The Pirate*, as in Gothic fiction, readers play a double role which makes them simultaneously detectives, actively piecing together evidence, and passive listeners, knowing that everything strange will eventually be explained. After a brief introduction to the geography and social conditions of Zetland at the end of the seventeenth century, *The Pirate* confronts its readers with a series of mysteries, which are presented as imaginatively compatible with its desolate and recess-riddled scenery. In the order in which they

[25] WN xxv. 221.

are introduced, these mysteries are: Basil Mertoun's misanthropic gloom, misogyny, and indifference towards his son Mordaunt;[26] the instinctive enmity between Mordaunt Mertoun and the pirate, Clement Cleveland; Mordaunt's sudden expulsion from the charmed circle of the Troil household; and the 'fatal secret' of Norna's alienation from society. When introducing the first of these, the strange isolation and misanthropy of Basil Mertoun, Scott acknowledges the special imaginative appeal of the principle of mystery itself. Deciding that none of Basil Mertoun's qualities equals in the eyes of the Zetlanders the mystery surrounding him, the narrator concludes: 'Above all, Mr Mertoun's secret seemed impenetrable, and his presence had all the interest of a riddle, which men love to read over and over, because they cannot find out the meaning of it.'[27] These are highly reader-conscious terms. They also anticipate the strong interest shown throughout The Pirate in riddles, 'wild' rhymes, and mysterious withheld speech. Not only is the narrative itself a triumph of rational explanation over riddling mystery. The novel's restructuring of social and domestic life after the mysteries in which it begins also follows the principles established by clear and direct speech. Language triumphs over gesture. Open communication replaces rumour and incantation.

In the imagination of Mordaunt Mertoun, also, mystery is given a special prominence. He is seen meditating the secrets of the ocean, 'aided by the dim twilight, through which it was imperfectly seen for more than half the year'. Vividly the narrator describes the creatures thought to inhabit the 'bottomless depths and secret caves', the mermaid, kraken, and sea-snake, sometimes glimpsed by mariners through banks of fog.[28] Scott presents Zetland as a land enshrining secrets. And it is significant that the man who both casts dissension into the community of Zetland and eventually brings about its more lasting harmony—the pirate himself—is plucked from the sea by Mordaunt in contravention of all the islanders' convenient taboos about sea-rescue. Through this as-

[26] Not really a problem, according to Nassau Senior in his review of The Pirate, Quarterly Review, xxvi (Oct. 1821), 456, where he notes Mertoun's misanthropy and silence, 'which, at once, indicate, to a practised novel-reader, one of the numerous family of retired criminals, or injured lovers'.
[27] WN xxiv. 8.
[28] All quotations from WN xxiv. 25.

sociation Cleveland himself becomes a sort of kraken, rising from the secrets of the past.

The mysteries of *The Pirate* are capable of being solved at any moment by a few words uttered by two characters, Norna of the Fitful Head and Basil Mertoun, who have been lovers many years before and have had an illegitimate child. Norna believes this child to be Mordaunt, who is assumed by the Zetlanders to be Mertoun's only son, but it transpires that Mordaunt is Mertoun's second son, his child by a failed later marriage. Norna discovers too late that her son is in fact the pirate, Cleveland, whose schemes she has worked so hard to frustrate. One part of the mystery, then, is their youthful love-affair and the extreme distrust of women it has produced in Mertoun. The second is Norna's conviction that she is to blame for the death of her father, which leads to her self-imposed isolation and necromantic 'enthusiasm'. These mysteries are linked thematically by the moral and social question of the proper relationship between father and child.

When the novel opens, Norna and Mertoun are living as strangers to each other in a community ignorant of their secret but intrigued by their different styles of linguistic indirectness. The misanthropic Mertoun is nicknamed the 'Silent Man of Sumburgh'.[29] Norna, in her role as 'Sibyl', 'Pythoness', 'Reimkennar', speaks predominantly in riddles or in a form of inspired private language. Her closest tie is with her dumb servant, Nick Strumpfer (or 'Pacolet', one of Scott's favourite nicknames for minor characters). In a rhetoric which recalls *Melmoth the Wanderer*, and all the traditions of Faustian overreaching which lie behind it, she repeatedly hints that the reason for her outcast speech is a pact made with the dark powers and 'a sacrifice which human tongue can never utter'.[30] The two interviews between these cryptic recluses are neatly designed as complementary exercises in linguistic indirection and revelation. In the first, Mertoun meets Norna at the ruinous church of St Ninian, hoping to hear news of his missing son. Ignorant of Norna's true identity and failing to recognize in the mysterious sibyl his former beloved, Mertoun conjures her disdainfully to speak plainly, to 'Lay aside this useless affectation of mystery'.[31] Norna complies, but only by whispering words to him which are withheld from the reader:

[29] *WN* xxiv. 80.   [30] *WN* xxiv. 175.   [31] *WN* xxv. 94.

'Hearken, then!' said the old woman. 'The word which I speak shall touch the nearest secret of thy life, and thrill thee through nerve and bone.'

So saying, she whispered a word into Mertoun's ear, the effect of which seemed almost magical.[32]

In their second meeting, this time in the cathedral of St Magnus in Kirkwall, it is Mertoun's turn to break the silence by revealing that Cleveland, not Mordaunt, is Norna's son. His explanation breaks the spell of what Mertoun calls 'the legerdemain of lunacy—the mere quackery of insanity'.[33] Realizing the true limits of her power and knowledge, Norna resumes her name and her original place in society.

The Zetland community as a whole is beset by other silences and mysterious forms of speech or riddles. In the central chapter of the novel (chapter 21 out of forty-two), Magnus Troil asks his guests, and obliges his daughters, to take part in a traditional fortune-telling conducted through riddling rhymes, and in a later explanation of the mysteries of Norna's wonderful knowledge and power, the narrator demonstrates how the everyday instances of Norna's dealings with the supernatural powers depend upon pacts of silence. The islanders who provide her with information are ignorant of each other's actions, and, 'as her orders were generally given under injunctions of the strictest secrecy, men reciprocally wondered at occurrences, which had in fact been produced by their own agency, and that of their neighbours, and in which, had they communicated freely with each other, no shadow of the marvellous would have remained'.[34] As the love-story of *The Pirate* emphatically declares, only when characters communicate freely are they able to break the spells which surround them. *The Pirate* is torn between the recognition that sociability and speech are essential to happiness and stability, and a fascination with anti-social, secretive, and silent characters.

On the one hand, the narrative voice insistently denies the fanciful claims of the superstitious and romantic characters, repeatedly explaining, for example, that Norna's supernatural powers are

---

[32] *WN* xxv. 95.

[33] *WN* xxv. 355.

[34] *WN* xxv. 212: the link is reinforced by the presence of Norna's dumb dwarf, 'Pacolet', xxv. 122–3.

merely delusions of her imagination, and can be explained by reference to the specific historical and cultural conditions of Zetland. It makes Norna's addiction to mysterious speech both comic and maddening, as in the scene soon after Mordaunt becomes an unwelcome guest at Burgh-Westra, when she tries to warn Mordaunt of 'the machinations of a villain',[35] without giving him enough information to be of practical use. To Norna's fanciful description of the adder who has crept into the eagle's nest, Mordaunt replies: 'You must speak more plainly, Norna . . . if you would have me understand or answer you. I am no guesser of riddles.'[36] The same sceptical narrative voice exposes the connections between superstition, madness, and imagination.[37] It insists that Norna's imagination has led to madness and alienation, and that the same fate threatens 'the high-minded and imaginative Minna', as a result of her 'unusual intensity of imagination'.[38] Minna is constitutionally inclined to the sublime scenery of 'solitary and melancholy grandeur' suited to her 'wild and poetical visions'.[39] When she falls into a nervous illness brought on by her consciousness of the secret (as she thinks it) that Cleveland has murdered Mordaunt, her plight is described in terms which closely echo Norna's description of the secret of her parricide. It is a 'horrible secret, which haunted her while awake, and was yet more tormenting during her broken and hurried slumbers'. The narrator underlines the point: 'There is no grief so dreadful as that which we dare not communicate.'[40] Minna is taken to Norna's strange outpost dwelling, a place described in terms which make literal the threat of division imperilling her, and defining Norna:

This natural fosse, which seemed to have been the work of some convulsion of nature, was deep, dark, and irregular, narrower towards the bottom, which could not be distinctly seen, and widest at top, having the appearance as if that part of the cliff occupied by the building had been half rent away from the isthmus which it terminated,—an idea favoured

[35] WN xxiv. 177.
[36] WN xxiv. 176.
[37] WN xxv. 99, 225, 354–5: on Minna, xxiv. 333, xxv. 36, 66, 112, 130, 148, 371: contrast Brenda, xxiv. 353, xxv. 106, 370–1: Halcro's alternative opinion, xxiv. 228.
[38] WN xxv. 371, xxiv. 333.
[39] WN xxiv. 36, 40.
[40] Both quotations from WN xxv. 98.

by the angle at which it seemed to recede from the land, and lean towards the sea, with the building which crowned it.[41]

Norna's unnatural (though unintentional) crime against her father is repeated in the image of the rock torn away by natural convulsion, and leaning out towards the sea which (conventionally enough) is the source of passion and secrecy in the novel.

On the other hand, however, Scott shows that imagination and desire are stimulated by denial and silence, a recognition which, as I have suggested, is implicit in the organization of his own mystery-novel. He describes Mordaunt's distress when the Troil sisters withdraw their friendship:

Mordaunt felt, as it were, assured upon the instant, that the regard of Minna was extinguished, but that it might be yet possible to recover that of the milder Brenda; and such is the waywardness of human fancy, that though he had never hitherto made any distinct difference betwixt these two beautiful and interesting girls, the favour of her, which seemed most absolutely withdrawn, became at the moment the most interesting in his eyes.[42]

The whole imaginative venture of *The Pirate* is based on the same association between what is withheld and what is desired. Scott's readers, like Mordaunt Mertoun, are to be shown that it is wrong to equate denial with desire.

At all its stages the story told in *The Pirate* constructs this lesson by contrasting the powers of communication and silence. Near the end of the first volume in the Magnum Opus edition, Minna and Brenda tentatively discuss the barriers to their free communication which have been created by their love for two men who are enemies. This scene is contrasted to the failures of communication between Mordaunt and Basil Mertoun, and between Mordaunt and Magnus Troil. Soon afterwards, Minna and Brenda take part in a fortune-telling scene in which Norna foretells in rhyme their future lives and loves. Finally, the romantic entanglements of the plot are explicable in terms of communication and silence. Minna and Cleveland never communicate directly enough to establish the differences between her ideals of an ancient sea-king and the reality of his life as a pirate. Mordaunt's imagination is stimulated by Minna's silence, and his emotions baffled by his father's silence, but his love is fixed by Brenda's speech. Only Brenda risks her family's displeasure to explain to Mordaunt the reasons for his fall from favour, and tries to help Minna by discussing her fears with Mordaunt. Minna, by contrast, is nearly driven mad because she must not communicate her own 'fatal secret'.[43] Brenda, the heroine of communication, and the sociable Mordaunt, break out of the bond of secrecy and silence which holds other characters fatally entranced.

Even in their dreams, Minna and Brenda are contrasted in terms of speech and silence. Before they awake to discover Norna sitting by the hearth, singing, her voice has become interwoven with their dreams. Each dream is symbolic of one sister's situation. Minna dreams that she is alone in a desolate cavern by the seashore, and is beckoned by a mermaid who sings to her a prophetic song of 'calamity and woe'. Brenda dreams that she is sitting in a bower surrounded by her father and his friends. She tries to entertain them with her favourite lively song, but loses control of her voice, which assumes, 'in her own despite, the deep tones and wild and melancholy notes of Norna of Fitful-head'.[44] Brenda is the heroine of society and also its entertainer, its speaker and singer. Minna is silent while another sings. Brenda's dream is also expressive of her plight while forbidden by her father to communicate with Mordaunt, to assume cold words which are not her own. Since Norna is about to tell the story of her demonic pact and supposed parricide, it is also significant that it is her song which intrudes in each sister's dream. Norna is the mermaid tempting Minna from society, the voice she must resist. She is also the doleful voice against which Brenda must struggle to assert her own right of social, harmonious speech.

The drama of language, imagination, and desire conducted in *The Pirate* touches on some of the most prevalent concerns of Scott's fiction. Although all the Waverely Novels demonstrate Scott's interest in language as the primary medium of social inter-action, and his commitment to finding a suitable language of fiction to achieve the same ends, most also contain one or more characters whose non-conforming speech, or whose refusal or inability to speak, is a threat. Some of these are characters whose language does not seem to obey the conventions of social speech

---

[43] WN xxv. 98–101 (100).   [44] The dreams passage, WN xxiv. 331–2.

(like the songs of Davie Gellatley in *Waverley* and Madge Wildfire in *The Heart of Midlothian*) although it is later discovered to be meaningful in its own way. Other characters harbour terrible secrets which they must eventually tell, such as Elspeth Mucklebackit in *The Antiquary* and Norna in *The Pirate*. A third, and especially threatening, group consists of mute or seemingly mute characters. It includes Norna's dumb dwarf Nick Strumpfer and the fake mute Fenella in *Peveril of the Peak*, supported in the introduction to the Magnum Opus by the tale of the servant girl 'Dumb Lizzie' from Scott's own family history. This is the context of debate about society and language in which one should position *The Pirate*'s contrast between Minna and Brenda Troil, and between the characters in the novel who take to extremes the principles by which this contrast is governed (Norna being the correlative of Minna's guilty silence and Magnus Troil, or less flatteringly the gossip Bryce Snailsfoot, being the correlative of Brenda's social speech). Equally complex is Scott's evaluation of imagination in the context of secrecy or of what is tantalizingly withheld. The plots of the Waverley Novels usually punish anti-social and secretive characters who misuse imagination, like George Staunton in *The Heart of Midlothian* and Richard Middlemas in *The Surgeon's Daughter*, crushed to death by a ceremonial elephant which is a kind of grotesque symbol of his Indian fantasy-life. More sentimental images of the romantic imagination (usually feminized, although Scott's most savage portrayals of imagination also take female form), such as Minna Troil, prove problematic, however. Minna's renunciation of her dreams at the end of *The Pirate* is a particularly sour version of the conflict between 'romance' and 'real history' which, since Edward Waverley, Scott's imaginative characters had had to negotiate. Minna declares to Cleveland: 'The delusions which a solitary education and limited acquaintance with the modern world had spread around me, are gone and dissipated forever.'[45] Scott recognizes the harshness of this, however, and is anxious to reassure. 'Reader, she *was* happy', declares the narrator, making an unusually direct and decisive intervention.[46] In *The Pirate*, Scott restricts his characters' imaginative indulgences, exposing the dangers of allowing the world of private imagination to

---

[45] WN xxv. 365.   [46] WN xxv. 371.

dominate the social, public world. Clearly there is much more at stake in the novel's creation of an alternative, extra-rational, highly charged world of the imagination than critics usually grant.

The Pirate, in conclusion, is a deconstruction of fictions based on mystery but also a powerful reinvention and redirection of Gothic plotting. It replaces silence with speech and secrecy with openness, but in doing so it continues rather than discredits Gothic aesthetics as typified by Radcliffe. As in Gothic, the genuine complications are to be found not in the explicit statements made by the narrative voice but in the imaginative activity prompted in the reader. Readers of *The Pirate* are engaged in solving mysteries while its hero is being taught that such fascinations are delusive. In a more subtle way, however, they are engaged in a fiction which accepts conventions—including novelistic ones—as a precondition of social interaction. The contrast with the 'unutterable' in *Melmoth the Wanderer* is instructive. In this novel, Maturin celebrates a private language, exemplified by Immalee-Isidora who learns social corruption as she learns a system of speech but who always retains a degree of linguistic as well as moral purity. Maturin shows language to be necessarily social but ideally also personal, and ultimately a private instrument of communication with God. In *The Pirate* Scott rejects a range of private, 'secret' languages and in the marriage of his hero and heroine enshrines the sociability of speech. To do so, however, he is forced to deploy all the authority of his narrating voice: 'Reader, she *was* happy.' Not all his novels choose to make so unequivocal an intervention.

2. Rob Roy: *'The Secrets of this Fearful Prison House'*

During that same interview, some one having observed that the next Waverley novel was to be 'Rob Roy,' Wordsworth took down his volume of Ballads, and read to the company 'Rob Roy's Grave;' then, returning it to the shelf, observed, 'I do not know what more Mr. Scott can have to say upon the subject.'

(Keats to Cowden Clark, 1817)[47]

---

[47] Quoted by Robert Gittings, *John Keats* (London, 1968), 168.

According to Keats, Wordsworth considered Scott's attempt at the subject of Rob Roy to be pitifully belated. Criticism of the novel, likewise, has often seemed predetermined by the strong pull of Lukácsian analysis. For Lukács, *Rob Roy* was the perfect illustration of Scott's interest in conflicting cultural forces and representative historical types.[48] Subsequently, it has been described as more of a thesis than a novel, 'an analysis, in historically realistic terms, of the state of English society in the first half of the eighteenth century'.[49] This emphasis on its social analyses has led some critics to underestimate its interest in individual psychology. In an article on *Wuthering Heights*, Robin Gilmour has claimed that it 'took a genius of the order of Emily Bronte to bring out the deeper possibilities latent in the cultural contrasts of *Rob Roy*'. Scott—'large, genial, fertile, but somehow unselfconscious and undeveloped'—was unable to tap the fearful resources of his fiction.[50] Yet *Rob Roy* is also the central text of Welsh's analysis of 'tentative fiction', by which the hero is continually anxious about events which never happen. Its subtexts of anxiety have been analysed by Jane Millgate and Marilyn Orr, among others, but there has been no sustained attention to the relationship between what Orr calls 'the abyss that opens between the lines' and its markedly self-conscious deployment of literary convention.[51]

The plot of *Rob Roy* is notoriously problematic.[52] It begins conventionally enough with the disagreement between a romantic young man and his father. Frank Osbaldistone's rebellion against paternal authority—which also represents a transgression against an entire social and economic order—is followed by expulsion and trial in the wildernesses of romance. In this, the novel follows the biblical patterns of *Robinson Crusoe* and *Caleb Williams* and

---

[48] Lukács, *Historical Novel*, 63–4: Donald Davie, *The Heyday of Sir Walter Scott* (London, 1961), 56–64; D. D. Devlin, *The Author of Waverley: A Critical Study of Walter Scott* (London, 1971), 93–7; David Daiches, 'Scott's Achievement as a Novelist' (1951), repr. in his *Literary Essays* (Edinburgh, 1956), 88–121 (esp. 110–13); Laurence Poston III, 'The Commercial Motif of the Waverley Novels', *ELH* xlii (1975), 62–87.

[49] Davie, *Heyday*, 59.

[50] Robin Gilmour, 'Scott and the Victorian Novel: The Case of "Wuthering Heights"', in *Scott and His Influence*, 363–71 (371).

[51] See Millgate, *Making of the Novelist*, ch. 7; Orr, 'Voices and Text', 47.

[52] The problem of plot was raised by early reviewers. See E. T. Channing's review for *North American Review*, vii (July 1818), 149–84, and Nassau Senior, Review of *Rob Roy*, *Tales of My Landlord*, 2nd ser., *Tales of My Landlord*, 3rd

SECRECY, SILENCE, AND ANXIETY

the educational model of sentimental fiction.[53] Frank is slow to recognize that his expulsion is more than just a token ordeal: 'It must be but a trial of my disposition, which, endured with patience and steadiness on my part, would raise me in his estimation, and lead to an amicable accommodation of the point in dispute between us.'[54] The unexpected violence of this 'trial', however, unhinges Frank's rational self-control to a point at which the 'amicable accommodation of the point in dispute' seems an irrelevance, a side-issue in a heavily stylized cultural compromise. The novel ends with a self-conscious fictional flourish in which all the obstacles to Frank's double inheritance (land and family business) are magically removed in the course of a few paragraphs.

The disconcerting shift into self-conscious fictionality, moreover, is firmly embedded in the narrating voice of Frank Osbaldistone himself. An old man looking back, relating his life-story for the benefit of his younger business partner, Will Tresham, he is continually in danger of having his leisurely retrospect hijacked by a heightened literary language of fear and oppression. This literary language is strongly—even dangerously—indebted to the stylized representation of loss, sexual betrayal, emasculation, enforced childishness, and helplessness in Gothic. If Frank's consciousness is a desperate effort to retain control over pain, loss, and meaninglessness, the novel which so presents it is a comparably embattled form, in which the novelistic forms of *Bildungsroman* and picaresque struggle with a subversive form of nightmare Gothic. Throughout the novel, Frank's feelings, his 'restless and feverish

---

ser., *Ivanhoe, The Monastery, The Abbot, Kenilworth, Quarterly Review*, xxvi (Oct. 1821), 109–48, esp. 110–15. In more recent criticism, see Lars Hartveit, *Dream Within a Dream: A Thematic Approach to Scott's Vision of Fictional Reality*, Norwegian Studies in English, No. 18 (Bergen, 1974), 73; Avrom Fleishman, *The English Historical Novel: Walter Scott to Virginia Woolf* (Baltimore, 1971), 69–70; Welsh, *Hero of the Waverley Novels*, 186; Davie, *Heyday*, 57–8; Devlin, *Author of Waverley*, 94; Gordon, *Under Which King?*, 78; Brown, *Historical Imagination*, 92–111; A. O. J. Cockshut, *The Achievement of Walter Scott* (London, 1969), 153–4, 160. Solutions are proposed by Wilson, *Laird of Abbotsford*, 183–4; William Cadbury, 'The Two Structures of *Rob Roy*', *MLQ* xxix (1968), 42–60; and F. R. Hart, *Scott's Novels: The Plotting of Historic Survival* (Charlottesville, Va., 1966), 37–9.

[53] WN vii. 28, viii. 69. This is a commercial version of original sin, according to Fiedler, *Love and Death*, 177. R. C. Gordon sees Frank as the Prodigal Son, *Under Which King?*, ch. 5.

[54] WN vii. 37–8.

anxiety',[55] are painfully detached from his ability to understand. His imagination and emotions are cut adrift from his reason, resulting in a nightmare of unreality, confusion, and nameless terror, for which his favourite metaphor is that of fog. The most revealing of all his anxious monologues describes his feelings after his first declaration of love to Diana:

A chaos of thoughts intruded themselves on me at once, passing hastily through my brain, intercepting and overshadowing each other, and resembling those fogs which in mountainous countries are wont to descend in obscure volumes, and disfigure or obliterate the usual marks by which the traveller steers his course through the wilds. The dark and undefined idea of danger arising to my father from the machinations of such a man as Rashleigh Osbaldistone,—the half-declaration of love which I had offered to Miss Vernon's acceptance,—the acknowledged difficulties of her situation, bound by a previous contract to sacrifice herself to a cloister, or to an ill-assorted marriage,—all pressed themselves at once upon my recollection, while my judgment was unable deliberately to consider any of them in their just light and bearings.[56]

These fogs of the understanding become literal when Frank is due to meet Rob Roy at midnight on Glasgow bridge, and during the surprise encounter with Diana and her father near Aberfoyle. As Radcliffe had already insisted in *The Mysteries of Udolpho*, 'human reason cannot establish her laws on subjects, lost in the obscurity of imagination, any more than the eye can ascertain the form of objects, that only glimmer through the dimness of night'.[57] As the novel progresses, the external world of *Rob Roy* increasingly resembles a psychologized landscape of romance in which Frank must act out his punishment and exile, rather than actively engage with the forces threatening him.

When Frank's father banishes him from London to his uncle's estate in Northumberland—a banishment which Frank interprets, romantically, as a return to his cultural and imaginative inheritance—he banishes him from adult opportunity and endeavour to the mysteries and powerlessness of childhood. Frank's journey north is punctuated by memories of his old nurse's tales, and Osbaldistone Hall itself, with its genial uncle, six bumptious sons, and one Snow White of a cousin, is a world of licence and misrule which contrasts sharply with his father's habits of caution and

[55] WN viii. 296.   [56] WN vii. 245.   [57] Udolpho, ii. 449.

restraint. Everything which happens there confirms his humiliating regression to childish dependence. Among his uncle's family, Frank is isolated and ignorant, treated with some indulgence, and subject to sudden wild suspicions of the adult world, which lead to anxiety and resentment. He contrasts his weakness with Diana's 'superior manliness'.[58] Later, Rob Roy speaks of him as a child who has stumbled into an adult mystery and is in danger of paying too high a price for the inconvenience he has caused: 'my conscience winna see this puir thoughtless lad ill-guided'.[59] Rashleigh taunts him with being lost in a 'world of poetical imaginations': 'leave the business of life to those who understand and can conduct it'.[60] This is the male nightmare of *Coriolanus* ('Name not the god, thou boy of tears').[61]

In Frank's heightened imaginative and emotional sensitivity, Osbaldistone Hall comes to resemble a Gothic house of mystery, or a psychological prison. As Diana reminds him, echoing *Hamlet*, 'you do not know half the secrets of this fearful prison-house'.[62] Its very architecture intensifies his insecurity. The library, which Frank believes to be a sanctuary in which he can further his romantic friendship with Diana, is surrounded by secret passageways from which their meetings may be observed by her father or by Rashleigh. Frank keeps watch on the library in an attempt to discover the secret of its mysterious visitors, but they, all the time, are spying on him.

In *Melmoth the Wanderer*, Monçada comes to realize that 'The drama of terror has the irresistible power of converting its audience into its victims'.[63] The same transformation is central to the experience of many Scott heroes, and is particularly clear in *Rob Roy*. It may be understood as a perverse twisting of the comfortable assumption of spectatorship and readership: that is, the assumption that the protagonist observes but does not act. For this reason, many of Scott's heroes are tourists who become entangled in local crises, only to discover that these crises are

---

[58] *WN* vii. 241; and see Diana's request to be known as 'Tom Vernon', vii. 81–2, and freedom from 'the nervous emotions of her sex', vii. 246.
[59] *WN* viii. 114.
[60] *WN* viii. 108.
[61] *Coriolanus*, v. vi. 100.
[62] *WN* vii. 200; referred to again as a prison house, vii. 206: and see nuns, 'imprisoned singing birds', vii. 69–70, and Diana's 'nets', vii. 142–3.
[63] *Melmoth*, iii. 34.

fundamental to the discovery of their personal identities and social roles. The nightmare possibilities of the Waverley Novels begin when the roles of the observer and the observed are suddenly reversed. In *Rob Roy*, Frank is accused, involved, forced out of his spectator's role. When, soon after his arrival at Osbaldistone Hall, Frank is charged with having robbed his timid fellow-traveller, Morris, his role as mocking observer is suddenly reversed, forcing him to revise his contempt for 'the terrible bugbears which haunted his [Morris's] imagination' and his complacent conviction that causeless fear is 'the most irritating, busy, painful, and pitiable' of human self-torments.[64] Later, he identifies himself with Morris, intervening ineffectually in the terrifying scene of Morris's execution. At the very end of the novel, he confesses himself still troubled by nightmares about Morris's death: significantly, in the version of this nightmare which he suffered before his marriage to Diana, *he*, not Morris, had been the victim and Diana's father the remorseless Helen MacGregor. Frank is the leisured spectator perversely forced into action and complicity. To adapt Monçada's words from *Melmoth the Wanderer*, Frank—the audience, as he first supposes, of a romantic spectacle—becomes its victim.

This reversal is especially traumatic in two scenes, one in which Rob Roy whispers his mysterious warning to Frank in the vaults of Glasgow Cathedral, and the other their subsequent meeting on Glasgow bridge. In the cathedral, Frank finds himself confronted directly by a physical analogue of the obscurity and confusion which frighten and fascinate him. The 'waste regions of oblivion', the caverns of the vaults in which the service is held, are vast in relation to the small congregation and lighted space.[65] The description of how these vaults appear to Frank is symbolic of his anxiety:

Such was the group of countenances, rising tier on tier, discovered to my critical inspection by such sunbeams as forced their way through the narrow Gothic lattices of the Laigh Kirk of Glasgow; and, having illuminated the attentive congregation, lost themselves in the vacuity of the vaults behind, giving to the nearer part of their labyrinth a sort of imperfect twilight, and leaving their recesses in an utter darkness, which gave them the appearance of being interminable.[66]

[64] WN vii. 41, 46.   [65] WN viii. 33.   [66] WN viii. 37–8.

As in the passages describing mysterious architecture in Gothic literature, the reactions of the hero are pointedly analogous to those of the reader:

and when my eyes took that direction, I found it difficult to withdraw them; such is the pleasure our imagination receives from the attempt to penetrate as far as possible into an intricate labyrinth, imperfectly lighted, and exhibiting objects which irritate our curiosity, only because they acquire a mysterious interest from being undefined and dubious.[67]

The analogy between mind and architecture, unfolding plot and withheld secrets, questing hero and questing reader, draws attention to the enforced obscurity which the reader shares with the hero. The withheld secret of the plot is not a clear fact which can be uncovered to the satisfaction of all, but a continuing mystery, always just beyond comprehension; a mystery in which discovery does little to dispel the sense of threat and powerlessness. Just as the reader feels that the ending of Rob Roy fails to solve the imaginative issues raised, and as Frank is trapped in obsessive but uncomprehending retelling of his personal history, so the vaults of Glasgow Cathedral hold out to the reader's imagination a fleeting glimpse of a possibility which the plot never fulfils. The whole scene is redolent of the aesthetic which Scott analyses in his 'Life' of Radcliffe, in which 'obscurity and suspense' are recognized as 'the most fertile source, perhaps, of sublime emotion', and readers are kept in suspense about mysteries which can never compensate for the emotion they arouse.

As Frank indulges his spectator's pleasure in the appearance of Glasgow Cathedral, he is once more suddenly implicated in the scene. Rob Roy steps unseen from the vaults to warn him that he is 'in danger in this city'.[68] Frank's fears overcome his reason. He is immediately suspicious of MacVittie's 'sinister expression', although he lacks 'any rational ground of dislike or suspicion'.[69] When Rob Roy meets Frank on Glasgow bridge, he is astonished at Frank's overwrought state: 'What is it you fear?'[70] The records of anxiety are especially concentrated at this stage of the novel:

---

[67] WN viii. 38.
[68] WN viii. 40; and see deliberately supernatural overtones in the description of Rob's exit, viii. 41.
[69] WN viii. 42.
[70] WN viii. 54; and see the details of atmosphere, viii. 51–4.

'My anxiety now returned on me with such violence', 'a state of incredible anxiety and vexation', 'so much had my anxiety been wound up by protracted expectation'.[71] The reader fears with Frank because the episode, as Frank describes it, so nearly fits the literary frame of Gothic. In his anxiety, Frank invests the mysterious warning with supernatural significance. The figure of Rob Roy, which he attempts to pursue, 'vanished in the vaulted cemetery, like the spectre of one of the numerous dead who rested within its precincts'.[72]

The plot element of the mysterious warning is familiar enough from romance, but had been much enhanced by its common use in Gothic. To a contemporary reader, this scene would have recalled memories of many others: perhaps the key scene in Eliza Parsons's *Mysterious Warning* (1796), in which the hero, Ferdinand, receives a timely but enigmatic warning about the perils which await him. From more mainstream Gothic, Frank's plight repeats patterns familiar from Radcliffe's work, including the scene in *The Mysteries of Udolpho* in which a mysterious figure glides between the pillars in the aisle while Emily seeks the grave of her father; or Emily's midnight meeting with Barnardine in the vaults of Udolpho; or the warnings given to Vivaldi from the shadows of Paluzzi, in the early chapters of *The Italian*, when Vivaldi, like Frank, surrenders to superstitious dread reluctantly, hastily deciding that the monk of Paluzzi is a ghost, but never relinquishing his grasp of more probable rational explanations.[73] The imaginative connection is strengthened by the terms in which Scott comments on Vivaldi and the Monk of Paluzzi in his 'Life' of Radcliffe. Vivaldi, explains Scott, is 'blindfolded' and hears 'the voice of a mysterious agent, who had repeatedly crossed his path, and always eluded his search'.[74] Both Scott and Radcliffe force their readers to interpret events in the terms offered by the heightened and strained individual imagination, which they, as narrators, choose not to endorse. Both introduce a comic perspective on their heroes' imaginings in the form of a pragmatic servant. Both, also, dislocate their heroes into situations in which their normal social

---

[71] *WN* viii. 39, 52: closely paralleled later, viii. 296, 307.
[72] *WN* viii. 41.
[73] *Udolpho*, i. 242–3, iii. 6–19; *Italian*, i. 21, 27–8. Compare Frank's long monologue, *WN* viii. 44–6, with *Italian*, i. 195–6.
[74] *MPW* iii. 352–3 (352).

experience offers no guidance to the motivations of those who persecute them, and which they are therefore inclined to interpret in the most extreme ways. They, and their readers, are allowed escape routes from the extremes of possibility, and allowed to reinterpret events from the security of retrospect. In both cases, however, the rationalist retrospective fails to remove entirely the memory of the language into which they were forced by heightened and confused perception, nightmare, and anxiety.

The passage in which Frank describes his night journey back to the protection of the Duke, in the middle of which he is unexpectedly overtaken by Diana and her father, represents the climax of his confused and benighted wanderings of mind and emotion. Diana continues to use parallels with romance quest to describe his experience, although, ironically, Frank is now the very opposite of a purposeful questing knight: 'But there were giants and dragons in the way; and errant-knights and damsels of modern times, bold though they be, must not, as of yore, run into useless danger.'[75] Her chiding, protective tones emphasize Frank's childishness. Frank's breakdown into hysterical tears marks the climax of his senseless, incomprehensible ordeal of childlike isolation and exclusion. He calls it 'a flood of the first and most bitter tears which had flowed from my eyes since childhood'. After this, Frank clings even to Rob Roy in the faint hope 'that through his means I might obtain some clew of guidance through the maze in which my fate had involved me'.[76] It is his fate not to act but to be rescued, however. He never re-emerges from the childhood to which his rejection of his father's protection condemns him, although he succeeds in finding strong characters capable of looking after him. He sits passively by while Rob Roy kills Rashleigh. He is married to the 'superior manliness' of Diana Vernon. He is restored to his father's business and (by default) inherits his uncle's estate. Frank's true comprehension of the events which have shaped his life lies outside this public realm, however, in his 'strange agony', the dream of Morris's death which symbolizes his own persecution at the hands of unyielding authority.

The volume structure of *Rob Roy* reinforces this analysis of its central emotional scenes. Scott believed, or affected to believe, that *Rob Roy* required a fourth volume, and the novel has some-

[75] *WN* viii. 270–1.   [76] *WN* viii. 275.

times been condemned as structurally inept.[77] Its coherent and highly effective patterning, however, emerges clearly in the three-volume first edition of 1818.[78] The first volume of the three contains thirteen chapters. In the central chapters, Frank is accused of highway robbery, and is only rescued by the appearance of Campbell (Rob Roy) in chapter 8. Volume One ends with a summary of Frank's feelings for Diana, and with his assuming a more active role, warning his father and Owen not to trust Rashleigh. This links back to the commercial affairs with which the novel opened, and marks Frank's first lesson in the reappraisal of commerce and filial loyalty. Volume Two again contains thirteen chapters, and in the central chapter, chapter 7—which is also the central chapter of the novel as a whole—comes the scene in Glasgow Cathedral, in which Frank is again exposed to danger within an apparently stable and secure setting. As in the first volume, Rob Roy reveals his identity more fully in chapter 8, this time after the meeting on Glasgow bridge. The volume ends with Frank, Jarvie, and Fairservice on their way to the Highlands, neatly closing the Glasgow scenes. The third volume contains twelve chapters, and in chapter 6 comes the most emotionally charged scene of Frank's isolation in an alien world which operates by its own hidden rules, the parting from Diana in the Highlands after Frank has unwittingly become implicated in Rob Roy's escape. At the very centre of this volume, the end of chapter 6, Frank breaks down in tears by the roadside. Structurally, *Rob Roy* resembles the technique of gradually dissolving certainties used in *The Mysteries of Udolpho*. The emotional centre of each volume is the same, and the three centres can be read as extensions of each other, each gradually extending the implications of the one preceding it. At each crisis, Frank finds himself bewilderingly at the centre of a stage, approached from the surrounding darkness by figures in disguise. The scenes of Frank's confusion and anxiety are structurally as well as emotionally central.

The romance resolution which makes the reconciliation between Frank and his father strangely insignificant in fact signals that the

---

[77] Scott's opinions, *Letters*, i. 521, v. 37, 50.

[78] In concentrating on the first edition, I aim to counter the interpretation offered by Marian H. Cusac, *Narrative Structure in the Novels of Sir Walter Scott*, De Proprietatibus Litterarum, edenda curat C. H. Van Schooneveld, Series Practica, No. 6 (The Hague, 1969), 36–9. Cadbury locates the three crises, 'Two Structures of *Rob Roy*', 55, but does not link them to the volume structure.

true resolution has taken place on the symbolic and figurative levels. The secret observers of Osbaldistone Hall turn out to be figures of the past, both familial and cultural. Diana's father, who has been disguised as the mysterious Catholic priest Father Vaughan, steps from a secret panel in the library dressed in the clothes shown in a portrait of his ancestor. Frank believes for a moment that the figure in the portrait has stepped down into the room. In this scene, he is a model of paternal, religious, and historical guilt, embodying constraint and repression. *Rob Roy* considers how far the past, emotionally accepted as the source of authority, is justified in repressing the present. The debates between commerce and the heroic, law and barbarism, the individual and the group, are expressions and repetitions of Frank's quest for the limits of his filial duty.

As he describes it in the preface to the Standard Novels edition of *Fleetwood* in 1832, Godwin came to believe that he had composed *Caleb Williams* so as to provide a plot 'adequate to account for' the psychological extremes which he wanted to portray.[79] *Rob Roy* is one of the many Waverley Novels in which psychological response is always out of proportion to external cause, and in which the reader is left with a residue of anxiety and doubt which the reassurances of the ending are only partially adequate to resolve. One recalls Coleridge's analysis of the 'jagged edge' of a lack of proportion between 'antecedents' and 'consequents'. As his career progressed, Scott became increasingly unwilling to assert at the end of his novels the necessary victory of morality and justice, or, at least, to assert this victory in terms consistent with the rest of the novel. In detailing the deaths of Frank's cousins, Scott seems to defy the reader to believe that the problems raised by his plot could ever be resolved in life. In the narrative present, Diana Vernon has been dead for several years, and Frank still suffers nightmares of guilt and sacrifice triggered by his memories of Morris's death. The unresolved sense of loss and pain suggests that the mind may not always be able to reassert control. It implies that a rational perspective on imaginative fear may never be attained, or may be possible only through the imposition of blatant fiction.

---

[79] As described in the preface of *Fleetwood; or, the New Man of Feeling: Revised, Corrected, and Illustrated with a New Preface, by the Author*, Standard Novels, No. 22 (London, 1832), p. vii.

3. Peveril of the Peak: 'Dimly Seen by Twilight'

Peveril of the Peak opens with a memorable realization of social
disorder during the last years of the Protectorate and the first of
the Restoration. The impetus for writing the novel came from
Scott's sense of the instability of 'that tumultuary & agitated
period of Charles 2ds reign which was disturbed by the popish
plot'.[80] From the confusion of the social world sketched in the
opening chapters the novel traces a quest for the restoration of
order and authority. It does this through the journeys of the young
hero and heir, Julian Peveril, who encounters a succession of
political and spiritual despots (the Countess of Derby, Bridgenorth,
Ganlesse-Christian) who claim his unquestioning allegiance. The
novel is patterned by contrasting states of independence and
domination, which are sometimes imagined in striking meta-
phorical terms. Alice Bridgenorth, for example, warns Julian that
her father will try literally to stamp on him an identity and a set of
loyalties which are not his own: '"... If you meet at all, you must
be the wax, he the seal—you must receive—he must bestow an
absolute impression."'[81] Sometimes the spell is imagined in terms
of enchantment, as in the *Comus*-like moment when Julian is so
spell-bound by Bridgenorth that he seems chained to his chair.[82]
The goal of Julian's quest for an authority which is not tyranny,
however, is the disconcerting monarch Charles II, who rules, as
far as Julian can see, by whim and favouritism. Losing the guiding
light of the Peveril 'star' of constancy, Julian makes his way
through countryside and city imagined persistently in terms of
labyrinths and mazes, only to have the quest end ironically with
the complex and apparently arbitrary codes of authority favoured
by Charles.[83]

One of the false trails of this quest is the female authority of the

[80] *Letters*, vii. 82.
[81] WN xxix. 56: for Julian's unease and guilt in Bridgenorth's company, see
WN xxviii. 248, xxix. 62.
[82] WN xxviii. 267–8.
[83] Of particular relevance to the concerns of this section of my argument are
Graham McMaster's comments on the mazes and labyrinths of *Peveril of the Peak*;
on its scenes of mob violence and hysteria, Caroline plots and Popish plots; and its
prison scenes, particularly the moment at which Sir Geoffrey Peveril is symbolically
shrunk into the shape of Sir Geoffrey Hudson. He pays no attention, however, to
the function of Gothic in such scenes.

Countess of Derby, the 'Queen in Man' who has assumed royal authority in order to accomplish the execution of Christian. This is the crime which generates the plot of the novel: the intrigues of Christian's brother, the disguise of Fenella, and the rupture between the families of Peveril and Bridgenorth. Bridgenorth taunts Julian Peveril with his subjection to womanish authority.[84] The crisis of authority experienced by the nation as a whole is repeated in miniature on the Isle of Man. The Countess's son, the young, careless, and dissolute Earl of Derby, neglects his responsibilities for the pleasures of London, and makes jokes about the monarchy. He gives his father's signet to his pet monkey as a plaything. Like Charles II, the Earl prefers pleasure to good government. Like Charles I, his mother holds out for the old principles of absolute rule. The disagreements between them are enacted again between the Countess and the King when she appears before him at court.

It comes as a surprise, looking back over *Peveril of the Peak*, to discover that none of the characters has, after all, seen a ghost. Supernatural confrontations seem to be expected at every turn. Early in the novel, young Julian and Alice are frightened by the sudden appearance of the Countess of Derby from behind the wall-hangings in the gilded chamber of Peveril Castle. In the Magnum Opus edition, Scott adds in support of this incident a story from the childhood of his aunt Margaret Swinton, which he embroiders with remembrances of Coleridge's 'Christabel'. Next, it is Lady Peveril's turn to experience momentary fear of the supernatural when she unexpectedly encounters Bridgenorth by moonlight in a deserted avenue near the castle. The narrator's language in this passage repeatedly hints at far more than he is prepared to deliver. He includes the detail of Lady Peveril's attendant, for example, who shivers with such fear as he enters the 'Dobby's [Goblin's] Walk' that Lady Peveril is reminded of the tradition that the ghost of the first Squire of Moultrassie 'was supposed to walk in this sequestered avenue, accompanied by a large headless mastiff'.[85] The reader is invited by the setting, Lady Peveril's solitude, and the half-glimpsed figure of the fanatic whom she must confront in order to defy, to expect some ominous or perhaps supernatural appearance. Even when the figure has been identified, Lady Peveril is described as 'anxious still to escape from this strange conference, though scarce knowing what to apprehend'.[86]

Throughout the novel, the narrator describes in some detail events in which the reader is expected simultaneously to believe and disbelieve, a technique which is strongly reminiscent of the way in which Radcliffe withholds information in *The Mysteries of Udolpho*, and seems to approve the false conclusions suggested by the heroine's disordered imagination. Twice during the chapters set in the Isle of Man, Julian feels that he is being watched by the portrait of Christian in Alice Bridgenorth's cottage. On both occasions the appearance of living threat is explained away as a momentary deception of imagination, but the impression hints that some harm will befall him from the Christian faction. Scott adds an appetizer of superstition to his story with the solemn impression of 'the fixed, chill, and ominous glance, which announced to the enemy of his race mishap and misfortune'.[87] In the Countess of Derby's castle of Peel-holm, sentinels claim to see the ghost of Eleanor of Gloucester haunt the battlements until cock-crow. Superstitions and mistrust surround Fenella, the Countess's 'Elf', and Julian himself is superstitious enough to imagine for a moment that Fenella is the prophetic spirit of his house, boding disaster.[88] The narrator disavows such fantasies, but sometimes he deliberately misleads readers in order to do so. When the supposedly dumb Fenella cries out to Julian as she is forced to leave the boat taking him from Man to England, he construes her cries into the voice of Alice Bridgenorth. (This is not the first or the last time that the two central female characters blend in his or the reader's imagination.) Wrongly identifying this as the problem, Julian sets out to find a rational explanation which is then heartily, but entirely falsely, endorsed by the narrator:

His dream was thus fully explained. Fancy had caught up the inarticulate and vehement cries with which Fenella was wont to express resistance or displeasure—had coined them into language, and given them the accents of Alice Bridgenorth. Our imagination plays wilder tricks with us almost every night.[89]

[86] *WN* xxviii. 183.

[87] *WN* xxviii. 229.

[88] *WN* xxix. 98; see the beginning of the next chapter, p. 99, on momentary superstitious fear, and Julian's general state of anxiety, pp. 102–3.

[89] *WN* xxix. 113.

In fact, as the reader already suspects, the voice is indeed Fenella's. The narrator's emphasis on the 'full' explanation of the 'dream' is a calculated deception.

Scott's heroes are frequently forced to place themselves in the control of an older man whose motives and sincerity they are unqualified to judge, but who knows every detail of their histories. In his dealings with Bridgenorth before he leaves the Isle of Man, Julian feels that this authoritative man has spoken to him in riddles.[90] Later, on his way to Martindale Castle, Julian unexpectedly finds himself in the company of an unknown horseman, who ignores his express desire to travel alone and insists on keeping him company. This happens once at night and again the following morning, by which time the ominous shadowing is reinforced by literary hints of magical or demonic agency. Julian starts 'like a guilty thing' on being rejoined by Ganlesse in the morning. His reasoned protests repeatedly expose the anxiety he is at pains to conceal:

'I understand not your threat,' answered Peveril, 'if a threat be indeed implied. I have done no evil—I feel no apprehension—and I cannot, in common sense, conceive why I should suffer for refusing my confidence to a stranger, who seems to require that I should submit me blindfold to his guidance.'[91]

The appeal to 'common sense' sits oddly with the language of suffering and subjection. As Julian finally frees himself, Ganlesse bids him an ominous farewell by echoing the prophecy of the witches in *Macbeth*: 'Farewell, then, Sir Julian of the Peak—that may soon be.'[92] The hints of a secretly desired parricide, though unintended by speaker and unnoticed by hearer, are unmistakable. In contemporary literature, Julian's predicament particularly recalls the scene in *Melmoth the Wanderer* in which Melmoth meets Don Francisco di Aliaga on the road to Madrid, and troubles him with strange hints about what he will find when he reaches his home.[93] Once again the associations of the scene carry the reader far beyond the parameters of likely outcomes.

[90] WN xxix. 73.
[91] WN xxix. 182; and see 'the influence of undefinable apprehension', xxix. 186.
[92] WN xxix. 182–3: *Macbeth*, I. iii. 48–50.
[93] Compare esp. WN xxix. 154–5, *Melmoth*, iv. 346.

Although *Peveril of the Peak* is shaped by parricidal fantasies, as Graham McMaster has argued, they are fantasies which—as in many Gothic novels and novels of political protest from the 1790s—take the specific shape of fears about the legal system, mistaken identity and false imprisonment. The evil father acts through the law. The prison becomes the symbol of personal helplessness and vulnerability to faceless figures of authority. The scenes in which Julian Peveril is imprisoned in Newgate awaiting trial for events which he seems unable to comprehend (in what Scott presents as the frenzy of suspicion and overreaction of the Popish Plot of 1678) repeat a common plot situation in Scott's fiction, but also include half-submerged references to a much more sensationalized treatment of the theme of false imprisonment: Radcliffe's account of Vivaldi's experiences in the prisons of the Inquisition, in *The Italian*.

The parallel brings out important similarities and differences in the heroes' situations and the literary conventions used to suggest them. After descriptions of gloomy gates, conventionally likened to the gates of Dante's Hell, both prisoners are ushered through a maze of dark passages leading to a central chamber.[94] At this point, Radcliffe's Vivaldi reflects in high moralistic fashion on the inhumanity of imprisonment:

While meditating upon these horrors, Vivaldi lost every selfish consideration in astonishment and indignation of the sufferings, which the frenzied wickedness of man prepares for man, who, even at the moment of infliction, insults his victim with assertions of the justice and necessity of such procedure.[95]

Scott, however, glances ironically at such an improbability:

had Peveril come thither as an unconcerned visitor, his heart would have sunk within him at considering the mass of human wretchedness which must needs be registered in these fatal volumes. But his own distresses sat too heavy on his mind to permit any general reflections of this nature.[96]

---

[94] For descriptions of the gates, compare WN xxx. 50–1 and *Italian*, ii. 186; for the passages and chamber, WN xxx. 51–3 and *Italian*, ii. 197–9: humorously, Scott likens his officials to those of the Inquisition, WN xxx. 87.

[95] *Italian*, ii. 190–1.

[96] WN xxx. 53. In *Power and Punishment in Scott's Novels* (Athens, Ga., 1992), 119, Bruce Beiderwell has recently suggested that the Newgate scenes are part of Scott's 'conspicuous avoidance of prison meditation' which must be read politically, as a refusal to question the legal operations of power, in contrast to

After a series of questions in which his answers, like those of Vivaldi, are deliberately misinterpreted by the gaoler, Julian is placed in the cell, not of his father, but of Queen Henrietta Maria's dwarf, Sir Geoffrey Hudson. As Hudson is revealed, rolled up in a huge red cloak in a corner, the reader expects some such gruesome discovery as the bundle of bloodied clothes which Vivaldi and Paulo discover in a corner of the dungeon of Paluzzi. The scene acts instead as a parody of such discoveries. The momentary fear that Julian's father has been murdered is succeeded first by a confused idea that he has somehow been mutilated to dwarf shape and then by comic relief. The close literary debts of this part of *Peveril of the Peak* disorientate the reader, by suggesting fears and evils which are never confronted by the rational narrator. This literary disorientation continues with the mysterious midnight visits to Julian's cell, which imitate the appearances of Nicola, the Monk of Paluzzi, to Vivaldi in the prisons of the Inquisition.[97] Like Radcliffe, Scott evokes the twilight between sleep and consciousness before the visitations, so that the figures of the two strangers assume some of the horrific explicitness of dream:

He dreamed of gliding spirits, gibbering phantoms, bloody hands, which, dimly seen by twilight, seemed to beckon him forward like errant-knight on sad adventure bound. More than once he started from his sleep, so lively was the influence of these visions on his imagination; and he always awaked under the impression that some one stood by his bedside.[98]

Throughout the prison sequence, Scott uses echoes of Gothic simultaneously to heighten the reader's sense of Julian's difficulties and to mock them. As in *Rob Roy*, Gothic echo complicates the overt social and political messages of *Peveril of the Peak* by insisting on the abyss of isolation, incomprehension, and helplessness which underlies the hero's experience and which threatens to

---

novels such as *Caleb Williams* and *The Wrongs of Woman*. This is a useful reminder of the broader context in which *The Italian* and *Peveril of the Peak* alike might be set; but the pseudo-supernatural complications in Scott's scene strongly suggest that the political has again been re-imagined using Gothic literary models of conspicuous excess.

[97] WN xxx. 79–84, 88–97.
[98] WN xxx. 79: compare *Italian*, iii. 167–8.

distort permanently his perception of that ordered and comprehensible social world in which the 'Author of *Waverley*' repeatedly announces his trust. At the same time, the self-consciously literary emotional environment of 'the abyss' is continually subverted by its very self-consciousness. In a way which the next chapter will reveal to be far more prevalent in Scott's work, it is left open to the reader to dismiss fear as a literary convention, to insist upon a ranking of descriptive conventions by which the Newgate scenes fade in historical significance and Sir Geoffrey Hudson is never more than a butt of crude humour. As some of the details selected in this discussion will have suggested, it would be very easy to make the Waverley Novels sound like terror-romances. It is much more difficult to describe the complex stance towards literary convention by which Scott allows certain parts of his works to be dismissed as derivative and secondary.

Scott's choice of literary models for his presentation of these themes draws attention to the close interdependence of the devices of narrative discussed in this chapter and the broader political and cultural criticisms in which he was engaged. For the Newgate and courtroom scenes of *Peveril of the Peak* touch on many topics of contemporary concern. The mockery of legal process in the courts presided over by 'the Lord Chief-Justice (the notorious Scroggs)'[99] echoes the peremptoriness of legal action during the Terror (and suggests a neglected precedent for the English and French trial scenes in *A Tale of Two Cities*). Scott's descriptions of Newgate, the gaoler who 'growled to himself as he turned the leaves of his ominous register',[100] and the trial of suspected Catholic conspirators by a prejudiced and perjured jury, suggest the influence of the Terror over his imagination: a suggestion which is strengthened by his decision to pause in the middle of setting the scene of trial to contrast the English moderation in punishment with the blood-letting favoured by other nations, which he likens to 'the tamed tiger, which, when once its native appetite for slaughter is indulged in one instance, rushes on in promiscuous ravages'.[101] The involvement of *The Italian* in readings of the Newgate scenes of *Peveril of the Peak* is not a dead-end of literary enquiry but calls into question the purpose of the complex allusions and imaginative associations set up at so many points in the Waverley Novels.

[99] *WN* xxx. 191.   [100] *WN* xxx. 108.   [101] *WN* xxx. 187.

Having established that Gothic devices in the novels studied so far represent a positive aesthetic fashioning rather than a negative lapse into mechanical populism, it is possible to examine in rather more detail the purposes for which they exist. Clearly it is not advisable to link any parts of the Waverley Novels too simply with Scott's subconscious, the darker impulses of his imagination (as set out in many accounts of the composition of *The Bride of Lammermoor*, for example) with any particular group of literary or (more narrowly) narratorial conventions. If anxiety is to be discerned it is of a far more general nature. In his 'Letter on Scott', Coleridge provocatively characterized the entire period of Scott's popularity as 'an age of *anxiety* from the crown to the hovel, from the cradle to the coffin; all is an anxious straining to maintain life, or *appearances*—to *rise*, as the only condition of not falling'. The reader in this age, he argues, wishes 'to be *amused*, and forget himself'. In this context, Coleridge proposes that Scott's popularity is due to his avoiding 'the higher beauties and excellencies of style, character, and plot'.[102] Coleridge's accusations of political irrelevance and literary complacency are closely connected. The next chapter aims to make the connection clearer by re-examining those elements in the Waverley Novels which might easily be dismissed as intrusive and irrelevant literary extravagances, but which call into question their declared solutions to social and political problems.

[102] Coleridge, *Misc. Crit.* 335.

5
Phantoms of Revolution: Five Case-Studies of Fictional Convention and Social Analysis

> I am unable to dispute with you in metaphor, sir; but I must say, in discharge of my conscience, that you stand much censured for adulterating the pure sources of historical knowledge. You approach them, men say, like the drunken yeoman, who, once upon a time, polluted the crystal spring which supplied the thirst of his family, with a score of sugar loaves and a hogshead of rum . . .
>
> (Dr Dryasdust to the 'Author of *Waverley*', 1822)[1]

ACCORDING to the pedantic antiquarian Jonas Dryasdust, the 'Author of *Waverley*'s respect for the pure sources of history is fatally compromised by his fondness for the sweeteners and intoxicants of fiction. This chapter focuses on some elements in Scott's novels which remain defiantly conventional in terms of the fashionable literature of his day, and which have largely succeeded in de-selecting themselves from subsequent critical scrutiny as marginal, inferior, or uninspired. Critical dissatisfaction with these apparent lapses is not obtuse, but rather too sensitive to the narrator's implied system of values. Scott is able to use Gothic conventions as variously and experimentally as he does precisely because he always leaves it open to readers to dismiss them as inauthentic. This process is especially complex in works which, like *The Antiquary* and *The Heart of Midlothian*, contain sustained parodies of sensationalist fiction and use its conventions to signal ideologies their narrators want to expose as false. It may seem perverse to read *The Antiquary* for the Glenallans rather than for the Mucklebackits, *The Bride of Lammermoor* through *The*

---

[1] In the Prefatory Epistle of *Peveril of the Peak*, WN xxviii, p. lxxix. The polluted spring or well is a favourite metaphor, prominent for example in Scott's first extended consideration of the rules of historical fiction in the Dedicatory Epistle from Templeton to Dryasdust in *Ivanhoe* (WN xvi, p. xxxii).

Castle of Otranto and *The Milesian Chief* rather than through *Romeo and Juliet* and *Hamlet*, or *The Fortunes of Nigel* through Radcliffean Gothic rather than through Jonson and Shadwell. Doing so, however, draws attention to long sections of these novels which are regularly dismissed as inferior and derivative (and, in the case of *Anne of Geierstein*, to an entire novel dismissed as such). Chapter 2 has already argued, using Godwin's novels as examples, that Gothic conventions should never be too readily explained away as automatic concessions to public taste, even if (as in *Fleetwood*) they are used as tropes of cultural malaise. If Scott's political fictions are to be seen as anything like as complex as his representations of historical authenticity or his response to a Burkean aesthetic of 'silence, fear, and vacuity', it is essential to avoid any rigid distinctions between those sections which have always been regarded as innovative and significant, and those which are constructed (and hence re-described by critics) as concessions to the market and to what the introductory chapter of *The Heart of Midlothian* describes as 'the public's all-devouring appetite for the wonderful and horrible'.

1. *The Dead Past and a Misbegotten Present:* The Antiquary

Styles of literature and styles of appropriating the past are a constant focus of interest and discussion in *The Antiquary*. In keeping with the period in which it is set, the 1790s, the novel refers particularly frequently to the fashion for Gothic and for ballads and histories of the wonderful and supernatural. It features a quack German adept, Hermann Dousterswivel, and a hero whose assumed name (Lovel) is a kind of literary in-joke, being, as the narrator comments, a fashionable choice among novelists of the time.[2] (It is also the name of Clara Reeve's hero in *The Old English Baron*, who of course shares Lovel's calling as the Lost Heir and redeemer of his house.) As well as necromancy and redeeming heroes, ballad-collecting is in vogue in *The Antiquary*. Oldbuck himself hies to the hearthside of Elspeth Mucklebackit in the hope of taking down notes of the ancient ballads she recites, just like a younger Scott in pursuit of material for the *Minstrelsy*.

[2] *WN* v. 59.

Other characters, meanwhile, tell strange tales of supernatural agency. Oldbuck's sister Griselda tells Lovel the mysterious story of the haunted chamber at Monkbarns, while the novel's heroine, Isabella Wardour, entertains a group outing to the local picturesque abbey with a Germanic folktale, 'The Tale of Martin Waldeck'. When she has finished, all her companions except the Antiquary himself express their admiration:

Oldbuck alone curled up his nose, and observed, that Miss Wardour's skill was something like that of the alchemists, for she had contrived to extract a sound and valuable moral out of a very trumpery and ridiculous legend. 'It is the fashion, as I am given to understand, to admire those extravagant fictions—for me,

———————————I bear an English heart,
Unused at ghosts and rattling bones to start.'

Oldbuck's reference comes, topically given the period in which the novel is set, from T. J. Mathias's attack on Lewis in his satirical poem *The Pursuits of Literature*, the same poem to which Scott refers in his 'Life' of Radcliffe to support his high opinion of her work.[3]

In another of his diatribes against modern bad taste, Oldbuck expresses outrage at the proposal that his local town of Fairport should be graced by a monument of a knight-templar placed on each side of a Grecian porch, with a Madonna on top: 'Lord deliver me from this Gothic generation!', he exclaims.[4] The novel itself, however, mixes styles in a comparable way, abjuring formal correctness to produce a novelistic version of Oldbuck's own irregular, cluttered house, Monkbarns. It tells of friendship, reconciliation, and the reintegration of two solitary individuals (Lovel and his father, the Earl of Glenallan) to the community. It also held a special place both in Scott's affections and in the antiquarian frames of his later works.[5] *The Antiquary* also, however, ex-

---

[3] *WN* v. 266; T. J. Mathias, *The Pursuits of Literature: A Satirical Poem in Dialogue, with Notes*, pt. 4 (London, 1797), lines 69–70. Mathias discusses *The Monk*, pp. ii–v. Scott later defends Lewis against the charges of indelicacy brought by Mathias, in 'Essay on Imitations of the Ancient Ballad', *PW* iv. 47–8.

[4] *WN* v. 218. See also Oldbuck on modern literature, v. 227.

[5] On friendship, see Wilson, *Laird of Abbotsford*, 71–3: for *The Antiquary*, legitimacy, and the 'pickling' of the past, see Wilt, *Secret Leaves*, 157–70; on the relationship between past and present, see Brown, *Historical Imagination*, ch. 3; also Hart, *Scott's Novels*, 251–4; Johnson, 536–43; Levine, *Realistic Imagination*,

presses varying intensities of loneliness, emotional deprivation, and cultural loss, which are concentrated in the story which Lockhart called 'the stately gloom of the Glenallans'.[6] Hazlitt thought that for 'sublime, heart-breaking pathos' and 'terrific painting', nothing that Scott had published could surpass the Glenallan story, 'the most harrowing in all these novels'.[7] The Glenallans strongly prefigure both the prevailing atmosphere and the cultural implications of the stately, sterile, Dedlock household in *Bleak House*, and, like the Dedlocks, they represent social and emotional states which the outcome of the novel's plot strongly suggests to be obsolete.

The mixed style or generic identity of *The Antiquary*, like the plot of *Rob Roy*, is a familiar critical problem. A. N. Wilson notes that it seems to be made up of two different novels, one a tale of convincing provincial character-types and the other 'a Gothic Romance by Mrs Radcliffe' in which the Countess of Glenallan weaves her villainous plots and her son ekes out 'a life of pious gloom analogous to Philip II's solitude in the Escorial'.[8] Wilson's instinct is to allow the two novels to lack coherence and to find their purpose elsewhere, in the celebration of the character of the Antiquary, friendship, and conversation. Edgar Johnson, on the other hand, strives to reconcile the two plots by emphasizing their common concern with the theme of time. Is there any way of interpreting the function of the Glenallan plot in *The Antiquary* which allows the novel a greater degree of formal inventiveness and imagination than Wilson's description of a conversation-novel suggests, but which does not fall back simply on the general humanistic themes proposed by Johnson?

The Glenallan plot is very different from the rest of *The Antiquary*, and it is abruptly introduced into a narrative which is at first exclusively concerned with the families of Oldbuck and Wardour, Sir Arthur Wardour's emotional and intellectual dependence on Dousterswivel's trickeries, and the ill-starred ro-

---

121–3. Key readings of the social messages of the Glenallan sections of the novel are given by Joan S. Elbers, 'Isolation and Community in *The Antiquary*', *Nineteenth-Century Fiction*, xxvii (1972–3), 405–23, and Millgate, *Making of the Novelist*, 98–103.

[6] Lockhart, v. 145.
[7] Hazlitt, *Works*, xviii. 301–2.
[8] *Laird of Abbotsford*, 70–4 (70).

mance of Lovel and Isabella. In the middle of the farcical double-crossings of Dousterswivel and Edie Ochiltree in the Gothic ruins of St Ruth's, a funeral procession is introduced, in darkness and secrecy, which evokes all the associations of a moribund past of 'popery' and superstition. In contrast to the funeral of Steenie Mucklebackit, in which Scott invokes Wilkie, this burial is invested with all the vague unspoken horrors of the burial of Madame Montoni in *The Mysteries of Udolpho*. It appears incongruous and modishly unreal:

> a man, of a figure once tall and commanding, but now bent with age or infirmity, stood alone and nearest to the coffin, attired in deep mourning— such were the most prominent figures of the group.... The smoky light from so many flambeaus, by the red and indistinct atmosphere which it spread around, gave a hazy, dubious, and, as it were, phantom-like appearance to the outlines of this singular apparition.[9]

The uncertainty extends to the identity of the person being buried. Exploiting the atmospherics of mystery to make the most of his disconcerting change of subject and style, Scott keeps the reader in suspense on this matter for several pages. Indeed, he drops hints which can only suggest that Isabella Wardour herself has died. Vague references to 'the leddy's burial' can imply nothing else at this stage, when the reader has been introduced to only one 'leddy' of any note or interest. The suspense continues over the chapter-break, as the narrator teasingly turns to introduce an entirely different family, the Mucklebackits. Only then does he explain that the dead woman is the dowager Countess of Glenallan and the chief mourner her reclusive elder son. The abrupt introduction of the Glenallan plot might suggest that it is indeed the contrived and melodramatic afterthought which most critics have thought it. Instead its clearly signalled disjointedness is characteristic of its relationship to some of the most persistent moral and artistic concerns of *The Antiquary* as a whole. There is no need to dismiss it, as Virginia Woolf did, as false and unnatural, but there is every need to register its consciously tangential position.[10]

The plot eventually revealed to Lord Glenallan by Elspeth Mucklebackit (in a chapter heralded, significantly, by a quotation

---

[9] WN vi. 59–60. Scott argues in his *Journal* (127–8) that funerals have greater aesthetic effect when seen from a distance.
[10] Woolf, *Collected Essays*, i. 142–3.

from *The Mysterious Mother*) tells how, twenty years before the novel opens, the old Countess of Glenallan destroys her son's marriage by convincing him that his new wife, Eveline Neville, is also his half-sister. (A similar plot is used in Maturin's tale of the Widow Sandal in the fourth volume of *Melmoth the Wanderer*, published four years after *The Antiquary*.) Eveline, heartbroken and suicidal, does not survive the birth of her child, while Lord Glenallan retreats into a gloomy world of seclusion and extreme Catholic piety. Their child escapes the death planned by the Countess but is brought up to believe himself doubly stained as the illegitimate child of incestuous parents. He re-emerges as Lovel, the novel's hero. Meanwhile, the Countess's servant and accomplice, Elspeth Mucklebackit, carries the secret of the plot with her into a twilight old age of guilt and alienation. In the novel's narrative present, this story of the guilty past, conventionally melodramatic though it is, leaves a taint of psychological pain and distortion which is unusually intense for this stage of Scott's career. It also intensifies some of the novel's most important preoccupations. One of these is Scott's interest in states of unnaturally arrested and obsessive psychology. Many of the characters are enclosed in psychological prisons or houses which have become prisons. The Glenallan plot produces two. The first is the dead environment of Glenallan House, enclosing the living prison of Glenallan's mind. The second, more extreme and more chilling, is Elspeth Mucklebackit's closed imagination. According to Edie Ochiltree, Elspeth's entire psychology is a kind of Gothic ruin:

auld Elspeth's like some of the ancient ruined strengths and castles that ane sees amang the hills. There are mony parts of her mind that appear, as I may say, laid waste and decayed, but then there's parts that look the steever, and the stronger, and the grander, because they are rising just like to fragments amang the ruins o' the rest—She's an awful woman.[11]

Elspeth's punishment for her complicity in the Countess's crime is an extreme mental isolation from community, a death in life. In her 'hollow and sepulchral voice', she speaks not of the present but of the obsessive images of her imagination and memory. As Jenny Rintherout says: 'it's awsome to hear your gudemither break out in that gait—it's like the dead speaking to the living'.[12]

[11] *WN* vi. 98.
[12] *WN* vi. 72; Jenny on Elspeth and the uncanny, vi. 72; see also vi. 133, 136. Hazlitt likens Elspeth to 'a speaking corpse', *Works*, xviii. 302.

The presentation of the Earl of Glenallan has much in common
with the death-in-life of Elspeth. He likewise is enclosed in a mental
prison of guilt converted to fanaticism, this time a fanaticism
of extreme Catholic piety and penance governed by what Scott
presents as the very strictest forms of Catholic ritual. If Elspeth's
isolation is imagined in architectural terms by Edie, the isolation
of the Earl takes the form of a gloomy and oppressive house. By
the dowager Countess's insistence, Glenallan House has not been
modernized. The paintings which dominate it demonstrate 'the
gloomy taste of the family'. There are works by Van Dyck (associated with the Caroline court and its doomed principles of monarchic absolutism and divine right) and the Catholic martyrdoms
of Domenichino, Velasquez, and Murillo ('awful, and sometimes
disgusting, subjects').[13] In the Earl's private chamber are stained
glass windows depicting the life of Jeremiah, and a Spagnoletto
painting of the martyrdom of St Stephen. If the Mucklebackit
family is commonly associated with Wilkie, Scott has chosen
Rembrandt (his favourite for dark, gloomy subjects) for the
Glenallans. Living like a recluse in these tomb-like chambers is the
cadaverous figure of the Earl himself: 'The inhabitant and lord
of this disconsolate chamber was a man not past the prime of
life, yet so broken down with disease and mental misery, so
gaunt and ghastly, that he appeared but a wreck of manhood.'[14]
Scott has carefully planned that the man sent to meet this pre-
maturely wasted figure should be the 'hale' mendicant, Edie
Ochiltree.

If Elspeth Mucklebackit's occasional outbursts sound like 'the
dead speaking to the living', the language of the Earl of Glenallan
is moribund in a highly literary manner. His form of speech is as
formal, literary, and dead, as his palace of gloomy Catholic art
suggests:

'tell me, do you come to say, that all that has been done to expiate guilt
so horrible, has been too little and too trivial for the offence, and to point
out new and more efficacious modes of severe penance?...'[15]

'Ay,' said the appalled nobleman, as his countenance sunk, and his cheek
assumed a hue yet more cadaverous; 'that name is indeed written in the
most tragic page of a deplorable history...'[16]

13 WN vi. 91.   14 WN vi. 94.
15 WN vi. 95.   16 WN vi. 97.

The Antiquary is the novel which led Virginia Woolf to lament the astonishing dead language of Scott's lovers ('when, with a dismal croaking and cawing, they emit the astonishing language of their love-making').[17] On rereading it, she had perhaps compounded the linguistic sins of Lovel with those of his father.

One fairly well-established way of reintegrating the Glenallan story, with its insistence on the subjects of incest and illegitimacy, with the novel which keeps it in abeyance for so long, is to argue that it is one of several stories in *The Antiquary* which signal failed relationships with the past. It might be regarded as a modern version of the story of Malcolm the Misbegot, to which Sir Arthur Wardour traces 'that horror and antipathy to defiled blood and illegitimacy, which has been handed down to me from my respected ancestry'.[18] The Glenallan plot might easily be assimilated, therefore, to what critics have seen as the dominant preoccupation of *The Antiquary*, the discrimination between good and bad ways of living with the past. It might serve to suggest stylized images of certain repressive forces in the Scottish past: particularly that past's Catholicism (reduced to ritual and secrecy, and associated with darkness and death in contrast to the robust Protestantism of the Oldbuck line),[19] and the dangers of a closed aristocratic system, one of the points constantly in dispute between Sir Arthur Wardour and Oldbuck. The novel insists that society must limit the power of an outdated, inward-looking aristocracy cut off from the changing world. Eventually, the Earl regains friends, national feeling, and a son, undergoing a comprehensive re-socialization. Lovel, the outcast who threateningly declares his detachment from society in contrast to Ochiltree's role at the centre of his community, is the 'phoenix Lovel'[20] who rises at the end of the novel as the military saviour of Fairport, discovers his rightful inheritance, and removes through his Protestantism the most lasting spiritual scar of the Glenallan inheritance. The true 'misbegot', after all, the usurper of the Wardour inheritance far back in the past, ended his days as Prior of St Ruth's. The purification of the

[17] Woolf, *Collected Essays*, i. 140.
[18] *WN* v. 181.
[19] On Oldbuck and Protestantism, see *WN* v. 18; Catholicism, 'darkness', and 'secrecy', vi. 71. Ironically, however, there are similarities in the situations of Oldbuck and Glenallan. Both loved Eveline Neville, and both have buried themselves in obsessions about the past in an attempt to overcome her loss.
[20] *WN* vi. 188.

Glenallan line is linked through Lovel to a myth of national
regeneration and reunion. The illegitimate and oppressive past
which it rejects—the closed mind of half-living, half-dead Elspeth
Mucklebackit who offers a false route back to the traditional
Scottish past (her ballads and stories, coveted by Oldbuck); the
tyranny of her obsessive mistress, now disposed of by secret burial
in a deserted abbey—is made accessible to Scott's readership of
1816 through the stylized exaggerations of Gothic.

To assimilate the story too neatly in this way, however, is to fail
to respond to its distinctive disjointedness and to smooth over the
aesthetic and political problems which are raised by its inclusion
in *The Antiquary*. Thematically the Glenallans do not threaten the
novel's ideological closures, but technically they do. They force
the recognition that Scott's novels are not seamless endorsements
of the rational and the normative but experimental, questioning,
and aesthetically disruptive.

The political argument conducted through the aesthetic becomes
comparably complex and restless. The preoccupations found concentrated in the Glenallan story make especially interesting reading in the political context of the years immediately following
Waterloo, in which the new European order was establishing itself
and the forces for monarchic legitimacy becoming strongly associated in France and in most countries of the anti-Napoleonic
alliance with a return to religious orthodoxy. On the surface, the
political references of *The Antiquary* fight battles long since won.
They allude to the wartime fears of the 1790s and to the immediate
post-Revolutionary debate. Oldbuck suggests the topicality of an
epic poem to be entitled 'The Caledoniad; or, Invasion Repelled',
and muses on the contrast between the rational principles and the
bloodthirsty actions of the revolutionaries in France. During the
very first conversation between Oldbuck and Sir Arthur Wardour,
Sir Arthur responds to threats of 'invasion from abroad and insurrection at home', arguing that they all 'ought to resist *cum toto
corpore regni*,—as the phrase is, unless I have altogether forgotten
my Latin—an enemy who comes to propose to us a Whiggish sort
of government, a republican system, and who is aided and abetted
by a sort of fanatics of the worst kind in our own bowels'.[21] Later,
the Earl of Glenallan expresses from his Catholic and aristocratic

21 *WN* v. 78.

standpoint an extreme horror of the French Revolution, and his dead mother is reported to have been outraged that 'the authority which the nobles of the land should exercise is delegated to quibbling lawyers and their baser dependents'.[22] The world of Fairport is, also appropriately for its imagined time, a world of spies and gossip, of mysterious intelligences (between Lovel and Edie Ochiltree) and not-so-mysterious efforts at investigation (as made by the ladies of the Fairport post office).

In addition, however, the topics debated in the novel have a distinct relevance to the post-Revolutionary order evolving (or imposed) at the time of its composition. Scott seems to be creating an alternative version of what a Protestant legitimacy might involve, centred on the interdependence of all strata within the social order and explicitly rejecting the Catholicism of the Glenallans by association with secrecy, anti-social activity and a melodramatic conspiracy based on incest and illegitimacy. The way forward endorsed by the plot of The Antiquary is obviously based on a reconciliation with the past, but it is equally based on a dynastic legitimacy which, it insists, and in spite of examples elsewhere in Europe, can be both Protestant and progressive. The bolstering of Britain at the end of The Antiquary presents itself as a defence against outside attack during the revolutionary wars with France. It is also, however, highly relevant to the situation which confronted Britain at the end of those wars. The Glenallans, like that later line of Catholic reactionaries, the Redgauntlets, must be reconciled to the present day by way of a hero brought up in ignorance of his identity and inheritance, a legitimate representative but an ideological opponent of the dead past which he alone can revitalize.

2. An Apostate Spirit Incarnate: The Heart of Midlothian

> Cockades and banners are not trifles, Sir, when they become the badge of peculiar opinions. A white ribband made treason in the year forty-five, to display a red cap announces a republican ever since 1792.
>
> (Scott on Peterloo, 1819)[23]

[22] WN vi. 156. Oldbuck and Glenallan discuss the French Revolution, vi. 186.
[23] Letter to Editor of the Edinburgh Weekly Journal, quoted by McMaster, Scott and Society, 231.

The self-conscious literariness found in the Glenallan plot has
been lamented in all the scenes in *The Heart of Midlothian* which
involve George Staunton. Critics have almost unanimously declared him to be the novel's fatal flaw, a betrayal of the new
standards of characterization and historical imagination achieved
in Scott's portrayal of the peasant heroine, Jeanie Deans.[24] Not
surprisingly, an authoritative explanation for his disruptive effect
on the novel is close at hand, for Scott had always lamented his
liking for the dark villains who turned out to be more interesting
than his heroes. He chose to present this as a personal quirk over
which he had little control. The effects of Staunton on the novel's
ideology are not so easily explained away, however. Literary to
the point of being blatantly derivative, his role in the novel is a
significant and troublesome addition to the source tale of Helen
Walker.

It is not difficult to determine the social and political opinions
which Scott satirizes in his portrayal of Staunton. No critic has
failed to register the satire on Byronism (to which, I shall claim,
should be added a critique of an earlier influence, Schiller).
Staunton is destructive, unprincipled, self-indulgent, and subversive. He combines social authority and anti-social alienation, taking
conscious pleasure in the assumed role of criminal outcast, and
telling Jeanie Deans: 'When you see owls and bats fly abroad, like
larks, in the sunshine, you may expect to see such as I am in the
assemblies of men.'[25] Scott's portrait of the revolutionary strongly
recalls Milton's Satan and the literary traditions he inspired. Self-
dramatizing, self-pitying, Staunton is a rebel against a loving father
and a master of disguise: a 'wretch, concentred all in self', to
quote the Miltonic echoes of the most famous section of *The Lay*

[24] The following critics give key interpretations of Staunton: Mayhead notes
Staunton's similarities to Schedoni, *Walter Scott*, 4–5; Brown argues that Scott
lacked interest in Staunton, *Historical Imagination*, 126; Millgate comments on
Staunton's melodrama, *Making of the Novelist*, 165; Lamont denounces Staunton
as a character-creation in the introd. to her edn. of *The Heart of Midlothian*
(Oxford, 1982), p. xvii; Kerr interprets Staunton as a 'Gothic straw man', *Fiction
against History*, 78; Harry E. Shaw gives the most weighty single interpretation,
The Forms of Historical Fiction: Sir Walter Scott and His Successors (Ithaca, NY,
1983), 234–8. Scott's treatment of the sources of *The Heart of Midlothian* is most
fully discussed by Mary Lascelles in *The Story-Teller Retrieves the Past: Historical
Fiction and Fictitious History in the Art of Scott, Stevenson, Kipling and Some
Others* (Oxford, 1980), 84–102.
[25] WN xii. 17.

of the Last Minstrel.[26] He is an actor of consummate ability (like
Lovelace, Henry Crawford, and many of Scott's dark heroes), and
one of his gestures of rebellion is to work as a travelling player.
The styles of his letters to Effie and to the Edinburgh court are
self-consciously dramatic, and he even admits to Jeanie that his
letter to Effie recommending Meg Murdockson as midwife was
written in the character of Macheath. His only magnanimous
words during the Porteous murder, delivered in theatrical fashion
to the crowd, are taken from *Othello* ('we will not kill both his
soul and body').[27] The echo subtly suggests his social superiority,
his exploitation of it, and his fantasies of power. He has clearly
developed a highly literary self-image, evident in his attempt to
reassure Jeanie at Muschat's Cairn: 'Mad, frantic, as I am, and
unrestrained by either fear or mercy, given up to the possession of
an evil being, and forsaken by all that is good, I would not hurt
you, were the world offered me for a bribe!'[28] Other characters
are flatteringly willing to accept this self-image. Even the prosaic
Reuben Butler—steeped, perhaps, in Milton—waxes lyrical about
him:

The fiery eye, the abrupt demeanour, the occasionally harsh, yet studiously
subdued tone of voice,—the features, handsome, but now clouded with
pride, now disturbed by suspicion, now inflamed with passion—those
dark hazel eyes which he sometimes shaded with his cap, as if he were
averse to have them seen while they were occupied with keenly observing
the motions and bearing of others—those eyes that were now turbid with
melancholy, now gleaming with scorn, and now sparkling with fury—was
it the passions of a mere mortal they expressed, or the emotions of a
fiend, who seeks, and seeks in vain, to conceal his fiendish designs under
the borrowed mask of manly beauty?[29]

Many of these descriptions of Staunton sound clichéd to the point
of pastiche. In this passage, for example, Butler can find no better
adjective than 'fiendish' to describe the designs of a 'fiend'.

The literary affiliations of Scott's presentation of Staunton repay
a little further elaboration. As commonly noted, Staunton is a
thoroughgoing parody of the rhetoric of Byron's heroes as found

[26] *PW* vi. 187.
[27] *WN* xi. 262, referring to *Othello*, v. ii. 32.
[28] *WN* xii. 12. The problems of Staunton's self-image were shrewdly described
by Nassau Senior, *Quarterly Review*, xxvi. 119.
[29] *WN* xi. 356.

in such early works as *Childe Harold* I and II, *The Giaour*, and *The Corsair*; and he registers particularly clearly Scott's irritation at the combination of liberalism and aristocratic disdain in Byron's work. Scott reacted angrily, for example, against the ennui of aristocratic privilege which he thought indulged in *Childe Harold* I and II, and later maintained that he always thought Byron 'a patrician on principle'.[30] Like many contemporary readers, Scott underestimated Byron's doubts about his heroes, apparently failing to register the strong indications of self-parody in the early parts of *Childe Harold* and the Turkish tales, but he clearly recognized the contradictions and uncertainties in Byron's political stance. Staunton, therefore, is what Scott saw as the most dangerous type of demagogue: the self-indulgent man of leisure, born to an independence which he can afford to abuse. There is more to Staunton than a satire on Byronism, however. He is also a close imitation of an earlier villain-hero who had been one of the common sources for the heroes of Byron's and Scott's own verse romances: Karl von Moor in Schiller's play *Die Räuber*. Scott's enthusiastic early reading of *Die Räuber* during the 'German mad' phase of his youth is well attested. His interest in German literature was aroused by Alexander F. Tytler's translation of *Die Räuber* in 1792, and by Mackenzie's 'Account of the German Theatre' read to the Royal Society of Edinburgh in 1788 and printed in its *Transactions* ii (1790). Schiller's play was, in addition, widely read as a fiction of revolution. Elements in Staunton's story directly recall the plot of *Die Räuber*. Karl von Moor's wildness tortures his doting father. Staunton, similarly, repays indulgence with neglect and disobedience. Karl von Moor saves Roller from the gallows, and Roller, in return, is loyal to him. Staunton and Wilson behave with similar loyalty to each other. Staunton does not kill Effie Deans, but he is very fond of seeing her as his tragic victim, in a role comparable to that of Karl von Moor's Amalia. However, Scott pointedly challenges the political implications of *Die Räuber*. Like Karl von Moor, Staunton is subversive and destructive, but Scott misses no opportunity to expose him as an actor, a devil, and a madman: a 'maniac, or an apostate spirit incarnate'.[31]

---

[30] *Letters*, iii. 98–9, 114–15, 123, 135, 137, 217–18, 454; Scott on Byron, cited by Lockhart, v. 40.
[31] *WN* xii. 10.

Staunton, therefore, is a satire on the masquerading revolutionary, as perfect a combination as any anti-Jacobin could desire of indulgent bourgeois upbringing (spoiled by his mother), adolescent rebellion, promiscuity, and sentimental attachments posing as egalitarian principles. Dressed in Madge Wildfire's clothes to lead the storming of the Tolbooth, he recalls those women revolutionaries of France who came to symbolize the struggle for liberty:

Several of those who seemed most active were dressed in sailors' jackets, trowsers, and sea caps; others in large loose-bodied great-coats, and slouched hats; and there were several who, judging from their dress, should have been called women, whose rough deep voices, uncommon size, and masculine deportment and mode of walking, forbade them being so interpreted. They moved as if by some well-concerted plan of arrangement. They had signals by which they knew, and nicknames by which they distinguished each other. Butler remarked, that the name of Wildfire was used among them, to which one stout Amazon seemed to reply.[32]

The scenes surrounding the Porteous riots and the mob advance on the Tolbooth are charged with revolutionary implications.[33] Scott describes them in such politically loaded terms that one constantly expects him to draw the comparison with the storming of the Bastille or the march on Versailles, which he describes so vividly in the 'Preliminary View of the French Revolution' in his *Life of Napoleon Buonaparte*. Closely indebted to Burke's rhetoric in the *Reflections on the Revolution in France*, Scott's account of the events of 5 and 6 October 1789 bristles with references

---

[32] WN xi. 245.

[33] In his discussion of *The Heart of Midlothian* in *Revolution as Tragedy*, Farrell parallels Scott's Tolbooth and the Bastille and describes Staunton as 'a terminal type of the revolutionary' (p. 104); while Donald D. Stone, in *The Romantic Impulse in Victorian Fiction* (Cambridge, Mass., 1980), suggests that Scott offers two versions of Romanticism in *The Heart of Midlothian*, 'a Burke-derived loyalty to the structures of political and religious restraint, and an almost Byronic fascination with the disruptive energies of the individual' (p. 12). See K. J. Logue's 'Anatomy of the Scottish Crowd', in *Popular Disturbances in Scotland, 1780–1815* (Edinburgh, 1979), ch. 9. David Lodge briefly places the Porteous riots alongside Carlyle's *French Revolution* and scenes of mob violence in early Victorian fiction, in which he argues that the French Revolution had changed the idea of the power of crowds, 'Crowds and Power in the Early Victorian Novel' (1989), repr. in his *After Bakhtin: Essays on Fiction and Criticism* (London, 1990), 100–15 (114).

to 'Amazons', 'female demons', 'murderous bacchantes', and 'drunken females'.[34]

The novel also contains its idyll of the counter-revolution, an image of the benevolent forces of community, and again this image is significantly feminized. In heroic contrast to Staunton, Jeanie Deans is a peasant heroine whose story puts the case *against* revolutionary struggle. Staunton is confined to his sickbed in a passion of resentment and guilt while Jeanie makes her pragmatic way to London in quest for Effie's pardon. She travels away from Edinburgh with its simmering resentment, aided by the down-trodden laird, Dumbiedikes. She falls alternately into rebel hands (Meg Murdockson and the robbers) and into the control of figures of benevolent, but impotent, authority. She progresses through the village in which Staunton's father is the model of an upright Anglican clergyman, and finds not only Staunton but also the complications and upsets caused by Madge Wildfire. The village itself, and its simple rural ceremonies, are seen as something which might be good, but which Jeanie is forced to experience through the hysteria of the woman its principles have failed to protect. After this, she travels through London, where she meets the foil of revolutionary 'Madge' in the figure of Queen Caroline. She progresses, finally, to the protection of the ideal aristocrat, Argyle. If *The Heart of Midlothian* opens with an uneasy question—what is to prevent mob rule, especially in a land unjustly governed?—it closes with the answer of the new integrated society represented

---

[34] *Life of Napoleon*, i. 185–200. Burke's account of the October days is discussed by Tom Furniss, 'Gender in Revolution: Edmund Burke and Mary Wollstonecraft', in *Revolution in Writing: British Literary Responses to the French Revolution*, ed. Kelvin Everest, Ideas and Production (Milton Keynes, 1991), 65–100. There is a growing literature on the role of women in the French Revolution. What has been described recently as the 'first generation' of this scholarship includes Paule-Marie Duhet, *Les Femmes et la Révolution, 1789–1794* (Paris, 1971), and Darline Gay Levy, Harriet Bronson Applewhite, and Mary Durham Johnson, *Women in Revolutionary Paris, 1789–1795: Selected Documents Translated with Notes and Commentary* (Urbana, Ill., 1979). More recent discussions include Joan B. Landes, *Women and the Public Sphere in the Age of the French Revolution* (Ithaca, NY, 1988); Darline Gay Levy and Harriet Applewhite, 'Women and Militant Citizenship in Revolutionary Paris', in *Rebel Daughters: Women and the French Revolution*, ed. Sara E. Melzer and Leslie W. Rabine, Publications of the University of California Humanities Research Institute (New York, 1992), 79–101. Logue comments on the role of women in crowd violence during Scott's time in *Popular Disturbances in Scotland*, 199–203. See also Jon Thompson's discussion 'Sir Walter Scott and Madge Wildfire: Strategies of Containment in *The Heart of Midlothian*', *Literature and History*, xiii (1987), 188–99.

by Jeanie's new home. Jeanie's quest takes her to the centre of the unjust authority which sparked the problems of the novel's beginning, through episodes which reflect different aspects of the legal, ecclesiastical, and aristocratic establishment.

This description of the contrast between Staunton and Jeanie Deans makes the messages of *The Heart of Midlothian* seem simple. There are complications in the novel's ideological stance, however. Effie Deans, for example, who starts out as 'this untaught child of nature', ends up as a false creature of 'artificial breeding'. Metaphors of nature and art used in this moralistic way are most often associated with Rousseau-inspired Jacobin fiction of the 1790s, with Bage's *Hermsprong* or with Inchbald's *Nature and Art*, which takes as its heroine a village girl, the pastorally named Hannah Primrose, seduced by the young squire William Norwynne.[35] The plot of the seduced village maiden has strong sentimental and implicit political connotations. In these novels evil is firmly associated with aristocratic principles. Radcliffe had addressed the same concern in her complex meditations on nature and art in *The Romance of the Forest*, where the contrast ranges from architectural description (the Marquis of Montalt's baroque palace of vice and art versus the pastoral idyll of the Leloncourt scenes and the forest setting of the early meetings of Theodore and Adeline) to a debate on medicine.[36] The pathos of female innocence exploited by aristocratic licentiousness had been a feature of many moral tales of social life, from *The Man of Feeling* to 'The Deserted Village', the novels of Wollstonecraft and Hays, and the poems of Crabbe. Scott may have wanted to discredit one kind of revolutionary, but he knew (as he was to show clearly in *The Fortunes of Nigel* four years later) that the greatest danger to his society came from the misuse of the authority which accompanies wealth and high birth. As a consequence, *The Heart of Midlothian* negotiates a troubled relationship to the desirability of social and political change. Staunton and Effie are both familiar literary types, but their stories pull in quite different political

[35] See Spencer, *Rise of the Woman Novelist*, ch. 4. A broad account of the social implications of tales of seduction is given by Anna Clark in 'The Politics of Seduction in English Popular Culture, 1748–1848', *The Progress of Romance: The Politics of Popular Fiction*, ed. Jean Radford, History Workshop Series (London, 1986), 47–70.
[36] *Romance of Forest*, i. 4–5, 19, 21–2, 186, ii. 117–20, 133–4 (Montalt's mansion), ii. 125–6, 189–90 (art and nature in healing), iii. 54, 283.

directions. The problem becomes pressing when one considers the
sequence of cause and effect leading up to Staunton's murder by
his long-lost child, an outlaw known only as 'The Whistler'.
Critics have no difficulty in establishing the poetic justice of the
murder itself. The Whistler is a parodic child of nature, a product
of the anarchy in which Staunton dabbles, and a suitable agent
of his punishment. Although the Whistler unknowingly kills his
father, however, he is set free to do so by Jeanie Deans. The
Whistler is not just (unknowingly) taking his own revenge on a
father who deserted him. He is also acting as the agent of Jeanie's.

This ambiguity extends to Scott's apparently straightforward
satire on the romantic revolutionary. Staunton creates tensions in
The Heart of Midlothian because Scott, for all his careful emphasis
on the social and spiritual dangers which Staunton represents,
continually reinforces Staunton's self-image by giving him a role
which corresponds to his own inflated imaginings:

> This sentence was spoken with the bitterness of self-upbraiding, and a
> contortion of visage absolutely demoniacal. Butler, though a man brave
> by principle, if not by constitution, was overawed; for intensity of mental
> distress has in it a sort of sublimity which repels and overawes all men,
> but especially those of kind and sympathetic dispositions.[37]

All generalizations about Staunton indicate Scott's disapproval,
but the minutiae of description and authorial comment, shown in
this passage, indicate a much more ambivalent response. Scott's
mixture of disapproval and attraction suggests a difficulty which
threatens to disrupt the declared moral scheme of *The Heart of
Midlothian*. The simple moral at the end of the novel, which
resembles those used by Radcliffe, is a strikingly incomplete response to the complicated issues with which it had begun. The
'placid loves' of Jeanie and Butler have satisfied very few readers
(although some recent critics have helpfully clarified the political context of Scott's creation of pastoral in the Knocktarlitie
episodes).[38] What most readers have regarded as the inferior
quality of the fourth volume seems to be an indictment of what
Scott saw when he projected Jeanie and Reuben into married
security, financial ease, and the property market. Critical revaluation of the fourth volume, however, can best proceed by an
emphasis on genre and convention, comparable to that proposed

---

[37] *WN* xi. 354.
[38] See esp. Kerr, *Fiction against History*, ch. 3.

here as a way of understanding Staunton's role in the novel. Both the Knocktarlitie idyll and the demonic Staunton register cultural desiderata in self-consciously stereotyped literary terms which both state and (through an excess which begins to parody itself) refute the novel's interpretation of society and politics.

One other issue draws attention to the complexity of the issues at stake in *The Heart of Midlothian*. While Scott was working on *The Heart of Midlothian*, he was following with interest the Scottish state trials of 1817, an attempt by the Lord Advocate, Alexander Maconochie, to justify the reports of dangerous radical conspiracy in Glasgow, especially among the group of radicals infiltrated by the government informer, Alexander Richmond. Two Glasgow radicals, one defended by Francis Jeffrey, were convicted, but were given prison sentences so short that they have been regarded by most historians as indictments of the legal system and its administrators rather than as evidence of the reality of radical threat. Fears about insurrection did not die down, and were in part justified by the so-called Radical War in 1820, which led to three executions. Scott himself was clearly convinced of the revolutionary threat, and his opinions about its supposed perpetrators are more than clear in letters of the time which refer to 'the Bonnymuir warriors' and 'the Radical row'.[39] But it is surely significant that the novel which emerges in this confused period is concerned not only with mob violence and conspiracy, but also with the conflicts between truth and justice. John Campbell, a witness for the prosecution at the trial of John McKinlay in July 1817, told the truth to devastating effect when asked whether he had been bribed: 'To the bench's customary opening question, "Has anybody given you a reward, or promise of a reward, for being a witness?", Campbell replied in the affirmative and pointed out as the person who had approached him the advocate-depute.'[40]

[39] Scott comments on the delayed trials of 'the Bonnymuir warriors', as he contemptuously describes them, in a letter to his son Walter in June 1820 (*Letters*, vi. 209). He also writes at length to Thomas Scott on 'the Radical row' and the gallantry of the yeomanry, which reminds him of the loyalty of his great-grandfather, his proudest family tale (vi. 234–5).

[40] William Ferguson, *Scotland 1689 to the Present*, The Edinburgh History of Scotland, iv (1968; repr. Edinburgh, 1978), 282. Francis Jeffrey acted as counsel for the defence at the trial of McKinlay. In *Power and Punishment in Scott's Novels*, 78, Bruce Beiderwell suggests as an alternative context for Effie's trial the charge of 'constructive treason' brought against Lord George Gordon, 'instigator' of the anti-Catholic riots in 1785.

Some of the ideological tensions in *The Heart of Midlothian*, which ends, far more than most Scott novels, as a resoundingly bourgeois rather than aristocratic idyll, are especially appropriate to a period in which Scott clearly feared mob violence but also saw the difficulties caused by trying to deal with it in courts of law. At a time when the Scottish legal system was having such difficulty in bringing a case against supposed radical insurrectionists, it is significant to find Scott being so strongly drawn to the story of a criminal trial in which the defendant must produce evidence that she has *not* committed murder, instead of the prosecutors proving that she *has*. The threat to the balance between law and justice in *The Heart of Midlothian* is that the law must make its case by proving a negative, an act omitted (Effie telling Jeanie she is pregnant) rather than committed (Effie murdering her child). Jeanie's quest is a redemption of law. It translates into personal, spiritual (and female) terms what has conspicuously failed in the public, pragmatic (and masculine) world of organized justice.

3. Re-Plotting Nationalist Rebellion:
The Bride of Lammermoor *and* The Milesian Chief

It is instructive to move from *The Heart of Midlothian* to *The Bride of Lammermoor*, published with its companion tale *A Legend of Montrose* in the year of Peterloo. *The Heart of Midlothian* begins with a breakdown in civil obedience and moves on to problematize the legal system which must attempt to resolve or at least to contain it. In *The Bride of Lammermoor*, also, from a situation which might be interpreted as an incitement to revolt (and which is so interpreted, briefly at least, in the riot following the funeral of Lord Ravenswood), the adequacy of legal redress is brought under scrutiny, and found wanting—or, perhaps worse, irrelevant. Both novels put the case against violent revolt to restore usurped social and political powers, without finding an adequate compensatory faith in the rule of law. Both draw extensively on literary models with striking, though not always consistent, political implications. The argument which follows examines *The Bride of Lammermoor* from the perspectives of (first, and briefly) *The Castle of Otranto* and (second and in detail) Maturin's *The Milesian*

Chief (1812). *The Milesian Chief* has occasionally been suggested as a possible source for *The Bride of Lammermoor*, but no sustained investigation of the likelihood of this, or its implications, has yet been attempted.

Of all Scott's novels, *The Bride of Lammermoor* follows most closely the historicizing of terror which characterizes Gothic.[41] In the terms established by Walpole in the preface to the second edition of *The Castle of Otranto*, it explains away superstition as the product of the age in which its story is set, and examines suffering as the result of crimes committed by previous generations. Although it follows the details of an established oral and written tale (the history of Janet Dalrymple, described in the introduction to the Magnum Opus), it also self-consciously organizes itself according to a range of other literary patterns from *Romeo and Juliet* to *The Castle of Otranto*.[42] The novel's narrator, Peter Pattieson, insists towards the end of his story that he has based it on an 'OWER TRUE TALE', and attempts to distinguish it from novels which describe sensational events only to gratify 'the popular appetite for the horrible', a category of romance obviously dominated by Gothic.[43] This belated appeal to historical fact, however, only draws attention to the way in which the tale has, in practice, both fallen into the narrative patterns of sensationalist fiction and become dependent on these patterns for its retelling. As in the opening preamble of *The Heart of Midlothian*, the narrator deliberately juxtaposes the public appetite for horror and 'true stories' from history so that they re-define each other. In *The Bride of Lammermoor* the 'OWER TRUE TALE' is bolstered by historical reference but structured by techniques of suspense and foreboding. It also has clear thematic links with Gothic plots, telling a story of usurpation which immediately recalls the lasting

---

[41] For the consensus of opinion in older critical studies on *The Bride of Lammermoor* as Scott's 'only Gothic novel' (Birkhead, *Tale of Terror*, 153), see Ernest A. Baker, *The History of the English Novel*, 10 vols. (London, 1924–39), vi. 168; and Edward Wagenknecht, *Cavalcade of the English Novel* (1943; new edn. with supplementary bibliography, New York, 1954), 156. Among recent studies, see Hart, *Scott's Novels*, 328–37; Punter, *Literature of Terror*, 164–5; Levine, *Realistic Imagination*, 107–21; Kerr, *Fiction against History*, ch. 3.
[42] Details of the novel's complex literary echoes and allusions, including its references to Walpole's romance, are given in the introd. and notes of my edn. of *The Bride of Lammermoor* (Oxford, 1991).
[43] *WN* xiv. 357.

impact of *The Castle of Otranto*, and the weight of Shakespearian
convention which accompanies it, on Scott's imagination. In Scott's
version, unlike Walpole's, neither usurper nor true heir succeeds in
winning lasting possession of the estate he disputes. Instead of
having his rank reaffirmed and his line secured by marriage, the
heir dies in a quicksand which metaphorically suggests his shifting
and ambiguous social status. Both feuding families are left barren
at the end of the novel. In spite of these differences of emphasis,
The Bride of Lammermoor is, like *The Castle of Otranto*, a
political romance which ultimately (though with reservations) puts
forward an ideal for social progress based on respect for the past.
Not all the literary sources of *The Bride of Lammermoor* are so
easily assimilated to its patterns of progress within the bounds of
the law and existing social conventions. One literary source, in
particular, tells the story of an entirely different response to the
problem of a land unjustly usurped: Maturin's rebel tale, *The
Milesian Chief*.

There has always been a loose critical consensus linking *The
Bride of Lammermoor* to the main plot of *The Milesian Chief*,
although the debts have not been analysed in any detail. David
Garnett states in the *Dictionary of National Biography* that Scott
unconsciously based his plot on Maturin's work, and several
critics, particularly those interested in Maturin, have taken up the
suggestion.[44] These supporters of Maturin's work clearly wish to
avoid the implications of Garnett's insistence on an *unconscious*
(blameless) debt. They tend to assume, however, that the best way
of enhancing Maturin's reputation is to show that Scott paid him
the compliment of imitation. Critics of Scott have been less than
forthcoming on the subject, treating it, if they mention it at all, as
a superficial coincidence of plot which has no bearing on the
essential subject-matter of Scott's novel.

The Milesian Chief, however, is anything but a neutral source
and could never have been regarded as such in Scott's time. In
order to adapt its main love-story Scott would have had to swerve
consciously aside from the novel's sustained and impassioned

---

[44] *DNB* xiii. 74. The claim has also been made by Baker, *History of the English
Novel*, v. 220; by Willem Scholten, *Charles Robert Maturin: The Terror-Novelist*
(Amsterdam, 1933), 26; and by Niilo Idman, *Charles Robert Maturin: His Life
and Works* (Helsinki, 1923), 97–8. In *The Literature of Terror* (163), Punter
notes that the plot of Scott's novel 'bears some similarity' to Maturin's.

rhetoric of tragic rebellion. Although the link between the two novels has been stated as fact by some critics, the evidence that Scott had read *The Milesian Chief* by the time he began work on *The Bride of Lammermoor* is not conclusive. When Maturin first wrote to Scott in December 1812, the year of *The Milesian Chief*'s publication, he referred to himself as 'an obscure Irishman— the author only of two trifling performances, the Romance of "Montorio" and of the "Milesian"'.[45] In his reply, Scott remarks that his 'attention was indeed very strongly excited both by the House of Montorio and the Irish tale which it was impossible to confound with the usual stile of novels'.[46] In their edition of the correspondence between Scott and Maturin, Ratchford and McCarthy gloss this 'Irish tale' as *The Wild Irish Boy*, and Grierson's edition of Scott's *Letters* makes the same identification. Maurice Lévy disagrees, however, and there is evidence to support his dissent.[47] 'Irish tale' certainly recalls the title of *The Wild Irish Boy*, but *The Milesian Chief* was Maturin's latest work and also the novel to which he had specifically drawn Scott's attention. The terms in which Scott writes of the novels he has read are very similar to the terms in which he reviewed *Fatal Revenge* for the *Quarterly Review* ('the redundancies of a powerful fancy', and 'very deep though painful interest'), so there is nothing here which can be linked specifically to any one work by Maturin.[48] The *Abbotsford Library Catalogue* records no copy of either *The Wild Irish Boy* or *The Milesian Chief*, and in Scott's review of *Women; or, Pour et Contre* for the *Edinburgh Review* in June 1818, Maturin is introduced as the author of *Fatal Revenge*, *The Wild Irish Boy*, 'and other tales'.[49] On the other hand, Scott was sufficiently familiar with Maturin's writings as a whole to agree to prepare a collected edition of them after the death of his 'troublesome correspondent' in 1825. His sense of responsibility for Maturin's work and well-being was clearly based on a respect for his artistic potential combined with an amused dread of the extravagances into which Maturin's overactive imagination might

---

[45] *Scott–Maturin Correspondence*, 6.
[46] Ibid. 7.
[47] Grierson's comment in *Letters*, xii. 339 n.; Lévy's in his introd. to *Fatal Revenge*, foreword Henry D. Hicks (New York, 1974), pp. vii–viii.
[48] *Scott–Maturin Correspondence*, 7.
[49] *MPW* xviii. 173.

lead him next. Although there are no specific discussions of *The Milesian Chief* in Scott's correspondence with Maturin, therefore, there is evidence to support a working assumption that he did read the novel, although it is not possible to assign the date of reading with any certainty.

The Bride of Lammermoor repeats the central situation of *The Milesian Chief*, which, in both novels, owes much to *Romeo and Juliet*. An ancient landed family is displaced by newcomers who represent the social changes sweeping the land. The surviving members of the old family retreat to a ruined watchtower on the edge of a cliff. The heir of the old line falls in love with the daughter of his displacer, and she with him. As a result, the heir is torn between his sense of his family's fate and his modern instinct for social integration, and the daughter is subjected to persecution from her family, and especially from her mother, who attempts to force her into marriage with another (and succeeds in doing so in *The Bride of Lammermoor*). In *The Milesian Chief*, Armida narrowly avoids being tricked into marriage with Connal's younger brother, Desmond, but only after she has swallowed the poison which will kill her. The madness which destroys Lucy Ashton is reserved in *The Milesian Chief* for Armida's sister, Ines. (The main difference between the two love-stories is that Maturin divides the implications of tragedy between two very different couples whose stories closely echo each other.) Most importantly of all, both *The Milesian Chief* and *The Bride of Lammermoor* use love-stories to symbolize and then to analyse the shifting states of power and legitimacy in a nation which is legally and politically, but not emotionally or culturally, united to England. In this they share one literary source which is rather more recent than either *Romeo and Juliet* or *The Castle of Otranto*, and which accounts for some of the difficulty in yoking too firmly together the plots of *The Bride of Lammermoor* and *The Milesian Chief*. The common source is Lady Morgan's highly sentimental nationalist tale, *The Wild Irish Girl* (1806), set like *The Milesian Chief* in Connaught and involving a culturally significant romance between the inheritor of a usurped estate and the daughter of the ancient family which has been displaced.[50] It is interesting that both Scott and Maturin, in

[50] In *The Irish Novelists 1800–1850* (New York, 1959), the classic study which explicitly excludes Maturin from the main part of its survey, Thomas Flanagan argues that both Maturin's *Wild Irish Boy* and *Milesian Chief* are 'bizarre imita-

their imaginative reactions to *The Wild Irish Girl*, reverse the gender terms of Morgan's original formulation. The romantic aura of the dispossessed is made masculine, and leads decisively to tragedy rather than reconciliation. Morgan's hero Horatio Mortimer already has social power, enough to marry Glorvina and establish for them both a renewed cultural heritage. Scott's Edgar Ravenswood and Maturin's Connal O'Morven lack the power to make such renewal possible. To look at these three novels together is to see that the threatened culture, if feminized, may be reassimilated: if masculine, must be lost and also more powerfully mourned.

The Milesian Chief, therefore, is already a strategic reworking of another novel's materials by the time it becomes an aesthetic and nationalistic context for *The Bride of Lammermoor*. Armida Fitzalban, Maturin's heroine, has a mixed literary and biographical genealogy. She is an idealized image of Maturin's talented and beautiful wife, Elizabeth, but also an imitation of the 'inspired' heroine of de Staël's novel *Corinne* (1807) and of Morgan's heroine Glorvina. Maturin presents her as a combination of the forms of classical harmony and grace with modern romantic sensibility. In the first two chapters of the novel she is seen being fêted in Naples and Paris, admired throughout the best society for her creativity and grace. Fashionable London, however, significantly ignores her. Throughout her Continental triumphs she is shadowed by melancholy, which one observer, the sinister Father Morosini, traces to an unfulfilled capacity for feeling: 'Armida has never loved, and the energies of her heart are too powerful to be wasted

tions' of Morgan (p. 46). In relation to Morgan, however, he draws attention to the significance of her (and thus Maturin's) choice of setting (p. 117): 'Of the four provinces, Connaught had come most recently and most imperfectly under English government.' A fuller account of Maturin's relationship to Irish nationalism and reworking of Morgan's ideas is provided by Barry Sloan in *The Pioneers of Anglo-Irish Fiction 1800–1850*, Irish Literary Studies, No. 21 (Gerrard's Cross, Buckinghamshire, 1986), 41–50. Sloan summarizes (p. 48): 'Maturin's nationalism emerges through his portrayal of the relationships of his characters rather than being a subject in its own right, as for example it was for Lady Morgan, and in this respect *The Milesian Chief* is his most revealing book.' The present discussion shows that nationalism is much more of a 'subject in its own right' in *The Milesian Chief* than Sloan allows here. To turn to Morgan's importance for Scott, Ina Ferris (in one of the few sustained discussions Morgan's novel has received) suggests *The Wild Irish Girl* as a model for the cultural contrasts and storyline of *Waverley* (*Achievement of Literary Authority*, 124–5).

even upon acquirements as splendid as hers.'[51] Her admirer, the Englishman Wandesford, thinks of her artistic displays, the tableaux in which she represents the classical muses, or Niobe, as all 'a piece of mechanism'.[52] Although this worldly and self-possessed heroine is in almost every other way the opposite of Lucy Ashton, one recalls the narrator's comment near the beginning of *The Bride of Lammermoor* that 'Lucy's sentiments seemed chill, because nothing had occurred to interest or awaken them'.[53] Armida and Lucy begin their stories in comparable states of emotional and spiritual vacancy.

After becoming engaged to Wandesford, Armida journeys back from the sophisticated civilization of court life to her father's castle in Connaught, which he has recently purchased from 'a ruined Milesian family', the O'Morvens. Here in Ireland, her imagination is awakened anew by the wild scenery and raw loyalties of the place, and by the heir of the family her father has displaced. Always an admirer of Ossian, she is now in a position to see Ossianic characters come to life. The imaginative framework of Edward Waverley and his successor tourists-of-the-heart is not far away. As Armida absorbs the old stories and traditions of the Irish, the artificial modern eloquence for which she had been famous falters. Later, she reflects:

'Alas! how different are the impressions we receive from imagination and passion. Educated in a celestial climate, where every object excited the mind and senses, my young and ardent mind reflected every image presented to it brighter than the original: every effort I made to express my sensations increased them; the images multiplied, the language coloured and kindled as I spoke, and the praises I received won the race for me before it was concluded. But now my imagination is gone: an object without dimensions and without colour seems to occupy my mind's eye: I want strength to conceive the extent of my misery: when I would speak of it, I have no words; when I would paint it, the picture is black, and a voice from the bottom of my heart tells me death alone can penetrate or express the depth of feeling there.'[54]

---

[51] *Milesian*, i. 19. Connal later remarks on Armida's 'abused capacity', i. 105.
[52] *Milesian*, i. 14. Her detractors in Ireland are even more direct about the affectations of her manner.
[53] *WN* xiii. 302.
[54] *Milesian*, ii. 170–1.

Armida struggles to express in language the failure of language: even the attempt to turn to metaphors of painting (favourites in Gothic) produces only blackness and void. Her false artistic sensibilities, her notions of dignity and decorum, break down under the pressure of her passion for Connal and all he represents.

What Connal represents, however, is not nearly as simple as Armida, in her innocence of Irish politics and her narrow notions of heroism, supposes. In a novel dominated by aesthetic debate—in which characters discuss, among other topics, theories of the picturesque and the rival claims of romantic and classical art—Maturin persistently weaves together political and aesthetic ideals, insisting on the close connection between art and political action. Early in the Irish chapters, the tale of avenged usurpation in *The Castle of Otranto* is explicitly recalled.[55] The figures of Ossian and Scott's Last Minstrel dominate Connal's political consciousness, and make his vision of rebellion self-consciously literary.[56] By using such parallels, Maturin implies that this educated man can only act as his countrymen's leader in the form laid down by a work of literature. This, of course, places a great responsibility on writers of literature, and Scott could not have avoided noticing that Connal's artistic vision of politics prominently combines his own *Lay of the Last Minstrel* with Macpherson's Ossian poems, which he preferred to associate with the enthusiasms of much more simple-minded patriots, such as Hector McIntyre in *The Antiquary*. As imagined through *The Milesian Chief*, Scott's poem suddenly becomes a piece of direct political propaganda, all the more powerful for containing so many artistic asides about pale moonlight and romantic ruins. Connal's sensibilities anticipate scenes like Edward Waverley's meeting with Flora MacIvor in *Waverley*, when a love of the picturesque and the romantic is exploited in the service of Jacobite politics. In a sneering reference which can be read as a challenge to the form of this romantic novel itself, Connal's time-serving father Randall O'Morven (a sort of Richard Waverley) asks him:

Do you think that poring over an old Irish manuscript, or wandering over these wild shores, listening to an old harp with hardly a string to it will

---

[55] *Milesian*, i. 52.
[56] Connal's literary sensibility, *Milesian*, i. 179–80: see Maturin's literary images of him, ii. 202 (Satan's revolt), ii. 38 (Ossianic nationalist hero), ii. 63, 84.

put a potatoe in your mouth, or give one stone to repair those ruins you live in, or bring you back your land to you again?[57]

With Wolfe Tone and Robert Emmet overshadowing Connal's rebellion and Ossianic heritage-fantasies shaping its presentation of Irish culture, *The Milesian Chief* reflects intently on usurpation, dependence, and cultural revival. It also questions the basis and the practical effects of the relationship between literature and political struggle.

When Armida falls in love with Connal, however, she, like Lucy Ashton, glories in what seems like a marvellous coincidence between romance and real life. The lovers first meet when Connal saves Armida from certain death, risking his own life to pull her from a carriage which is hurtling down the cliff side, its horses having taken fright and bolted. Her father has leapt clear. Ravenswood and Lucy Ashton, similarly, first meet when, again in dereliction of his declared plans to revenge himself on her family, he rescues her from the charge of a wild bull. Like Ravenswood, Connal carries Armida only as far as is absolutely necessary to secure her safety, then leaves without a word, conspicuously failing to take advantage of his gallantry or her gratitude. Although it is conventional enough to suggest several literary sources, the first meeting of Connal and Armida in *The Milesian Chief* is strikingly reminiscent of the accident which first brings hero and heroine together in Bage's *Hermsprong* (1796). The parallel is significant, for it suggests that Armida, like Caroline Campion, is about to meet not just a new lover but an entire set of new ideological principles which will radically alter her views on society. At the time, however, she is only conscious of Connal's impressive physical presence and his air of mystery and romance:

Her senses failed her when she felt him snatch her from the carriage through the door, which was still open, nor did she recover them until she found herself in her father's arms: she had then a faint recollection of a tall figure bending over her, and a long curl of raven hair touching her cheek as in a dream. . . . No one knew who he was, but from his silence, his figure, and a romantic dress which none of them could describe, all concluded him to be the grandson of the old Milesian.[58]

Again, several of these details anticipate the equivalent rescue scene in *The Bride of Lammermoor*.

[57] *Milesian*, i. 66.   [58] *Milesian*, i. 58–9.

The romantic image of Connal rapidly displaces Armida's cultivated but passionless aesthetic ideals. On seeing him, she says, she
ceases to admire works of art.[59] She listens to the tales and
prophecies of the O'Morvens' blind harper, a traditional figure
regarded as the 'visionary being' of their family and modelled on
the character of Scott's Minstrel in *The Lay*.[60] The lovers struggle
against an ominous array of prophecies, warnings, and omens,
and the imperious interventions of Armida's betrothed, Wandesford, who refuses to free her from her engagement. During one of
their arguments, Armida describes the kind of bride she will be for
him, in a passage made literal in the wedding scenes of *The Bride
of Lammermoor*:

> 'Oh, no!' said Armida, smiling with high disdain: 'Oh, no, thou honour-
> able lover! I will fulfil the bond: my person and fortune will be your's
> [*sic*]: you shall bear about this wretched, faded figure, in all the heartless
> pageantry of splendid misery; but take care that even before your victim
> is bound she does not escape.'[61]

After extended trials and doubts, Armida abandons her family to
follow Connal, now the leader of a rebel group openly fighting for
Irish independence. Maturin carefully minimizes Connal's direct
responsibility for the revolt, presenting him as caught up in it by
almost an Edward-Waverley-like series of special circumstances.
He shows (and has Connal acknowledge) the futility of the attempt. The novel closes with an agonizingly paced execution-scene
which strikingly anticipates Maturin's powers of gruesome suspense (already discussed in relation to *Melmoth the Wanderer*).

In many ways *The Milesian Chief* is the impassioned novel of
'heath and moor, of ruins and moonlight'[62] which many readers
expect *The Bride of Lammermoor* to be, and it would be easy to
set extracts next to Scott which would suggest that Maturin poured
forth ideas and images which Scott then calmed and rationalized.
Yet this would be inaccurate, and would particularly impoverish
the complex way in which Maturin presents Connal's rebellion.
Connal is passionate, imaginative, but also rational, resourceful,

---

[59] *Milesian*, i. 159.
[60] On linguistic struggles and silences, *Milesian*, ii. 170–1; and see the eventual
association with death, iii. 28: Armida's reaction to the blind harper, i. 62–4: see
also the similarities in Connal's description of the family 'visionary being', i. 177,
to Scott's portrayal of Blind Alice.
[61] *Milesian*, ii. 167.
[62] *Milesian*, ii. 177.

and well educated. He is caught up in a rebellion which he has outgrown intellectually and emotionally, and, like Ravenswood, he is tied to a past which demands allegiance and revenge while trying to commit himself to a future of love and reconciliation. Also like Ravenswood, he has severe misgivings about the simplified role of rebel aristocrat which his circumstances oblige him to perform (a simplified role which, as I have suggested, is made more difficult by Armida's belief in it). If Maturin's hero bears comparison with Scott's, so does his evocation of social ills. *The Milesian Chief* is a serious novel about the problems facing Ireland under English rule. Maturin's reflections on the plight of his nation are wide-ranging and often moving, especially when they are seen in the context of his extended debate on the Irish situation, which runs from *The Wild Irish Boy* through *Women; or, Pour et Contre* to the first section of *Melmoth the Wanderer*. Connal gives Maturin an outlet for his nationalistic sympathies, and allows him to glorify, at the safe distance of elegy, the opportunity for self-determination which he regarded as lost for ever in Ireland after the Union: 'It seemed like Emmet's insurrection, the isolated and hopeless attempt of a single enthusiast.'[63] By elevating and rarefying Connal's revolt in this way, as well as by showing that it is doomed to failure, Maturin avoids advocating mass rebellion, but his presentation of Connal as a daring romantic enthusiast carries unmistakable emotional commitment, especially when set against the novel's insistent rhetoric of romantic loss, renunciation, and despair. The result is a complex blend of idealization and detachment which makes available a romantic (and highly eroticized) image of rebellion without giving it authorial endorsement.

Although the plot and situations of *The Milesian Chief* strongly anticipate *The Bride of Lammermoor*, the two novels make significantly different uses of similar material. Most importantly, Scott avoids the subject which takes up the greater part of Maturin's four volumes, the Irish nationalistic revolt led by Connal. Ravenswood is not a political idealist waging a hopeless battle against the necessities of centralized administration, and Scott is at some pains to emphasize that this heroic extremism would be a simplification of a complicated historical situation. Not only does he avoid the kind of political engagement hinted at by the drunken

[63] *Milesian*, ii. 143.

mourners at his father's funeral, but he also avoids for as long as possible the legal rebellion for restoration of his estate by due legal process. The Marquis of A——, not Ravenswood, is responsible for pursuing this goal. The only signs of rebellion are the debased Jacobitism of Craigengelt and the concealed Jacobite loyalties of the Marquis of A——. Nor, in spite of Ravenswood's stirring rhetoric at the scene of Lucy's betrothal to Bucklaw, do Scott's lovers manage to do more than fantasize about the passionate rebellion against all convention and decorum which Connal and Armida enact. In these ways, Scott's reformulation represents a significant struggle against the social, psychological, and political implications of *The Milesian Chief*. The most important link between the two novels is their description of imaginative potential brought into contact with passion and politics. In both novels, the lovers form imaginative ideals which are insufficient to bring them happiness within the social world, and these imaginative ideals can only be expressed in the strained rhetoric of defiant love. Maturin transcribes rather more of this rhetoric than Scott, but Ravenswood's grand gestures, inspired alternately by love and by haughty renunciation, suggest a world of absolutes which cannot coexist in the cynical social worlds which both Scott and Maturin depict. There are also similarities in the two novels' tactics of shifting the weight of political complaint on to a story of romantic love. Maturin closes his novel with a glorified image of romantic devotion, allowing the safe excesses of passion to replace the controversial excesses of nationalism. Readers of *The Bride of Lammermoor* have willingly avoided its political implications in a comparable manner, by presenting Edgar Ravenswood's ride into the Kelpie's Flow as a culmination of family fate and hopeless passion. In both novels, however, political ideals are shown to be closely related to ideals of art and imagination, and art itself to be almost too potent a political force for comfort. Art is eroticized as a motivation for political action, which in turn is sublimated to erotic tragedy.

4. *Phantoms of Revolution:* The Fortunes of Nigel

'. . . Tell me, proud lords,' she added, wiping away the tears as she spoke, 'by what earthly warrant can liege subjects

pretend to challenge the rights of an anointed Sovereign—to
throw off the allegiance they have vowed, and to take away
the crown from the head on which Divine warrant had
placed it?'

(Mary Stewart, *The Abbot*)[64]

The Fortunes of Nigel was inspired by Scott's detailed knowledge
of Jacobean and Caroline literature, especially the plays of Jonson,
and large sections of it draw extensively on Shadwell's *The Squire
of Alsatia*. Following Scott's comments in the introduction to the
Magnum Opus, its success is commonly ascribed to his ease with
the period and confident re-creation of its atmosphere.[65] Lockhart
praises his reconstruction of life at the court of James VI and I as
'all so easily and naturally' executed, and James himself has been
described as a 'natural' subject for Scott's pen.[66] The novel's
commitment to realistic historical reconstruction seems clear.

In the Introductory Epistle to *The Fortunes of Nigel*, Scott
admits that the White Lady of *The Monastery* has been a failure,
and promises that his new novel will include nothing which a
Scots metaphysician might not believe. No ghosts are introduced
in *The Fortunes of Nigel*, but Lady Hermione, the mysterious
recluse who occupies the Foljambe apartments in Heriot's house,
shares some of the functions of the White Lady and is accorded,
by superstitious characters at least, more than a few of her supernatural powers. Her pallor is repeatedly remarked by the narrator
and by other characters. She is said to look like a ghost and
rumoured to sleep in a coffin. Hermione herself admits 'that the
few who now see me, look upon me as a bloodless phantom'.[67]
Her presence is curiously negative and life-denying. Discussing
with Margaret Ramsay the relative merits of real and embroidered
flowers, for example, she espouses the cause of death, turning
away from the variety and unpredictability of life. The secret story
of her past, when she finally explains it to Margaret, is a miniature
Radcliffean romance of religious and sexual persecution, of a type
much imitated by followers of Radcliffe and indebted to a tradi-

[64] *WN* xxi. 32.
[65] *WN* xxvi, pp. xiv–xvi (the debt to Shadwell): see Gordon, *Under Which
King?*, 128–38; Hart, *Scott's Novels*, 198.
[66] Lockhart, vii. 26.
[67] *WN* xxvii. 44: see also xxvi. 133–5, 142, 143.

tion in the novel traceable ultimately to Richardson's *Pamela*.[68] It is an odd challenge to the credulity of the Scots metaphysician.

Hermione's classically Radcliffean story, set in Spain, is a cautionary tale of misplaced trust and undeserved persecution. After the death of her Catholic father, a Genoese merchant who has fallen badly into debt, her Protestant mother is left vulnerable to persecution, and soon afterwards dies. Hermione makes a secret marriage to a young Englishman, and is soon pregnant. She takes temporary refuge in a convent, where the evil Abbess, discovering both her secret Protestantism and her secret pregnancy, tries to force her to take the veil. She escapes with the help of her husband, but is passed over to the protection of his friend, who, with her husband's permission, tries to make her his mistress. Eventually Hermione wins the protection of the King's goldsmith, George Heriot, and takes up residence in his London house, in a set of secret rooms known as the Foljambe apartments, previously used to shelter Roman Catholics during the Reformation. The history of the Foljambe apartments is very reminiscent of that of the secret dens of Sophia Lee's *Recess*. All these details of plot, of course, might be narrated in a style which strips them of sensationalism. Yet this is not what Scott chooses to do. Something of the tone in which Hermione's history is told is obvious in the following passage, which describes her stay in the Spanish convent:

As I was soon discovered to have shared my mother's heresy, I was dragged from her dead body, imprisoned in a solitary cloister, and treated with severity, which the Abbess assured me was due to the looseness of my life, as well as my spiritual errors. I avowed my marriage, to justify the situation in which I found myself—I implored the assistance of the Superior to communicate my situation to my husband. She smiled coldly at the proposal, and told me the church had provided a better spouse for me; advised me to secure myself of divine grace hereafter, and deserve milder treatment here, by presently taking the veil.[69]

---

[68] Hermione is 'totally unconvincing', according to C. Hugh Holman, '*Nigel* and the Historical Imagination', in *The Classic British Novel*, ed. Howard M. Harper, Jr., and Charles Edge (Athens, Ga., 1972), 65–84 (79: and this in an article which argues for *The Fortunes of Nigel*'s 'ominous historical overtones'). Merrill, 'A Reappraisal of Sir Walter Scott', notes that Hermione's tale is an 'interpolated Gothic story' (p. 121), but offers no interpretation of it in the context of the rest of the novel.
[69] *WN* xxvii. 42–3.

Scott could never have hoped to pass off such a story as anything other than stylized to the point of pastiche. Hermione's tale is so conventionally Gothic that it raises serious questions about his reasons for including it.

To answer them one needs an overview of the issues debated in the novel as a whole, and some sense of why they might be contentious. It is not difficult to see that *The Fortunes of Nigel* concerns itself explicitly with the moral and social decay of the seventeenth-century aristocracy, or that it does so in the spirit of historical explanation. As the introduction to the Magnum Opus version of the novel suggests, moreover, the problems of aristocratic haughtiness and selfish luxury, of the neglect for land and the ancient responsibilities associated with land, continued to be relevant to Scott's reflections on his own society as well as on the ways of the past.[70] In his 'Life' of Bage for *Ballantyne's Novelist's Library*, and in spite of his fundamental disagreement with most of Bage's political views, Scott praises Bage's skills in satirizing the vices of the modern aristocracy in terms which are highly relevant to *The Fortunes of Nigel*. Summarizing Bage's criticisms, he explains:

Men of rank, in the present day, are too indifferent, and too indolent, to indulge any of the stormy passions, and irregular but vehement desires, which create the petty tyrant, and perhaps formerly animated the feudal oppressor. Their general fault is a want of energy, or, to speak more accurately, an apathy . . .[71]

The Fortunes of Nigel presents a similiar opposition between the plausible sophisticates of Dalgarno's generation, scornful of effort and preserving a sham hauteur, and their more worthy fathers. The character of Dalgarno, in fact, includes all the vices which Scott blamed for the downfall of the monarchy in 1649: selfish pursuit of pleasure, false graces, neglect of the responsibilities imposed by the inheritance of land, and the moral corruption of the lower orders (represented here by Dame Nelly) by the upper. The aristocracy in *The Fortunes of Nigel* is clearly hastening to a fall, undermined by its own failures of principle and practice. It has become a force for corruption. The young apprentice Jenkin Vincent, for example, is ruined by his attempts to become a

---

[70] *WN* xxvii. 190, v, x, xiii.   [71] *MPW* iii. 454.

'gentleman' and to vie with Nigel, Lord Glenvarloch, for the affections of the enterprising bourgeois heroine, Margaret Ramsay. Nigel himself clings to an empty ideal of gentlemanly behaviour, unable at first to believe that gentlemanliness and deception can be in any way or any circumstances connected. At the very pinnacle of this precarious system, James VI and I lazily and ominously declares for an easy solution to the Glenvarloch problem: 'let the land gang'.[72]

Problematic elements in the novel, such as the lengthy opening description of two characters, Jenkin Vincent and Frank Tunstall, who seem irrelevant to the development of the plot, make sense when one recognizes Scott's overriding moral and political concern with aristocratic decay and its effects on the artisan class. The well-born Tunstall depends on the active intervention of Vincent to preserve his place in the rough world of apprentices, until, 'without showing any formal symptoms of disease, [Tunstall] grew more thin and pale as he grew older, and at length exhibited the appearance of indifferent health, without any thing of the habits and complaints of an invalid, excepting a disposition to avoid society'.[73] This image of aristocratic decline is strikingly physical. Tunstall, like Hermione, is thin, wasted, and bloodless, and, in the symbolic economy of Scott's novel, the reasons for their weakness are very similar.

The action of *The Fortunes of Nigel* is overshadowed by the crisis of 1649. When James VI and I is introduced, Scott notes that he is at that time planning the building of Whitehall, 'little suspecting that he was employed in constructing a palace, from the window of which his only son was to pass in order that he might die upon a scaffold before it'.[74] There are many more asides of this kind, foreshortening and distorting historical process. Scott introduces 'the Prince of Wales, afterwards the most unfortunate of British monarchs' with his face already marked by melancholy.[75] Introducing Buckingham, Scott's mind leaps forward to his assassination by Felton.[76] He is restless and uneasy in giving the slightest impression of successful stability in the court of James, repeatedly emphasizing the approaching collapse. When, much later in the novel, Nigel reminds Charles that one day he will

[72] *WN* xxvi. 187.   [73] *WN* xxvi. 10.   [74] *WN* xxvi. 93.
[75] *WN* xxvi. 302.   [76] *WN* xxvi. 303.

plead in vain to be heard, he refers to divine justice, while the reader and Scott think of Charles's trial and execution.[77] James worries about the 'dragon's teeth' in the time to come, while Charles despises his weakness and speaks of the near-divinity of kings.[78] In the contrast between these views, Scott summarizes the main issues of the Civil Wars. He uses retrospect to the same end, as when Nigel discovers the writing of Lady Jane Grey, another executed monarch, on his prison wall.[79]

All these links support the view that Scott was considering the problem of the causation of historical events which might appear inevitable from the retrospect of a comfortable age. The unvoiced fear is the possibility that history will repeat itself, particularly in the downfall of kings who fail to adapt to changing social conditions. Scott never directly addresses himself in fiction to the downfall of Charles I. In *Woodstock*, it has already happened, and there is a sense in which it has also already happened in *The Fortunes of Nigel*. The novel is overshadowed by revolution in France and the royal executions of 1793. This in itself is not unique in Scott's work. A more immediately striking reference to revolution in France occurs in the Liège scenes of *Quentin Durward*, in which a bishop named Louis Bourbon is executed by a violent mob after a parody-trial. *Quentin Durward* considers the problem of declining aristocratic loyalty and chivalric ideals, but its implications are less troubling, partly because they are deflected on to France, and partly because they do not include the specific problem of aristocratic decline in relation to responsibilities of land and family. In *The Fortunes of Nigel*, Scott cannot escape the haunting image of royal death which lies at the end of the vista. His insistence on looking forward to this end gives it the quality of inescapable nightmare, inescapable because the links between aristocratic indulgence and selfishness in Jacobean times and in his own time inevitably bring to mind the connected images of an executed king, and the chaos of civil war to come. Scott describes Enfield Chase, the scene of the death of Dalgarno and an example of the results of aristocratic decline: 'A wild woodland prospect

---

[77] WN xxvii. 196.

[78] WN xxvii. 200, 315.

[79] WN xxvii. 208 (suggesting that *The Fortunes of Nigel* may have helped to inspire the detail of the documents which Dr Manette leaves behind in his prison cell in *A Tale of Two Cities*).

led the eye at various points through broad and seemingly interminable alleys, which, meeting at this point as at a common
centre, diverged from each other as they receded.'[80] The fearful
prospects at the end of such a landscape recur in Scott's writing.
His novels are drawn towards a historical horror which they
cannot articulate, or articulate in a distanced way by using literary
convention to heighten the reader's imaginative apprehension of
horror. In this context, the significance of Hermione's tale, and the
reason for its self-conscious conventionality, may be more clearly
understood.

Hermione functions first of all as a parallel for Nigel's experiences at the hands of Dalgarno and his friends. Like the hero, she
is the victim of Dalgarno's greed, ambition, and treachery. The
friend for whom Dalgarno attempts to procure her after her escape
from the Spanish convent is the Duke of Buckingham, the same
friend for whose idle sport he schemes to procure Nigel's ancestral
estate. Both she and Nigel are deceived by Dalgarno to promote
the luxurious pleasures of Buckingham, and thereby to advance
Dalgarno's influence at court. Hermione's importance is more
pervasive than this, however. As the daughter of a Scottish heiress
and a Catholic merchant prince of Genoa, she is haunted by a
strong Catholic inheritance, but adheres to the Protestant faith.
Her history is connected with Bothwell and Queen Mary, and she
has a divided inheritance nationally and religiously. Her history
therefore repeats the divided religious and social inheritance of
King James. She also functions as a symbol of the fading aristocracy, a role shared by the wasted apprentice of good birth, Frank
Tunstall. She is a ghost of history, an aristocratic presence which,
like the power of the absolute monarchy maintained by James and
Charles, seems almost to be vanishing before the eyes of her
staunch bourgeois protectors. More specifically still, Hermione is
a spectral anticipation of the fate awaiting the future Charles I.
Like Charles, as the novel presents him, she is melancholy, severe,
and mysterious. He alone matches her extreme but uncompromis-
ingly sincere views on rank. She advises Margaret to 'seek a match
among [her] equals' rather than raise her ambitions to Nigel, a
social rigidity which the novel's ending emphatically rejects.[81]
From being 'immured within the Bastile of his rank' (perhaps an

accidental, but certainly not a neutral, image),[82] Nigel is dramatically if rather comically rescued by the devotion of Margaret Ramsay. Their marriage firmly endorses the values of the emergent bourgeoisie. Even the comedy of Margaret's love is ideologically significant in a novel so highly charged with tragic anticipations which it presents as character-traits of the doomed ruling order. Given that the reader's first reaction to Hermione and Margaret must be that they are to be rivals for the hero's love, Nigel's marriage to a living, rather than a dead, woman is a macabre version of the culturally significant marriages which heroes of the Waverley Novels are apt to make.

The associations by which Hermione comes to represent the dying force of absolute monarchy are appropriate to a novel in which so many verbal details of description are echoed, and in which parody commonly suggests sinister imaginative affiliations. Hermione herself finds an echo in the faded figure of Martha Trapbois, daughter of the moneylender in Alsatia who, it turns out, is the source of the funds with which Heriot supplies the king. In the criminal mirror-world of Alsatia, Martha's position repeats several aspects of Hermione's. James calls her a spectre, and she herself bitterly remarks to Nigel after the murder of her father: 'A spectre arising from the dead were more unwelcome than I should be at the doors of those who have disclaimed us.'[83] The tale of Hermione, therefore, presents in safely stylized miniature the main points of anxiety and political debate in *The Fortunes of Nigel*. In its submerged but highly suggestive symbolism it is characteristic of a much-underestimated technique in the Waverley Novels: the use of highly stylized anticipations of plot, and unexpected links between characters, suggested by verbal echo, parallel situations, and shared details of description. Scott often uses hunting scenes, for example, as concentrated anticipations of, or reflections on, the central conflicts in his works. The stag at bay in *Waverley* suggests the heroic but ill-fated courage of the Jacobites. In *Rob Roy*, the fox hunted as Frank reaches Osbaldistone Hall is spent and soiled, a description echoed much later in the death of Sir Hildebrand. In *The Bride of Lammermoor*, the Master of Ravenswood and Bucklaw join in a stag-hunt which ends with strong prefigurings of the stabbing scene at the wedding of Lucy and Bucklaw, and Lucy herself is repeatedly imagined (and imagines

---

[82] *WN* xxvii. 168.   [83] *WN* xxvii. 146.

herself) as a hunted animal, particularly (Dido-like) as a white
doe. The salmon hunt in *Redgauntlet* is a confrontation of the
ways of old and new, and the heron hunt in *The Betrothed* is a
strikingly intricate allegory of the social and sexual traps which
threaten Eveline Berenger throughout the novel. The most closely
allegorical example is the boar hunt near the beginning of *Quentin
Durward*, in which the later movements of the major political
characters are precisely anticipated in the cuts and thrusts of
the kill.[84] In *The Fortunes of Nigel*, Hermione's tale is a highly
stylized and potently symbolic Gothic miniature used to reinforce
a disturbing interpretation of history. Its stylization is as important as its symbolism. As in *The Antiquary*, thematic significance is there to be detected but it is also presented in a
manner which justifies rejection. As in all these interpolations of
Gothic, it is essential to register disruption as well as to suggest
possible routes to significance.

5. *Ritual and Trial:* The House of Aspen *and* Anne of Geierstein

> The history of my eventful life proves how little all human
> strength, and a well tried and circumspect experience, can
> prevail over the secret plans of certain unknown persons,
> who, behind the impenetrable veil of mystic concealment,
> invisibly watch over a great part of the world.
>
> (Grosse, in Will's translation, *Horrid Mysteries*, 1796)[85]

Scott adapted his tragedy *The House of Aspen* in 1799 from *Die
Heilige Vehme*, a play in the sixth volume of Veit Weber's *Sagen
den Vorzeit*.[86] He intended it for the stage, but it was rejected by

---

[84] WN i. 251–4 (*Waverley*); vii. 63, viii. 336–7 (*Rob Roy*); xxxv. 41–2
(*Redgauntlet*); xxxvii. 339–44 (*The Betrothed*); xxxi. 179–82 (*Quentin Durward*):
The Fortunes of Nigel also uses hunting symbolically, xxvii. 187, 225.

[85] Peter Will's translation of the Marquis of Grosse's work typifies the politicized presentation of secret societies in 1790s terror-fiction: *Horrid Mysteries: A
Story; From the German of the Marquis of Grosse*, ed. Devendra P. Varma, The
Northanger Set of Jane Austen Horrid Novels (London, 1968), 3; and see Translator's Preface on secret societies, pp. xv–xviii.

[86] A long romantic drama set in 1438. Scott omits many of the minor characters
in Weber's work, and changes several names: see Arthur Melville Clark, *Sir Walter
Scott: The Formative Years* (London, 1969), 263–6, and Bertrand Evans, *Gothic
Drama from Walpole to Shelley*, University of California Publications in English,
No. 18 (Berkeley, Calif. 1947), 224–8.

Kemble and was not performed until 1829, when much of its relevance to the political situation of the late 1790s had been lost. After working on the play from time to time for thirty years, he gave it to Charles Heath for publication in *The Keepsake for 1830* (1829). The Advertisement which he wrote for *The Keepsake* records his disillusionment with the outdated 'German' dramatic model of his youth, but remarks:

Very lately, however, the writer chanced to look them over with feelings very different from those of the adventurous period of his literary life during which they had been written, and yet with such as perhaps a reformed libertine might regard the illegitimate production of an early amour. There is something to be ashamed of, certainly; but, after all, paternal vanity whispers that the child has a resemblance to the father.[87]

Four weeks after this, he finished *Anne of Geierstein*, in which he returns to the central subject of *The House of Aspen*, the Germanic Secret Tribunal or Vehme Gericht with which he had first worked in his translation of Goethe's *Götz von Berlichingen* and first discussed in his preface to that translation.[88] Obviously the 'reformed libertine' was not yet to be trusted. More importantly, and in defiance of Edgar Johnson's suggestion, already quoted in Chapter 1, that he made a steady recovery from the 'German measles' of his youth, the Vehme Gericht plays an important part in the imaginative and narrative schemes of *Anne of Geierstein*. It is not there simply to be a prop of sensationalist fiction (in fact it would have been rather out of date if so designed), or to take advantage of the Germanic setting of the novel. As used in *The House of Aspen*, the Vehme Gericht figures the threat to individual thought and conscience, and to the stability of society as a whole, posed by the powers invested in a secret organization. In *Anne of Geierstein*, it functions as culmination and symbol of a

---

[87] *PW* xii. 367: see dismissive references to the play, *Letters*, i. 124, ii. 89, 495.
[88] He worked on *Anne of Geierstein* from the autumn of 1828 to the end of Apr. 1829. The preface to Scott's *Goetz of Berlichingen, with the Iron Hand* describes the Vehme Gericht as an extra-judiciary force, with only a slight suggestion of the sinister overtones of corruption which become so important in his imaginative uses of the Tribunal in *The House of Aspen* and *Anne of Geierstein* (*PW* xii. 445–50).

narrative pattern dominated by repeated situations of loss, insecurity, and live burial.

The play and the novel, separated by thirty years of social and political change, predictably make significantly different uses of the potent political and judicial symbol of the Vehme Gericht. The differences make it clear that Scott's interest in sensationalist motifs was neither static, nor, by the time when he was avowedly writing in order to pay off his financial debts, either jaded or derivative. In fact, even after its rejection by Kemble, Scott continued to tinker with *The House of Aspen*, making it no bad register of his changing views about dramatic style and the role of the modern dramatist. At one time he redrafted it under the title *Mother and Son*, signalling a shift of interest away from the Vehme Gericht towards the type of psychological drama most stridently advocated in this period by his friend Joanna Baillie. The crisis between mother and son (Isabella and George of Aspen) still seemed to Scott in 1811 to provide the play's 'only tolerable scene . . . which I think would have a dramatic effect'.[89] A play about conspiracy and betrayal had been refocused as a domestic psychodrama. Despite these sporadic reworkings, however, the original conception of *The House of Aspen* centres on the social, political, and legal implications of the Secret Tribunal. The play contrasts different forms of ritual, justice, and conscience, highlighting the differences between secret sin and open feud. The battle between the troops of Aspen and Maltingen, for example, is contrasted with the revenge treacherously enacted under cover of Vehmic ritual. Although the young heroine, Gertrude, idealistically describes the Tribunal as an instrument of divine vengeance, it is in fact a travesty of her elevated image of silent retribution. The judges of the Tribunal, in their cowls and long black robes, meeting before an altar in a ruined chapel, are types of the priesthood in its most sinister role. Like the officers of the Inquisition in *The Italian* and *Melmoth the Wanderer*, they also suggest social and political threat which springs from the organization of individuals in groups which are not governed by the normal rules of their society. As the tragic hero, George of Aspen, states, the Tribunal works to deny the free moral choice of the individuals of which it is composed, a denial dramatized in the dilemma of the Eldest of the Secret

[89] *Letters*, ii. 495; see also ii. 520 on the same scene.

Judges who is forced to carry out the ritual killing of George against the promptings of his own conscience.[90]

Scott's opinion of *The House of Aspen* was always closely related to his views on German literature in general. He describes it in letters as being written 'upon the vile German plan', as his 'Germanized brat', 'a sort of half-mad German tragedy'.[91] However, one must not forget Coleridge's insistence that: 'The so-called *German* drama, therefore, is *English* in its *origin*, *English* in its materials, and *English* by re-adoption'.[92] Long before the first English translation of *Die Raüber* (by A. F. Tytler in 1792) a number of plays had appeared which established a British tradition of Gothic drama. In the mid-1790s the conventions of German and British Gothic plays, many of them adaptations of successful Gothic novels, became hopelessly entangled, partly because of their common origins in Shakespearian and later Jacobean tragedy. When looking at Scott's models in the 1790s, therefore, it is important to remember the Gothic as well as the German. *The House of Aspen* evokes the atmospherics of many Gothic novels and plays with its ruined chapel, hemlock marsh, forced marriage, moody hero, stories of ghosts and magic mirrors, wailing spirits, and the terrible dream which Isabella's niece, Gertrude, relates somewhat tactlessly to her, in which Isabella is buried alive beneath the tomb of her first husband. Scott's 'Germanized brat' also has close links in subject-matter with Walpole's *The Mysterious Mother*, and, beyond it, to classical tragedy. As I have already mentioned, Scott's 'Essay on Drama' in 1819 makes a spirited defence of *The Mysterious Mother* when considering the 'genteel' traditions of the eighteenth-century stage between 1714 and 1760. He is not able to approve its subject-matter, which he describes as 'a theme not only totally unfit for representation, but from which the mind shrinks in private study'. Yet Walpole treats it, he insists, 'as a man of genius, free from the trammels of habit and of pedantry'.[93] With John Home's *Douglas* (1757), the play which

---

[90] George's attacks, *PW* xii. 416–17, 431: the Eldest Judge, 431–2; see also 438–9 in which he refuses to murder Rudiger, and asserts the values of compassion and companionship.

[91] *Letters*, ii. 89, i. 124, ii. 495.

[92] *Biographia Literaria*, ii. 212. Coleridge mentions Young's *Night Thoughts*, Harvey's *Meditations*, Richardson's *Clarissa*, and *The Castle of Otranto* itself as the works which have had such an impact on German literature.

[93] *MPW* vi. 378.

sparked his enthusiasm for the theatre as a child in Bath, Scott presents *The Mysterious Mother* as an effort to restore 'truth and passion' to tragedy. Both plays are significant in the imaginative prehistory of *The House of Aspen*.

Like *The Mysterious Mother* and *Douglas*, *The House of Aspen* hinges on an event in the past which returns to threaten the present, and visits upon the children the sins of the parents. Also like *The Mysterious Mother* and *Douglas*, its central character is a woman unable to forget or to confess the sins of the past. Isabella of Aspen has murdered her first husband, in fear for her own life, and has married the man from whom she was forcibly separated in her youth. The moral crisis comes when her crime is discovered by her eldest son, George, who, unknown to his mother, is a member of the Secret Tribunal and bound to reveal any crime which comes to his knowledge. George must either denounce his mother to the Tribunal or face execution himself for breaking his vows to them. By George's self-sacrifice, Isabella's husband Rudiger is prevented from learning of her crime, and the inheritance of Aspen passes from the gloomy elder son to his cheerful younger brother. The Secret Tribunal itself is cleansed of the corruption introduced by Roderic of Maltingen by the Duke of Bavaria, who functions much like the Duke of Vienna in *Measure for Measure*, a prototype for many Gothic plays, and, indeed, novels. The forms of Roman Catholic worship are, directly and indirectly, a target in both *The Mysterious Mother* and *The House of Aspen*. Both plays are deeply suspicious of the attempt to absolve sin through organized penance. The individual conscience is explicitly raised above all religious system, and of course the Secret Tribunal itself, described by one character as 'the holy and invisible circle', is a quasi-religious institution, a warning about organized ritual which compromises individual moral choice. The closest parallel is with the representation of the Inquisition in so many Gothic novels, but what is most interesting about the Secret Tribunal as it appears in Scott's work and elsewhere is that its members are all ordinary men, not specialized investigators and punishers but an extension of the usual organizations of society as a whole. Barruel's accusation that Rosicrucians, Illuminati, free-masons, and other secret societies fostered Jacobinism is an attempt to explain revolution without implicating ordinary domestic and social groups. In *The House of Aspen*, however, this

reassurance that the everyday man is not after all to blame is
entirely lacking.

The reference to Barruel and to the way in which British commentators extended his theories about the origins of revolution
provides an important context for Scott's work on *The House of
Aspen*. Not only does the type of secret organization depicted in
Scott's play recall Barruel's theories. It also acts as a possible
representation of political groups in Britain in the late 1790s.
Robert Clifford, the translator of Barruel's *Memoirs, Illustrating
the History of Jacobinism* (1798), goes on to extend Barruel's
theories to apply also to secret societies in Britain, singling out for
comment the Society for Constitutional Reform and the London
Corresponding Society.[94] With this in mind, some of Rudiger's
speeches about secret organizations in *The House of Aspen* make
interesting reading in the context of Pitt's Combination Acts,
passed in the same year, 1799: 'we only know that it has taken
deep root, and spread its branches wide. I sit down each day in my
hall, nor know I how many of these secret judges may surround
me, all bound by the most solemn vow to avenge guilt.'[95]

It has been claimed that *The House of Aspen* reveals no ideas or
techniques peculiar to Scott.[96] It is, however, a play steeped in
anxieties highly characteristic of the late 1790s. These can best be
seen by contrasting it to the play which introduced the Vehme
Gericht to the English stage in 1795, James Boaden's *The Secret
Tribunal*.[97] The Tribunal motif adapted from Boaden, Goethe,
Naubert's *Herman of Unna* (1788), and Weber allowed Scott to
express his current fears for his society in recognizable literary
form. Boaden's play expresses a less troubled belief in the forms of
British justice, and ends happily.[98] Ida's speech contrasting the

---

[94] *Application of Barruel's Memoirs of Jacobinism, to the Secret Societies of
Ireland and Great Britain* (London, 1798). Especially significant in the present
context is Clifford's closing address and appeal to English law and justice, pp.
48–50. See also J. M. Roberts, *The Mythology of the Secret Societies* (London,
1972), ch. 6.

[95] *PW* xii. 380–1.

[96] Evans, *Gothic Drama*, 227–8.

[97] Boaden's play loosely follows the plot of C. B. E. Naubert, *Herman of Unna:
A Series of Adventures of the Fifteenth Century, In Which the Proceedings of the
Secret Tribunal Under the Emperors Wincaslaus and Sigismond, Are Delineated*
(1788), trans. anon., 3 vols. (London, 1794); admired by Scott, *Letters*, ii. 495.

[98] See Boaden's complacent assertion in his Epilogue of the imaginative effort
needed to appreciate these 'dread scenes of a benighted age', *The Secret Tribunal:
A Play* (London, 1795), 71.

secret trials with the ideal of justice may be taken as representative:

> O, if there be a land, where equal laws
> And open judgment are the claims of all,
> Where those of our own rank pronounce upon us,
> There true decision calls on punishment,
> Temper'd in anger by enthroned Mercy.[99]

In *The House of Aspen*, the luxury of private conscience, however tortured, is replaced by public examination against which it struggles to assert itself, anticipating the misunderstandings and misrepresentations suffered by heroes of the Waverley Novels.

As already stated, there is a coincidence between Scott's work on *The House of Aspen* in preparation for its submission for publication in 1829 and his work on *Anne of Geierstein*. Although he had great difficulties in writing *Anne of Geierstein*, he took some care in researching once again the subject of the Vehme Gericht, relying not simply on earlier reading but consulting the latest scholarly sources on the subject.[100] The Magnum Opus introduction for *Anne of Geierstein*, which Scott prepared rapidly, and in poor health, is largely taken up with quotation from the latest work of scholarship on the Tribunal, Francis Palgrave's *The Rise and Progress of the English Commonwealth*, at that time awaiting publication.[101] Scott also refers in retrospect to the literary vogue through which the Vehme Gericht had 'again been revived in public fancy with a full share of its ancient terrors', acknowledging the influential example of Goethe.[102] The scholarly value of the section of Palgrave's work which deals with 'The Vehmic, or Secret Tribunals of Westphalia' lies in its systematic correction of the prevalent notion that the Vehme Gericht was a mysterious, secretive institution, alien from all forms of judicial custom established in other lands. As Palgrave emphasizes, 'the celebrated Vehmic tribunals' were 'well known from Romance; but the pro-

---

[99] Ibid. 27.
[100] Difficulties of composition: *Letters*, xi. 164, 166–7, 171–2; *Journal*, 510, 524, 526, 553–4. Scott asked James Skene for his paper on Secret Tribunals for Memoirs of the Society of Antiquaries while working on the novel, as Skene recalls in *Memories of Sir Walter Scott*, 155–6.
[101] WN xliv, pp. vi–xxv. *The Rise and Progress of the English Commonwealth: Anglo-Saxon Period: Containing the Anglo-Saxon Policy, and the Institutions Arising out of Laws and Usages which Prevailed Before the Conquest*, 2 vols. (London, 1832), ii, pp. cxliv–clvii.
[102] WN xliv, p. vi.

tocols of their proceedings do not altogether realize the popular
idea of their terrors and tyranny'.[103] In a passage which Scott
places in italics as being 'the most important' of his extracts,
Palgrave suggests that the Vehmic system may have influenced the
early forms of justice in England, and that both are linked to an
older religious ritual:

The singular and mystic forms of initiation, the system of enigmatical
phrases, the use of the signs and symbols of recognition, may probably be
ascribed to the period when the whole system was united to the worship
of the Deities of vengeance, and when the sentence was promulgated by
the Doomsmen, assembled, like the Asi of old, before the altars of Thor
or Woden.[104]

Despite the scholarly information provided by Palgrave, the Vehme
Gericht is used, as in *The House of Aspen*, to suggest the threat
posed to the individual by the group, and, through extensive
patterning of events and reactions of the sort easier (for Scott, at
least) to achieve in prose narrative than in stage drama, intensifies
the psychological implications of the threat. As in *The House of
Aspen*, the Tribunal in *Anne of Geierstein* is threatening largely
because of its combination of secrecy, the social authority of its
leaders, and the domination of individual will by a group identity
and morality. The President of the Tribunal is the Black Priest
of St Paul's, Anne of Geierstein's father, who represents a combination of spiritual, paternal, and social authority, and is cast
physically in the mould of Schedoni, with his haggard face and
compelling eyes. He is a familiar Waverley-Novel figure of authority, and must be resisted, especially since he comes charged
with the meanings of a suspect ritualistic fraternity imaginatively
equated with Catholicism. Gothic novels and plays present their
own versions of this Protestant heroism in the face of Catholic
temptation, as in *Melmoth the Wanderer* and *Bertram*. The
spiritual associations of the Tribunal in *Anne of Geierstein* are in
line with Gothic practice, and with the recurrent motif of threat to
the individual conscience in Scott's own work. Heroes of the
Waverley Novels must always resist forces which threaten to deny
the Protestant independence of faith and conscience.

---

[103] Palgrave, *Rise and Progress of the English Commonwealth*, ii, p. cxlix.
Palgrave refers to Scott's use of the Vehme Gericht, ii, p. cxlvii n.
[104] Ibid., ii, p. clvi, quoted with one variant in *WN* xliv, p. xxiii.

Despite these broad similarities, there are important differences in presentation and emphasis between *The House of Aspen* and *Anne of Geierstein*, and these are best understood not as a recovery from 'German measles' but as responses to changed social and political problems. The heroic words of the oppressed are far closer to the tone of Boaden's *The Secret Tribunal* than the agonized words of characters in *The House of Aspen* had ever been. The greater part of Philipson's addresses to the Tribunal is taken up with an appeal to true justice on the paradigmatic English system, which strongly recall Boaden. He declares: 'My answer to the accusation is, that I am an Englishman, one of a nation accustomed to yield and to receive open-handed and equal justice dealt forth in the broad light of day.'[105] Warming to his theme, he moralizes:

'... No laws or judicial proceedings can be just or commendable, which exist and operate by means of a secret combination. I said, that justice could only live and exist in the open air, and that when she ceased to be public, she degenerated into revenge and hatred. I said, that a system, of which your own jurists have said, *non frater afratre, non hospes a hospite, tutus*, was too much adverse to the laws of nature to be connected with or regulated by those of religion.'[106]

The fear of secret political association has mellowed into pleasure at the contemplation of English justice. *Anne of Geierstein* is centrally concerned with the rights of individuals in social groups, investigated through the cause of the Swiss burghers against the feudal, aristocratic rule of Burgundy. The cause of individual liberty which Scott espouses through the Secret Tribunal scenes is expressed with a complacency very different from the tone of *The House of Aspen*. At the same time, the emphasis on the workings of law during a scene which plays upon *religious* fears inevitably recalls the way in which the Secret Tribunal functioned in *The House of Aspen* as a symbol not just of legal but also of religious organization. *Anne of Geierstein* is an important demonstration of the ways in which the influences of the early years were not rejected or made blandly respectable in later work, but formed the basis of new experiment. The two uses of this potent symbol of legal and political oppression, separated by thirty years, disrupt

[105] *WN* xlv. 46.
[106] *WN* xlv. 47.

any simple scheme of a progression from immature sensationalism to mature 'good sense', and show how Scott responded both overtly and covertly to changing political, social, and personal conditions.

The importance of the Tribunal scenes in *Anne of Geierstein* is reinforced by a second, new element, best summarized as the physical and psychological insecurity of the individual. The readings of *Rob Roy* and *Peveril of the Peak* in Chapter 4 have demonstrated that anxieties about personal safety were often fundamental to the emotional effect of Scott's work. The description of the elder Philipson's descent into the vaults used by the Tribunal is closely connected to an ominously recurrent situation in *Anne of Geierstein*, by which a character is suddenly faced with an abyss or precipice, which may be superficially naturalistic (as in the account of Arthur Philipson's perilous climb in the opening chapter of the novel), or highly improbable (as in the scene in Arthur's dungeon, in which the ground suddenly opens before him). At the start of *Anne of Geierstein*, Scott seems to have brought his readers back to Charles Brockden Brown's Norwalk:

It is a tedious maze, and perpetual declivity, and requires, from the passenger, a cautious and a sure foot. Openings and ascents occasionally present themselves on each side, which seem to promise you access to the interior region, but always terminate, sooner or later, in insuperable difficulties, at the verge of a precipice, or the bottom of a steep.[107]

One wonders whether Scott recalled the adventure of the tree-bridge in Brown's novel (as indeed he seems to do in the scenes at the Black Linn of Linklater towards the end of *Old Mortality*). The suggestion that *Anne of Geierstein*'s land of precipices and sudden abysses is in part a landscape of the mind and spirit lingers throughout the striking opening adventure on the rock face. Until rescued by Anne of Geierstein, Arthur Philipson is in a perilous situation indeed:

The solid rock had trembled and rent beneath his footsteps, and although, by an effort rather mechanical than voluntary, he had withdrawn himself from the instant ruin attending its descent, he felt as if the better part of him, his firmness of mind and strength of body, had been rent away with the descending rock, as it fell thundering, with clouds of dust and smoke, into the torrents and whirlpools of the vexed gulf beneath.[108]

[107] *Edgar Huntly*, 92.   [108] WN xliv. 35.

However conventional it may at first seem, Arthur's intense association here between the falling rock and 'the better part' of himself initiates what becomes a powerfully threatening series of images. In *Anne of Geierstein*, the ground is never very firm underfoot. Even the monastery of Mont Saint Victoire, to which Margaret of Anjou retreats, overhangs a 'fearful gulf' from which (in echo of *Vathek*) demonic 'subterranean voices' are said to issue.[109] At Margaret of Anjou's funeral, Scott describes how priests carry the body 'down a private staircase which yawned in the floor to admit their descent'.[110] In this context, the circumstances of Philipson's descent to the Tribunal, in which the floor of his chamber literally splits open, taking him and his bed down to the vaults, can be seen as part of a developing pattern which strongly expresses the insecurities which underlie the novel.[111] The overt investigations of *Anne of Geierstein* concern the rights and responsibilities of a free people, and the burgher class. The imagery and scenery, however, repeatedly return to death and burial, to mental and physical collapse, and to the ignominy of being suddenly helpless and immobile.

As in many Gothic novels, a descent into the vaults for a confrontation with the forces of retribution and death had been used many times in Scott's previous work. The trial and live-burial of Constance in *Marmion*, and the grim wedding-scene at the end of *The Black Dwarf*, are only the most obvious examples. In *Anne of Geierstein*, however, the motifs of sudden descent and immurement are unusually prevalent. They most ominously recall the concealed trap-door which, at the end of *Kenilworth*, pitches Amy Robsart to her death, and the terrible fears of Cromwell's search-party in *Woodstock* that they are about to plunge through concealed traps in the secret labyrinth leading to Rosamond's Tower. The curious return to the live-burial motif in *The Betrothed*, two

<hr/>

[109] WN xlv. 254, 261.
[110] WN xlv. 317.
[111] Daniel Cottom comments that the descent into the abyss before the Vehme Gericht is 'almost a symbolic description of the nightmarish depths of law not only in this book but throughout Scott's novels' (*Civilized Imagination*, 178). Graham McMaster comments on the importance of the abyss in *Anne of Geierstein*, and Gary Kelly, in *English Fiction of the Romantic Period*, 175–6, discusses the settings of mountain and prison. Kelly also argues, pp. 163–4, that images of the abyss are more prominent in Scott's novels of the 1820s, and suggests links between this and the Reform Bill crisis.

years earlier, touches on the same preoccupation. Looking at
Scott's *Journal* for these years, it is clear that similar metaphors
had permeated his private thoughts: 'In my better days I had
stories to tell but death has closed the long dark avenue upon
loves and friendships and I can only look at them as through the
grated door of a long burial place filld with monuments of those
who were once dear to me.'[112] As they appear in his fiction,
however, they become ways of suggesting more general cultural
fears. The next chapter is concerned with a novel which is not
only about days in which there are 'stories to tell' but also about
the experience of having the grated door which separates the dead
from the living lifted; not from the perspective of an old man
who welcomes the opportunity to re-enter his past but from the
perspective of a young one who finds himself alternately beckoned
and threatened by a past he finds unexpectedly alien.

The case-studies in this chapter have set out to demonstrate the
complexity of Gothic's involvement in the settings, character-
studies, and plots of the Waverley Novels. It would be very easy to
set up a model of the Waverley Novels as rational texts fissured by
the return of the literary repressed in the shape of sensationalist
Gothic sub-plots or secondary characters who can be rapidly
sketched as Radcliffean villains. Yet literary subversion is not the
same as political subversion and sub-plots are not the province
of the subconscious. Nor, for all Wordsworth's anxieties in the
Preface to *Lyrical Ballads*, is there any straightforward or inevitable connection between sensational plots, social escapism, and
moral quiescence. Scott's openness to all the competing and
sometimes conflicting elements in his novels suggests that, for
the course of each novel at least, he was not interested in setting
up hierarchies among possible modes of fiction. What interests
him—as in the mixed modes of *The Antiquary*, the complex
evaluation of revolutionary and nationalistic passions in *The
Heart of Midlothian* and *The Bride of Lammermoor*, and the
conspicuously stylized echoes of terror-fiction in *The Fortunes of
Nigel* and *Anne of Geierstein*—is disjunction and the narrative
energies it generates. It is the stylistic equivalent of the working
process which Scott describes so vividly in the *Journal* in 1827:

[112] *Journal*, 254–5 (18 Dec. 1826).

There is one thing I believe peculiar to me—I work, that is meditate for the purpose of working, best when I have a *quasi* engagement with some other book for example. When I find myself doing ill or like to come to a still stand in writing I take up some slight book, a novel or the like, and usually have not read far ere my difficulties are removed and I am ready to write again. There must be two current[s] of ideas going on in my mind at the same time . . . I always laugh when I hear people say do one thing at once. I have done a dozen things at once all my life.[113]

In the Introductory Epistle to *The Fortunes of Nigel*, Scott professes to regard the incongruities of his plots, their lack of shape and strict economy, as 'a Gothic anomaly' without purity or integrity in either style or form. Yet the formal incongruities of the Waverley Novels, so casually and so characteristically dismissed by Scott as a failure of his art and commitment, are the source of much that is most complex in their reworkings of social, moral, and political crisis.

[113] *Journal*, 391. See also 523, 551.

6
'Ripping Up Auld Stories': Exhumation and the Gothic Imagination in *Redgauntlet*

Ye should mind there are some auld stories that cannot be ripped up again with entire safety to all concerned.

(Pate-in-Peril, *Redgauntlet*)[1]

'Behold me'—he said; 'see you not my hair streaming with sulphur, my brow scathed with lightning?—I am the Arch-Fiend—I am the father whom you seek—...'

(General Witherington, *The Surgeon's Daughter*)[2]

IN June 1824, the month in which the 'Author of *Waverley*' published his last Jacobite romance, *Redgauntlet*, his friend James Hogg published (also anonymously) *The Private Memoirs and Confessions of a Justified Sinner*. Hogg's novel takes up a story which he had launched in August 1823 by writing a letter to *Blackwood's Edinburgh Magazine* about a bizarre case of grave-robbing.[3] In this letter Hogg had described for the benefit of *Blackwood's* readers the discovery of a remarkably well-preserved corpse in an unmarked grave, believed to be that of a suicide, in the south-west of Scotland. In a macabre search for souvenirs, Hogg relates, the local people had twice partially exhumed the body and taken away fragments of its clothing. In *Confessions of a Justified Sinner* the Editor quotes this letter towards the end of his narrative, and goes on to describe how it inspired him and a party of fellow gentleman-amateurs to set out in search of the grave and its treasures. Their progress is hindered by Hogg him-

---

[1] WN xxxvi. 84.
[2] WN xlviii. 324.
[3] 'A Scots Mummy', *Blackwood's Magazine*, xiv (Aug. 1823), 188–90. In 'The Three Burials in Hogg's *Justified Sinner*', *Studies in Scottish Literature*, xiii (1978), 15–23, Michael York Mason notes the inconsistencies and contradictions in the three accounts of the burial (the editor's exhumation, the exhumation described in Hogg's letter, and the local traditions given in the letter and enlarged on by the guide), and argues that these must be read into the larger structure of the novel.

self, who churlishly refuses to guide them to the correct site. Undeterred, they complete the exhumation of the lower half of the body and take away further samples of clothing and a printed memoir which they discover in a leather tobacco-pouch. Anxious to possess the physical evidence of the past, they actually expose it to decay. As the Editor watches the exhumation of the lower parts of the body, he comments: 'All the limbs, from the loins to the toes, seemed perfect and entire, but they could not bear handling. Before we got them returned again into the grave, they were all shaken to pieces, except the thighs, which continued to retain a kind of flabby form.'[4] This occasion has, in fact, fulfilled Hogg's warning as given in his original letter to *Blackwood's*:

These young men meeting with another shepherd afterwards, his curiosity was so much excited, that they went and digged up the curious remains a second time, which was a pity, as it is likely that by these exposures to the air, and from the impossibility of burying it up again as closely as it was before, the flesh will now fall to dust.[5]

While the evidence which he supposedly values is falling into dust, the Editor takes upon himself the task of 'explaining' the suicide's memoir for modern readers, although he is eventually forced to confess himself unequal to it. The story of the respectable gentlemen who dig up the past then rob its body is a paradigm of the dangers of antiquarianism when it is not mediated by a respect for the integrity of the past. The story is especially resonant when one recalls, first, the description of the Rankleburn expedition and the discovery of the old tar-pot with which I began this study, and, second, the uncovering of more exotic relics than a suicide's manuscript in parallel tomb-robbings and raids on culture in Greece and Egypt.[6] The Editor and his accomplices like to see their actions as comfortably local and benign, a small-scale depredation by respectable amateurs. The *Confessions*, however, obliges readers to think rather more seriously about the motivation of those who want to rewrite the past according to their own cultural (to include moral and political) preoccupations.

[4] *Confessions*, 251.
[5] Ibid. 245.
[6] See John Whale's discussion of Belzoni and cultural grave-robbing, 'Sacred Objects and the Sublime Ruins of Art', in Copley and Whale (eds.), *Beyond Romanticism*, 218–36.

Possible links between the composition of *Redgauntlet* and *Confessions of a Justified Sinner* are frustratingly obscure. According to the Advertisement to the version of the *Confessions* published in the 1837 *Novels and Sketches*, Scott had been involved in revising Hogg's manuscript after its original publication. The links of theme and treatment, however, are illuminating. *Redgauntlet* is preoccupied by the problems of 'ripping up auld stories', as the old Jacobite Pate-in-Peril describes it, and also by the senses in which storytelling can indeed be 'perilous'. In *Confessions of a Justified Sinner*, Hogg marks his distrust of attempts to 'explain' the past by divorcing his conventional, moralizing Editor from his troubled, haunted Sinner, and by setting up a host of other commentators and interpreters, from Mrs Logan to Samuel Scrape, narrator of the 'Auchtermuchty Preachment'. The narrative fissures of *Redgauntlet* are just as complex, and just as distrustful of easy explanation. Both Hogg and Scott show that in attempting to explain we actually rewrite, and that any rewriting has to be performed in conventions and forms which may seem deeply incongruous with the events they try to revive. In the *Confessions* this incongruous form is the moral tale constructed by the Editor. In *Redgauntlet* it is the literature of terror.

At key points in the telling of *Redgauntlet*, the past is figured as a dead body to be exhumed, just as the past is exhumed in the body of Hogg's Sinner. 'You'll as soon raise the dead as raise the Highlands', warns Nanty Ewart.[7] Before his adventures begin, Darsie Latimer (who admits to a passion for deciphering the lettering on old tombstones) believes that Jacobitism is dead: 'The Pretender is no more remembered in the Highlands, than if the poor gentleman were gathered to his hundred and eight fathers, whose portraits adorn the ancient walls of Holyrood.'[8] What Darsie experiences as the plot unfolds, however, is the uncanny resurrection of the past, and the political passion, which he thinks dead and buried. In *Redgauntlet*, as in *Melmoth the Wanderer*, two images of the past uncannily confront each other: one which is painted, framed, and believably dead; and one which is all too aggressively alive.

---

[7] *WN* xxxvi. 160.
[8] *WN* xxxv. 34 (a favourite reflection: see Sir Arthur Wardour on the paintings, *WN* v. 65).

In case these reflections on bodies seem far distant from what actually happens in *Redgauntlet*, it is worth noting the implications of one conversation which takes place between Alan Fairford and his father. Saunders Fairford persuades Alan to advance his education in the law, to 'cure Lazarus' (an interesting association of ideas) and take on the case of the crazy litigant Peter Peebles:

'... the chirurgeons have an useful practice, by which they put their apprentices and *tyrones* to work upon senseless dead bodies, to which, as they can do no good, so they certainly can do as little harm; while at the same time the *tyro*, or apprentice, gains experience, and becomes fit to whip off a leg or arm from a living subject, as cleanly as ye would slice an onion.'[9]

The principle holds true for the romantic historian Darsie Latimer as well as for the apprentice advocate Alan. While Alan Fairford experiments on the cadaver of the Peebles–Plainstanes lawsuit, his friend Darsie Latimer works through his fantasies of the family past on the dead body of Jacobitism. Peter Peebles proves Alan's legal flair, while Charles Edward Stewart, his fellow 'wanderer and litigant', proves Darsie's manhood and citizenship. Although Saunders Fairford thinks that practising on 'senseless dead bodies' is safe enough, however, the novel shows that 'raking up old matters, and mixing them with new subjects of disaffection', as Nicholas Faggot describes Hugh Redgauntlet's Jacobitism, can be a perilous occupation.[10] For Redgauntlet, as for the Editor of Hogg's *Confessions of a Justified Sinner*, there are clear dangers as well as a compulsive attraction in 'ripping up auld stories'.

In *Redgauntlet* Scott examines the appeal of history to the imagination through the invention and narration of striking stories, which unify and explain, but also distort and misrepresent, the mass of circumstantial detail on which they depend. The novel is itself a misrepresentation, a notorious example of what Mary

---

[9] WN xxxv. 225.
[10] WN xxxvi. 15. Chris Baldick has drawn attention to Marx's use of the imagery of vampires and raised corpses, and 'the delight ... with which he portrays the Legitimist party as a corpse which needs to be galvanized back to life', in *In Frankenstein's Shadow*, ch. 6 (p. 125). Although it is tempting to see Hugh Redgauntlet as a vampire, and although it would certainly be productive to consider Scott alongside Marx in Baldick's meditations on the use of the Frankenstein myth, I have focused on the revived body of the past as part of Scott's reflections on historical method rather than as a type of psycho-political threat.

Lascelles has called 'the historical event that never happened'.[11] It invests with impressive circumstantial particularity an entirely fictitious Jacobite plot in 1765. In 'Wandering Willie's Tale', Sir John Redgauntlet warns Steenie Steenson that 'if there be a knave amongst us, it must be he that tells the story he cannot prove'.[12] By Sir John's criterion, many of *Redgauntlet*'s cast of storytellers are knaves: most of all, Scott himself. There are, in fact, uncomfortably close parallels between Scott and Hugh Redgauntlet, the novel's most insistent fantasist about historical renewal. Redgauntlet is a storyteller who insists on retelling a tale which has lost its audience and its relevance. Scott, also, was conscious of retelling the Jacobite tale in defiance of Constable's calls for new material, yet he gives fictional reality to Redgauntlet's greatest dream, the return of Charles Edward Stewart (determined, like Redgauntlet, that Jacobitism's day is not yet dead). Like the other narrators of *Redgauntlet*, Scott embellishes stories about the past to make an impression on the present. Redgauntlet does this for political ends; Darsie, for personal gratification; Pate-in-Peril, because he endlessly relives the moment which has given him his name. Scott's motivation was perhaps a mixture of these, perhaps a mystery which only the unravelling of his own history in later years would explain. As he comments in the *Journal* on his love for Williamina Belsches: 'Yet what a romance to tell and told I fear it will one day be. And then my three years of dreaming and my two years of wakening will be chronicled doubtless. But the dead will feel no pain.'[13] Faced with this other form of exhumation, Scott is relieved to remember that he will finally be out of reach of the storytelling he fears most.

Redgauntlet considers how and why stories are told, what purposes they serve, politically and psychologically, and how storytelling about the past affects the freedom of the imagination in the present. Throughout, it reduces action to storytelling and makes storytelling an active force. Characters tell stories about the past to influence the present. According to Nanty Ewart, Redgauntlet 'is stirring up all the honest fellows who should be drinking their brandy quietly, by telling them stories about their ancestors

---

[11] *Storyteller Retrieves the Past*, ch. 5.
[12] WN xxxv. 180.
[13] *Journal*, 375.

and the forty-five'. Similarly, Redgauntlet initiates Darsie into his family by telling the story of his ancestor, Alberick. Alan Fairford works his way into the favour of Pate-in-Peril by listening to the story of his past, and into the confidence of 'Father Buonaventure' by giving a professionally brief account of himself.[14] Stories are rarely reliable. As Joshua Geddes tells Darsie, in words which might serve as a summary of the entire narrative mode of *Redgauntlet*: 'I have heard various stories of my neighbour; of most of which I only believe a small part, and even then they are difficult to reconcile with each other.'[15]

Some of the intensity of *Redgauntlet*'s reflections upon story-telling can be traced to the repetition of key images and descriptive motifs in parts of the novel which are not obviously related to the preoccupation with storytelling, its imprecisions and delays. The complex structure of the novel's different narrative forms—hearsay, legendary tale, confession—is constantly reflected on the levels of plot and description. Certain key images and phrases recur many times. Most important are the repeated descriptions of frustrated journeys and circuitous approaches, mazes, and labyrinths. These can only be negotiated without danger by figures of control and authority, just as Redgauntlet, in the paradigmatic scene of rescue from the Solway, finds a 'devious' route out of the quicksands and makes a headlong assault on the confused pathways back to his hut. Examples include: the 'perilous passages' and 'labyrinth of dark and deep lanes' of the Solway; the vaults and secret passageways of Trumbull's retreat, which remind Alan of Peter Peebles's lawsuit; the labyrinth of lanes on the way to Fairladies; the 'intricate avenues' of this house itself; the back-streets of London; and the irregular passages of Crackenthorp's Inn.[16] In this 'murkily symbolic' novel, the reader must submit in patience to the narrator's circuitous routes, just as Alan Fairford must submit to the indirect navigation of the 'Jumping Jenny':

He called to Nanty Ewart, and expressed his surprise at the course they were pursuing, and asked why they did not stand straight across the Frith for some port in Cumberland.

[14] Kerr points out that Alan Fairford combines the roles of lawyer and story-teller, both of which are based on skills in interpretation and retelling (*Fiction against History*, 110–13).
[15] WN xxxv. 90.
[16] WN xxxv. 306; xxxvi. 125, 172, 202, 239–41, 273.

'Why, this is what I call a reasonable question, now,' answered Nanty; 'as if a ship could go as straight to its port, as a horse to the stable, or a free-trader could sail the Solway as securely as a King's cutter!...'[17]

This insistence on circuitous routes is repeated in the narrative strategies of the novel as a whole. It is not only that interpretation is difficult, as Darsie implies when describing his attempt to alert Wandering Willie to his plight by taking up snatches of song, Blondel-style:

notwithstanding the mode of intercourse we had adopted was both circuitous and peculiarly liable to misapprehension, I saw nothing I could do better than to continue it, trusting my own and my correspondent's acuteness, in applying to the airs the meaning they were intended to convey.[18]

They also need to be circuitous in order to remain safe. In linguistic terms just as in the navigational terms of Nanty Ewart's boat, straight courses are shown to be dangerous. As Lilias warns Alan, 'The word may cost you your life.'[19] Social as well as personal safety depends on not describing things, not giving them names, or giving them so many names that names become meaningless.[20] Those who succeed in social and personal life are masters of linguistic moderation. Saunders Fairford is careful to refer to Charles Edward Stewart as 'the Chevalier', neither 'King' nor 'Pretender'. Moderate language is the governing principle of Alan's careful speech: 'I should not hold it prudent to make them much the subject of conversation.'[21] The sanctimonious smuggler, Thomas Trumbull, survives by preserving a strict distinction between what he knows and what he might infer.

The primary protagonist of such a novel, appropriately, is an accomplished and determined narrator. Darsie, to Alan's ex-

---

[17] WN xxxvi. 157: 'murkily symbolic' is quoted from McMaster, Scott and Society, 9.

[18] WN xxxvi. 52.

[19] WN xxxvi. 356.

[20] On names, WN xxxv. 116, 307, 320, 323, 327–30, xxxvi. 14–15, 63, 110, 117, 128–9, 293. For alternative readings of language, the 'problem of civil and humane speech' in Redgauntlet, see Hart, Scott's Novels, 51–5, and Mary P. Cullinan, 'History and Language in Scott's Redgauntlet', Studies in English Literature 1500–1900, xviii (1978), 659–75.

[21] WN xxxvi. 160. See Wilt on 'the language of carnal reason', Secret Leaves, ch. 3.

asperation, has 'the highest knack at making histories out of nothing', and for imbuing everything with his taste for 'the wonderful and the sublime'.[22] He writes in order to gain control over experiences which become increasingly puzzling and threatening. His very first letter finds him musing: 'I repeat the little history now, as I have a hundred times done before, merely because I would wring some sense out of it.'[23] He analyses the importance of writing, apologizes for the lack of grand circumstances in his story, ponders why a record of events and words is inadequate to the impression gained by the protagonist at the time, and asserts the appeal of 'writing history (one's self being the subject)'.[24] He writes as a romantic novelist (moodily setting the scene of his first encounter with Redgauntlet on the shores of the Solway, for example) and jokes, in *Tristram Shandy* fashion, about the discordances between experiencing, narrating, and reading. Some of his defences resemble the passages in letters, *Journal*, and Introductory Epistles in which Scott defiantly announces that he will plague the public with novels for as long as he chooses:

And so, despite thy solemn smile and sapient shake of the head, I will go on picking such interest as I can out of my trivial adventures, even though that interest should be the creation of my own fancy; nor will I cease to inflict on thy devoted eyes the labour of perusing the scrolls in which I shall record my narrative.[25]

Darsie's efforts to gain control of his experiences by narrating them have become essential to his survival by the time he begins his journal, which begins as an appeal for help but rapidly becomes a substitute for help. Struggling to deal with his sudden imprisonment by command of the tyrant, Herries, Darsie soon discovers that writing is a more profitable expenditure of energy than anxiety, and by the end of the first entry he can refer more comfortably to the 'rage of narration'. Later, the journal elicits response ('My heart rises against it, especially when I sit down to record my sufferings in this Journal').[26] It imposes order. Darsie

[22] WN xxxv. 66.
[23] WN xxxv. 12.
[24] WN xxxv. 122 (a phrase close to Frank Osbaldistone's at the start of *Rob Roy*). See also xxxv. 12, 14, 48, 53, 200, and a highly self-conscious mockery of the suspense of reading from letter to letter, xxxv. 96.
[25] WN xxxv. 201.
[26] WN xxxv. 316.

spends more than an hour after the meeting with Foxley, for example, 'reducing to writing the singular circumstances which I had just witnessed'.[27] Eventually, it becomes a necessary part of each day, and, significantly, a means of retreat and healing: 'the exercise of the pen seems to act as a sedative upon my own agitated thoughts and tumultuous passions'.[28]

In recent years *Redgauntlet* has become Scott's most widely admired essay in metafiction.[29] Deciding that it is a story about telling stories, however, should not preclude analysis of the particular fictional form the metafiction adopts. While the metafiction of *Redgauntlet* is debating the conditions for telling stories about the past, its fiction is modelling itself on tales of terror, and the place of the terror-romance in the middle of the Jacobite-romance has always caused problems. In a review of Hoffmann's *Die Elixiere des Teufels* (1815–16) for *Blackwood's* in July 1824, Lockhart confidently refers to Grierson of Lagg, the original of the Robert Redgauntlet of 'Wandering Willie's Tale', as a classic of horror: 'We like to be horrified—we delight in Frankenstein—we delight in Grierson of Lagg—we delight in the Devil's Elixir.'[30] Mary Lascelles, however, criticizes the legend of Alberick and the horseshoe mark as being in Scott's 'worst early German manner'. Scott had not needed to describe any legendary curse when he created the Bertrams of Ellangowan, she points out.[31] This suspicion that Scott returned to weak fictional conventions which he had not needed when at his imaginative peak has continued to influence readings of *Redgauntlet*. Yet in this novel Scott firmly

---

[27] *WN* xxxvi. 24.

[28] *WN* xxxvi. 47. All these functions have parallels in Scott's own journal, begun a year later in 1825. See e.g. his measured account of his decision to keep a journal, *Journal*, 1, and later analysis, 296; ordering his reactions to the financial crash through writing, 39, 41, 42; writing himself into a good humour, 54; on the journal's power to 'write down my resolution', 145; its power to fix misery, 367; its selfishness, 590.

[29] Relevant discussions include Kathryn Sutherland's introd. to her edn. of *Redgauntlet* (Oxford, 1985); Kerr, *Fiction Against History*, ch. 4, where the artist-figures are seen as 'metafictional instruments for the author' (p. 122); Susan Manning's analysis of the two heroes' complementary roles as readers and writers in *The Puritan-Provincial Vision: Scottish and American Literature in the Nineteenth Century*, Cambridge Studies in American Literature and Culture (Cambridge, 1990), 88–96.

[30] Review of *The Devil's Elixir*, assigned to Lockhart, *Blackwood's Edinburgh Magazine*, xvi (July 1824), 55–67 (56).

[31] *Storyteller Retrieves the Past*, 116–17 (116).

places Gothic and other samples of the 'worst early German manner' among the literary and imaginative conventions needed to understand and to represent the past. If, as Scott insists in his 'Life' of Clara Reeve, the depiction of the past must necessarily be mediated through present tastes, the way in which the individual imagination approaches the past must be shaped by current models for that relationship. For Darsie Latimer, the past *is* Gothic, in mood, setting, and style of command.

Part of the difficulty of allowing this aspect of the novel its say can be traced once again to tensions introduced by the introduction to the Magnum Opus version of the novel. It is a function of many of the introductions to the Magnum Opus edition to privilege certain readings of the novels over others: usually, readings which place historical fact at the centre and fantasy at the margins. In the case of *Redgauntlet*, this privileging continues a process acted out in the novel's story itself, a move away from fantasizing about the past to living in the safe present, indulgently looking back. The fantasy which is driven out by the recognition of history (especially the family history of Darsie Latimer) is, specifically, a fantasy of persecution and miraculous restoration based on Gothic. In the Magnum Opus introduction to *Redgauntlet* (1832), Scott provides a fine account of the decline of Jacobitism and reflects detachedly upon its merits as 'a theme, perhaps the finest that could be selected, for fictitious composition, founded upon real or probable incident'.[32] He projects a comfortable, unthreatening image of Jacobites from fond personal memory:

and although their political principles, had they existed in the relation of fathers, might have rendered them dangerous to the existing dynasty, yet, as we now recollect them, there could not be on the earth supposed to exist persons better qualified to sustain the capacity of innocuous and respectable grandsires.[33]

The dignified formality of this description enhances its complacency. When the novel opens, it is clear that Darsie and Alan share the comfortable assumption that Jacobitism is a distant, spent force. As the action develops, however, heroes, narrator, and reader are forced to reconsider the past. *Redgauntlet* does

---

[32] *WN* xxxv, p. iii.
[33] *WN* xxxv, p. xxii.

not read like an investigation of declining political fervour in enthusiastic but powerless characters, and Darsie Latimer is hardly confronted with an image of Jacobite enthusiasts as 'innocuous and respectable grandsires'. His struggle to assert himself in the face of his uncle's domination has much more in common with Victor Frankenstein's struggle against a monster which he alone has called into life, and which he imagines as 'my own vampire, my own spirit let loose from the grave, and forced to destroy all that was dear to me'.[34] Darsie enters freely into the lawless society of the Solway, driven by an inner compulsion to discover the secret of his birth. Redgauntlet does not rise up to persecute him until rashly invited to do so. Alternatively, and following through the vampire suggestion, Darsie's situation recalls that of another young orphan fascinated by the dark romanticism of an increasingly sinister nobleman—Aubrey in Polidori's fragment 'The Vampyre: A Tale', first published in the *New Monthly Magazine* in 1819. Challenging and qualifying the social discourse of *Redgauntlet* is a tale of terror in which the family past and an outdated political ideal threaten to rob the individual of his will, his social identity, his adulthood, and his masculinity.

From this perspective, *Redgauntlet* is a study in the perception of authority by an imagination repeatedly trivialized as childish and impotent. It is haunted by anxieties about physical pain and privation, including blindness, blindfolding, madness, fever, and imprisonment. Buildings become prisons, and windows are grated at Fairladies and at the house in Cumberland. Alan is kept to his desk by a father who little thinks that he is a variation upon the tyranny of his haughty guest, Redgauntlet, and Cristal Nixon unnerves Darsie by telling him of *lettres de cachet* and French prisons. In one passage, Darsie expresses his fears about his illegal imprisonment in terms which strongly recall the story of Stanton's imprisonment in the madhouse in *Melmoth the Wanderer*:

I have heard—dreadful thought!—of men who, for various reasons, have been trepanned into the custody of the keepers of private madhouses, and whose brain, after years of misery, became at length unsettled, through irresistible sympathy with the wretched beings among whom they were

---

[34] *Frankenstein*, i. 149. The monster, as the product of imagination, delivers the imagination's ultimatum: 'You are my creator, but I am your master;—obey!' (iii. 47).

classed. This shall not be my case, if, by strong internal resolution, it is in human nature to avoid the action of exterior and contagious sympathies.[35]

Darsie, like Stanton, struggles to maintain his sanity. Other characters in *Redgauntlet* have found that the 'strong internal resolution' surfaces as monomania. In a novel which is greatly concerned with freedom and restraint, imagination assumes differing constructive and obsessional forms. The image of Peter Peebles associates excessive imagination with madness, 'the tendency of madness to eddy about one idea', as De Quincey calls it in his 1824 article 'Madness'.[36] The law itself is dangerously allied to monomania, madness, and misrule, and subjected to its own testing in the land of disorder. The 'Great Causes' of the two 'Wanderers' and 'litigants', Peebles and Charles Edward, are closely linked.[37]

Like *Rob Roy*, and like Radcliffean Gothic, *Redgauntlet* generates a sense of vulnerability which is never fully objectified or articulated. The two heroes describe their mental experiences in the direst terms: 'These were awful apprehensions; but it pleased Providence to increase them to a point which my brain was scarcely able to endure.'[38] Time is distorted for Darsie by 'horror and agony'.[39] He is shocked by the 'appalling', 'dreadful vision of infancy', the horseshoe mark.[40] It is important that these fears beset both heroes: Alan, perhaps, even more than Darsie. Alan, similarly, describes 'pain of a distressing and oppressive character', high fever, and 'involuntary shuddering'.[41] He is 'disabled by dizziness', 'stunned with pain and noise':

Fairford could not withstand the passing impulse of terror which crossed him, when thus reminded that he was so absolutely in the power of a man, who, by his own account, had been a pirate, and who was at present, in all probability, an outlaw as well as a contraband trader.[42]

---

[35] *WN* xxxv. 321.
[36] *The Collected Writings of Thomas De Quincey*, ed. David Masson, 14 vols. (Edinburgh, 1889–90), x. 445–7 (447): exemplified by Peebles, *WN* xxxvi. 352.
[37] The 'great causes', *WN* xxxvi. 10–11, directly linked in the year 1745, and xxxvi. 360: litigants and wanderers, xxxvi. 286, 332, 341. Geddes unwittingly makes them sound very similar, xxxvi. 353–4. See Johnson, 926.
[38] *WN* xxxv. 303–4.
[39] *WN* xxxv. 306.
[40] *WN* xxxv. 334–5.
[41] *WN* xxxvi. 139.
[42] *WN* xxxvi. 157–8. For previous references, see xxxvi. 163–5, 171–2, 157–8.

Whatever it reveals about Alan's veneration for the legal system, the term 'impulse of terror' is not quite what one would expect as a description for this spectacle of villainy. It overstates his anxiety.

The same can be said of Darsie Latimer's way of describing his experiences. The story which Darsie has to tell, rather like that of Morton and Julian Peveril (and of politicized Gothic fictions stretching back at least as far as *Paradise Lost*), is of authority which must be resisted and which thinks itself absolute. A. N. Wilson has noted that Darsie's fears 'seem to draw on a different *genre* altogether', and briefly suggests possible links with Maturin and Hogg. He concludes, however, that it is 'only in the most skeletal form that the fantastic conventions of horror literature shape the story. Scott is concerned to show the powerful attraction, not of evil, but of nobility distorted into fanaticism'.[43] The conventions of horror literature are more than 'skeletal', however, because they are the governing principle of Darsie's over-stimulated imagination. Wilson may distinguish sharply between the attractions of 'evil' and 'nobility distorted into fanaticism', but Darsie, in the extremes of his anxiety, tends not to.

Redgauntlet relates how Darsie wins inheritance and identity through an ordeal of passive resistance, in which he believes himself inexplicably tormented by a figure of gloomy authority. Scott uses Darsie's experiences to suggest the problems which beset the imaginative discovery and accommodation of the past. At first, Darsie wants to repossess his past only on his own terms, and is not prepared to accept the demands which it might make of him in return.[44] He finds, however, that his past threatens to assimilate, not to complete, him, and that he has to struggle against a doctrine of historical determinism rigidly adhered to by his authoritarian uncle. Hugh Redgauntlet treats Darsie as if he had no power of independent choice, strongly recalling the situations of heroes and heroines in many Gothic novels. Monçada, in *Melmoth the Wanderer*, for example, has to struggle against his father's language of fatalism and absolute authority: 'My son, all opposition is unavailing, all discussion fruitless. Your destiny is decided, and though your struggles may render it wretched, they cannot reverse it.'[45] As in *The Recess* and *The Romance of the*

[43] Wilson, *Laird of Abbotsford*, 80, 85.
[44] WN xxxv. 34–6; and Alan's perceptive criticism of Darsie's approach to the past, xxxv. 26–7.
[45] *Melmoth*, i. 220.

Forest, the discovery of identity also involves the discovery of a way of relating to the past which does not stultify and destroy the present.

In his account of Redgauntlet's first address to him, Darsie is tempted to make him sound more like a spectre than a fisherman. He checks himself, but the uncertain fear lingers: 'I turned my head and looked at him without answering; for, to my thinking, his sudden appearance (or rather, I should say, his unexpected approach) had, amidst the gathering shadows and lingering light, something in it which was wild and ominous.'[46] Next, he attempts to comprehend Redgauntlet's sinister and world-weary presence by assimilating him to a literary tradition of dark heroism. Consciously, he debates whether Coriolanus or Marius comes closer to the mark, but unconsciously he has already imagined for Redgauntlet a much more menacing and disturbing authority. 'The rider sat like a tower',[47] he writes of the first meeting on the Solway shore, sounding the first note of the associations with Milton's Satan which become more insistent as the novel progresses. These associations have become explicit by the time of Darsie's imprisonment:

However little Peter Peebles might resemble the angel Ithuriel, the appearance of Herries, his high and scornful demeanour, vexed at what seemed detection, yet fearless of the consequences, and regarding the whispering magistrate and his clerk with looks in which contempt predominated over anger or anxiety, bore, in my opinion, no slight resemblance to

——'the regal port
And faded splendour wan'——

with which the poet has invested the detected King of the Powers of the Air.[48]

Here, Darsie does not sound at all like a young man in danger, recording his impressions in a secret journal. He indulges in literary decoration in a way which lessens the impression of immediate danger in his situation. Even the reference to Milton's Satan is embroidered by other literary conventions of description ('fearless of the consequences', 'contemptuous'). As a result, the reader can only see Redgauntlet through Darsie's spirited but anxious and obscuring attempts to make him imaginable.

---

[46] *WN* xxxv. 43.   [47] *WN* xxxv. 45.
[48] *WN* xxxvi. 13, quoting *Paradise Lost*, iv. 869–70.

It is also important to discriminate between the effect of the easy multiplication of tales in oral tradition and the cultivated literary imagination of Darsie Latimer. Scott based many details of *Redgauntlet* on local demonological tradition. Tales of Sir Robert Grierson of Lagg provided the source for 'Wandering Willie's Tale', and the horseshoe mark on the brow has a local Scottish precedent in witchcraft tales. He originally intended to write a novel called 'The Witch'.[49] Darsie's attempts to imagine his uncle, however, draw not on these local or traditional sources but on highly literary notions of the Satanic (specifically, Milton's), the heroic (a more mixed group here), and the predatory.

For all his resistance to his uncle's dominance and politics, Darsie is recognizably a Redgauntlet in his habits of imagination. His letters reveal that he is particularly susceptible to scenes and characters of grandeur and terror. Alan specifically remarks this tendency towards the dark and mysterious in Darsie's account of the Laird ('you can work mysterious and romantic heroes out of old crossgrained fishermen').[50] Describing his own reaction to Herries (Redgauntlet) in Edinburgh, Alan remarks: 'If I had thy power of imagination and description, Darsie, I could make out a fine, dark, mysterious, Rembrandt-looking portrait of this same stranger.'[51] Darsie meets exactly the dark adventure and the brooding villain-hero which he most desires, an evil genius conjured and defined by himself. His uncle, invested with a sinister spiritual authority which exceeds his physical power to kidnap, emasculate, and imprison, answers all too literally his romantic yearning for historical identity. Darsie's highly self-conscious and literary description of his as yet motiveless apprehension about Redgauntlet mark the Gothic bent of his imagination:

> Why was it, Alan, that I could not help giving an involuntary shudder at receiving an invitation so seasonable in itself, and so suitable to my naturally inquisitive disposition?[52]

> Alan, there is something terrible about this man.[53]

---

[49] As Constable reports to Cadell, 9 Sept. 1823, quoted in *Letters*, viii. 85 n. An account of a witch with a horseshoe mark on her forehead is endorsed in Scott's hand, 'Red Gauntlet. Major Weir.', NLS MS 905, fo. 24. The demonological background of *Redgauntlet* is described by Coleman Oscar Parsons, *Witchcraft and Demonology in Scott's Fiction: With Chapters on the Supernatural in Scottish Literature* (Edinburgh, 1964), 26–7, 179–84, 284–5.

[50] *WN* xxxv. 69.   [51] *WN* xxxv. 75.   [52] *WN* xxxv. 47.

[53] *WN* xxxv. 63.

For Darsie, Redgauntlet's is the 'voice of menacing authority': 'The cause for his inveterate persecution I cannot pretend even to guess at.'[54] He repeatedly casts Redgauntlet as an object of fear who represents total, arbitrary, and motiveless tyranny: 'I was in the power of one whose passions seem as violent as his means of gratifying them appear unbounded.'[55]

Darsie, however, is not the only Redgauntlet to be enamoured of images of dark heroism. His uncle has a highly developed and self-conscious imagination, and, Darsie records, can speak 'in a tone of enthusiasm which, joined to some other parts of his conduct, seems to intimate an over-excited imagination, were it not contradicted by the general tenor of his speech and conduct'.[56] This 'over-excited imagination' tends to express itself in terms which endorse Darsie's wildest fears about limitless authority. Uncle and nephew share a rhetoric of power and subjection (to fate, to a political cause, and to the past), as well as an obsession with the historical determinism of identity, free will, and the 'privilege of free action'. Darsie imagines himself as a tethered horse, a moth drawn to the candle, an underground river with its sense of remorseless and hidden destination, although he comes to recognize the dangers of giving up his freedom too easily. His romantic self-indulgence reinforced by Redgauntlet's fatalism, Darsie describes his decision to suspend active resistance: 'My story, long a mysterious one, seems now upon the verge of some strange developement; and I feel a solemn impression that I ought to wait the course of events, to struggle against which is opposing my feeble efforts to the high will of fate.'[57] This 'passive acquiescence, which has sunk down on me like a benumbing torpor',[58] is the result of the submission of his imagination to the dark heroism of its creation. He is dealing, after all, with a man whose rigid adherence to the laws of historical necessity recalls Maturin's interest in automata:

'... Meanwhile, be assured that you are a prisoner for the time, by competent authority, and that such authority is supported by adequate power. Beware, therefore, of struggling with a force sufficient to crush you, but abandon yourself to that train of events by which we are both swept along, and which it is impossible that either of us can resist.'[59]

---

[54] WN xxxv. 302–3.   [55] WN xxxv. 322.   [56] WN xxxvi. 36.
[57] WN xxxv. 315.   [58] WN xxxv. 315.   [59] WN xxxv. 323.

As in the following exchange, both Darsie and Redgauntlet indulge what seems to be a family passion for the dark and mysterious, modelled on the dark hints of the Gothic 'secret sin':

'Mysterious man,' I replied, 'I know not of what you speak; your language is as dark as your purposes.'
'Sit down, then,' he said, 'and listen; thus far, at least, must the veil of which you complain be raised. When withdrawn, it will only display guilt and sorrow—guilt, followed by strange penalty, and sorrow, which Providence has entailed upon the posterity of the mourners.'[60]

Darsie and Redgauntlet, therefore, have significant imaginative affinities, and it is the Redgauntlet side of his imagination, as well as his uncle's political claims, which Darsie, and the historical novelist who wishes to reach the 'truth' about political motivation, must confront and exorcize. In the plan of *Redgauntlet*, Peter Peebles challenges and eventually validates the legal training of Alan Fairford. Redgauntlet performs the same function for the romantic imagination of Darsie Latimer.[61] Peebles exasperates and pursues Alan, but eventually makes him a finer lawyer. Redgauntlet pursues Darsie, throwing into disarray his self-indulgent romanticism and exposing the inadequacy of his reactions, but eventually becomes the main subject and the main attraction of the narrative based on that romanticism.

The battle between Darsie and Redgauntlet, in other words, is more profound than has been recognized. Redgauntlet seeks to assimilate his apparently helpless nephew to a political cause which carries a concealed threat to his self-sovereignty. Darsie, meanwhile, wielding the new but potent weapons of novelistic convention, seeks to assimilate Redgauntlet to a literary tradition in which he can be packaged for the modern reader: a reader who, like Darsie's immediate narratee, Alan Fairford, may be strongly disposed to reject the fanciful images he conjures up.

Darsie's highly literary ways of describing and attempting to

---

[60] WN xxxvi. 28, closely related to Sir Richard Glendale's outburst on the crime of the Stewart ancestry, xxxvi. 340. Wilt comments on the secret sin of *Redgauntlet* in *Secret Leaves*, 128–9.
[61] Daiches, 'Scott's *Redgauntlet*', in *From Jane Austen to Joseph Conrad: Essays Collected in Memory of James T. Hillhouse*, ed. Robert C. Rathburn and Martin Steinmann, Jr. (Minneapolis, 1958), 55, claims 'there is a sense in which Peter and Redgauntlet are the same character'. McMaster qualifies, suggesting that the parallel was an 'afterthought', *Scott and Society*, 34.

understand his uncle are significantly, and necessarily, out of keeping with this uncle's social and historical significance, just as the Editor's comments in *Confessions of a Justified Sinner* are necessarily inadequate as explanations of the Sinner's tale. Perhaps the fact that Redgauntlet has far more in common with Darsie's habits of perception than he realizes is another sign that his Jacobitism is no longer a thing of action, but a thing of imagining. Near the end of the novel, Darsie's and Alan's imagined horrors fade away as Scott turns his attention to another version of the event desired by the imagination but denied by history. Colonel Campbell, the master of evasive speech ('I do not know . . . this gentleman'),[62] walks in on the novel's carefully created mock-historical tableau, and Charles Edward and Redgauntlet, Scott's versions of Arthur and Bedivere, sail away from Scotland for ever. Unlike the Arthur who will come again, this sailing into the mists of legend features a Pretender who could never return, except in the fantasies of historical romancers like Scott. In one sense, *Redgauntlet* denies the confrontation towards which it had seemed to build, since Darsie and Alan fade in importance as the stage on which they act becomes more crowded. In another, however, the fantasy in which they had been engaged reaches its own climax in imagined history. Scott's romantic imagination takes over as Darsie's fades.

Clearly *Redgauntlet* invites its readers to appraise the romantic imagination and the romantic approach to the past as perfected by Darsie Latimer, and to find them in some ways inadequate or at least evasive. In his discussion of *Redgauntlet*, A. O. J. Cockshut remarks that many of the later historical novelists who set out to imitate Scott were actually much closer to the imagination of the romantic Darsie Latimer, and he is right to draw distinctions between the two.[63] Much of the complexity of *Redgauntlet*, however, lies in the fact that Darsie's romantic perceptions are never absolutely invalidated. Instead, the outcome of the plot shows that they have never been very far from the truth. Gothic conventions of seeing and describing may partially misrepresent the past— as they certainly, for Darsie, conveniently obscure its political urgency—but they are no more 'inauthentic' than any other set of

---

[62] WN xxxvi. 366.
[63] Cockshut, *Achievement of Walter Scott*, 196.

conventions. Gothic may seem to align itself with 'fake' history and the distortions of the 'Claude Lorraine glass' as extravagances which Darsie must learn to set aside. As *Redgauntlet* unfolds, however, Gothic is increasingly validated as one of the ways in which a modern imagination like Darsie's, or Scott's, or the early nineteenth-century reader's, can best perceive and represent the past and the experience of being persecuted by it. Jacobite fanatics in *Redgauntlet* are allowed to be both 'respectable grandsires' and vampires, and it is surely fitting that at the very end of the novel, after Dr Dryasdust has reported what he has been able to gather about the likely later lives of Darsie, Alan, and Lilias, the reader is left with one striking last image, of a dead body and its authentic testimony. Hugh Redgauntlet dies as Prior of a monastery in Ratisbon, so strictly devout that he is considered for canonization. Those who prepare his body for the grave, however, find concealed beneath his robes a small silver box containing a lock of his executed brother's hair, and inscribed with the motto '*Haud obliviscendum*'. They have ripped up another auld story and another undead past.

Conclusion
Labyrinth, Origin, and the Gothic House of Mystery: *Woodstock*

His labours seem as if they were employed to diversify or adorn a long strait avenue of yews and cypresses, terminating in the full view of a sepulchre.

(Scott's review of Maturin's *Women; or, Pour et Contre,* 1818)[1]

THIS chapter aims by way of conclusion to draw together the main proposals made in this study by examining the questions of Gothic form, suspenseful narrative, and legitimacies novelistic and political as raised by one last novel, *Woodstock.* It is instructive to move from one much-admired novel, *Redgauntlet,* in which Gothic has been seen to offer valid imaginative ways of understanding the past and presenting it to a modern audience, to another, less admired, which seems to swerve abruptly back to the classic settings and situations of Radcliffean Gothic—so much so that Scott was moved to defend himself against Ballantyne's imputations of plagiarism. The move is prompted by something like a desire not to let Gothic benefit merely by the fact of its inclusion in *Redgauntlet. Redgauntlet*'s reputation now stands so high among Scott scholars that anything it includes—even Gothic extravagances and horseshoe marks—is likely to find favour. Can Gothic really sustain serious attention as either a narrative strategy or a complex of images in a novel not yet enshrined by critics, such as *Woodstock*?[2]

Woodstock was published six years before Scott's death. After

---

[1] *MPW* xviii. 201.

[2] Although *Woodstock* has not featured prominently in discussions of Scott's work, it has recently attracted attention because of its relationship to contemporary politics and Scott's work on *The Life of Napoleon.* Significantly, it is one of the Waverley Novels singled out for special attention in Gary Kelly's survey of the period, *English Fiction of the Romantic Period,* 165–73. See also Christopher Worth's account, 'Scott, Story-Telling and Subversion: Dialogism in *Woodstock*', in *Scott '91,* ed. J. H. Alexander and David S. Hewitt (Edinburgh, forthcoming).

it, the public had yet to encounter the imagery of graves and precipices in *Anne of Geierstein*, the dead-end quests and oppressive entrapments (in prisons, in combat-enclosures) of *The Fair Maid of Perth*, the parodies of history and history-telling of *Count Robert of Paris*, and more. It is not a conclusion. However, some of its governing themes and metaphors make *Woodstock* an appropriate novel on which to end this particular discussion. It highlights Scott's interest in frames, narrative and pictorial, in significant symbolic and metonymic structure, and in the figure of the labyrinth. It is also a good example of the way in which historical events are re-imagined as tales of mystery. Judith Wilt has drawn attention to the importance of fakes in *Woodstock*, and the winding passages which lead to a figure of legitimacy (Charles II) which is absent, impersonated by Albert Lee.[3] The present reading examines with rather different intentions the intense and repetitive imagery which leads up to these fake confrontations.

Although *Woodstock* is not a valedictory novel, it contains elements of a personal sense of ending, and indeed has often been read as testimony to Scott's pain and fear (aroused by public as well as private matters) at the time of its composition.[4] It also carries forward elements drawn from many other works. In places, indeed, and especially in the first and third volumes of its original three-volume format, it reads as an intensification of key moments and images from earlier Waverley Novels. The painting of Victor Lee recalls the ancestral portrait of Malisius de Ravenswood from *The Bride of Lammermoor*, which, after Lucy Ashton's wedding-feast, is popularly rumoured to have descended from its frame and walked among the revellers. The Countess of Man appears in a similar fashion in the wainscoted chamber of Peveril Castle in *Peveril of the Peak*, as does Diana Vernon's father at the end of *Rob Roy*. All these scenes are indebted to the impact made on Scott's imagination by *The Castle of Otranto*, and by his obvious sensitivity to the spookiness of portraits which

---

[3] *Secret Leaves*, 161–2, 172–6, in a discussion of fake history and legitimacy which draws together *Woodstock* and *The Antiquary*. Wilt's attention to the 'feminized' forms of monarchy represented by the disguised Charles II also suggest how close *Woodstock* is to similar images of a degenerate male line in *Redgauntlet*.

[4] Kenneth M. Sroka analyses its links with Scott's personal situation in 1826 in 'Fairy Castles and Character in *Woodstock*', *Essays in Literature*, xiv (1987), 189–205.

seem to watch and track the living (and would-be detached) observer. The extended sequence involving the portrait of Victor Lee in *Woodstock* elaborates and literalizes the implications of several of these earlier scenes. Instead of the past stepping out of its frame, however, the present is invited in to search through ever more complex recesses and labyrinths for its living embodiment. In another significant re-imagining, the figure of the man disguised as a woman, wearing a red cloak and giving away the secret of his gender by his harsh features, ungainly carriage, and 'prodigious long unwomanly strides', is not now the revolutionary George Staunton dressed in Wildfire garb, but the ultimate counter-revolutionary figure of Charles II. In terms of the three-volume structure of *Woodstock*, this figure of comic resolution appropriately appears at the heart of the maze (in the sixth chapter out of twelve in the second volume of three, to be precise). This entire scene, in which Alice Lee meets one of the 'denaturalized women' on whom Scott dwells in his account of the French Revolution in the *Life of Napoleon*, supplies a powerful metaphor for the spring 'unrivalled in purity' of Charles's ancestry and his present unworthy appearance before it. Here, in a description which strongly recalls that of the broken-down Mermaiden's Well in *The Bride of Lammermoor*, one finds an alternative centre for all the framed approaches to the labyrinth, 'gushing out amid disjointed stones, and bubbling through fragments of ancient sculpture'.[5] In its latest incarnation, however, the legitimate has become both ludicrous and threatening.

The opening chapters of *Woodstock*, and especially the unusually long and detailed approach to the central chambers of the old hunting lodge itself, set up patterns of deferral and elaborate framing which shape the novel as a whole. The lodge of Woodstock, as Wilt has shown, contains a labyrinth and a secret. It can be interpreted as a house which formalizes the approach to the hidden past, a house in which surfaces slide apart to reveal passages of access to what everyone knows must be there—the approach to Rosamond's Tower—but which are only known to the antiquarian cleric, Dr Rochecliffe, on whose manuscripts the novel purports to be based. Rochecliffe is custodian of the secrets of the past. His character, in fact, has obvious points of

[5] WN xxxix. 356.

resemblance to the presentation of the 'Eidolon' of the 'Author of *Waverley*' as found at the centre of the maze of passages in the frame narrative of the first-edition *Fortunes of Nigel*. Dr Rochecliffe's 'secret appartment' is to be found only after winding through many confusing passageways, and the chamber itself is described as having 'walls of great thickness, within which were fabricated various issues, leading in different directions, and communicating with different parts of the building'.[6] 'Rochecliffe the Plotter', as he is significantly nicknamed, is also the 'busy and all-directing Doctor' who stage-manages the final charades and bluffs of Charles II's escape.[7] With this figure of quasi-authorial authority at their centre, it is no surprise to find the labyrinths of *Woodstock* described in a way which recalls the figures of narrative analysed in Chapter 2 in relation to Gothic:

the fact was undeniable, that in raising the fabric some Norman architect had exerted the utmost of the complicated art which they have often shown elsewhere, in creating secret passages, and chambers of retreat and concealment. There were stairs, which were ascended merely, as it seemed, for the purpose of descending again—passages, which, after turning and winding for a considerable way, returned to the place where they set out—there were trapdoors and hatchways, panels and portcullises. . . . so that the party blundered on in the dark, uncertain whether they were not going farther from, rather than approaching, the extremity of the labyrinth.[8]

This house of secrets, however, is itself approached just as elaborately as the secret chamber, Rosamond's and Rochecliffe's chamber, at the heart of the deceptive maze. The reader first finds the approach framed by the ornate old gates of the lodge:

A battlemented portal of Gothic appearance defended the entrance to the avenue. It was of mixed architecture, but on the whole, though composed of the styles of the different ages when it had received additions, had a striking and imposing effect. An immense gate composed of rails of hammered iron, with many a flourish and scroll, displaying as its uppermost ornament the ill-fated cipher of C. R., was now decayed, being partly wasted with rust, partly by violence.[9]

When seen at the end of the avenue, the hunting lodge of Woodstock is of similarly mixed architecture. It abounds in winding

[6] WN xl. 65.   [7] WN xl. 67, 174.   [8] WN xl. 333.
[9] WN xxxix. 25–6.

corridors, and at one end of the Great Hall stands a chimney-piece which takes up the description of the lodge-gates already quoted. It too is 'adorned with many a cipher, and many a scutcheon of the Royal House of England'.[10] Following a passageway leading out of the Great Hall, the reader comes to the chamber which dominates the action of *Woodstock*, the room named after the portrait which it contains, of the triumphant (and resonantly named) royalist ancestor, Victor Lee. This portrait exercises a powerful hold over the imagination of the novel's hero, Markham Everard, and it is this image of past security which conceals the entrance to the secrets of the labyrinth. It would be tedious to go through all the novel's other references to mazy passageways, man-made wildernesses in the grounds, and paintings (framed, unframed, reversed, hollow), but their cumulative force is considerable, and their implications disturbing. The emotional power exercised by paintings is especially marked during the scene at Windsor when Cromwell turns round an old portrait to illustrate the face of Charles II, only to discover that it is in fact a portrait of the executed king, Charles I. Cromwell's prey here, as at the end of the novel, eludes him, and leaves him only with the evidence of what he describes as his 'parricide'. Among the mazes and wildernesses, Wildrake's description of Woodstock may serve as summary of many. For him, it is an 'old mansion . . . having abundance of backstairs, also subterranean passages, and all the communications under ground, which are common in old ravennests of the sort'.[11] In these passages and from these apparently static representations of a dead past, however, Markham Everard confronts the mock-ghosts which take a disturbingly familiar form. The description of the painting of Victor Lee makes it sound promisingly like the portrait of Melmoth as seen by John Melmoth near the start of Maturin's novel. As John Melmoth reads Stanton's manuscript:

he raised himself with an involuntary start, and saw the picture gazing at him from its canvas. He was within ten inches of it as he sat, and the proximity appeared increased by the strong light that was accidentally thrown on it, and its being the only representation of a human figure in the room. Melmoth felt for a moment as if he were about to receive an explanation from its lips.[12]

[10] *WN* xxxix. 61.   [11] *WN* xxxix. 156.   [12] *Melmoth*, i. 145.

In terror, he destroys the painting, only to receive, at the novel's end, exactly what this scene anticipates—an explanation from the lips of its demonic original. Like John Melmoth in the secret closet of his uncle, Everard is of course psychologically keyed up for some supernatural occurrence, despite his avowed scepticism about ghosts: 'There rushed on his mind the various traditions of Victor Lee's chamber, which, though he had often despised them as vague, unauthenticated, and inconsistent rumours . . . had yet something in them, which did not tend to allay the present unpleasant state of his nerves.'[13] He thinks he sees the form of Victor Lee before him, anxiously examines the portrait on the following day, and addresses it aloud.

Although the 'supernatural' events which occur in the lodge of Woodstock are shown to be just as illusory as anything in Radcliffe, one should not underestimate Woodstock's claims to be a model Gothic house of horror, a concentration of Gothic devices of description and suggestion. Rochecliffe's horrified account of the appearance in his mirror of a man he has believed long since dead recalls many a crisis of identity in Gothic:

It was then that something seemed to pass behind me, casting a reflection on the great mirror before which I had placed my writing-table, and which I saw by assistance of the large standing light which was then in front of the glass. And I looked up, and I saw in the glass distinctly the appearance of a man—as sure as these words issue from my mouth, it was no other than the same Joseph Albany—the companion of my youth—he whom I had seen precipitated down the battlements of Clidesthrough Castle into the deep lake below![14]

The dead past comes to life in *Woodstock*: glimpsed in mirrors, framed in pictures, rising by the side of a well or Gothic font. The rational narratorial clamps on the supernatural are as pronounced as ever, but the story itself, like *Melmoth the Wanderer*, is always threatening to break free of them and become genuinely the story of supernatural confrontation which its narrator is so anxious to discredit. The extent to which the patterns of suspense-fiction effectively supersede the known outcomes of history was acknowledged in the comments of one perceptive contemporary reader. When Lady Louisa Stuart wrote to Scott in May 1826 to

---

[13] WN xxxix. 285.
[14] WN xxxix. 333.

congratulate him on this latest novel, she praised the degree of excitement which he had managed to instil into known historical events: 'All I shall say about it is this, that I felt as anxious for Charles the Second's escape, and held my breath, as if I had not known he did escape, and been sure he must.'[15] *Woodstock* may be a novel on the margins of historical event, but it is also structured as a narrative of persecution and suspense. Stuart was always one of Scott's most perceptive readers, and her sense here of possible tensions between the reader's knowledge of history and willing suspension of it in the cause of enjoyable 'anxiety' brings into focus some of the arguments put forward in this study.

First of all, *Woodstock* is a timely demonstration of the continuing vitality and experimentation of Scott's work. Chapter 1 examined a complex set of associations by which Gothic has been equated with the 'sickly' part of Scott's imagination and has therefore seemed more likely to dominate works of which his healthy self was not fully in control. It also cited critics who have argued that Gothic was simply a popular fictional style to which Scott became more inclined at times of financial crisis. *Woodstock* would be an obvious target for both of these views, yet, as my analysis in this chapter has tried to show, its use of Gothic is much more imaginative and less opportunistic than they might suggest. There were more obvious ways for Scott to maximize his popularity and his earnings. He noted in his *Journal* in July 1826, when he was at work on the First Series of *Chronicles of the Canongate*, that 'J. B. [James Ballantyne] roars for chivalry', and Scott himself was interested in bringing 'the Highlanders' back on his imaginative stage.[16] Instead, novels like *Woodstock* and *Anne of Geierstein*, just as much as the more celebrated example of *Redgauntlet*, are vitally preoccupied with testing out received fictional formulas.

A close reading of the Gothic settings and narrative ploys of *Woodstock*, and their links to those used elsewhere in the Waverley Novels, also makes less convincing any attempt to see Gothic in this novel, or in Scott's work as a whole, as an instantiation of personal anxieties and sadnesses. Scott was certainly thinking about Maida when he made the death of the old dog Bevis suggest a whole lost world of fidelity at the end of *Woodstock*. But *Woodstock* is not just a narrative about loss, but

---

[15] *Stuart Manuscripts*, 232. [16] *Journal*, 169.

an almost obsessively patterned series of *approaches to* loss (hence this chapter's epigraph from Scott's review of Maturin, which is so expressive of his sensitivity to analogies between narrative and architecture), and thus part of a tradition which both enshrines and distances objects of dread. Obviously *Woodstock* can function perfectly convincingly as a psychobiographical exercise, but one first has to accept, as I suggested in Chapter 4 in relation to the 'Caliph Vathek' passage from the *Journal*, that Gothic tropes and conventions had come to serve as psychological shorthand for Scott. If one does choose to read *Woodstock* as a metaphor of mind, however, in which characters struggle to find ways through the maze to the secret chamber at the centre, one is led to other ideas put forward in this study. One is that the centre turns out not to be central after all, but to be peripheral. Another is that the maze leads to the chamber of the antiquarian and author, Dr Rochecliffe, and to Albert Lee dressed up as the king. The end of the quest is the source, and a fake.

Within *Woodstock* itself, characters both exemplify and explicitly debate the relationship between language and political opinion. They also consider the part played in revolution—and, by implication, restoration—by works of literature. In the terms laid out in my Introduction, *Woodstock* is the classic fiction of restoration, closing as it does with an idealized but worryingly static tableau of restored legitimacy. In other words, the novel participates in the literary-political process it analyses. The role of Gothic in this process is interesting, for, as I have shown in analyses of *Rob Roy* and *Peveril of the Peak*, among other works, Gothic tropes of anxiety throw into question the political solutions offered in Scott's novels, even as Gothic novels themselves can be seen as engaged in ritualizing and familiarizing such anxiety. *Woodstock* shows Scott examining in a particularly close way the relationship between political and novelistic legitimacies. When one recalls his indignant remark to Ballantyne about setting Radcliffe up as a 'potatoe-bogle' to warn other writers away from the explained supernatural, it might seem that Scott had decided to write about an outlawed king in an outlawed literary style, determined that both, for all their awkward disguises, were to be liberated by the schemes of 'Rochecliffe the Plotter'.

Scott is not, then, either intimidated by the potatoe-bogle or inclined to concede the field as somebody else's property. His use of Gothic is diverse, opportunistic in the best sense, and flexible. It is also based on a conscious contract with the reader, a willingness to play upon conventions and expectations, and a sensitivity to literary form. Like Scott's presentation of himself as artist, the Waverley Novels strive conscientiously to be conservative. The endings of most of them affirm a few central social and personal values: moderation, continuity, social stability combined with a new recognition of the responsibilities brought by power. At the same time, they develop disconcerting and divisive ways of challenging these certainties, through images of loss and death, through unresolved psychological and emotional crises, and, most of all, through histories which ostentatiously declare themselves to be improbable fictions.

Bibliography

1. MANUSCRIPT MATERIALS

SCOTT, SIR WALTER, BT., 'Commonplace Book' (1792–1803), NLS MS 1568.

—— '"Emma Darcy, or, the Manners of Old Times." Drafts and Notes [1801–2] of Joseph Strutt for the novel which Scott completed and published as *Queenhoo-Hall* in 1808', NLS MS 878.

—— 'List of Works of C. R. Maturin, perhaps drawn up in connexion with a project that Scott should edit them', NLS MS 891, fo. 64.

—— 'Witches and Ghosts. Extracts from records of trials for witchcraft, etc., and from printed books on witches, with a list of works, endorsed by Scott "Ghost Books," in part used for the *Letters on Demonology*', NLS MS 905.

—— Introductions to *Chronicles of the Canongate*, NLS MS 911, fos. 264–71.

STUART, LADY LOUISA, 'Letter to Sir Walter Scott', NLS MS 3898, fo. 244.

2. PUBLISHED MATERIALS AND DISSERTATIONS

ABRAMS, M. H., *Natural Supernaturalism: Tradition and Revolution in Romantic Literature* (1971; repr. New York, 1973).

ADOLPHUS, JOHN LEYCESTER, *Letters to Richard Heber, Esq. Containing Critical Remarks on the Series of Novels Beginning with "Waverley," and an Attempt to Ascertain their Author* (London, 1821).

AIKIN, JOHN, and AIKIN, ANNA LAETITIA, *Miscellaneous Pieces, in Prose* (London, 1773).

ALEXANDER, J. H., 'A Study of Scott's Poetic Treatment of the Middle Ages and its Relation to the Poetry of the "Medieval Revival"', B.Litt. Dissertation (Oxford University, 1965).

—— *Two Studies in Romantic Reviewing: Edinburgh Reviewers and the English Tradition; The Reviewing of Walter Scott's Poetry: 1805–1817*, Salzburg Studies in English Literature under the direction of Professor Erwin A. Stürzl, Romantic Reassessment, ed. James Hogg, No. 49, 2 vols. (Salzburg, 1975).

—— *The Lay of the Last Minstrel: Three Essays*, Salzburg Studies in English Literature under the direction of Professor Erwin A. Stürzl, Romantic Reassessment, ed. James Hogg, No. 77 (Salzburg, 1978).

—— '"Only Connect": The Passionate Style of Walter Scott', *Scottish Literary Journal*, vi/2 (Dec. 1979), 37–54.

—— *Marmion: Studies in Interpretation and Composition*, Salzburg Studies in English Literature under the direction of Professor Erwin A. Stürzl, Romantic Reassessment, ed. James Hogg, No. 30 (Salzburg, 1981).

—— and HEWITT, DAVID S. (eds.), *Scott and His Influence: The Papers of the Aberdeen Scott Conference, 1982*, Association for Scottish Literary Studies Occasional Papers, No. 6 (Aberdeen, 1983).

ALLAN, GEORGE [and WEIR, WILLIAM], *Life of Sir Walter Scott, Baronet; With Critical Notices of His Writings* (Edinburgh, 1832–4).

ALTER, ROBERT, *Partial Magic: The Novel as a Self-Conscious Genre* (Berkeley, Calif., 1975).

ANDERSON, BENEDICT, *Imagined Communities* (London, 1983).

ANDERSON, JAMES, 'Sir Walter Scott as Historical Novelist', *Studies in Scottish Literature*, iv (1966–7), 29–41, 63–78, 155–78; v (1967–8), 14–27, 83–97, 143–66. Repr. in his *Sir Walter Scott and History: With Other Papers* (Edinburgh, 1981).

ARAC, JONATHAN, *Commissioned Spirits: The Shaping of Social Motion in Dickens, Carlyle, Melville, and Hawthorne* (New Brunswick, NJ, 1979).

ASH, MARINELL, *The Strange Death of Scottish History* (Edinburgh, 1980).

ASHTON, ROSEMARY D., 'The Reception of German Literature in England from the founding of *Blackwood's Magazine* (1817) to the time of Carlyle and his Disciples', Ph.D. Dissertation (Cambridge University, 1974).

—— *The German Idea: Four English Writers and the Reception of German Thought 1800–1860* (Cambridge, 1980).

ASTLE, RICHARD SHARP, 'Structures of Ideology in the English Gothic Novel', Ph.D. Dissertation (University of California at San Diego, 1978).

AUERBACH, NINA, *Romantic Imprisonment: Women and Other Glorified Outcasts*, Gender and Culture Series, ed. Carolyn G. Heilbrun and Nancy K. Miller (New York, 1985).

AUSTEN, JANE, *Novels of Jane Austen*, ed. R. W. Chapman, 3rd edn., 5 vols. (London, 1932–4).

BAGE, ROBERT, *Hermsprong; or, Man as He is Not: A Novel*, 3 vols. (London, 1796).

BAGEHOT, WALTER, Review of *The Waverley Novels*, *The National Review*, vi (Apr. 1858), 444–72.

BAILLIE, JOANNA, *The Dramatic and Poetical Works of Joanna Baillie* (London, 1851).

BAKER, ERNEST A., *The History of the English Novel*, 10 vols. (London, 1924–39).

BAKHTIN, MIKHAIL, *The Dialogic Imagination: Four Essays*, ed. Michael Holquist, trans. Caryl Emerson and Michael Holquist (Austin, Tex., 1981).

BALDICK, CHRIS, *In Frankenstein's Shadow: Myth, Monstrosity, and Nineteenth-Century Writing* (Oxford, 1987).

BALL, MARGARET, *Sir Walter Scott as a Critic of Literature* (1907; repr. Port Washington, NY, 1966).

BANN, STEPHEN, *The Clothing of Clio: A Study of the Representation of History in Nineteenth-Century Britain and France* (Cambridge, 1984).

—— 'The Sense of the Past: Image, Text, and Object in the Formation of Historical Consciousness in Nineteenth-Century Britain', in H. Aram Veeser (ed.), *The New Historicism* (New York, 1989), 102–15.

[BARON-WILSON, MARGARET], *The Life and Correspondence of M. G. Lewis, Author of "The Monk," "Castle Spectre," &c. With Many Pieces in Prose and Verse, Never Before Published*, 2 vols. (London, 1839).

BARRUEL, AUGUSTIN, *Memoirs, Illustrating the History of Jacobinism*, trans. Robert Clifford, 4 vols. (London, 1797–8).

BARTHES, ROLAND, *Mythologies* (1957), selected and trans. Annette Lavers (New York, 1972).

—— 'Historical Discourse', in Michael Lane (ed.), *Introduction to Structuralism* (New York, 1970), 145–55.

BAS, KLAAS, *Religious Creeds and Philosophies as Represented by Characters in Sir Walter Scott's Works and Biography* (Amsterdam, 1932).

BATHO, EDITH C., *The Ettrick Shepherd* (Cambridge, 1927).

—— 'Scott as a Medievalist', in H. J. C. Grierson (ed.), *Sir Walter Scott To-Day* (London, 1932), 133–57.

BAYER-BERENBAUM, LINDA, *The Gothic Imagination* (London, 1987).

BEATTIE, JAMES, *Dissertations Moral and Critical* (London, 1783).

—— *The Poetical Works of James Beattie* (London, 1866).

BECKFORD, WILLIAM, *An Arabian Tale, From An Unpublished Manuscript: With Notes Critical and Explanatory* [by Samuel Henley], (London, 1786). [*Vathek*, ed. and introd. Roger Lonsdale (Oxford, 1970).]

—— *Modern Novel Writing; or, The Elegant Enthusiast; And Interesting Emotions of Arabella Bloomville: A Rhapsodical Romance; Interspersed with Poetry, By the Right Hon. Lady Harriet Marlow*, 2 vols. (London, 1796).

—— *Azemia: A Descriptive and Sentimental Novel; Interspersed with Pieces of Poetry, By Jacquetta Agneta Mariana Jenks, of Bellegrove Priory in Wales: Dedicated to the Right Honourable Lady Harriet*

Marlow; To which are added, Criticisms Anticipated, 2 vols. (London, 1797).

BEIDERWELL, BRUCE, *Power and Punishment in Scott's Novels* (Athens, Ga., 1992).

BELL, ALAN (ed.), *Scott Bicentenary Essays: Selected Papers Read at the Sir Walter Scott Bicentenary Conference* (Edinburgh, 1973).

BERGER, DIETER A., ' "Damn the Mottoe": Scott and the Epigraph', *Anglia*, c (1982), 373–96.

BIRKHEAD, EDITH, *The Tale of Terror: A Study of the Gothic Romance* (London, 1921).

BLAKEY, DOROTHY, *The Minerva Press, 1790–1820* (London, 1939).

BLAND, D. S., 'Endangering the Reader's Neck: Background Description in the Novel', *Criticism*, iii (1961), 121–39.

BLOCK, ANDREW, *The English Novel 1740–1850: A Catalogue Including Prose Romances, Short Stories, and Translations of Foreign Fiction* (1939), introd. John Crow and Ernest A. Baker (London, 1961).

BLOEDÉ, BARBARA, 'The Gothic Antecedents of *The Three Perils of Man*', *Studies in Hogg and His World*, No. 3 (1992), 76–86.

BLONDEL, JACQUES, 'On "Metaphysical Prisons"', *Durham University Journal*, lxiii (1970–1), 133–8.

BLOOM, HAROLD, *The Ringers in the Tower: Studies in Romantic Tradition* (Chicago, 1971).

—— *The Anxiety of Influence: A Theory of Poetry* (New York, 1973).

—— *Poetry and Repression: Revisionism from Blake to Stevens* (New Haven, Conn., 1976).

—— *Agon: Towards a Theory of Revisionism* (Oxford, 1982).

BOADEN, JAMES, *The Secret Tribunal: A Play* (London, 1795).

BOATRIGHT, MODY C., 'Scott's Theory and Practice Concerning the Use of the Supernatural in Prose Fiction in Relation to the Chronology of the Waverley Novels', *PMLA* l (1935), 235–61.

BOGEL, FREDRIC V., 'Structure and Substantiality in Later Eighteenth-Century Literature', *Studies in Burke and His Time*, xv (1973–4), 143–54.

BOSWELL, GEORGE W., 'Supernaturalism in Scott's Novels', *Mississippi Folklore Register*, viii (1974), 187–99.

BOTTING, FRED, *Making Monstrous: 'Frankenstein', Criticism, Theory* (Manchester, 1991).

BRADLEY, PHILIP, *An Index of the Supernatural, Witchcraft and Allied Subjects in the Novels, Poems and Principal Works of Sir Walter Scott*, 2 vols. (High Wycombe, 1966).

—— *An Index to the Waverley Novels* (Metuchen, NJ, 1975).

BRAUDY, LEO, *Narrative Form in History and Fiction: Hume Fielding and Gibbon* (Princeton, NJ, 1970).

BRIGGS, JULIA, *Night Visitors: The Rise and Fall of the English Ghost Story* (London, 1977).

BRONTË, EMILY, *Wuthering Heights* (1847), ed. Hilda Marsden and Ian Jack, The Clarendon Edition of the Novels of the Brontës (Oxford, 1976).

BROOKE-ROSE, CHRISTINE, *A Rhetoric of the Unreal: Studies in Narrative Structure, Especially of the Fantastic* (Cambridge, 1981).

BROOKS, PETER, 'Virtue and Terror: *The Monk*', ELH xl (1973), 249–63.

—— 'Godlike Science/Unhallowed Arts: Language and Monstrosity in *Frankenstein*', NLH ix (1977–8), 591–605.

BROWN, CHARLES BROCKDEN, *Edgar Huntly; or, Memoirs of a Sleep-Walker* (1799), ed. and introd. Norman S. Grabo (Harmondsworth, 1988).

BROWN, DAVID, *Walter Scott and the Historical Imagination* (London, 1979).

BROWN, IAIN GORDON (ed.), *Scott's Interleaved Waverley Novels (The 'Magnum Opus': National Library of Scotland MSS. 23001–41): An Introduction and Commentary* (Aberdeen, 1987).

BUCHAN, JOHN, *Sir Walter Scott* (London, 1932).

BUCKLE, HENRY THOMAS, *On Scotland and the Scotch Intellect*, from his *History of Civilization in England*, 2 vols. (1857 and 1861), Classics of British Historical Literature, ed. and introd. H. J. Hanham (Chicago, 1970).

BUCKLEY, JEROME HAMILTON, *Season of Youth: The Bildungsroman from Dickens to Golding* (Cambridge, Mass., 1974).

BURKE, EDMUND, *A Philosophical Enquiry into the Origin of our Ideas of the Sublime and Beautiful* (1757), ed. and introd. J. T. Boulton (London, 1958).

—— *Reflections on the Revolution in France and on the Proceedings in Certain Societies in London Relative to that Event* (1790), ed. and introd. Conor Cruise O'Brien (1968; repr. Harmondsworth, 1981).

BURNS, ROBERT, *The Poems and Songs of Robert Burns*, 3 vols., ed. James Kinsley (Oxford, 1968).

BURY, LADY CHARLOTTE, *Diary Illustrative of the Times of George the Fourth, Interspersed with Original Letters from the late Queen Caroline, and from Various Other Distinguished Persons*, 4 vols., vols. iii and iv ed. John Galt (London, 1838–9).

BUTLER, MARILYN, *Romantics, Rebels and Reactionaries: English Literature and its Background 1760–1830* (Oxford, 1981).

—— 'Against Tradition: A Case for a Particularized Historical Method', in Jerome J. McGann (ed.), *Historical Studies and Literary Criticism* (Madison, Wis., 1985), 25–47.

—— 'Repossessing the Past: The Case for an Open Literary History', in

Marjorie Levinson *et al.* (eds.), *Rethinking Historicism: Critical Readings in Romantic History* (Oxford, 1989), 64–84.

—— 'Plotting the Revolution: The Political Narratives of Romantic Poetry and Criticism', in Kenneth R. Johnston *et al.* (eds.), *Romantic Revolutions: Criticism and Theory* (Bloomington, Ind., 1990), 133–57.

BYRON, GEORGE GORDON NOEL, 6TH BARON, *Don Juan* (1819–24), ed. T. G. Steffan and W. W. Pratt (Harmondsworth, 1977).

—— *Byron's Letters and Journals,* ed. Leslie A. Marchand, 12 vols. (London, 1973–82).

—— *The Complete Poetical Works,* ed. Jerome J. McGann (Oxford, 1980–).

CADBURY, WILLIAM, 'The Two Structures of *Rob Roy*', *MLQ* xxix (1968), 42–60.

CALDER, ANGUS, and CALDER, JENNI, *Scott,* Literature in Perspective (London, 1969).

CAMERON, DONALD ALLAN, 'Studies in the Structure of Six Major Novels of Sir Walter Scott', Ph.D. Dissertation (London University, 1967).

—— 'History, Religion and the Supernatural: The Failure of *The Monastery*', *Studies in Scottish Literature,* vi (1968–9), 76–90.

CAMIC, CHARLES, *Experience and Enlightenment: Socialization for Cultural Change in Eighteenth-Century Scotland* (Edinburgh, 1983).

CAMPBELL, THOMAS, *The Complete Poetical Works of Thomas Campbell,* ed. J. Logie Robertson (London, 1907).

CANTOR, PAUL A., *Creature and Creator: Myth-Making and English Romanticism* (Cambridge, 1984).

CARGILL, ALEXANDER, 'Sir Walter Scott and his "Anonymous" Quotations', *The Scotsman,* No. 24175 (20 Nov. 1920), 9.

CARLYLE, THOMAS, *The Works of Thomas Carlyle,* Centenary Edition, ed. H. D. Traill, 30 vols. (London, 1896–9).

CARNOCHAN, W. B., *Confinement and Flight: An Essay on English Literature of the Eighteenth Century* (Berkeley, Calif., 1977).

CARSWELL, DONALD, *Sir Walter: A Four-Part Study in Biography (Scott, Hogg, Lockhart, Joanna Baillie)* (London, 1930).

CASERIO, ROBERT L., *Plot, Story, and the Novel: From Dickens and Poe to the Modern Period* (Princeton, NJ, 1979).

CASTLE, TERRY, 'The Spectralization of the Other in *The Mysteries of Udolpho*', in Felicity Nussbaum and Laura Brown (eds.), *The New Eighteenth Century: Theory Politics English Literature* (New York, 1987), 231–53.

CAWS, MARY ANN, *Reading Frames in Modern Fiction* (Princeton, NJ, 1985).

CECIL, LORD DAVID, *Sir Walter Scott,* The Raven Miscellany (London, 1933).

CERVANTES SAAVEDRA, MIGUEL DE, *The Adventures of Don Quixote* (1605, 1615), trans. J. M. Cohen (Harmondsworth, 1950, 1988).

CHAMBERS, ROBERT, *Life of Sir Walter Scott, With Abbotsford Notanda by Robert Carruthers*, ed. W. Chambers (Edinburgh, 1871).

CHANDLER, ALICE, *A Dream of Order: The Medieval Ideal in Nineteenth-Century English Literature* (London, 1971).

CHANDLER, JAMES K., 'The Historical Novel Goes to Hollywood: Scott, Griffith, and Film Epic Today', in Gene W. Ruoff (ed.), *The Romantics and Us: Essays on Literature and Culture* (New Brunswick, NJ, 1990), 237–73.

CHANNING, EDWARD TYRRELL, Review of *Rob Roy*, *North American Review*, vii (July 1818), 149–84.

CHATTERTON, THOMAS, *Poems, Supposed to have been written at Bristol, by Thomas Rowley, and Others, in the Fifteenth Century; The Greatest Part now First Published from the Most Authentic Copies, with an Engraved Specimen of one of the MSS. To which are added, a Preface, an Introductory Account of the Several Pieces, and a Glossary* (London, 1777).

—— *Miscellanies in Prose and Verse* (London, 1778).

Review of *Chronicles of the Canongate*, 1st ser., *The Scotsman*, xi, No. 816 (3 Nov. 1827), 697.

CIXOUS, HÉLÈNE, 'Fiction and Its Phantoms: A Reading of Freud's *Das Unheimliche* (The "Uncanny")', *NLH* vii (1975–6), 525–48.

CLARK, ANNA, 'The Politics of Seduction in English Popular Culture, 1748–1848', in Jean Radford (ed.), *The Progress of Romance: The Politics of Popular Fiction*, History Workshop Series (London, 1986), 47–70.

CLARK, ARTHUR MELVILLE, *Sir Walter Scott: The Formative Years* (London, 1969).

CLARK, KENNETH MCKENZIE, LORD, *The Gothic Revival: An Essay in the History of Taste* (1928), 3rd edn. (London, 1962).

CLEMENS, SAMUEL LANGHORNE [MARK TWAIN], *Life on the Mississippi* (1883), introd. James M. Cox (Harmondsworth, 1984).

—— *The Adventures of Huckleberry Finn* (1884), ed. and introd. Peter Coveney (Harmondsworth, 1966).

CLIFFORD, ROBERT, *Application of Barruel's Memoirs of Jacobinism, to the Secret Societies of Ireland and Great Britain* (London, 1798).

COATES, PAUL, *The Realist Fantasy: Fiction and Reality Since 'Clarissa'* (London, 1983).

COCHRANE, J. G., *Catalogue of the Library at Abbotsford* (Edinburgh, 1838).

COCKBURN, HENRY, *Memorials of His Time* (Edinburgh, 1856).

COCKSHUT, A. O. J., *The Achievement of Walter Scott* (London, 1969).

COLBY, ROBERT A., *Fiction with a Purpose: Major and Minor Nineteenth-Century Novels* (Bloomington, Ind., 1967).

COLEMAN, WILLIAM EMMET, *On the Discrimination of Gothicisms*, Gothic Studies and Dissertations (New York, 1980).

COLERIDGE, SAMUEL TAYLOR, *Biographia Literaria: or Biographical Sketches of My Literary Life and Opinions* (1817), ed. James Engell and W. Jackson Bate, 2 vols., *The Collected Works of Samuel Taylor Coleridge*, vii, Bollingen Series lxxv, gen. ed. Kathleen Coburn (Princeton, NJ, 1983).

—— *Coleridge's Miscellaneous Criticism*, ed. Thomas Middleton Raysor (London, 1936).

—— *Collected Letters of Samuel Taylor Coleridge*, ed. Earl Leslie Griggs, 6 vols. (Oxford, 1956–71).

COLLINS, NORMAN, *The Facts of Fiction* (London, 1932).

COLLYER, J. M, ' "The Catastrophe" in "St Ronan's Well" ', *Athenaeum* (4 Feb. 1893), 154–5.

CONGER, SYNDY M., *Matthew G. Lewis, Charles Robert Maturin and the Germans: An Interpretative Study of the Influence of German Literature on Two Gothic Novels*, Salzburg Studies in English Literature under the direction of Professor Erwin A. Stürzl, Romantic Reassessment, ed. James Hogg, No. 67 (Salzburg, 1977).

CONRAD, JOSEPH, *Victory: An Island Tale* (1915), ed. John Batchelor, introd. Tony Tanner (Oxford, 1986).

'Conversations of Maturin', *New Monthly Magazine*, xix (May and June 1827), 401–11, 570–7. 'Recollections of Maturin', *New Monthly Magazine*, xx (Aug. and Oct. 1827), 146–52, 370–6.

COOKE, ARTHUR L., 'Some Side Lights on the Theory of the Gothic Romance', *MLQ* xii (1951), 429–36.

COONEY, SEAMUS, 'Narrative Voice, Personae, and Frame Stories in Scott's Fiction', Ph.D. Dissertation (University of California at Berkeley, 1971).

—— 'Scott's Anonymity—Its Motives and Consequences', *Studies in Scottish Literature*, x (1972–3), 207–19.

COPLEY, STEPHEN, and WHALE, JOHN (eds.), *Beyond Romanticism: New Approaches to Texts and Contexts 1780–1832* (London, 1992).

CORSON, JAMES C., *A Bibliography of Sir Walter Scott: A Classified and Annotated List of Books and Articles Relating to his Life and Works 1797–1940* (Edinburgh, 1943).

—— *Notes and Index to Sir Herbert Grierson's Edition of the Letters of Sir Walter Scott* (Oxford, 1979).

COTTOM, DANIEL, *The Civilized Imagination: A Study of Ann Radcliffe, Jane Austen, and Sir Walter Scott* (Cambridge, 1985).

CRAIG, DAVID, *Scottish Literature and the Scottish People 1680–1830* (London, 1961).

CRAWFORD, THOMAS, *Scott* (1965), rev. edn., Scottish Writers Series (Edinburgh, 1982).

CRISCUOLA, MARGARET MOVSHIN, 'The Porteus Mob: Fact and Truth in *The Heart of Midlothian*', *ELN* xxii/1 (Sept. 1984), 43–50.

CRUSE, AMY, *The Englishman and his Books in the Early Nineteenth Century* (London, 1930).

CULLINAN, MARY P., 'History and Language in Scott's *Redgauntlet*', *Studies in English Literature*, xviii (1978), 659–75.

CURTIES, T. J. HORSLEY, *The Monk of Udolpho; A Romance*, 4 vols. (London, 1807). [Foreword Devendra P. Varma, introd. Mary M. Tarr (New York, 1977).]

CUSAC, MARIAN H., *Narrative Structure in the Novels of Sir Walter Scott*, De Proprietatibus Litterarum, edenda curat C. H. Van Schooneveld, Series Practica, No. 6 (The Hague, 1969).

DACRE, CHARLOTTE, *Confessions of the Nun of St Omer: A Tale*, 3 vols. (London, 1805). [Introd. Devendra P. Varma (New York, 1972).]

—— *Zofloya; or, The Moor: A Romance of the Fifteenth Century*, 3 vols. (London, 1806). [Foreword G. Wilson Knight, introd. Devendra P. Varma (New York, 1974).]

—— *The Passions*, 4 vols. (London, 1811). [Foreword Sandra Knight-Roth, introd. Devendra P. Varma (New York, 1974).]

DAICHES, DAVID, 'Scott's Achievement as a Novelist' (1951) (repr. in his *Literary Essays* (Edinburgh, 1956), 88–121.

—— 'Scott's *Redgauntlet*', in Robert C. Rathburn and Martin Steinmann, Jr. (eds.), *From Jane Austen to Joseph Conrad: Essays Collected in Memory of James T. Hillhouse* (Minneapolis, 1958), 46–59.

—— *The Paradox of Scottish Culture: The Eighteenth-Century Experience*, The Whidden Lectures for 1964 (London, 1964).

—— 'Sir Walter Scott and History', *Études Anglaises*, xxiv (1971), 458–77.

—— 'Scott's *Waverley*: The Presence of the Author', in Ian Campbell (ed.), *Nineteenth-Century Scottish Fiction: Critical Essays* (Manchester, 1979), 6–17.

DAVIE, DONALD, *The Heyday of Sir Walter Scott* (London, 1961).

DAVIS, LENNARD J., 'A Social History of Fact and Fiction: Authorial Disavowal in the Early English Novel', in Edward W. Said (ed.), *Literature and Society*, Selected Papers from the English Institute, 1978, NS, No. 3 (Baltimore, 1980), 120–48.

—— *Factual Fictions: The Origins of the English Novel* (New York, 1983).

—— *Resisting Novels: Ideology and Fiction* (London, 1987).

DAY, WILLIAM PATRICK, *In the Circles of Fear and Desire: A Study of Gothic Fantasy* (Chicago, 1985).

DE BEER, E. S., 'Gothic: Origin and Diffusion of the Term; The Idea of Style in Architecture', *Journal of the Warburg and Courtauld Institutes*, xi (1948), 143–62.

DEKKER, GEORGE, *The American Historical Romance*, Cambridge Studies in American Literature and Culture (Cambridge, 1987).

DELAMOTTE, EUGENIA C., *Perils of the Night: A Feminist Study of Nineteenth-Century Gothic* (New York, 1990).

DE QUINCEY, THOMAS, *The Collected Writings of Thomas De Quincey*, ed. David Masson, 14 vols. (Edinburgh, 1889–90).

DEVLIN, D. D., 'Scott and History', in A. Norman Jeffares (ed.), *Scott's Mind and Art* (Edinburgh, 1969), 72–92.

—— *The Author of Waverley: A Critical Study of Walter Scott* (London, 1971).

DICKENS, CHARLES, *Bleak House* (1853), ed. Norman Page, introd. J. Hillis Miller (Harmondsworth, 1971).

—— *A Tale of Two Cities* (1859), ed. and introd. George Woodcock (Harmondsworth, 1970).

DICKSON, BETH, 'Sir Walter Scott and the Limits of Toleration', *Scottish Literary Journal*, xviii/2 (Nov. 1991), 46–62.

DOODY, MARGARET ANNE, 'Deserts, Ruins and Troubled Waters: Female Dreams in Fiction and the Development of the Gothic Novel', *Genre*, x (1977), 529–72.

DORSCH, T. S. (trans. and introd.), *Classical Literary Criticism: Aristotle: On the Art of Poetry; Horace: On the Art of Poetry; Longinus: On the Sublime* (Harmondsworth, 1965).

DOWSON, LEVEN M., '*Melmoth the Wanderer*: Paradox and the Gothic Novel', *Studies in English Literature 1500–1900*, viii (1968), 621–32.

DRAKE, NATHAN, *Literary Hours: or Sketches Critical and Narrative* (London, 1798).

DUFF, WILLIAM, *An Essay on Original Genius; and its Various Modes of Exertion in Philosophy and the Fine Arts, Particularly in Poetry* (London, 1767).

DUHET, PAULE-MARIE, *Les Femmes et la Révolution, 1789–1794* (Paris, 1971).

DUNLOP, JOHN, *The History of Fiction: Being a Critical Account of the Most Celebrated Prose Works of Fiction, From the Earliest Greek Romances to the Novels of the Present Age*, 3 vols. (London, 1814).

DURANT, DAVID S., JR., 'Ann Radcliffe and the Conservative Gothic', *Studies in English Literature 1500–1900*, xxii (1982), 519–30.

EDGEWORTH, MARIA, *Castle Rackrent: An Hibernian Tale* (1800), ed. and introd. George Watson (Oxford, 1964).

EDWARDS, SIMON, 'Producing Voices: The Discursive Art of Walter Scott', in Kathleen Parkinson and Martin Priestman (eds.), *Peasants and Countrymen in Literature* (London, 1982), 123–52.

ELBERS, JOAN S., 'Isolation and Community in *The Antiquary*', *Nineteenth-Century Fiction*, xxvii (1972–3), 405–23.

ELLIS, KATE FERGUSON, *The Contested Castle: Gothic Novels and the Subversion of Domestic Ideology* (Urbana, Ill., 1989).

EMERSON, OLIVER FARRAR, 'The Early Literary Life of Sir Walter Scott', *JEGP* xxiii (1924), 28–62, 241–69, 389–417.

ERMARTH, ELIZABETH DEEDS, *Realism and Consensus in the English Novel* (Princeton, NJ, 1983).

EVANS, BERTRAND, *Gothic Drama from Walpole to Shelley*, University of California Publications in English, No. 18 (Berkeley, Calif., 1947).

FARRELL, JOHN P., *Revolution as Tragedy: The Dilemma of the Moderate from Scott to Arnold* (Ithaca, NY, 1980).

FERGUSON, MARY LOUISE DECHERT, 'My Spectre Around Me: The Reluctant Rebellion of the Gothic Novelists', Ph.D. Dissertation (Vanderbilt University, 1981).

FERGUSON, WILLIAM, *Scotland 1689 to the Present*, The Edinburgh History of Scotland, iv (1968; repr. Edinburgh, 1978).

FERRIS, INA, *The Achievement of Literary Authority: Gender, History, and the Waverley Novels* (New York, 1991).

FIEDLER, LESLIE A., *Love and Death in the American Novel* (1960; rev. edn. London, 1967).

FINLEY, C. STEPHEN, 'Scott, Ruskin, and the Landscape of Autobiography', *Studies in Romanticism*, xxvi (1987), 549–72.

FITZPATRICK, WILLIAM JOHN, 'Were all "the Waverley Novels" Written by Sir Walter Scott?', *Notes and Queries*, xii (1855), 342–3.

—— *Who Wrote the Waverley Novels? Being an Investigation into Certain Mysterious Circumstances Attending their Production, and an Inquiry into the Literary Aid which Sir Walter Scott may have received from Other Persons* (London, 1856).

FLANAGAN, THOMAS, *The Irish Novelists 1800–1850* (New York, 1959).

FLEENOR, JULIANN E. (ed.)., *The Female Gothic* (London, 1983).

FLEISHMAN, AVROM, *The English Historical Novel: Walter Scott to Virginia Woolf* (Baltimore, 1971).

FORBES, DUNCAN, 'The Rationalism of Sir Walter Scott', *Cambridge Journal*, vii/1 (Oct. 1953), 20–35.

FOSTER, JAMES R., *History of the Pre-Romantic Novel in England*, MLA Monograph Series, No. 17 (New York, 1949).

FOUCAULT, MICHEL, *Madness and Civilization: A History of Insanity in the Age of Reason* (1961), trans. Richard Howard, introd. David Cooper (London, 1967).

FOWLER, KATHLEEN, 'Hieroglyphics in Fire: *Melmoth the Wanderer*', *Studies in Romanticism*, xxv (1986), 520–39.

FRANK, FREDERICK S., 'From Boudoir to Castle Crypt: Richardson and the Gothic Novel', *Révue des Langues Vivantes*, xli (1975), 49–59.

—— *Guide to the Gothic: An Annotated Bibliography of Criticism* (Metuchen, NJ, 1984).

—— *The First Gothics: A Critical Guide to the English Gothic Novel* (New York, 1987).

FRANKL, PAUL, *The Gothic: Literary Sources and Interpretations through Eight Centuries*, trans. Priscilla Silz (Princeton, NJ, 1960).

FRANKLIN, CAROLINE, 'Feud and Faction in *The Bride of Lammermoor*', *Scottish Literary Journal*, xiv/2 (Nov. 1987), 18–31.

FRASER, W. HAMISH, 'Patterns of Protest', in Thomas Martin Devine and Rosalind Mitchison (eds.), *People and Society in Scotland, 1760–1830*, i (Edinburgh, 1988), 268–91.

FRAZER, ALLAN (ed.), *Sir Walter Scott 1771–1832: An Edinburgh Keepsake* (Edinburgh, 1971).

FRENCH, GILBERT JAMES (ed.), *Parallel Passages from Two Tales Elucidating the Origin of the Plot of Guy Mannering* (Manchester, 1855).

—— *An Enquiry Into the Origin of the Authorship of Some of the Earlier Waverley Novels* (Bolton, 1856).

FREUD, SIGMUND, *The Standard Edition of the Complete Psychological Works of Sigmund Freud*, ed. James Strachey, 24 vols. (London, 1953–74).

FREYE, WALTER, 'The Influence of "Gothic" Literature on Sir Walter Scott', Inaugural Dissertation (Rostock, 1902).

FRYE, NORTHROP, *Fables of Identity: Studies in Poetic Mythology* (New York, 1963).

—— *The Secular Scripture: A Study of the Structure of Romance*, The Charles Eliot Norton Lectures, 1974–5 (Cambridge, Mass., 1976).

FURNISS, TOM, 'Gender in Revolution: Edmund Burke and Mary Wollstonecraft', in Kelvin Everest (ed.), *Revolution in Writing: British Literary Responses to the French Revolution*, Ideas and Production (Milton Keynes, 1991), 65–100.

GARBER, FREDERICK, 'Meaning and Mode in Gothic Fiction', in Harold E. Pagliaro (ed.), *Racism in the Eighteenth Century*, Studies in Eighteenth-Century Culture, iii (Cleveland, 1973), 155–69.

GARDEN, MARY GRAY (ed.), *Memorials of James Hogg, the Ettrick Shepherd*, Preface by [J.] Veitch (Paisley, [1885]).

GARRETT, JOHN, *Gothic Strains and Bourgeois Sentiments in the Novels of Mrs. Ann Radcliffe and her Imitators*, Gothic Studies and Dissertations (New York, 1980).

GARSIDE, PETER D., 'Intellectual Origins of Scott's View of History in the

Waverley Novels', Ph.D. Dissertation (Cambridge University, 1970).
—— 'Scott, the Romantic Past and the Nineteenth Century', *RES* NS xxiii (1972), 147–61.
—— 'Scott and the "Philosophical" Historians', *Journal of the History of Ideas*, xxxvi (1975), 497–512.
—— 'Redgauntlet and the Topography of Progress', *Southern Review*, x (1977), 155–73.
—— 'Rob's Last Raid: Scott and the Publication of the Waverley Novels', in Robin Myers and Michael Harris (eds.), *Author/Publisher Relations During the Eighteenth and Nineteenth Centuries* (Oxford, 1983), 88–118.
—— 'Union and *The Bride of Lammermoor*', *Studies in Scottish Literature*, xix (1984), 72–93.
GASTON, PATRICIA S., *Prefacing the Waverley Prefaces: A Reading of Sir Walter Scott's Prefaces to the Waverley Novels*, American University Studies, Series IV, English Language and Literature, vol. cxxx (New York, 1991).
GAYOT DE PITAVAL, FRANÇOIS, *Causes célèbres et intéressantes avec les jugemens qui les ont décidées*, Nouvelle édition, revûe, corrigée et augmentée de plusieurs piéces importantes qu'on a recouvrées, 20 vols. (Paris, 1738–40).
GEARHART, SUZANNE, *The Open Boundary of History and Fiction* (Princeton, NJ, 1984).
GENETTE, GÉRARD, *Palimpsestes: la littérature au second degré* (Paris, 1982).
—— *Introduction à l'architexte* (Paris, 1986).
The Genius and Wisdom of Sir Walter Scott, Comprising Moral, Religious, Political, Literary, and Social Aphorisms, Selected Carefully from his Various Writings: With a Memoir (London, 1839).
GIBSON, JOHN, *Reminiscences of Sir Walter Scott* (Edinburgh, 1871).
GIFFORD, DOUGLAS, *James Hogg* (Edinburgh, 1976).
GILBERT, SANDRA M., and GUBAR, SUSAN, *The Madwoman in the Attic: The Woman Writer and the Nineteenth-Century Literary Imagination* (New Haven, Conn., 1979).
GILFILLAN, GEORGE, *Life of Sir Walter Scott, Baronet* (Edinburgh, 1870).
[GILLIES, R. P.], *Recollections of Sir Walter Scott, Bart.* (London, 1837).
GITTINGS, ROBERT, *John Keats* (London, 1968).
GLEIG, GEORGE ROBERT, *The Life of Sir Walter Scott: Reprinted with Corrections and Additions from the Quarterly Review* (Edinburgh, 1871).
GODWIN, WILLIAM, *Enquiry Concerning Political Justice and its Influence on Modern Morals and Happiness* (1793), 3rd edn. (1798) ed. and introd. Isaac Kramnick (Harmondsworth, 1976).

—— *Things as They Are; or, The Adventures of Caleb Williams*, 3 vols. (London, 1794).

—— *St Leon: A Tale of the Sixteenth Century*, 4 vols. (London, 1799).

—— *Fleetwood; or, The New Man of Feeling*, 3 vols. (London, 1805).

—— *Fleetwood; or, The New Man of Feeling: Revised, Corrected, and Illustrated with a New Preface, by the Author*, Standard Novels, No. 22 (London, 1832).

—— *Cloudesley: A Tale*, 3 vols. (London, 1830).

GOFFMAN, ERVING, *Frame Analysis: An Essay on the Organization of Experience* (1974; repr. Harmondsworth, 1975).

GORDON, ROBERT C., '*The Bride of Lammermoor*: A Novel of Tory Pessimism', *Nineteenth-Century Fiction*, xii (1957), 110–24.

—— 'In Defence of *Rob Roy*', *Essays in Criticism*, xviii (1968), 470–5.

—— *Under Which King? A Study of the Scottish Waverley Novels* (Edinburgh, 1969).

—— 'The Marksman of Ravenswood: Power and Legitimacy in *The Bride of Lammermoor*', *Nineteenth Century Literature*, xli (1986), 49–71.

GOSLEE, NANCY MOORE, 'Witch or Pawn: Women in Scott's Narrative Poetry', in Anne K. Mellor (ed.), *Romanticism and Feminism* (Bloomington, Ind., 1988), 115–36.

GOSSMAN, LIONEL, 'History and Literature: Reproduction or Signification', in Robert H. Canary and Henry Kozicki (eds.), *The Writing of History: Literary Form and Historical Understanding* (Madison, Wis., 1978), 3–39.

GRANT, ANNE MACVICAR, OF LAGGAN, *Essays on the Superstitions of the Highlanders of Scotland: To which are added, Translations from the Gaelic; and Letters connected with those formerly published*, 2 vols. (London, 1811).

GREEN, MARTIN, *Dreams of Adventure, Deeds of Empire* (London, 1980).

GREEN, SARAH, *Scotch Novel Reading; or, Modern Quackery: A Novel Really Founded on Facts*, 3 vols. (London, 1824).

GRIEDER, THEODORE, 'The German Drama in England, 1790–1800', *Restoration and 18th Century Theatre Research*, iii/2 (Nov. 1964), 39–50.

GRIERSON, H. J. C., *Sir Walter Scott, Bart: A New Life Supplementary to, and Corrective of, Lockhart's Biography* (London, 1938).

GRIEVE, CHRISTOPHER MURRAY [HUGH MACDIARMID], *Lucky Poet: A Self-Study in Literature and Political Ideas: Being the Autobiography of Hugh MacDiarmid (Christopher Murray Grieve)* (London, 1943).

'GRILDRIG, SOLOMON' [pseud.], 'Remarks on Novels and Romances.— Receipt for a Modern Romance', *The Miniature, A Periodical Paper*, No. 2, 30 Apr. 1804 (Windsor, 1805), 13–22.

GRIXTI, JOSEPH, *Terrors of Uncertainty: The Cultural Contexts of Horror Fiction* (London, 1989).

GROVES, DAVID, 'Parallel Narratives in Hogg's *Justified Sinner*', *Scottish Literary Journal*, ix/2 (Dec. 1982), 37–44.

—— *James Hogg: The Growth of a Writer* (Edinburgh, 1988).

Review of *Guy Mannering*, *Augustan Review*, i (July 1815), 228–33.

—— *British Critic*, NS iii (Apr. 1815), 399–409.

—— *Monthly Review*, NS lxxvii (May 1815), 85–94.

—— *Quarterly Review*, xii (Jan. 1815), 501–9.

—— *Scots Magazine*, lxxvii (Aug. 1815), 608–14.

HABER, TOM B., 'The Chapter Tags in the Waverley Novels', *PMLA* xlv (1930), 1140–9.

HADLEY, MICHAEL, *The Undiscovered Genre: A Search for the German Gothic Novel*, Canadian Studies in German Language and Literature, No. 20 (Berne, 1978).

HAMILTON, ELIZABETH, *The Cottagers of Glenburnie; A Tale for the Farmer's Ingle-Nook* (Edinburgh, 1808).

HARKIN, PATRICIA, 'The Fop, the Fairy, and the Genres of Scott's *Monastery*', *Studies in Scottish Literature*, xix (1984), 177–93.

HARLEY, MRS, *St Bernard's Priory: An Old English Tale; Being the First Literary Production of a Young Lady* (London, 1786).

HART, F. R., *Scott's Novels: The Plotting of Historic Survival* (Charlottesville, Va., 1966).

—— 'The Experience of Character in the English Gothic Novel', in Roy Harvey Pearce (ed.), *Experience in the Novel: Selected Papers from the English Institute* (New York, 1968), 83–105.

—— *Lockhart as Romantic Biographer* (Edinburgh, 1971).

—— 'Limits of the Gothic: The Scottish Example', in Harold E. Pagliaro (ed.), *Racism in the Eighteenth Century*, Studies in Eighteenth-Century Culture, iii (Cleveland, 1973), 137–53.

—— *The Scottish Novel: A Critical Survey* (London, 1978).

—— 'Scott's Endings: The Fictions of Authority', *Nineteenth-Century Fiction*, xxxiii (1978–9), 48–68.

HARTVEIT, LARS, *Dream Within a Dream: A Thematic Approach to Scott's Vision of Fictional Reality*, Norwegian Studies in English, No. 18 (Bergen, 1974).

HARVIE, CHRISTOPHER, *Scotland and Nationalism: Scottish Society and Politics, 1707–1977* (London, 1977).

HAWTHORNE, NATHANIEL, *The House of the Seven Gables* (1851), *The Centenary Edition of the Works of Nathaniel Hawthorne*, ed. William Charvat *et al.*, ii (Columbus, Oh., 1965).

HAYDEN, JOHN O., 'The Satanic School, Sir Walter Scott', in his *The Romantic Reviewers: 1802–1824* (London, 1969), 125–34.

HAZEN, A. T., *A Bibliography of Horace Walpole* (New Haven, Conn., 1948).

HAZLITT, WILLIAM, *The Complete Works of William Hazlitt*, Centenary Edition, ed. P. P. Howe, 21 vols. (London, 1930–4).

HEIDLER, JOSEPH BUNN, *The History, from 1700 to 1800, of English Criticism of Prose Fiction*, University of Illinois Studies in English Language and Literature, xiii/2 (Urbana, Ill., 1928).

HEILMAN, ROBERT B., 'Fielding and "the First Gothic Revival"', *MLN* lvii (1942), 671–3.

—— 'Charlotte Brontë's "New Gothic"', in Austin Wright (ed.), *Victorian Literature: Modern Essays in Criticism* (New York, 1961), 71–85.

HENDERSON, PETER MILLS, *A Nut Between Two Blades: The Novels of Charles Robert Maturin*, Gothic Studies and Dissertations (New York, 1980).

HENNELLY, MARK M., '*Waverley* and Romanticism', *Nineteenth-Century Fiction*, xxviii (1973–4), 194–209.

HEWITT, DAVID S. (ed.), *Scott on Himself: A Selection of the Autobiographical Writings of Sir Walter Scott*, The Association for Scottish Literary Studies, No. 10 (Edinburgh, 1981).

—— 'Scott's Art and Politics', in Alan Bold (ed.), *Sir Walter Scott: The Long-Forgotten Melody* (London, 1983), 43–64.

HILBISH, FLORENCE MAY ANNA, 'Charlotte Smith, Poet and Novelist (1749–1806)', Ph.D. Dissertation (University of Pennsylvania, 1941).

HILLHOUSE, JAMES T., *The Waverley Novels and Their Critics* (Minneapolis, 1936).

—— and WELSH, ALEXANDER, 'Sir Walter Scott', in Carolyn Washburn Houtchens and Lawrence Huston Houtchens (eds.), *The English Romantic Poets and Essayists: A Review of Research and Criticism*, rev. edn. (New York, 1966), 115–54.

HIRSCH, E. D., JR., *Validity in Interpretation* (New Haven, Conn., 1967).

—— 'The Politics of Theories of Interpretation', *Critical Inquiry*, ix (1982–3), 235–47.

HOGG, JAMES, 'Translation from an Ancient Chaldee Manuscript', *Blackwood's Edinburgh Magazine*, ii (Oct. 1817), 89–96.

—— *The Brownie of Bodsbeck; and Other Tales*, 2 vols. (Edinburgh, 1818).

—— 'A Scots Mummy', *Blackwood's Edinburgh Magazine*, xiv (Aug. 1823), 188–90.

—— *The Private Memoirs and Confessions of a Justified Sinner: Written by Himself: With a Detail of Curious Traditionary Facts, and Other Evidence, by the Editor* (London, 1824). [Ed. and introd. John Carey (Oxford, 1969, 1981).]

—— *Anecdotes of Sir W. Scott*, ed. Douglas S. Mack (Edinburgh, 1983).

HOGG, JAMES, *Memoir of the Author's Life* and *Familiar Anecdotes of Sir Walter Scott* (1834), ed. Douglas S. Mack (Edinburgh, 1972).

—— *The Works of the Ettrick Shepherd: A New Edition, Revised at the Instance of the Author's Family, by the Rev. Thomas Thomson*, 2 vols. (Glasgow, 1865–6).

—— *Selected Stories and Sketches*, ed. Douglas S. Mack, The Association for Scottish Literary Studies, No. 12 (Edinburgh, 1982).

—— *Tales of Love and Mystery*, ed. and introd. David Groves (Edinburgh, 1985).

—— *Selected Poems and Songs*, ed. David Groves, The Association for Scottish Literary Studies, No. 16 (Edinburgh, 1986).

HOGLE, JERROLD E., 'The Restless Labyrinth: Cryptonymy in the Gothic Novel', *Arizona Quarterly*, xxxvi (1980), 330–58.

HOLBROOK, WILLIAM C., 'The Adjective "Gothique" in the XVIIIth Century', *MLN* lvi (1941), 498–503.

HOLCROFT, THOMAS, *The Adventures of Hugh Trevor* (1794–7), ed. and introd. Seamus Deans (Oxford, 1973).

HOLLAND, NORMAN N., and SHERMAN, LEONA F., 'Gothic Possibilities', *NLH* viii (1976–7), 279–93.

HOLMAN, C. HUGH, '*Nigel* and the Historical Imagination', in Howard M. Harper, Jr., and Charles Edge (eds.), *The Classic British Novel* (Athens, Ga., 1972), 65–84.

HOME, JOHN, *Douglas: A Tragedy* (London, 1757).

HOOK, ANDREW D., '*The Bride of Lammermoor*: A Reexamination', *Nineteenth-Century Fiction*, xxii (1967–8), 111–26.

—— 'Jane Porter, Sir Walter Scott, and the Historical Novel', *Clio*, v (1976), 181–92.

HOWELLS, CORAL ANN, *Love, Mystery, and Misery: Feeling in Gothic Fiction* (London, 1978).

HUME, ROBERT D., 'Gothic versus Romantic: A Revaluation of the Gothic Novel', *PMLA* lxxxiv (1969), 282–90.

—— and PLATZNER, ROBERT L., '"Gothic versus Romantic": A Rejoinder', *PMLA* lxxxvi (1971), 266–74.

HURD, RICHARD, *Hurd's Letters on Chivalry and Romance: With the Third Elizabethan Dialogue* (1762), ed. and introd. Edith J. Morley (London, 1911).

IDMAN, NIILO, *Charles Robert Maturin: His Life and Works* (Helsinki, 1923).

Impartial Strictures on the Poem Called 'The Pursuits of Literature' and Particularly a Vindication of the Romance of 'The Monk' (London, 1798).

INCHBALD, ELIZABETH, *A Simple Story*, 4 vols. (London, 1791).

—— *Nature and Art*, 2 vols. (London, 1796).

ISER, WOLFGANG, *The Implied Reader: Patterns of Communication in Prose Fiction from Bunyan to Beckett* (1972), trans. anon. (Baltimore, 1974).

JACK, IAN, *English Literature 1815–1832*, The Oxford History of English Literature, ed. F. P. Wilson and Bonamy Dobrée, x (Oxford, 1963).

JACKSON, ROSEMARY, *Fantasy: The Literature of Subversion* (London, 1981).

JACOBSON, SIBYL, 'The Narrative Framing of History: A Discussion of *Old Mortality*', *Journal of Narrative Technique*, i (1971), 179–92.

JACOBUS, MARY, 'The Buried Letter: *Villette*' (1979), repr. in *Reading Woman: Essays in Feminist Criticism* (London, 1986), 41–61.

JAMESON, FREDRIC, 'Reification and Utopia in Mass Culture', *Social Text*, i (1979), 130–48.

—— *The Political Unconscious: Narrative as a Socially Symbolic Act* (London, 1981).

JARRETT, DAVID, *The Gothic Form in Fiction and its Relation to History*, Contexts and Connections: Winchester Research Papers in the Humanities, No. 5 (Winchester, 1980).

JAUSS, HANS ROBERT, 'Literary History as a Challenge to Literary Theory' (first trans. *NLH* 1970), in *Towards an Aesthetic of Reception*, trans. Timothy Bahti, introd. Paul de Man, Theory and History of Literature, No. 2 (Brighton, 1982).

JEFFREY, FRANCIS, Review of *The Lay of the Last Minstrel*, *Edinburgh Review*, vi (Apr. 1805), 1–20.

—— Review of *Marmion*, *Edinburgh Review*, xii (Apr. 1808), 1–35.

—— Review of *Waverley*, *Edinburgh Review*, xxiv (Nov. 1814), 208–43.

JOHNSON, EDGAR, *Sir Walter Scott: The Great Unknown*, 2 vols. (London, 1970).

JOHNSTON, ARTHUR, *Enchanted Ground: The Study of Medieval Romance in the Eighteenth Century* (London, 1964).

JOHNSTON, GEORGE P., 'The First Book Printed by James Ballantyne: Being an Apology for *Tales of Terror*; with Notes on *Tales of Wonder* and *Tales of Terror*', *Publications of the Edinburgh Bibliographical Society*, i (1896), 1–15.

—— 'Note to a Paper Entitled the First Book Printed by James Ballantyne', *Publications of the Edinburgh Bibliographical Society*, ix (1913), 90.

JORDAN, FRANK, 'Chrystal Croftangry, Scott's Last and Best Mask', *Scottish Literary Journal*, vii/1 (May 1980), 185–92.

—— 'The Vision of Pandemonium in Scott's Novels', *Scottish Literary Journal*, xix/2 (Nov. 1992), 24–35.

KARL, FREDERICK R., *The Adversary Literature: The English Novel in the Eighteenth Century: A Study in Genre* (New York, 1974).

KEITH, CHRISTINA, *The Author of Waverley: A Study in the Personality of Sir Walter Scott* (London, 1964).

KELLNER, HANS, *Language and Historical Representation: Getting the Story Crooked* (Madison, Wis., 1989).

KELLY, GARY, *The English Jacobin Novel 1780–1805* (Oxford, 1976).

—— '"A Constant Vicissitude of Interesting Passions": Ann Radcliffe's Perplexed Narratives', *Ariel*, x (1979), 45–64.

—— *English Fiction of the Romantic Period 1789–1830*, Longman Literature in English Series (London, 1989).

—— 'The Limits of Genre and the Institution of Literature: Romanticism between Fact and Fiction', in Kenneth R. Johnston *et al.* (eds.), *Romantic Revolutions: Criticism and Theory* (Bloomington, Ind., 1990). 158–75.

KERMODE, FRANK, *The Genesis of Secrecy: On the Interpretation of Narrative*, The Charles Eliot Norton Lectures, 1977–8 (Cambridge, Mass., 1979).

KERR, JAMES, 'Scott's Dreams of the Past: *The Bride of Lammermoor* as Political Fantasy', *Studies in the Novel*, xviii (1986), 125–42.

—— *Fiction against History: Scott as Storyteller* (Cambridge, 1989).

KIELY, ROBERT, *The Romantic Novel in England* (Cambridge, Mass., 1972).

KLANCHER, JON P., *The Making of English Reading Audiences, 1790–1832* (Madison, Wis., 1987).

—— 'English Romanticism and Cultural Production', in H. Aram Veeser (ed.), *The New Historicism* (New York, 1989), 77–88.

KLEPETAR, STEVEN F., 'Levels of Narration in *Old Mortality*', *Wordsworth Circle*, xiii/1 (Winter 1982), 38–45.

KLIGER, SAMUEL, 'The "Goths" in England: An Introduction to the Gothic Vogue in Eighteenth-Century Aesthetic Discussion', *Modern Philology*, xliii (1945), 107–17.

—— 'The Gothic Revival and the German *Translatio*', *Modern Philology*, xlv (1947–8), 73–103.

—— *The Goths in England: A Study in Seventeenth and Eighteenth Century Thought* (Cambridge, Mass., 1952).

KROEBER, KARL, *Romantic Narrative Art* (Madison, Wis., 1960).

KUNITZ, STANLEY J., and HAYCRAFT, HOWARD, *British Authors Before 1800: A Biographical Dictionary* (New York, 1952).

LAIDLAW, WILLIAM, *Recollections of Sir Walter Scott (1802–1804)*, ed. James Sinton, Transactions of the Hawick Archaeological Society (Hawick, 1905).

LAMB, CHARLES, and LAMB, MARY, *The Works of Charles and Mary Lamb*, ed. E. V. Lucas, 7 vols. (London, 1903–5).

LAMONT, CLAIRE, 'Scott as Story-Teller: *The Bride of Lammermoor*', *Scottish Literary Journal*, vii/1 (May 1980), 113–26.

—— (ed. and introd.), *The Heart of Midlothian* (1818), by Sir Walter Scott (Oxford, 1982).

LANDES, JOAN B., *Women and the Public Sphere in the Age of the French Revolution* (Ithaca, NY, 1988).

LANG, ANDREW, *Sir Walter Scott*, Literary Lives, ed. W. Robertson Nicoll (London, 1906).

LASCELLES, MARY, 'Scott and the Art of Revision' (1968), in her *Notions and Facts: Collected Criticism and Research* (Oxford, 1972), 213–29.

—— *The Story-Teller Retrieves the Past: Historical Fiction and Fictitious History in the Art of Scott, Stevenson, Kipling and Some Others* (Oxford, 1980).

LATHOM, FRANCIS, *The Midnight Bell, A German Story, Founded on Incidents in Real Life*, 3 vols. (London, 1798).

—— *The Impenetrable Secret, Find it Out! A Novel*, 2 vols. (London, 1805).

Review of *The Lay of the Last Minstrel*, British Critic, xxvi (Aug. 1805), 154–60.

—— Critical Review, 3rd ser. v (July 1805), 225–42.

—— Eclectic Review, ii, pt. 1 (Mar. 1806), 193–200.

LEE, SOPHIA, *The Recess; or, A Tale of Other Times*, 3 vols. (London, 1785). [Foreword J. M. S. Tompkins, introd. Devendra P. Varma (New York, 1972).]

LELAND, THOMAS, *Longsword, Earl of Salisbury: An Historical Romance*, 2 vols. (London, 1762). [Foreword Devendra P. Varma, introd. Robert D. Hume (New York, 1974).]

A Letter, Containing Some Remarks on the Tendency and Influence of the Waverley Novels on Society, From a Clergyman of the Church of England to a Younger Brother (London, 1832).

'Letters to Certain Persons. Epistle I. To Miss Jane Porter'. Signed 'Peter Puff'. *Aberdeen Magazine*, i (Oct. 1831), 552–7.

LEVINE, GEORGE, *The Realistic Imagination: English Fiction from Frankenstein to Lady Chatterley* (Chicago, 1981).

—— and KNOEPFLMACHER, U. C. (eds.), *The Endurance of Frankenstein: Essays on Mary Shelley's Novel* (Berkeley, Calif., 1979).

LEVINSON, MARJORIE, *The Romantic Fragment Poem: A Critique of a Form* (Chapel Hill, NC, 1986).

LEVY, DARLINE GAY, and APPLEWHITE, HARRIET, 'Women and Militant Citizenship in Revolutionary Paris', in Sara E. Melzer and Leslie W. Rabine (eds.), *Rebel Daughters: Women and the French Revolution*, Publications of the University of California Humanities Research Institute (New York, 1992), 79–101.

—— AND JOHNSON, MARY DURHAM, *Women in Revolutionary Paris, 1789–1795: Selected Documents Translated with Notes and Commentary* (Urbana, Ill., 1979).

LÉVY, MAURICE, Le Roman 'gothique' anglais, 1764–1824 (Toulouse, 1968).

LEWIS, MATTHEW GREGORY, The Monk: A Romance, 3 vols. (London, 1796). [Ed. and introd. Howard Anderson (Oxford, 1973).]

—— The Castle Spectre: A Drama, in Five Acts (London, 1798).

—— Adelmorn, the Outlaw: A Romantic Drama, in Three Acts (London, 1801).

—— Tales of Wonder; Written and Collected by M. G. Lewis, 2 vols. (London, 1801).

—— Adelgitha; or, The Fruits of a Single Error: A Tragedy, in Five Acts (London, 1806).

—— Journal of a West India Proprietor, Kept During a Residence in the Island of Jamaica (London, 1834).

LEWIS, PAUL, 'Fearful Lessons: The Didacticism of the Early Gothic Novel', College Language Association Journal, xxiii (1980), 470–84.

—— 'Mysterious Laughter: Humor and Fear in Gothic Fiction', Genre, xiv (1981), 309–27.

LOCKE, DON, A Fantasy of Reason: The Life and Thought of William Godwin (London, 1980).

LOCKHART, JOHN GIBSON, 'Goetz von Berlichingen, a Tragedy, by Goethe', Blackwood's Edinburgh Magazine, xvi (Oct. 1824), 369–85.

—— Review of The Devil's Elixir, Blackwood's Edinburgh Magazine, xvi (July 1824), 55–67.

—— Review of Lives of the Novelists, Quarterly Review, xxxiv (Sept. 1826), 349–78.

—— Life of Robert Burns, Constable's Miscellany of Original and Selected Publications in the Various Departments of Literature, Science, and the Arts, No. 23 (Edinburgh, 1828).

—— Memoirs of the Life of Sir Walter Scott, Bart., 2nd edn., 10 vols. (Edinburgh, 1839).

LODGE, DAVID, 'Crowds and Power in the Early Victorian Novel' (1989), repr. in his After Bakhtin: Essays on Fiction and Criticism (London, 1990), 100–15.

LOGUE, KENNETH JOHN, Popular Disturbances in Scotland, 1780–1815 (Edinburgh, 1979).

LONGUEIL, ALFRED E., 'The Word "Gothic" in Eighteenth Century Criticism', MLN xxxviii (1923), 453–60.

LOVEJOY, ARTHUR O., 'The First Gothic Revival and the Return to Nature', MLN xlvii (1932), 419–46. Repr. in his Essays in the History of Ideas (Baltimore, 1948).

LOVELL, TERRY, Consuming Fiction, Questions for Feminism (London, 1987).

LUKÁCS, GEORG, The Historical Novel (1937), trans. Hannah and Stanley Mitchell (London, 1962).

LYLES, W. H., *Mary Shelley: An Annotated Bibliography*, Garland Reference Library of the Humanities, No. 22 (New York, 1975).

LYONS, MARTYN, 'The Audience for Romanticism: Walter Scott in France, 1815–51', *European History Quarterly*, xiv (1984), 21–46.

MACANDREW, ELIZABETH, *The Gothic Tradition in Fiction* (New York, 1979).

MACARTNEY, M. H. H., 'Sir Walter Scott's Use of the Preface', *Longman's Magazine*, xlvi (1905), 366–75.

MACCARTHY, BARBARA G., *The Later Women Novelists 1744–1818*, The Female Pen, ii (Cork, 1947).

MCFARLAND, THOMAS, *Originality and Imagination* (Baltimore, 1985).

MCGANN, JEROME J., *The Romantic Ideology* (Chicago, 1983).

—— *The Beauty of Inflections: Literary Investigations in Historical Method and Theory* (Oxford, 1985).

MCGUIRE, SHIRLEE A., 'The Storytelling Impulse of Sir Walter Scott's Narrative Technique', Ph.D. Dissertation (West Virginia University, 1982).

MCINTYRE, CLARA FRANCES, *Ann Radcliffe in Relation to her Time*, Yale Studies in English, No. 62, ed. Albert S. Cook (New Haven, Conn., 1920).

—— 'Were the "Gothic Novels" Gothic?', *PMLA* xxxvi (1921), 644–67.

—— 'The Later Career of the Elizabethan Villain-Hero', *PMLA* xl (1925), 874–80.

MACK, DOUGLAS S., ' "The Rage of Fanaticism in Former Days": James Hogg's *Confessions of a Justified Sinner* and the Controversy over *Old Mortality*', in Ian Campbell (ed.), *Nineteenth-Century Scottish Fiction: Critical Essays* (Manchester, 1979), 37–50.

—— 'Hogg, Lockhart, and *Familiar Anecdotes of Sir Walter Scott*', *Scottish Literary Journal*, x/1 (May 1983), 5–13.

MACKENZIE, HENRY, *The Man of Feeling* (London, 1771).

MCKILLOP, ALAN D., 'Mrs. Radcliffe on the Supernatural in Poetry', *JEGP* xxxi (1932), 352–9.

MCLAREN, MORAY, *Sir Walter Scott: The Man and Patriot* (London, 1970).

MCMASTER, GRAHAM, *Scott and Society* (Cambridge, 1981).

MACNALTY, SIR ARTHUR SALUSBURY, *Sir Walter Scott: The Wounded Falcon* (London, 1969).

MCNUTT, DAN J., *The Eighteenth-Century Gothic Novel: An Annotated Bibliography of Criticism and Selected Texts*, foreword Devendra P. Varma and Maurice Lévy (New York, 1975).

MACPHERSON, JAMES, *The Poems of Ossian, Translated by James Macpherson, Esq. With the Translator's Dissertations on the Era and Poems of Ossian; Dr Blair's Critical Dissertation; and An Inquiry into the Genuineness of these Poems, Written Expressly for this Edition*, by the Rev. Alex. Stewart (Edinburgh, [1819]).

MADDOX, JAMES HUNT, 'The Survival of Gothic Romance in the Nineteenth-Century Novel: A Study of Scott, Charlotte Brontë, and Dickens', Ph.D. Dissertation (Yale University, 1970).

MADOFF, MARK, 'The Useful Myth of Gothic Ancestry', *Studies in Eighteenth-Century Culture*, viii, ed. Roseann Runte (Madison, Wis., 1978), 337–50.

MANNING, SUSAN, *The Puritan-Provincial Vision: Scottish and American Literature in the Nineteenth Century*, Cambridge Studies in American Literature and Culture (Cambridge, 1990).

—— (ed. and introd.), *Quentin Durward* (1823), by Sir Walter Scott (Oxford, 1992).

Review of *Marmion*, *The Satirist*, ii (Apr. 1808), 186–93.

—— *Universal Magazine*, NS, ix (May 1808), 410–20.

MARSHALL, ROSALIND, *Virgins and Viragos: A History of Women in Scotland 1080–1980* (Chicago, 1983).

MARTIN, PHILIP W., *Mad Women in Romantic Writing* (Brighton, 1987).

MARTIN, WALLACE, *Recent Theories of Narrative* (Ithaca, NY, 1986).

MASON, MICHAEL YORK, 'The Three Burials in Hogg's *Justified Sinner*', *Studies in Scottish Literature*, xiii (1978), 15–23.

MASSEY, IRVING, 'Mary Shelley, Walter Scott, and "Maga"', *Notes and Queries*, ccvii (1962), 420–1.

MASSIE, ALLAN, 'Scott and the European Novel', in Alan Bold (ed.), *Sir Walter Scott: The Long-Forgotten Melody* (London, 1983), 91–106.

MATHIAS, THOMAS JAMES, *The Pursuits of Literature: A Satirical Poem in Dialogue, with Notes*, pt. 4 (London, 1797).

MATTHEWS, GEORGE KING, *Abbotsford and Sir Walter Scott* (London, 1853).

MATURIN, CHARLES ROBERT, *Fatal Revenge; or, The Family of Montorio: A Romance*, 3 vols. (London, 1807). [Foreword Henry D. Hicks, introd. Maurice Lévy (New York, 1974).]

—— *The Wild Irish Boy*, 3 vols. (London, 1808). [Introd. Robert Lee Wolff, Ireland From the Act of Union, 1800, to the Death of Parnell, 1891: 77 Novels and Collections of Shorter Stories by 22 Irish and Anglo-Irish Novelists. A Garland Series, No. 11 (New York, 1979).]

—— *The Milesian Chief: A Romance*, 4 vols. (London, 1812).

—— *Bertram; or, The Castle of St Aldobrand: A Tragedy, in Five Acts* (London, 1816).

—— *Manuel: A Tragedy, in Five Acts* (London, 1817).

—— *Women; or, Pour et Contre: A Tale*, 3 vols. (Edinburgh, 1818).

—— *Melmoth the Wanderer: A Tale*, 4 vols. (Edinburgh, 1820). [Ed. and introd. Alethea Hayter (Harmondsworth, 1977).]

—— *The Albigenses: A Romance*, 4 vols. (London, 1824). [Foreword James Gray, introd. Dale Kramer (New York, 1974).]

MAY, LELAND CHANDLER, *Parodies of the Gothic Novel*, Gothic Studies and Dissertations (New York, 1980).

MAYER, ROBERT, 'The Internal Machinery Displayed: *The Heart of Midlothian* and Scott's Apparatus for the Waverley Novels', *Clio*, xvii (1987), 1–20.

MAYHEAD, ROBIN, *Walter Scott*, Profiles in Literature Series (London, 1968).

MAYO, ROBERT DONALD, 'The Waverley Novels in their Relations to Gothic Fiction', Ph.D. Dissertation (Princeton University, 1938).

—— 'How Long Was Gothic Fiction in Vogue?', *MLN* lviii (1943), 58–64.

—— *The English Novel in the Magazines, 1740–1815: With a Catalogue of 1375 Magazine Novels and Novelettes* (Evanston, Ill., 1963).

MEEKE, MARY, *'There is A Secret, Find It Out!': A Novel*, 4 vols. (London, 1808).

—— *The Veiled Protectress; or, The Mysterious Mother: A Novel*, 5 vols. (London, 1819).

MEHROTRA, K. K., *Horace Walpole and the English Novel: A Study of the Influence of 'The Castle of Otranto', 1764–1820* (Oxford, 1934).

Review of *Melmoth the Wanderer*, *Blackwood's Edinburgh Magazine*, viii (Nov. 1820), 161–8.

—— *Monthly Review*, ns xciv (Jan. 1821), 81–90.

'Memoir of the Rev. C. R. Maturin', *New Monthly Magazine*, xi (Mar. 1819), 165–7.

MERRILL, HERBERT J., 'A Reappraisal of Sir Walter Scott: His Commercial Motivation and His Reliance Upon Formula Fiction for Popular Markets', Ph.D. Dissertation (Indiana University, 1957).

MILLER, J. HILLIS, 'Narrative and History', *ELH* xli (1974), 455–73.

MILLER, KARL, *Doubles: Studies in Literary History* (1985; corr. edn. Oxford, 1987).

MILLGATE, JANE, 'Scott and the Dreaming Boy: A Context for *Waverley*', *RES*, ns xxxii (1981), 286–93.

—— *Walter Scott: The Making of the Novelist* (Edinburgh, 1984).

—— 'Adding More Buckram: Scott and the Amplification of *Peveril of the Peak*', *English Studies in Canada*, xiii (1987), 174–81.

—— *Scott's Last Edition: A Study in Publishing History* (Edinburgh, 1987).

Review of *Minstrelsy of the Scottish Border*, *British Critic*, xix (June 1802), 570–6.

—— *Edinburgh Review*, i (Jan. 1803), 395–406.

—— *Monthly Review*, ns xlii (Sept. 1803), 21–33.

—— *Scots Magazine*, lxiv, 3rd ser. i (Jan. 1802), 68–70.

MISE, RAYMOND WINFIELD, *The Gothic Heroine and the Nature of the Gothic Novel*, Gothic Studies and Dissertations (New York, 1980).

MITCHELL, JEROME, *Scott, Chaucer, and Medieval Romance: A Study in*

Sir Walter Scott's Indebtedness to the Literature of the Middle Ages
(Lexington, Ky., 1987).

MIYOSHI, MASAO, *The Divided Self: A Perspective on the Literature of
the Victorians* (New York, 1969).

'Modern Literature', *Aberdeen Magazine*, iii (July 1798), 338–40.

MODLESKI, TANIA, *Loving with a Vengeance: Mass-Produced Fantasies
for Women* (1982; repr. New York, 1988).

MOERS, ELLEN, 'Female Gothic', in her *Literary Women* (1976), introd.
Helen Taylor (London, 1986), 90–110.

MONK, SAMUEL H., *The Sublime: A Study of Critical Theories in XVIII-
Century England* (New York, 1935).

MONROE, JUDSON TAYLOR, *Tragedy in the Novels of the Reverend
Charles Robert Maturin*, Gothic Studies and Dissertations (New York,
1980).

MORETTI, FRANCO, 'The Dialectic of Fear', *New Left Review*, xvi (1982),
67–87.

MORGAN, PETER F., *Literary Critics and Reviewers in Early 19th-Century
Britain* (London, 1983).

MORGAN, SYDNEY OWENSON, LADY, *The Wild Irish Girl* (London, 1806).
[Introd. Brigid Brophy (London, 1986).]

MORRIS, DAVID B., 'Gothic Sublimity', *NLH* xvi (1984–5), 299–319.

MORSE, DAVID, *Perspectives on Romanticism: A Transformational
Analysis* (London, 1981).

—— *Romanticism: A Structural Analysis* (London, 1982).

MUIR, EDWIN, *Scott and Scotland: The Predicament of the Scottish
Writer* (London, 1936).

MURRAY, HUGH, *Morality of Fiction; or, An Inquiry into the Tendency of
Fictitious Narratives, with Observations on Some of the Most Eminent*
(Edinburgh, 1805).

NABOKOV, VLADIMIR, *Lolita* (1959; repr. Harmondsworth, 1980).

NAPIER, ELIZABETH R., *The Failure of Gothic: Problems of Disjunction
in an Eighteenth-Century Literary Form* (Oxford, 1987).

NAUBERT, C. B. E., *Herman of Unna: A Series of Adventures of the
Fifteenth Century, In Which the Proceedings of the Secret Tribunal
Under the Emperors Wincaslaus and Sigismond, Are Delineated* (1788),
trans. anon., 3 vols. (London, 1794).

NEEDLER, G. H., *Scott and Goethe* (Toronto, 1950).

NELLIST, BRIAN, 'Narrative Modes in the Waverley Novels', in
R. T. Davies and B. G. Beatty (eds.), *Literature of the Romantic Period,
1750–1850*, Liverpool English Texts and Studies (Liverpool, 1976),
56–71.

NELSON, LOWRY, JR., 'Night Thoughts on the Gothic Novel', *Yale
Review*, lii (1962–3), 236–57.

NEWMAN, BETH, 'Narratives of Seduction and the Seductions of Narrative: The Frame Structure of *Frankenstein*', *ELH* liii (1986), 141–63.

'Noctes Ambrosianae', No. 15, *Blackwood's Edinburgh Magazine*, xv (June 1824), 706–24.

—— No. 27, *Blackwood's Edinburgh Magazine*, xx (July 1826), 90–109.

NOVAK, MAXIMILLIAN E., 'Gothic Fiction and the Grotesque', *Novel: A Forum on Fiction*, xiii (1979), 50–67.

OCHOJSKI, PAUL M., 'Sir Walter Scott's Continuous Interest in Germany', *Studies in Scottish Literature*, iii (1965–6), 164–73.

OMAN, CAROLA, *The Wizard of the North: The Life of Sir Walter Scott* (London, 1973).

'On the Cause of the Popularity of Novels'. Signed 'Clio'. *The Universal Magazine of Knowledge and Pleasure*, ciii (Dec. 1798), 413–15.

'On Novels and Romances'. Signed 'W. W.' *Scots Magazine*, lxiv (June and July 1802), 470–4, 545–8.

'On the Writings of Mr Maturin, and More Particularly His Melmoth', *London Magazine*, iii (May 1821), 514–24.

ORR, MARILYN, 'Voices and Text: Scott the Storyteller, Scott the Novelist', *Scottish Literary Journal*, xvi/2 (Nov. 1989), 41–59.

The Other Sir Walter Scott: The Eighteen Twenties in Edinburgh. Law: Business: Banking: Insurance, Edinburgh College of Commerce Library (Edinburgh, 1971).

PALGRAVE, FRANCIS TURNER, *The Rise and Progress of the English Commonwealth: Anglo-Saxon Period: Containing the Anglo-Saxon Policy, and the Institutions Arising out of Laws and Usages which Prevailed Before the Conquest*, 2 vols. (London, 1832).

PALMER, JOHN, JR., *The Haunted Cavern: A Caledonian Tale* (London, 1796).

—— *The Mystic Sepulchre; or, Such Things Have Been: A Spanish Romance*, 2 vols. (London, 1807).

PARKER, WILLIAM MATHIE, 'The Origin of Scott's *Nigel*', *MLR* xxxiv (1939), 535–40.

PARR, NORAH, *James Hogg at Home: Being the Domestic Life and Letters of the Ettrick Shepherd* (Dollar, 1980).

PARREAUX, ANDRÉ, *The Publication of the Monk: A Literary Event 1796–1798*, Études de Littérature Étrangère et Comparée, No. 41 (Paris, 1960).

PARSONS, COLEMAN OSCAR, 'The Interest of Scott's Public in the Supernatural', *Notes and Queries*, clxxxv (1943), 92–100.

—— 'Scott's Fellow Demonologists', *MLQ* iv (1943), 473–94.

PARSONS, COLEMAN OSCAR, *Witchcraft and Demonology in Scott's Fiction: With Chapters on the Supernatural in Scottish Literature* (Edinburgh, 1964).

PARSONS, ELIZA, *Castle of Wolfenbach; A German Story*, 2 vols. (London, 1793).

—— *The Mysterious Visit: A Novel, Founded on Facts*, 4 vols. (Brentford, 1802).

PATTEN, JOHN ALEXANDER, *Sir Walter Scott: A Character Study* (London, 1932).

PAULSON, RONALD H., *Representations of Revolution (1789–1820)* (New Haven, Conn., 1983).

PEACOCK, THOMAS LOVE, *The Works of Thomas Love Peacock*, ed. H. F. B. Brett-Smith and C. E. Jones, Halliford Edition, 10 vols. (London, 1924–34).

PECK, LOUIS F., *A Life of Matthew G. Lewis* (Cambridge, Mass., 1961).

PHILLIPSON, N. T., 'Scott as Story-Teller; An Essay in Psychobiography', in Alan Bell (ed.), *Scott Bicentenary Essays: Selected Papers read at the Sir Walter Scott Bicentenary Conference* (Edinburgh, 1973), 87–100.

PIKOULIS, JOHN, 'Scott and *Marmion*: The Discovery of Identity', *MLR* lxvi (1971), 738–50.

PINKERTON, JOHN, *Dissertation on the Origin and Progress of the Scythians or Goths: Being an Introduction to the Ancient and Modern History of Europe* (London, 1787).

PITCAIRN, ROBERT, *Ancient Criminal Trials in Scotland; Compiled from the Original Records and MSS., with Historical Illustrations, &c.*, i, pts. 1, 2, 3; ii, pts. 1, 2; iii, pts. 1, 2 (Edinburgh, 1833).

PITTOCK, JOAN, *The Ascendancy of Taste: The Achievement of Joseph and Thomas Warton* (London, 1973).

PITTOCK, MURRAY G. H., *The Invention of Scotland: The Stuart Myth and the Scottish Identity, 1638 to the Present* (London, 1991).

PLATZNER, ROBERT LEONARD, *The Metaphysical Novel in England: The Romantic Phase*, Gothic Studies and Dissertations (New York, 1980).

POLIDORI, JOHN WILLIAM, *The Vampyre; A Tale* (1819), in *The Castle of Otranto by Horace Walpole; Vathek by William Beckford; The Vampyre by John Polidori; and a Fragment of a Novel by Lord Byron: Three Gothic Novels*, ed. E. F. Bleiler (New York, 1966).

POLITI, JINA, 'Narrative and Historical Transformations in *The Bride of Lammermoor*', *Scottish Literary Journal*, xv/1 (May 1988), 70–81.

POOVEY, MARY L., 'Ideology and "The Mysteries of Udolpho"', *Criticism*, xxi (1979), 307–30.

POPE-HENNESSY, UNA, *The Laird of Abbotsford: An Informal Presentation of Sir Walter Scott* (London, 1932).

PORTE, JOEL, 'In the Hands of an Angry God: Religious Terror in Gothic Fiction', in G. R. Thompson (ed.), *The Gothic Imagination: Essays in*

Dark Romanticism (Pullman, Wash., 1974), 42–64.

PORTER, JANE, *The Scottish Chiefs: A Romance*, 5 vols. (London, 1810).

—— *Thaddeus of Warsaw: Revised, Corrected, and Illustrated with a New Introduction, Notes, Etc. By the Author*, Standard Novels, No. 4 (London, 1832).

—— *The Scottish Chiefs*, 2 vols., Standard Novels, No. 7 (London, 1835).

—— *The Scottish Chiefs: Revised, Corrected, and Illustrated with A New Retrospective Introduction, Notes, &c., By the Author* (London, 1840).

POSTON III, LAWRENCE, 'The Commercial Motif of the Waverley Novels', *ELH* xlii (1975), 62–87.

POTTLE, FREDERICK A., 'The Power of Memory in Boswell and Scott' (1945), repr. in A. Norman Jeffares (ed.), *Scott's Mind and Art* (Edinburgh, 1969), 230–53.

PRAZ, MARIO, *The Romantic Agony* (1933), 2nd edn., trans. Angus Davidson (London, 1951).

—— *The Hero in Eclipse in Victorian Fiction*, trans. Angus Davidson (London, 1956).

PUNTER, DAVID, *The Literature of Terror: A History of Gothic Fictions from 1765 to the Present Day* (London, 1980).

—— 'Social Relations of Gothic Fiction', in David Aers, Jonathan Cook, David Punter, *Romanticism and Ideology: Studies in English Writing 1765–1830* (London, 1981), 103–17.

RADCLIFFE, ANN, *The Castles of Athlin and Dunbayne: A Highland Story* (London, 1789). [Foreword Frederick Shroyer (New York, 1972).]

—— *A Sicilian Romance*, 2 vols. (London, 1790). [Foreword Howard Mumford Jones, introd. Devendra P. Varma (New York, 1972).]

—— *The Romance of the Forest: Interspersed with Some Pieces of Poetry*, 3 vols. (London, 1791). [Ed. and introd. Chloe Chard (Oxford, 1986).]

—— *The Mysteries of Udolpho, A Romance; Interspersed with Some Pieces of Poetry*, 4 vols. (London, 1794). [Ed. Bonamy Dobrée, notes Frederick Garber (Oxford, 1966, 1970).]

—— *The Italian; or, The Confessional of the Black Penitents: A Romance*, 3 vols. (London, 1797). [Ed. and introd. Frederick Garber (Oxford, 1968, 1981).]

—— *Gaston de Blondeville; or, The Court of Henry III. Keeping Festival in Ardenne, a Romance; St Alban's Abbey, a Metrical Tale; With some Poetical Pieces: To which is prefixed a Memoir of the Author, with Extracts from her Journals*, 4 vols. (London, 1826). [Introd. Devendra P. Varma (New York, 1972).]

—— 'On the Supernatural in Poetry', *New Monthly Magazine*, xvi (Jan. 1826), 145–52.

RADCLIFFE, MARY-ANNE, *Manfroné; or, The One-Handed Monk: A*

Romance, 4 vols. (London, 1809). [Foreword Devendra P. Varma, introd. Coral Ann Howells (New York, 1972).]

RAILO, EINO, *The Haunted Castle: A Study of the Elements of English Romanticism*, trans. anon. (London, 1927).

RAY, WILLIAM, *Story and History: Narrative Authority and Social Identity in the Eighteenth-Century French and English Novel* (Oxford, 1990).

REDDIN, CHITRA PERSHAD, *Forms of Evil in the Gothic Novel*, Gothic Studies and Dissertations (New York, 1980).

REED, JAMES, *Sir Walter Scott: Landscape and Locality* (London, 1980).

REED, WALTER L., *An Exemplary History of the Novel: The Quixotic versus the Picaresque* (Chicago, 1981).

REEVE, CLARA, *The Champion of Virtue: A Gothic Story* (Colchester, 1777).

—— *The Old English Baron: A Gothic Story*, 2nd edn. (London, 1778). [Ed. and introd. James Trainer (London, 1967).]

—— *The Progress of Romance, Through Times, Countries, and Manners; With Remarks on the Good and Bad Effects of it, on them respectively; in a Course of Evening Conversations*, 2 vols. (London, 1785).

RICHARDSON, SAMUEL, *Clarissa; or, The History of a Young Lady* (1747–8), 8 vols. (Oxford, 1930).

RICHETTI, JOHN J., *Defoe's Narratives: Situations and Structures* (Oxford, 1975).

RICHTER, DAVID H., 'The Reception of the Gothic Novel in the 1790s', in Robert W. Uphaus (ed.), *The Idea of the Novel in the Eighteenth Century* (East Lansing, Mich., 1988), 117–37.

RIGNALL, J. M., 'The Historical Double: *Waverley, Sylvia's Lovers, The Trumpet-Major*', *Essays in Criticism*, xxxiv (1984), 14–32.

—— 'Walter Scott, J. G. Farrell, and the Fictions of Empire', *Essays in Criticism*, xli (1991), 11–27.

ROBERTS, BETTE B., 'Sophia Lee's *The Recess* (1785): The Ambivalence of Female Gothicism', *Massachusetts Studies in English*, vi/3–4 (1979), 68–82.

ROBERTS, J. M., *The Mythology of the Secret Societies* (London, 1972).

ROBERTS, MARIE, *Gothic Immortals: The Fiction of the Brotherhood of the Rosy Cross* (London, 1990).

ROBERTSON, FIONA (ed. and introd.), *The Bride of Lammermoor* (1819), by Sir Walter Scott (Oxford, 1991).

—— 'Castle Spectres: Scott, Gothic Drama, and the Search for the Narrator', in J. H. Alexander and David S. Hewitt (eds.), *Scott '91* (Edinburgh, forthcoming).

ROBINSON, MARY, *Hubert de Sevrac, a Romance of the Eighteenth Century*, 3 vols. (London, 1796).

ROCHE, REGINA MARIA, *The Children of the Abbey: A Tale*, 4 vols. (London, 1796).
—— *Clermont: A Tale*, 4 vols. (London, 1798). [*Clairmont: A Tale*, The Northanger Set of Jane Austen Horrid Novels, ed. Devendra P. Varma (London, 1968).]

RONALD, MARGARET A., *Functions of Setting in the Novel: From Mrs Radcliffe to Charles Dickens*, Gothic Studies and Dissertations (New York, 1980).

ROPER, DEREK, *Reviewing Before the 'Edinburgh' 1788–1802* (London, 1978).

ROUDINESCO, ELISABETH, *Théroigne de Méricourt: A Melancholic Woman During the French Revolution* (1989), trans. Martin Thom (London, 1991).

'The Rovers; or, The Double Arrangement', *The Anti-Jacobin; or, Weekly Examiner*, No. 30 (4 June 1798), 235–9; No. 31 (11 June 1798), 242–6.

RUBENSTEIN, JILL, *Sir Walter Scott: A Reference Guide*, A Reference Publication in Literature, ed. Marilyn Gaull (Boston, Mass., 1978).

RUFF, WILLIAM, 'A Bibliography of the Poetical Works of Sir Walter Scott, 1796–1832', *Transactions of the Edinburgh Bibliographical Society*, i (1938), 99–239.

RUSKIN, JOHN, *The Works of John Ruskin*, Library Edition, ed. E. T. Cook and Alexander Wedderburn, 39 vols. (London, 1903–12).
—— *Praeterita: Outlines of Scenes and Thoughts Perhaps Worthy of Memory in my Past Life* (1885–9), introd. Kenneth Clark (London, 1949).

RUSSELL, BERTRAND, *An Inquiry into Meaning and Truth: The William James Lectures for 1940* (1950; repr. London, 1980).

SADE, DONATIEN ALPHONSE FRANÇOIS, MARQUIS DE, *Selected Writings of De Sade*, selected and trans. Leonard de Saint-Yves (London, 1953).

SADLEIR, MICHAEL, ' "All Horrid?" Jane Austen and the Gothic Romance', in his *Things Past* (London, 1944), 167–200.

SAID, EDWARD W., 'Molestation and Authority in Narrative Fiction', in J. Hillis Miller (ed.), *Aspects of Narrative: Selected Papers from the English Institute* (New York, 1971), 47–68.
—— *Beginnings: Intention and Method* (1975; repr. New York, 1985).

Review of *St Ronan's Well*, *British Critic*, NS xxi (Jan. 1824), 16–26.
—— *Monthly Review*, NS ciii (Jan. 1824), 61–75.
—— *New European Magazine*, iv (Jan. 1824), 54–61.

SAINTSBURY, G. E. B. (ed.), *Tales of Mystery: Mrs. Radcliffe—Lewis—Maturin*, The Pocket Library of English Literature, i (London, 1891).

SALE, ROGER, *Literary Inheritance* (Amherst, Mass., 1984).

SANDY, STEPHEN MERRILL, *The Raveling of the Novel: Studies in Ro-*

mantic Fiction from Walpole to Scott, Gothic Studies and Dissertations (New York, 1980).

SCARBOROUGH, DOROTHY, *The Supernatural in Modern English Fiction* (1917; repr. New York, 1967).

SCHOLTEN, WILLEM, *Charles Robert Maturin: The Terror-Novelist* (Amsterdam, 1933).

SCHILLER, JOHANN CHRISTOPH FRIEDRICH VON, *The Robbers* and *Wallenstein* (1781 and 1799), trans. and introd. F. J. Lamport (Harmondsworth, 1979).

SCOTT, PAUL HENDERSON, *Walter Scott and Scotland* (Edinburgh, 1981).

SCOTT, SIR WALTER, BT., *The Chase, and William and Helen: Two Ballads, From the German of Gottfried Augustus Bürger* (Edinburgh, 1796).

—— *Minstrelsy of the Scottish Border*, 3 vols. (Edinburgh, 1803), ed. T. F. Henderson, 4 vols. (Edinburgh, 1902, 1932).

—— (ed.), *Sir Tristrem; A Metrical Romance of the Thirteenth Century, by Thomas of Ercildoune, called The Rhymer* (Edinburgh, 1804).

—— (introd.), *The Castle of Otranto: A Gothic Story* (Edinburgh, 1811).

—— *Paul's Letters to His Kinsfolk* (Edinburgh, 1816).

—— with W. ERSKINE and W. GIFFORD, Review of *Tales of My Landlord* [1st ser.], *Quarterly Review*, xvi (Jan. 1817), 430–80.

—— *Rob Roy*, 3 vols. (Edinburgh, 1818, for 1817).

—— *Tales of My Landlord, Second Series, Collected and Arranged by Jedediah Cleishbotham, Schoolmaster and Parish-Clerk of Gandercleugh*, 4 vols. (Edinburgh, 1818).

—— *The Visionary* (1819), ed. Peter D. Garside, Regency Reprints, No. 1 (Cardiff, 1984).

—— (ed.), *Ballantyne's Novelist's Library*, 10 vols. (Edinburgh, 1821–4).

—— 'A Character of Lord Byron', in *The Life and Genius of Lord Byron, With Additional Anecdotes and Critical Remarks from Other Publications; To which is Prefixed a Sketch on Lord Byron's Death, by Sir Walter Scott, Bart.*, by Sir Cosmo Gordon (Paris, 1824).

—— *The Life of Napoleon Buonaparte, Emperor of the French: With a Preliminary View of the French Revolution*, 9 vols. (Edinburgh, 1827).

—— *The Waverley Novels*, 48 vols. (Edinburgh, 1829–33).

—— *Letters on Demonology and Witchcraft, addressed to J. G. Lockhart, Esq.*, The Family Library, No. 16 (London, 1830).

—— *The Poetical Works of Sir Walter Scott, Bart.*, ed. J. G. Lockhart, 12 vols. (Edinburgh, 1833–4).

—— *The Miscellaneous Prose Works of Sir Walter Scott, Bart.*, ed. J. G. Lockhart, 28 vols. (Edinburgh, 1834–6).

—— *The Private Letter-Books of Sir Walter Scott: Selections from the Abbotsford Manuscripts; With a Letter to the Reader from Hugh Walpole*, ed. Wilfred Partington (London, 1930).

—— *Sir Walter's Post-Bag: More Stories and Sidelights from his Unpublished Letter-Books*, ed. Wilfred Partington, foreword Hugh Walpole (London, 1932).

—— *The Letters of Sir Walter Scott*, ed. H. J. C. Grierson *et al.*, 12 vols., Centenary Edition (London, 1932–7).

—— *Private Letters of the Seventeenth Century*, ed. Douglas Grant (Oxford, 1947).

—— *Sir Walter Scott on Novelists and Fiction*, ed. Ioan Williams (London, 1968).

—— *The Journal of Sir Walter Scott*, ed. W. E. K. Anderson (Oxford, 1972).

—— *Sir Walter Scott's Edinburgh Annual Register*, ed. Kenneth Curry (Knoxville, Tenn., 1977).

—— and MATURIN, CHARLES ROBERT, *The Correspondence of Sir Walter Scott and Charles Robert Maturin With a Few Other Allied Letters*, ed. Fannie E. Ratchford and William H. McCarthy, Jr. (Austin, Tex., 1937).

SEDGWICK, EVE KOSOFSKY, *The Coherence of Gothic Conventions* (1980; repr. New York, 1986).

SEED, DAVID, 'Gothic Definitions', *Novel*, xiv (1981), 270–4.

SENIOR, NASSAU WILLIAM, Review of *The Pirate*, *Quarterly Review*, xxvi (Oct. 1821), 454–74.

—— Review of *Rob Roy, Tales of My Landlord* 2nd ser., *Tales of My Landlord* 3rd ser., *Ivanhoe, The Monastery, The Abbot, Kenilworth, Quarterly Review*, xxvi (Oct. 1821), 109–48.

—— 'Sir Walter Scott', in his *Essays on Fiction* (London, 1864), 1–188.

SHAKESPEARE, WILLIAM, *The Riverside Shakespeare*, textual ed. G. Blakemore Evans, gen. introd. Harry Levin *et al.*, essay on stage history Charles H. Shattuck (Boston, Mass., 1974).

SHAW, HARRY E., *The Forms of Historical Fiction: Sir Walter Scott and His Successors* (Ithaca, NY, 1983).

SHELLEY, MARY WOLLSTONECRAFT, *Frankenstein; or, The Modern Prometheus*, 3 vols. (London, 1818). [Ed. James Rieger (1974; repr. Chicago, 1982).]

—— *The Fortunes of Perkin Warbeck: A Romance*, 3 vols. (London, 1830).

—— *The Letters of Mary Wollstonecraft Shelley*, ed. Betty T. Bennett, 3 vols. (Baltimore, 1980–8).

SHELLEY, PERCY BYSSHE, *The Complete Works of Percy Bysshe Shelley*, ed. Roger Ingpen and Walter E. Peck, Julian Edition, 10 vols. (London, 1926–30).

SHERWIN, PAUL, '*Frankenstein*: Creation as Catastrophe', *PMLA* xcvi (1981), 883–903.

SIMMONS, JAMES C., *The Novelist as Historian: Essays on the Victorian*

Historical Novel, Studies in English Literature, No. 87 (The Hague, 1973).

SIMPSON, LOUIS, *James Hogg: A Critical Study* (Edinburgh, 1962).

Sir Gawain and the Green Knight (c.1350–75), ed. E. V. Gordon and J. R. R. Tolkien (Oxford, 1925).

SISKIN, CLIFFORD, *The Historicity of Romantic Discourse* (New York, 1988).

SKENE, JAMES, *The Skene Papers: Memories of Sir Walter Scott* (c.1832), ed. Basil Thomson (London, 1909).

SLEATH, ELEANOR, *The Orphan of the Rhine: A Romance*, 4 vols. (London, 1798). [The Northanger Set of Jane Austen Horrid Novels, ed. Devendra P. Varma (London, 1968).]

—— *The Nocturnal Minstrel; or, The Spirit of the Wood*, 2 vols. (London, 1810). [Introd. Devendra P. Varma (New York, 1972).]

SLOAN, BARRY, *The Pioneers of Anglo-Irish Fiction 1800–1850*, Irish Literary Studies, No. 21 (Gerrards Cross, Buckinghamshire, 1986).

SMITH, CHARLOTTE, *The Romance of Real Life*, 3 vols. (London, 1787).

—— *Emmeline, The Orphan of the Castle*, 4 vols. (London, 1788). [Ed. and introd. Anne Henry Ehrenpreis (London, 1971).]

—— *The Old Manor House: A Novel*, 4 vols. (London, 1793). [Ed. and introd. Anne Henry Ehrenpreis (London, 1969).]

—— *The Letters of a Solitary Wanderer: Containing Narratives of Various Description*, 3 vols. (London, 1800–1).

SMITH, NELSON C., *The Art of Gothic: Ann Radcliffe's Major Novels*, Gothic Studies and Dissertations (New York, 1980).

SMOLLETT, TOBIAS GEORGE, *The Adventures of Ferdinand Count Fathom*, 2 vols. (London, 1753).

'Some Remarks on the Use of the Preternatural in Works of Fiction', *Blackwood's Edinburgh Magazine*, iii (Sept. 1818), 648–50.

SONTAG, SUSAN, *Illness as Metaphor* and *Aids and its Metaphors* (1978 and 1989) (Harmondsworth, 1991).

SOUTHEY, ROBERT, *Roderick, The Last of the Goths* (London, 1814).

—— *Poems of Robert Southey: Containing Thalaba, The Curse of Kehama, Roderick, Madoc, A Tale of Paraguay and Selected Minor Poems*, ed. Maurice H. Fitzgerald (London, 1909).

SPECTOR, ROBERT DONALD, *The English Gothic: A Bibliographic Guide to Writers from Horace Walpole to Mary Shelley* (Westport, Conn., 1984).

SPENCER, JANE, *The Rise of the Woman Novelist From Aphra Behn to Jane Austen* (Oxford, 1986).

SPENSER, EDMUND, *The Faerie Queene* (1590, 1596), ed. A. C. Hamilton, Longman Annotated English Poets (1977; corr. edn. London, 1980).

SROKA, KENNETH M., 'Fairy Castles and Character in *Woodstock*', *Essays in Literature*, xiv (1987), 189–205.

STALKER, ARCHIBALD, *The Intimate Life of Sir Walter Scott* (London, 1921).

STALLYBRASS, PETER, and WHITE, ALLON, *The Politics and Poetics of Transgression* (London, 1986).

STEPHEN, SIR LESLIE, 'Hours in a Library No. 3—Some Words About Sir Walter Scott', *Cornhill Magazine*, xxiv (Sept. 1871), 278–93.

STEVENSON, DAVID, 'Major Weir: A Justified Sinner?', *Scottish Studies*, xvi (1972), 161–73.

STEWART, DAVID, OF GARTH, *Sketches of the Character, Manners, and Present State of the Highlanders of Scotland: With Details of the Military Service of the Highland Regiments*, 2 vols. (Edinburgh, 1822).

STOKOE, F. W., *German Influence in the English Romantic Period 1788–1818, with Special Reference to Scott, Coleridge, Shelley and Byron* (Cambridge, 1926).

STONE, DONALD D., *The Romantic Impulse in Victorian Fiction* (Cambridge, Mass., 1980).

STROUT, ALAN LANG, *The Life and Letters of James Hogg, The Ettrick Shepherd*, i (1770–1825), Texas Technological College Research Publications No. 15 (Lubbock, Tex., 1946).

—— 'James Hogg's "Chaldee Manuscript"', *PMLA* lxv (1950), 695–718.

—— 'Writers on German Literature in *Blackwood's Magazine*, with a Footnote on Thomas Carlyle', *The Library*, 5th ser. ix/1 (Mar. 1954), 35–44.

—— *A Bibliography of Articles in Blackwood's Magazine Volumes i through xviii, 1817–1825*, Library Bulletin No. 5 (Lubbock, Tex., 1959).

—— 'Maga and the Ettrick Shepherd', *Studies in Scottish Literature*, iv (1966–7), 48–51.

STUART, LADY LOUISA, *Lady Louisa Stuart: Selections from her Manuscripts*, ed. James A. Home (Edinburgh, 1899).

SULTANA, DONALD E., *'The Siege of Malta' Rediscovered: An Account of Sir Walter Scott's Mediterranean Journey and His Last Novel* (Edinburgh, 1977).

—— *The Journey of Sir Walter Scott to Malta* (New York, 1986).

SUMMERS, MONTAGUE, *Essays in Petto* (London, 1928).

—— *The Gothic Quest: A History of the Gothic Novel* (London, 1938).

—— *A Gothic Bibliography* (London, [1940]).

SUTHERLAND, KATHRYN (ed. and introd.), *Redgauntlet* (1824), by Sir Walter Scott (Oxford, 1985).

—— 'Fictional Economies: Adam Smith, Walter Scott and the Nineteenth-Century Novel', *ELH* liv (1987), 97–127.

SWIFT, JONATHAN, *Gulliver's Travels and Other Writings*, ed. Louis A. Landa (Oxford, 1976).

SWINGLE, L. J., 'The Romantic Emergence: Multiplication of Alternatives and the Problem of Systematic Entrapment', *MLQ* xxxix (1978), 264–83.

SYPHER, WYLIE, 'Social Ambiguity in a Gothic Novel', *Partisan Review*, xii (1945), 50–60.

—— *The Obstinate Questionings of English Romanticism* (London, 1987).

Review of *Tales of My Landlord*, 2nd ser., *The Scotsman*, ii, No. 80 (1 Aug. 1818), 247.

Review of *Tales of My Landlord*, 3rd ser., *Blackwood's Edinburgh Magazine*, v (June 1819), 340–53.

—— *Edinburgh Magazine*, iv (June 1819), 547–54.

—— *Edinburgh Monthly Review*, ii (Aug. 1819), 160–84.

TARR, MARY M., *Catholicism in Gothic Fiction: A Study of the Nature and Function of Catholic Materials in Gothic Fiction in England* (Washington, 1946).

'Terrorist Novel Writing', *The Spirit of the Public Journals for 1797*, i, 3rd edn. (London, 1802), 227–9.

'Terrorist System of Novel Writing', signed 'A Jacobin Novelist', *Monthly Magazine*, iv (Aug. 1797), 102–4.

THOMPSON, E. P., *The Making of the English Working Class* (1963; rev. edn. Harmondsworth, 1968, 1980).

THOMPSON, JON, 'Sir Walter Scott and Madge Wildfire: Strategies of Containment in *The Heart of Midlothian*', *Literature and History*, xiii (1987), 188–99.

THORSLEV, PETER LARSEN, JR., *The Byronic Hero: Types and Prototypes* (Minneapolis, 1962).

—— *Romantic Contraries: Freedom versus Destiny* (New Haven, Conn., 1984).

TODD, WILLIAM B., 'The Early Editions and Issues of *The Monk*, with a Bibliography', *Studies in Bibliography: Papers of the Bibliographical Society of the University of Virginia*, ii (1949–50), 3–24.

TODOROV, TZVETAN, *The Fantastic: A Structural Approach to a Literary Genre* (1970), trans. Richard Howard (Cleveland, 1973).

TOMPKINS, JOYCE M. S., *The Popular Novel in England, 1770–1800* (London, 1932).

'TOUCHSTONE, TIMOTHY' [pseud.], *A Letter to the Author of Waverley, Ivanhoe, &c. &c. &c. on the Moral Tendency of those Popular Works* (London, 1820).

TRACY, ANN BLAISDELL, *Patterns of Fear in the Gothic Novel 1790–1830*, Gothic Studies and Dissertations (New York, 1980).

—— *The Gothic Novel 1790–1830: Plot Summaries and Index to Motifs* (Lexington, Ky., 1981).

TREVOR-ROPER, HUGH, 'The Invention of Tradition: The Highland Tradition of Scotland', in Eric Hobsbawm and Terence Ranger (eds.), *The Invention of Tradition* (Cambridge, 1983), 15–43.

TULLOCH, GRAHAM, *The Language of Sir Walter Scott: A Study of his Scottish and Period Language* (London, 1980).

TWISS, HORACE, Review of *Marmion*, *Le Beau Monde*, iii (May 1808), 263–70.

TYSDAHL, B. J., *William Godwin as Novelist* (London, 1981).

VAN LUCHENE, STEPHEN ROBERT, *Essays in Gothic Fiction: From Horace Walpole to Mary Shelley*, Gothic Studies and Dissertations (New York, 1980).

VARMA, DEVENDRA P., *The Gothic Flame: Being a History of the Gothic Novel in England: Its Origins, Efflorescence, Disintegration, and Residuary Influences*, foreword Herbert Read, introd. J. M. S. Tompkins (London, 1957).

VEDDER, DAVID, *Memoir of Sir Walter Scott, Bart. With Critical Notices of His Writings: Compiled from Various Authentic Sources* (Dundee, 1832).

WAGENKNECHT, EDWARD, *Cavalcade of the English Novel* (1943; new edn. with supplementary bibliography New York, 1954).

WAGNER, PETER, *Eros Revived: Erotica of the Enlightenment in England and America* (London, 1988).

WALPOLE, HORACE, *The Castle of Otranto: A Gothic Story* (1764, 1765), ed. and introd. W. S. Lewis (Oxford, 1964, 1982).

—— *The Mysterious Mother: A Tragedy* (London, 1781).

—— *The Castle of Otranto, with Sir Walter Scott's Introduction*, preface Caroline F. E. Spurgeon, The King's Classics (London, 1907).

—— *The Yale Edition of Horace Walpole's Correspondence*, ed. W. S. Lewis *et al.*, 48 vols. (New Haven, Conn., 1937–83).

WARD, WILLIAM SMITH, *Literary Reviews in British Periodicals 1798–1820: A Bibliography: With a Supplementary List of General (Non-Review) Articles on Literary Subjects*, 2 vols. (New York, 1972).

—— *Literary Reviews in British Periodicals 1821–1826: A Bibliography: With a Supplementary List of General (Non-Review) Articles on Literary Subjects*, Garland Reference Library of the Humanities, No. 60 (New York, 1977).

WARE, MALCOLM, *Sublimity in the Novels of Ann Radcliffe: A Study of the Influence upon Her Craft of Edmund Burke's 'Enquiry into the Origin of Our Ideas of the Sublime and Beautiful'*, Essays and Studies on English Language and Literature, No. 25 (Uppsala, 1963).

WARTON, THOMAS, *The History of English Poetry, From the Close of the Eleventh to the Commencement of the Eighteenth Century. To which are prefixed, Two Dissertations. I. On the Origin of Romantic Fiction in Europe. II. On the Introduction of Learning into England*, 3 vols. (London, 1774–81), iv (incomplete) (? London, 1789).

WASWO, RICHARD, 'Story as Historiography in the Waverley Novels', *ELH* xlvii (1980), 304–30.

WATT, IAN, *The Rise of the Novel: Studies in Defoe, Richardson and Fielding* (London, 1957).

WATT, WILLIAM WHYTE, *Shilling Shockers of the Gothic School: A Study of Chapbook Gothic Romances* (1932; repr. New York, 1967).

Review of *Waverley, Antijacobin Review*, xlvii (Sept. 1814), 217–47.

—— *British Critic*, NS ii (Aug. 1814), 189–211.

—— *The Champion* (24 July 1814), 238–9.

—— *Monthly Review*, NS lxxv (Nov. 1814), 275–89.

—— *The Port Folio*, 3rd ser. v (Apr. 1815), 326–33.

—— [Attributed to Croker], *Quarterly Review*, xi (July 1814), 354–77.

—— *Scots Magazine*, lxxvi (July 1814), 524–33.

WEINSTEIN, MARK A. (ed.), *The Prefaces to the Waverley Novels* (Lincoln, Nebr., 1978).

WEISKEL, THOMAS, *The Romantic Sublime: Studies in the Structure and Psychology of Transcendence* (1976), foreword by Harold Bloom (Baltimore, 1986).

WEISS, FREDRIC, *The Antic Spectre: Satire in Early Gothic Novels*, Gothic Studies and Dissertations (New York, 1980).

WELSH, ALEXANDER, *The Hero of the Waverley Novels*, Yale Studies in English, No. 154 (New Haven, Conn., 1963).

WEXELBLATT, ROBERT, 'The Ambivalence of *Frankenstein*', *Arizona Quarterly*, xxxvi (1980), 101–17.

WHITE, HAYDEN, *Metahistory: The Historical Imagination in Nineteenth-Century Europe* (Baltimore, 1973).

—— 'The Question of Narrative in Contemporary Historical Theory', *History and Theory*, xxiii (1984), 1–33.

WILL, PETER (trans.), *Horrid Mysteries: A Story; From the German of the Marquis of Grosse* (1796), ed. Devendra P. Varma, The Northanger Set of Jane Austen Horrid Novels (London, 1968).

WILLIAMS, IOAN (ed.), *Novel and Romance 1700–1800: A Documentary Record* (London, 1970).

WILLIAMS, RAYMOND, *Culture and Society 1780–1950* (1958; repr. with postscript Harmondsworth, 1963).

WILSON, A. N., *The Laird of Abbotsford: A View of Sir Walter Scott* (Oxford, 1980).

WILT, JUDITH, *Ghosts of the Gothic: Austen, Eliot and Lawrence* (Princeton, NJ, 1980).

—— *Secret Leaves: The Novels of Walter Scott* (Chicago, 1985).

WITTIG, KURT, *The Scottish Tradition in Literature* (Edinburgh, 1958).

WOLLSTONECRAFT, MARY, *Vindication of the Rights of Woman; With Strictures on Moral and Political Subjects* (1792), ed. and introd. Miriam Brody Kramnick (Harmondsworth, 1975, 1982).

—— *Mary* and *The Wrongs of Woman* (1788 and 1798), ed. James Kinsley and Gary Kelly (Oxford, 1976, 1980).

WOOLF, VIRGINIA, *Collected Essays*, 4 vols. (London, 1966–7).

WORDSWORTH, WILLIAM, *The Poetical Works of William Wordsworth*, ed. Ernest de Selincourt and Helen Darbishire, 5 vols. (Oxford, 1940–9).

—— *The Prose Works of William Wordsworth*, ed. W. J. B. Owen and Jane Worthington Smyser, 3 vols. (Oxford, 1974).

—— and WORDSWORTH, DOROTHY, *The Letters of William and Dorothy Wordsworth: The Middle Years Part II, 1812–1820*, ed. Ernest de Selincourt, rev. Mary Moorman and Alan G. Hill, 2nd edn. (Oxford, 1970).

WORTH, CHRISTOPHER, 'Scott, Story-telling and Subversion: Dialogism in *Woodstock*', in J. H. Alexander and David S. Hewitt (eds.), *Scott '91* (Edinburgh, forthcoming).

WORTHINGTON, GREVILLE, *A Bibliography of the Waverley Novels*, Bibliographia: Studies in Book History and Book Structure 1750–1900, No. 4, ed. Michael Sadleir (London, 1931, 1971).

Index

314

INDEX